MARKET THE ARTS!

Compiled and Edited by Joseph V. Melillo

Published by

FEDAPT

Foundation for the Extension
and Development of the
American Professional Theatre

Frederic B. Vogel, Executive Director

165 West 46th Street, Suite 310
New York, NY 10036
(212) 869-9690

1983

Library of Congress Catalog Card Number 83-81870

ISBN 0-9602942-4-4

$19.95

Design: David J. Skal Associates, New York

TABLE OF CONTENTS

PART III: GENERAL APPLICATIONS OF THE MARKETING PRINCIPLES

PART IV: SPECIFIC APPLICATIONS OF THE MARKETING PRINCIPLES BY DISCIPLINE

PART V: MARKETING PROBLEMS AND ALTERNATIVES

PART VI: APPENDICES

Frederic B. Vogel

FOREWORD

The gestation period for *Market the Arts!* has been six and a half years. It began in a snow-covered landscape on Long Island Sound, the site of the Eugene O'Neill Memorial Theatre Center. It was there, in January of 1977, that FEDAPT conducted its first middle-management program. Rather, I should say, FEDAPT conducted the program in conjunction with Theatre Communications Group (TCG) and the O'Neill Center itself with the most important cooperation of Peter Zeisler, the executive director of TCG, and George White, the executive director of the O'Neill Center.

The middle-management program was conceived to train the middle managements of theater companies throughout the country. By virtue of a three-year grant from the William H. Donner Foundation, the program was initiated with the first week-long sessions that January. The intensive sessions lasted from late Sunday evening through the following Saturday afternoon (from 9:00 in the morning until 10 or 11:00 at night). The subjects were Audience Development, Press, Publicity, Promotion, Group Sales, etc. In those days, none of us used the word "marketing." In attendance were fourteen members of fourteen different theater companies who were selected out of solicited nominations mostly from the LORT theaters throughout the country. The grant that Phillip Jessup of the Donner Foundation had helped devise allowed us to invite these fourteen people at no cost to their theaters other than the round-trip transportation to the Waterford, Connecticut site.

Joseph Melillo had just joined FEDAPT and was conducting the week with a co-director, Michalann Hobson. The speakers included Harry Clark, Charles Ziff, Douglas Eichten, David Skal, and William Stewart. Among the fourteen participants were Patricia Cox and Bill Rudman. When you start to read through *Market the Arts!* you will note that all of these nine people are contributors to this publication.

The week-long program had a profound effect on all of us. All of the participants learned not merely from the seminar leaders or speakers, but from one another. Most of them had only worked at one theater (the one at which they were presently employed), so that they had no point of reference, no comparisons, no understanding that what they were doing was a skill, a craft, a talent that in turn was applicable to other kinds of arts organizations and indeed, other kinds of endeavors.

Another very exciting revelation was the enthusiasm—in fact the passion—with which the speakers mentioned above projected in their sessions. They were in effect saying that the fourteen participants could only fail in their endeavors for the right reasons. That is, they might fail if they employed some kind of a process that had *never* been tried before and for which there were no case histories, no examples, no experiences to study before embarking on such a new path. There was absolutely no holding back on facts, figures, or information, by the speakers who shared as openly and as intimately as it was possible to do. FEDAPT had always used the working professionals as consultants. There was, however, something additional

Frederic B. Vogel has been Executive Director of FEDAPT since 1970. Prior to this, Mr. Vogel was Assisting Director of the Performing Arts Division at the Seattle World's Fair which presented more than 125 international theatrical and concert attractions. He was in charge of the International Special Events Program, and served as the Director of the Film Program. He was Special Events Director of the New York State Pavilion at the World's Fair from 1963 to 1965; General Manager for *Lumadrama* (a "Son et Lumiere") at Independence Hall in Philadelphia in 1963. Beginning his theatrical career as an actor at age 9, Mr. Vogel appeared on Broadway, off-Broadway, the summer stock circuit, television and film before switching his creative priorities to the "front office." He has held administrative positions in summer theatres, music tents, off-Broadway theatres, and has created and supervised several Broadway Theatre Leagues (CAMI). In addition, Mr. Vogel has worked in the professional theatre as a Stage Manager, Box-Office Treasurer, Subscription and Group Sales Manager, Box-Office Treasurer, Subscription and Group Sales Manager, Public Relations/Publicity Director, General Manager, and Producer.

happening here. There was such incredibly valuable information being shared that when the week ended with no documented records of the events, I felt that FEDAPT had not entirely done its job. There were no ''souvenir photographs'' of the information-exchanging experience the way there would have been if we had all been on a trip experiencing the Taj Mahal, the Grand Canyon, or another wonder of the world for the first time.

Without actually planning a book, Joe Melillo and I began to talk about ways in which we could gather all the information presented at the middle-management program, and put it in a form that would be useable by staff members of other theater companies and, in fact, by members of other performing-arts disciplines. FEDAPT began to work with dance companies in 1980, and middle-management staff from various dance companies have been included in the seminars conducted since then.

After our first week-long program, it was absolutely evident that FEDAPT had to do this book on marketing. We had to create a tool that would be useable for all sizes of theater and dance companies, and other kinds of performing-arts disciplines. We all needed more weapons to combat the problem of insufficient financial support, both contributed and earned, that plagues every arts organization in this country.

I myself had always had a reluctance to accept the term ''marketing,'' but I felt we had to devise whatever methods were necessary to see that our performing-arts treasures not only survived, but grew and strengthened.

I remember an experience I had on a trip to Europe some years ago. I walked out of my Helsinki hotel and saw staring me in the face a fast-food restaurant that was part of a U.S. chain. Here in this gorgeous, old, well-preserved city was this garish example of American culture. What the restaurant really represented was the power of astute, imaginative marketing by that fast-food chain. It occurred to me that if my favorite performing-arts organizations were to prosper and grow, I had to find a way to help theaters and dance companies become as adroit at selling an image as that food chain had.

It was not as truly difficult as it sounded. Once I began to talk to the men and women who were doing the marketing at the time and to those who ultimately swelled those ranks, I found the clue. In the heart of good marketing people, I realized, is a sensitivity toward the art form that is being marketed, a concern for it, a passion for it, and most importantly, a deep and abiding concern for its integrity and its uniqueness. I have translated that concern into what I hope is a highly useable tool—this book called *Market the Arts!*

In addition to the contributors of the book, I would like to express my appreciation and thanks to FEDAPT's staff—to Jessica Andrews, Alice Chebba, and Sheila Wood of the Theatre Program; to Nello McDaniel and Christopher Miller of the Dance Program; to Jillson Knowles, development director; to Madonna Ann Morrow, business manager/project coordinator, and to David Barbour, who, I hope, will soon be very busy filling orders for this book.

No book on marketing the arts would be at all complete without acknowledging the spirit and impact of Danny Newman, who, like Johnny Appleseed, planted the seeds in all of us which have grown into flowering sales campaigns.

But most importantly, I would like to thank those marketing people and other management staff members, board members, in fact, whomever will use this book to ensure the life of a theater company, a dance company, an opera company, an orchestra, a performing-arts center—anything that enriches our lives by offering performances of artistic quality.

Joseph V. Melillo

PREFACE

The *raison d'être* for this publication surfaced during my tenure with FEDAPT as the theater program director. Succinctly, the managements of not-for-profit performing-arts organizations were maturing daily, and several of the institutions were evidencing radical administrative changes. Simultaneously, our economy was pressuring all performing-arts organizations into looking more seriously at their earned income figures. This resulted in the direct transference from the corporate arena of the species commonly known as "marketing" to the performing-arts sector—the results of which have been less than terrific.

It is the basic premise of this book that the superimposition of standard corporate marketing processes and techniques on to a performing-arts organization is an error made out of naiveté. The performing arts, by their essential artistic nature, require the marketing principles (and the resulting processes and techniques) to go through a transformation before being inseminated into the creative process. Only then are they ready to offer a performing-arts event, an audience.

You will discover that the marketing principles have a constancy while the process continues to remain organic to the situation. The arts of each discipline possess a uniqueness. The temperaments, skills, imaginations, and communities will differ from person to person and locale to locale. The task of marketing becomes a series of creative people solving creative and challenging problems.

Market the Arts is a resource that seeks to alter people's perceptions of what they do professionally. It provides a context for the artists, managers, marketing directors, boards of trustees, students of all the represented disciplines, curious audience members, and generous donors, as well as anyone who ever desires to be a part of this startling, creative network of imaginations and skills.

I wish to extend my sincerest gratitude to all the contributors for their thoughts, work, and patience. And to FEDAPT for having the foresight and sensitivity in its continued mission of helping to fulfill artistic and managerial needs through its services, and in particular, for committing to publish this book you are about to read.

Former Theater Program Director of FEDAPT, Joseph V. Melillo is currently the Next Wave Festival Coordinator for the Brooklyn Academy of Music, Inc. (BAM). His experiences in the performing arts range from Producing Director, General Manager, and Marketing positions across the country. Several published articles on management issues have appeared in *Theatre Crafts* and his consultancies and teaching assignments have kept him committed to the survival of the performing arts in our society.

Charles Ziff

INTRODUCTION

As our art reflects ourselves, so our marketing of art reflects our art. For the making and marketing of art are similar disciplines, each requiring technique, imagination, experience, and conviction, applied in just the right balance. When a campaign is successful, we know immediately that it has worked. But how it works, and why, may not be as easy to understand.

This book describes the how and the why of good arts marketing. But in so doing, it suggests something more important: That the maker and the marketer of art must be in harmony to achieve success. Maker and marketer are sometimes uneasy partners, protective of their prerogatives, jealous of each other's turf, and occasionally competitive. Each is charting a course for which the outcome is uncertain, and each can be confused (especially when things don't go well), over who is in the lead and who should be in the lead.

The marketer of art is an interpreter of the work of the artist. As you read the chapters that follow, several themes will emerge over and over as central to the effective marketing of art:

- That the potential audience for any artistic work will be composed of two groups: those who know the work, understand its conventions and recognize its value, and those who do not. The marketing approach to each must be distinct.

- That our consumer-oriented, advertising-saturated society has trained us to style ourselves by what we consume. Thus, how you depict the consumer of the art you market will affect who the consumer turns out to be.

- That marketing must be based on constant and consistent measurement of the efficiency of everything you do. While you may choose to temper what the measurements suggest, that choice should be conscious and informed.

- That the quality of the marketing communications you create will represent the quality of your art.

- That you must bring artists and audiences together based upon mutual trust and respect. The artist who is abused by marketing will not return to produce good work again. The audience that is misled will not give you a second chance.

- That just as there is no substitute for imagination in art, there is no substitute for imagination in marketing.

- That achievement in marketing the arts requires diligence in execution. Day-dreaming is one thing; getting things done in something else.

> "The quality of the marketing communications you create will represent the quality of your art."

The presentation of art is rather like a trapeze act in which the artist is the flyer and the marketer is the catcher. The marketer must expect the unexpected and know that while the responsibilities are shared, the risks are not. While the appeal of the performance will be based primarily on the actions of the artist, he cannot work alone. He must remember that, though his marketer's resolve may be absolute, his strength and reach have limits.

In the pages that follow, you will learn something of technique, of imagination, of experience, and of conviction. You will pass through more than a full career's worth of wisdom in just a few hours. Be prepared to smile some smiles of self-recognition, and shudder some shudders of, "there but for the grace of God go I." Some of the chapters will touch you and some will not. Some will teach you and some will not. But each will have something to offer, in the successes they describe, or in the failures they do not.

PART I:
Artistic and
Management Perspectives
and Process Marketing:
A Professional View

Mark Lamos and William Stewart

THEATER: THE VITAL RELATIONSHIP

Messrs. Lamos and Stewart are responding directly to a set of questions that were posed to them by Joseph Melillo. Mr. Lamos specifically was asked about his art, how he defined the title "Artistic Director," what did he believe management to be, and what did he infer from the word marketing. *Whereas, Mr. Stewart was asked what he thought management was, the parameters of the job of a "Managing Director," the essentials of a relationship with an Artistic Director, what he believed* marketing *to be, and what qualities would he search for in a Marketing person for his performing arts institution.*

Mark Lamos:

If I knew what it meant to be an artist, I wouldn't be one anymore; I'd be on to something else. I think of myself as one who *learns.* I have visions and ideas that I wish to share with other artists and with an audience. I locate and define these visions by interperting the work of others.

Theater is my art form because I am no longer a musician, and because I cannot dance. It is my art form because I want to reevaluate experience. I want to recreate life by re-forming it within the precise confines of artifice. Artifice is one of the supreme achievements of civilization because you have to be able to see a thing truly and personally in order to reinvent it. Shakespeare understood this; Mozart understood this; Houdini, too.

I am currently an artistic director. Being an artistic director means that you head an organization that produces artistic experiences. Your name is on a letterhead. You are responsible for many people—for the audience, the community, and a staff of other artists, people who are creative in ways in which you are not. A successful artistic director has put together a staff that understands his needs as an artist and that understands the community he serves. To me, the job of artistic director is really a group effort on the part of a managing director, a literary manager, a production manager, etc. Though I am ultimately responsible for the work produced by the institution, I want to surround my being and my process with knowledgeable, trained people who also take responsibility and actively enjoy many of the aspects that go into the artistic experience. We also exist for ourselves, as people and artists; we exist to produce theatrical experiences for a community; and we exist to examine and honor the work.

Part of that also involves interpreting for a community the works of people who write or have written for the theater. I exist not solely to entertain an audience, but also to serve it. My mission is to fulfill myself as an artist, for if I do not do this, my work will be dishonest. I want to take people out of themselves, and put people back *into* themselves (i.e. reevaluate their life and being). In my work I wish to educate the audience as well as myself. Most of us live such narrow-minded lives; but the Theater says, "There is something else." In achieving this goal I become vulnerable, because I must open myself up, explore my nakedness, my intuition, my limits, and then show what I have learned by exploration.

Mark Lamos, Artistic Director of the Hartford Stage Company, made his professional acting debut at Academy Playhouse in Lake Forest, Illinois, and later appeared on Broadway in plays and musicals. For three seasons at the Guthrie Theater in Minneapolis, during Michael Langham's tenure as Artistic Director, he played many leading roles, and was encouraged to direct at Guthrie II. He also acted and directed at the Old Globe in San Diego. Mr. Lamos served as the Acting Artistic Director of the Arizona Theatre Company in Tucson, and then returned to New York to resume his career as an actor. He appeared at Circle-in-the-Square, Off Broadway, and at Stratford Connecticut's American Shakespeare Festival. In 1978, Mr. Lamos became the Artistic Director of the California Shakespearean Festival in Visalia, where he directed to international critical acclaim. In 1979, for San Francisco Opera's American Opera Project, he directed the world premiere of John Harbison's *Winter's Tale.* During the first two seasons at the Hartford Stage Company, he directed, among other works, the American premieres of *Undiscovered Country* and the three-evening compilation of plays by Aeschulus, Sophocles, and Euripides entitled *The Greeks.* Mr. Lamos has also directed for Opera Theatre of St. Louis, and for Santa Fe Opera. He graduated Northwestern University with a Bachelor of Science in Speech Education.

Photo: Lanny Nagler

"The more
I understand
marketing, the less
I can function as
an artist."

My mission is to validate existence and change minds. I don't particularly like being responsible for an institution, though I assume that responsibility. I do like being responsible for the work it produces. I dislike any thought of having an "image" in a community. The profile of the Hartford Stage Company is delineated by its productions, the production values, the choice of plays, the work of guest directors, designers, composers, writers, actors, and my own work. The artistic ego treads dangerous water when it gets involved in public relations.

A great manager is someone who not only loves and appreciates art and understands the temperaments of artists, but who also is constantly willing (like the audience) to be surprised, astonished, delighted. He does everything in his power to give the artist whose work he is managing, the tools with which to create. He literally "makes life manageable." When life becomes "unmanageable," he is capable of telling an artist why this is so and then leads the artist in new directions. Clearly, his task is promethean.

The audience exists as a sounding board for the artistic impulse. It is the receiver, the empty room in which the noise of the artist echoes. It is dangerous for an artist to want the audience to always be the "friend." An artist exists to shake an audience up, make noise, open unused doors, create spaces. The artist is the communicator; the audience is his other self.

Currently, we are part of a world that mistrusts the spoken word, mistrusts communication. Because of our politics, the actions of government leaders, the repression of free will in so many parts of the world, and because of the explosion of glib media forms, the audience has a hard time exercising its collective brain cells. A lot of people don't know what to think anymore. The theater is a forum for ideas, a place to question values. It is also a place to provide nourishment for the soul, to entertain, to validate and enhance life.

The audience you serve is only partially the particular community in which your institution operates. Your audience also consists of the larger community—the nation and the world. We have become part of a global village; therefore, the provincialism inherent in the words "Broadway" or "regional theater" is giving way to the idea that artists exist everywhere—in the neighborhood, in fact—and that the very words "art" and "artist" now represent something that can be understood and experienced by more people than ever before.

A true artist *shows* a community what it wants. Since the nature of art is to renew and rearticulate life, no audience can know what that experience is going to be. You don't go to a zoo expecting to see a tiger in every cage. After you "experience" tiger, you move on, you get into antelope, giraffe, monkey, eagle. Each is an animal, of course; and each can be seen at the zoo, but each is a totally different experience. Audiences need to understand this. An artist keeps searching and growing; he owes it to his gifts and his audience to keep moving and expanding his horizons.

Since my work is involved in communication, a great part of its dialectic would not exist without an audience. There has to be a receptor. Though the initial impulse of any artist is completely ego-oriented and most adult artists spent a good deal of their childhood alone in their rooms, creating puppet shows on makeshift theaters, listening to the radio, drawing pictures, all solely for their own enjoyment, the artist is now confronted with *communicating* his ideas. Though *he* wants to see something, *he* wants to create something, *he* wants to have a new experience, he must now pass that desire on to an audience (an act which is an art in itself).

"Marketing" is done so that people will pay money to experience what I want to share, experience, create, interpret, evaluate. "Marketing" is a mystery to me, and I wish it to remain so. It is what gets people into the theater seats to see something they've never seen before. The more I understand marketing, the less I can function as an artist, and I expect a good marketing person to understand my ignorance and my lack of desire to learn. One of the vicissitudes of marketing the work produced by a not-for-profit artistic institution is to transform an artistic impulse into a commodity that can be bought and sold. I expect the marketing director to take something he may loathe or love and figure out how to create an audience for it so that people will experience it, and so that the art itself can be complete. Without an audience, the process of the artist is incomplete. Someone who truly understands marketing understands this.

I feel that so much of what we attempt to do is sullied by "salesmanship." I know it's necessary, but when I get involved in it I begin to feel more like a salesman and less like an artist. The artistic impulse is so vulnerable and fragile anyway, that I feel we endanger it when we begin to think of a play we deeply love as a commodity. Marketing directors, it seems to me, are here to take some of this burden from the artist's shoulders, allowing the purest impulse to find its fulfillment in the work onstage rather than its packaging. If I chose to produce *A Midsummer Night's Dream,* for instance, I might do it because of a deep-seated personal idea about the work, or because the audience hasn't had the opportunity to see an Elizabethan comedy for a few years, but I would never program it to sell tickets.

I talk to the marketing director often, and at regularly scheduled meetings. I want each sales campaign to represent the show as correctly as possible. I give him as detailed a description as I can of the style and "feel" of each particular production so that he can represent the show properly in the media.

William Stewart:

Management is the handling, direction, and care of an institution. In the not-for-profit professional theater, this control and governance is most frequently centered in the persons of the artistic director and the managing director. However, because of the public nature of these organizations, the broad policy-making authority originates with the board of trustees who engages the executive management who implements this policy and directs the operation of the theater.

Management structure and policy should develop out of the artistic purpose of the theater. It is the responsibility of the managing director to understand the artistic director's determination of the character, spirit, and quality of the institution and to create the environment in which it can thrive. The choices the manager makes in organizing the direction of the theater are influenced by the artistic director's objectives. Management must provide the financial and physical resources and the personnel to create positive and responsive conditions that are both protective and liberating for the artists.

The managing director weighs the realities and establishes situations allowing for the extension of boundaries and the improvement of opportunities. While many of the duties of management of the institution are equally shared by the managing director and the artistic director, the former should continually be aware that he is in the service of an artist whose esthetic and vision are predominant. He must listen and come to understand the artist's needs and intents. Finally, the relationship between the two must be one of great trust and mutual respect.

A managing director is pragmatic and optimistic, which means that he always has a positive attitude when analyzing the dynamics of the institution's artistic and financial opportunities while remaining alert to the requirements of any given situation. It is the manager who provides the ongoing practical relationship between the institution and the community. This structured connection begins with the board of trustees and takes in the media, funding sources, patrons, and other community resources and agencies.

This is not to suggest that the artistic director shall have no contact with the community. It does mean that the manager will assist the artist by making use of his person and time in a productive, efficient, and protective manner. He will structure the circumstances in which the artist is able more fully to comprehend the community and in which the community can better understand and appreciate the artist. The aboved presupposes an artistic director of unusual talent, imagination, intelligence, and inspiration.

It is the responsibility of the managing director to assist the artistic dirfector in relating his vision and goals to the mission of the institution. A resident professional theater exists to serve its community, its artists, and dramatic art. The emphasis given each of these elements in the operation of the theater provides the creative tensions between the artistic director and his community. The manager's role is to establish an open and productive atmosphere in which those tensions can be explored and exploited in a positive manner, and where the artist is free to pursue his work fully as only he knows it. To this end, the managing director must be capable of spontaneity while exercising authority.

William Stewart has been Managing Director of the Hartford Stage Company since 1976 and held the same position there from 1969 to 1973. During the intervening three years he was Managing Director of the American Shakespeare Theatre, Stratford, Connecticut, where he had begun his career in 1962 as a Ford Foundation administrative intern. In 1967 Mr. Stewart went to the Cincinnati Playhouse as Managing Director. He has been a lecturer at the Yale School of Drama since 1974 and was appointed to the Theatre Administration faculty in 1981. He has served as a consultant for FEDAPT for eight years and is co-director of their Theatre Middle Management Program, Development and Institutional Planning.

"Marketing is a process of total institutional presentation and projection."

While the manager's function is to be totally supportive of the artistic director's role in leading the institution and producing its programs, he also has the principal responsibilities for its overall operation and administration. Included in those are the creation and control of the annual budget, the origination of all fund raising and development, the supervision of personnel other than artistic, and the coordination of all public relations, promotion, sales, and marketing.

In undertaking these activities, the manager will engage additional supervisory personnel. His first decision will relate to the use of his own time, energy, and abilities. He will have a reasonable understanding of his particular interests and his strengths and weaknesses. The manager will want to engage individuals who are better equipped and better able than he is to accomplish a particular job. Traditionally, the manager will separate his work into five general areas: facilities operation (security, maintenance, and front-of-house), production management (shared with the artistic director), financial and business management, planning and development, and marketing and publicity. Middle-management positions are established to supervise the more immediate duties in each of these areas.

The words used to define management in the first paragraph all suggest the most important function of the manager — to communicate. The middle-management staff, no matter how talented and aggressive, will be effective only when the planning process of the artistic and managing directors is fully and regularly communicated to them. In the same way, the institution will be successful only if its purpose and objectives are communicated carefully and skillfully to its community. Marketing is the method of this communication, and it relates to all areas of the operation. The communication originates with the initial understanding between the board, the artist, and the manager as to the nature of their individual theater. Only with clarity of thinking and its careful articulation can marketing begin to function throughout the organization.

Until recently, not-for-profit theater management thought of marketing as an individual function rather than the sum of its parts: public relations, promotion, sales, publicity, and advertising. The annual subscription campaign was a major promotion; single-ticket merchandising was a sales effort; occasional newspaper ads constituted advertising; weekly press releases provided publicity; newsletters and after-performance discussions were public relations. Each effort was appropriate and to a certain extent effective, but seldom was there an overall marketing strategy that could lead to long-term public understanding, commitment, involvement, and participation.

Marketing is a process of total institutional presentation and projection. It consists of long-range objectives for institutional prominence and recognition, and shorter-range goals for program acceptance and growth. The difficulty in implementing these concepts is that the more traditional marketing relationships between the product and the consumer do not apply to performing-arts activities. Not-for-profit theater marketing requires stronger product understanding and orientation and a lesser emphasis on the consumer.

Marketing is thought of as being product or consumer motivated, and it is important for the not-for-profit theater-marketing director to be well aware of the subtleties of difference in these approaches. Product orientation presupposes that something (in this instance, the work of an artistic director in an institutional environment) is being offered that is worthwhile and intrinsically beneficial. Consumer orientation suggests that after discovering the needs, interests, and demands of the consumer, that the product not only might be marketed differently, but also should be changed to accommodate those findings.

Proper not-for-profit resident theater marketing will remain product oriented. The marketing director must first understand the artistic director and the vision he develops for his theater. That artistic expression will be the source of the marketing plan. The role of marketing becomes one of first comprehending the artistic purpose and goals of the theater, and then determining the potential customers for that theater. Research is important in determining the methods of reaching these consumers and in better grasping their motivations for purchasing tickets and attending.

The old term "audience development" suggested that motivation was the result of promotion efforts somewhat disassociated from the work being presented. What is currently advocated is a more thorough understanding of the artist and the work, and a market plan that presents this reality to an identified consumer whose interests and expectations are addressed by the marketing effort.

The foregoing does not lessen the importance of market research and concerns for market position and consumer targeting—just the contrary. These aspects of marketing are most important. Research that enhances the knowledge of the institution's potential audience, its location, and its perceptions and concerns, is of the utmost importance. Such research must be framed by belief in the validity of the work and the philosophy of the artist.

The marketing director must be willing to investigate all potentials for the promotion of the institution within the context of a product that is artist-originated and oriented. The objectives of the institution might become:

1. To realize evolving artistic goals that merit national prominence and recognition while responding to the cultural interest of the community.

2. To serve the maximum audience consistent with the purpose, objectives, and goals articulated by the company.

These objectives evolve from a mission statement that might be phrased: "to offer a range of high-quality professional production of consistent significance."

Currently, too much marketing is being conducted by well-meaning and talented generalists who have been trained in the less exact disciplines of audience development, sales, and public relations. The complexities of today's marketplace, with its competition for the theatergoer's attention, time, and money, call for the most sophisticated methodology. Highly trained individuals are needed to engage in the demanding tasks of performing-arts marketing.

The marketing director should have an advanced degree with a concentration in marketing and some background in the performing arts. He must understand the values and limitations of research. He must know how to plan for its implementation and be able to evaluate its results. He should be skilled in the use of media (newspaper, radio, and television advertising) as well as direct mail. Most importantly, he must be a planner who can develop an overall marketing strategy that provides for public relations, specific promotion, and general sales.

These thoughts regarding management and marketing are directly related to a specific arts instituion—the resident professional theater. The ideas are rooted in a developing conception of institutional mission and long-range objectives informed by an examination of the place this art form occupies in current American culture. Not-for-profit arts managers are only beginning to understand the practical applications and adaptations of profit management and marketing, and they provide direction for continued exploration.

Robert Yesselman

DANCE: MANAGEMENT, MARKETING, AND SCHIZOPHRENIA

Introduction

This chapter is written from the perspective of the executive director of a modern dance company—an art form in which the creator, whose name the institution usually bears, traditionally takes dominance over all other facets of that institution's operations, particularly in marketing and advertising where the identification of name and institution is particularly sensitive. The lessons to be learned, if any, from what follows are, I believe, issues at the crux of the management of any artistic institution and hence of its marketing.

I. Art

A) Perception of the Artist by the Manager

To begin at the beginning, I believe that it is necessary for any arts administrator to examine closely the reasons he has chosen this schizophrenic profession for a career. Certainly there are rewards, but just as certainly, those rewards are more of the spirit than of the flesh. Most often, working conditions are dreadful, pay levels are pathetic, ''perks'' are non-existent, and the desire for the personal spotlight must be sublimated to the good of the institution. I describe the profession as essentially schizophrenic because the administrator is the man in the middle. Increasingly, because of the economic difficulties facing all of us, the administrator must be the rational, shrewd, and well-organized businessman running a fairly sizable business that is, at its base, non-rational. He must be the one to coordinate the basically conflicting points of view between the requirements of funders, boards of trustees (most often made up of successful business people), and sheer business necessities, with the needs of the artist or artists for whom the institution exists. Art, by its very definition, is non-rational communication, and the artist, with very few exceptions, is essentially non-rational in his response to and perception of the world—how else does he create his art? Thus, the administrator must coordinate and balance perceptively the needs of the artist he serves and the commercial world in which the institution that supports the artist exists. This is not easy. Often, it is not pleasant. But this is the world the arts administrator chooses for himself, and he must continually balance this conflict of essentially opposing forces.

What, then, is the reward? Indeed, what is the compulsion that drives us into this profession? I believe that the answer lies in the administrator's perception of the artist he serves. If one believes that art is as essential as daily bread or nuclear submarines, then the administrator is faced with necessity—the necessity to ensure the ability of the artist he serves who must fulfill his own necessity. The artist must create his art in his own way, on his own terms. Lincoln Kirstein, that greatest of arts administrators, in an article entitled ''The Performing Arts and our Egregious Elite,'' said:

If the defenders, patrons, and promotors of the performing arts ... have one salient, modest, persistent duty or objective responsibility, it is to reason and

Robert Yesselman, Executive Director of the Paul Taylor Dance Company, holds a BA in English/Theatre from the State University of New York College at Cortland, awarded in 1965; and an MA in Theatre from Adelphi University in Garden City, New York, awarded in 1968. Mr. Yesselman was a teacher of English, Theatre, and Speech at Bethpage High School in Bethpage, New York, where he organized and was the first Chairman of the Drama Department. While at Bethpage, Mr. Yesselman developed an interdisciplinary approach to the study of the Humanities, still in use at that school. Mr. Yesselman left teaching in 1971 to become Company Manager, then Manager of American Ballet Theatre's Ballet Repertory Company under Richard Englund. In 1975, he was appointed General Manager of the Paul Taylor Dance Company and, in 1983, was named Executive Director. Mr. Yesselman is listed in "Who's Who in America."

"What will sell is important, but not-for-profit organizations must have the ability to say no."

clarify their claims to be associated with a legitimate elite alongside ballplayers, brain surgeons, or brokers. It is time for the inventive, lyric, poetic, creative elite to come out of their closets and declare themselves — their worth, their difference in kind, their capacity, their energy, and their strength. Most of all — their necessity.

I was once in the initial planning stages of an advertising campaign with an agency that had no previous arts or not-for-profit experience and to whom I had given the mandate to "sell us" just as they would any other upscale consumer product. As we sat around the mile-long conference table, surrounded by acres of beige carpeting and rosewood panelling, I found myself rejecting idea after idea that made perfect marketing sense but that I knew would be unacceptable to my own artist's perception of himself and of his artistic image. As I watched these high-pressure professionals becoming increasingly annoyed with my restrictions, I found myself crystallizing for the first time what makes us different from the commercial world — we can say "no." What I said was, "You must understand that this is the very reason that we are a not-for-profit organization—we can, and indeed must, say no." Profit, and what will sell, is important and increasingly crucial to us, but we must have the ability to say no. We must state, "I fully understand that this will sell, that this will work, that XYZ detergent doubled its sales with this approach, but still we can and often, must, say no." This is frustration of the highest order, in fact, it leads to ulcers and early burn-out, but this is the job we choose for ourselves. We must feel that same necessity as the artists we serve.

And where does this sense of necessity come from? It comes from the administrator's own personal response to his artist's art.

For me, this sense of necessity comes from my own response to Paul Taylor's dances and dancers. I often tell prospective employees that their rewards must come from what happens to them when the curtain goes up. Their rewards cannot be monetary—our salaries are not high enough. Their rewards cannot be in making a name for themselves—there is only one name in the name of the company. They must take their reward, their justification, their *raison d'être* from what happens to them and, happily, to the audience, from what that one single man does and how his incredibly talented and dedicated and beautiful dancers show the world what he does.

For the thesis for my master's degree, I wrote on the Jungian elements in the work of a Polish director named Jerzy Grotowski. In my research for this project, I discovered the Jungian precept of the collective subconscious. Those elements in mythology or legend or art that communicate and appeal to all people, in all cultures, in all times. For example, the concept of the hero is one of these: It manifests itself most obviously to us in Greek myth and literature, but also manifests itself with the same characteristics in legends of the Australian aborigines, and the pygmies of Africa, and in Russian literature, and in John Le Carre spy stories. It is my personal belief that this is the essence of the artistic communication—the ability of art to touch us in an individual and non-rational way, the ability of art to stay with us, to enter into our dreams, our unconscious, our beings. And this is what Paul Taylor's work does for me. There are moments of his dances that are ineradicably etched into my subconscious—a little flick of a female dancer's hands in his beautiful *Aureole,* a bird-like and floating entrance for two women in a dance called *Images,* a solo for a blind and crippled dancer in *Dust,* and hundreds of others.

Lest this all sound too altruistic, there are other gratifications as well. In our self-produced home seasons, which occur only once a year, there is the tremendous satisfaction of watching the curtain go up in front of a sold-out house and knowing that I had something to do with this. There is the satisfaction of knowing that that very curtain is going up because of untold hours of planning, worrying, negotiating, bargaining, and dealing on the part of me and my wonderful staff. It is almost a physical sensation on opening night watching that curtain going up—an exhilaration, a relief, a deep sigh. There are few pleasures that can compare with the joy of seeing the work and its effects on that sold-out house.

There is, I suppose, a bit of Diaghilev in all successful arts administrators. Some administrators are more involved in the actual artistic product than I am—that varies greatly from company to company and artist to artist, but that sense of helping to make it happen, of smoothing over as many obstacles as possible for our artists in this commercial and mercenary world, of making it possible for that all-important curtain to go up, *that* must take the place of huge salaries and bonuses and of wide-scale personal recognition. If it doesn't, you are in the wrong business. Look elsewhere for a profession.

B) The Importance of the Artist's Work

Next in importance to one's own personal commitment to an artist's work is the response of the public. A philosopher once said in defining art, "Art endures." For this reason, the administrator must have a realistic understanding of the place of his artist in the greater scene. This is not to say that an artist must be popular—that he must "sell." We all know the stories of the artists who died unacknowledged, only to be discovered fifty years later as major contributors to world culture and man's understanding of himself. But this understanding must be present.

I have already spoken of my personal responses to Paul Taylor's work. It is my further good fortune to work for a man who is generally acknowledged to be one of the dominant forces in our art form. This is a great source of personal and professional pride. But more importantly, it gives me the ammunition I need to take my own love of the work to funders and supporters and audiences and sponsors and bookers and advertising people and P.R. people and the world in general to ensure the fulfillment of our own institution's goals.

Paul Taylor Dance Company. *Mercuric Tidings.* **Photo: Lois Greenfield.**

I am sometimes accused of having too much missionary zeal, of being too much "Paul Taylor's man," but I must say that I don't really understand how this can be otherwise. If your belief is deeply founded, if your dedication is such that you take the job for the reasons mentioned above, how can it be otherwise? To leave it unspoken is to deny why one becomes an arts administrator to begin with. It is this conviction that allows you to be the reconciler, the propagandist, the marketer, the advertiser, the advocate.

We have just created a new staff position and were able to attract an extremely effective and well-known candidate for the job. When she accepted, after, I know, many offers from other institutions, she said that the reason she accepted was the uncommon dedication of everyone in the company to Paul Taylor's work—not only my own dedication, but that of our board president, our board members, and every staff person who works here. It seems that in each interview she had with a member of the Taylor organization, each person started out by saying that requirement number one was an understanding of the work and the man who makes the work. She saw it in action.

C) Understanding the Needs of the Artist

Second in importance to the administrator's love and personal relationship to the art he administers, is an understanding of the artistic vision of the specific artist. Needless to say, individual artists want different things, and it is the responsibility of the administrator to understand clearly and intimately his own artist's method of working, his tools, the conditions necessary for him to create, and his perhaps unspoken desires in the public and private arenas.

As I mentioned earlier, perhaps the most difficult area of an arts administrator's job is to reconcile the rational needs of running a business with the often irrational needs of the artist for whom that business exists. An administrator who cannot find this reconciliation, who cannot balance these opposing forces in a sensitive and responsive way, is not a successful administrator. Those elusive rewards for all the hard work that makes up this job then become more than elusive — they no longer exist.

This reconciliation will often go against the grain of the individual administrator. Indeed, speaking of balance once again, the administrator must find within himself just how far he can bend in order to maintain this balance. Certainly, we must all bow to the demands of the artists for whom we work—sometimes we must bend a little, and sometimes we must bend a lot. Sometimes — and this is the crux of the balance question—we must decide that we cannot bend any further, and the only solution to this problem is to resign. Thus, the administrator's understanding of his artist's needs is at the core of his job description, and is crucial to his success.

What does the artist want for himself? What does he want for his institution? What are the conditions the artist must have to do his work? How much time does he need? Does the administrator understand these wants? Does he agree with them so that he can put his heart and mind into making them possible? Have the artist and the administrator ever spoken about them? How far is the artist willing to bend? Can the artist's often unspoken aims for himself be accomplished in the hard, cold "real world"? These are questions that must be asked and, I suspect, seldom are. It seems to me that the artist-administrator relationship is quite similar to a marriage—both sides must understand each other on the surface and below, because divorce is disruptive and unpleasant.

Summary: The Artist and the Manager

Thus, in modern dance, an art form in which the individual creator traditionally takes dominance over all areas of an institution's operations, the two crucial issues to be faced are:

1. The administrator's personal response to and understanding of his artist's work which must serve to provide him with the rewards and satisfactions any sensitive person needs from his daily work.

2. The absolutely essential ability of the administrator to balance the contradictory needs of running a business in a cold, hard world of diminishing financial resources with the often irrational needs of a creator who is creating an irrational yet essential product.

II. Marketing

For the administrator, all the issues referred to above—the manager's perception of the artist he serves, the manager's personal commitment to the artist's work, the manager's ability to reconcile the contradictory needs of art and business—come to the forefront over the issue of marketing. It is on this most sensitive issue that the latent conflict between manager and artist can turn into a monster and jump out of the closet. It is also in this area that a manager can have a profound effect on an institution's profile in two essential spheres:

1. The institution's recognition by its audience and the effects of that recognition on ticket sales, touring, and fundraising from individuals.

2. The institution's recognition by the professional funding community — the corporations, foundations, and governmental agencies that often do not understand the sensitivity of artists to the market place and do not understand why arts institutions won't and can't sell themselves in the same ways that are successful for those agencies.

In no other area of an institution's operations is there so much challenge for the administrator. In no other area is that challenge fraught with so much potential conflict and frustration.

A) Evolution of a Marketing Plan: The Campaign of 1982

Prior to its 1982 New York season, the Taylor Company had had a comfortable and by most standards, successful, history of home seasons. Using traditional marketing methods (to be discussed below), overall paid attendance had hovered around 70% of capacity. After a successful one-week season in 1976, an unbroken string of superb work from Mr. Taylor, unusually favorable critical reaction, an increasingly loyal and growing audience, respectable television exposure, and the generosity of funders, had contributed to permitting the company to comfortably manage self-producing four years of three-week seasons without putting itself out of business.

A turning point in my own attitude towards marketing was reached during the 1981 season with the premiere of a new dance by Mr. Taylor called *Arden Court*. Critical acclaim (Clive Barnes in the New York Post, said in the biggest type I've ever seen, something like, "Last night I myself had the experience of standing in front of a work of genius...") and audience reaction to this work was extraordinary. Lines formed at the box office, the office phones never stopped ringing, there was

"It is on the issue of marketing that the latent conflict between manager and artist can turn into a monster."

an excitement in the air at each performance of the dance. It was rather like going to bed one perfectly ordinary night, and waking up the next morning to discover you are the new toast of the town. Yet, when the season was over and the excitement was buried in the statistical analysis that should follow any season, three very disturbing facts were evident:

1. Overall attendance at the season increased only marginally over previous seasons, partly due to the six sold-out performances of *Arden Court* that had been scheduled.

2. Having spent much time in the box office savoring lines going out the lobby door (a rare and delicious experience for a modern-dance manager), I had made the upsetting observation that people were coming to the box office to ask for tickets for *Arden Court*. When told that all performances of the dance were sold out, they turned around and walked out. They showed no interest in the Taylor Company itself, and no interest in other works that had been just as rapturously received by both critics and audiences.

3. I had recently seen a performance of Bob Fosse's *Dancin'*, then in its sixth year on Broadway. The performance, on a weekday evening, was sold out, and the show, even that late in its run, was still pulling in substantial houses. The audience had, I think, a marvelous evening. My own reaction was less marvelous. I readily admit that I am prejudiced when it comes to looking at other people's choreography—my reaction to and close relationship with Mr. Taylor's work has given me something of a jaundiced eye—but most other dancing just doesn't look right. Yet, readily acknowledging my prejudice, I felt very deeply that if that audience watching *Dancin'* could be persuaded to go to City Center, they would have a better time, at lower cost, with more satisfaction, than they had had on Broadway.

Thus, there I was with a major success on my hands that had played to an overall average of 76% of the capacity of only 1,561 seats for eighteen performances. And there was *Dancin'* in its *sixth year* doing better business at higher prices. Something was wrong. I set out to find out what it was.

The basic problem, I thought, was in the public's perception not so much of the Paul Taylor Dance Company (although this had to be dealt with — despite our relative popularity in the dance world we are not exactly a household word — because we are still asked if Paul is any relation to June Taylor and *her* dancers), but of "modern dance," whatever that is. I suspected that when the general public heard that term what they saw was lots of blue stage light, Greek myths, writhing, masks—esoteric, dense, unfathomable, effete—definitely not something to be enjoyed, to be moved by, or something that made you laugh or cry.

The challenge then became how to communicate to the general public that Paul Taylor's work is not what they think of as "modern dance." How was I to let them know that they would be excited and stimulated, shown true beauty and true ugliness, that they would laugh and they would cry, that they could be touched and moved in ways they perhaps didn't know they could be—and have a good time as well.

B) The Marketing Plan

The answer, I thought, was to find a professional communicator who could look at dance from the outside, someone who had no preconceptions about the art form and the way "they" say it should be treated in marketing and advertising.

I began by going through a directory of advertising agencies, noting those whose advertising I remembered and admired. I wound up with a list of twenty-seven agencies and wrote to the creative director of each. I had chosen to write to the creative directors because of an observation I had made at the few advertising agencies with which I had worked in the past. Agencies, as you may know, are made up of two parts: the business end (account executives, vice presidents for this and that) and the "creative end" (art directors, copywriters, graphics people, etc.). With few exceptions, the "creative" people considered themselves failed artists and writers who had sold out for the offer they received from the big-bucks agencies and now had wives and children and mortgages and the like.

Our relatively small advertising budget, and my insistence that the agency work without the usual percentage applied to typesetting, mechanicals, space buys, etc.,

> "There is a bit of Diaghilev in all successful arts administrators."

would not be of interest to the agency's business people. My hope was to interest a strong creative type whom the agency's management felt they had to keep happy. I thought that if, at least, the agency didn't lose any money on our account, they would gain by letting their creative people be creative for a not-for-profit creative institution. This might result in benefits for the agency as a whole.

My letter to each of the agencies began with the following sentence: "With reviews like these, why ain't we rich?" and went on to detail the *Arden Court* season's sales results, advertising schedule and budget, my own description of Mr. Taylor's work ("witty, virile and athletic" was a key phrase), copies of the season's ads, an acknowledgement that they probably wouldn't make any money on us but what a challenge they'd have, etc. Of the twenty-seven agencies, eight responded, and I spent a giddy few weeks interviewing creative directors from agencies large and small, from boutique-style (2 or 3 member staffs) to multinational conglomerates. What was I looking for in these interviews? I'm not really sure. I was depending more on "vibes" than on anything else. I had a natural reluctance to go with the huge agencies, fearing that as very small fish we could easily get lost. I was looking for someone who specialized in fresh approaches, who looked at things in a slightly different way than anyone else. I found Don Staley.

Two of his previous ads had prompted me to write to him. The first was the rather famous campaign (in advertising circles, at least) for *U.S. News and World Report* that featured head shots of celebrities associated with a particular form (Craig Claiborne—"No Recipes." Andy Warhol—"No Gossip.") The second was for a small florist on the Upper West Side of New York. The ad featured exquisite line drawings of flowers with the price per stem given for each, under a huge headline reading: "STARTING TODAY, NEW YORKERS CAN LIVE ALMOST AS WELL AS THE MOST DEMANDING FRENCH PEASANTS." Both of these campaigns were extremely successful in accomplishing their aims.

Staley himself, had, in my mind, the right "vibes." He began his presentation to me by showing me a solid page of advertisements from the *Times* Arts and Leisure section. He described this page as "static." Not one ad stood out. Not one ad was essentially different from any other ad, whether it was for a Broadway show or for a "cultural event." His presentation crystallized thoughts that had been building in me for a long time. All arts advertising, and I know of no exceptions, has always consisted of precisely the same elements: a pretty picture, an esthetically pleasing typeface, a terrific quote from a terrific review from a well-known reviewer (preferably *The New York Times*), the dates, times, programs, and sometimes the prices. Take any arts ad from the newspaper you read today and see if this is not so. Transfer one pretty picture and one esthetically pleasing typeface, and one program—is there any difference? Imagine an entire page of these. This is static.

Let us consider each of these elements and its effectiveness:

1. A Pretty Picture:

The Problem: Photographs simply do not reproduce well in newspapers. Our eye almost automatically adjusts itself to see a newspaper photograph on the page not as it is printed, but "for real." In dance, the problem is compounded tenfold because dance is an art of movement and an art of the manipulation of depth; no photograph on earth can even begin to reproduce the experience of a live dancer moving through space, and yet this is how we represent ourselves to the general public—gray, drab, static, flat. Another dance complication is that the person who selects or approves the photograph to be used (and probably rightly so) is often more concerned with a step being executed perfectly or a pinkie being perfectly positioned than with what the photograph will say to the general public or how it will catch the eye when surrounded by many other photographs. This is probably justifiable, but it is as big a problem in the ballet world as it is here in the modern.

One Solution: Don't use a photograph. Capitalize on what newspaper printing can do well rather than what it does worst. Bold, highly contrasted line drawings or images reproduce well, particularly when surrounded by as much white space as possible, jump out from the page. Your art should jump out at the audience; so should your advertising.

Paul Taylor Dance Company. Elie Chaib, David Parsons, Kenneth Tosti and Thomas Evert in *Cloven Kingdom*. Photo: Jack Mitchell.

2. An Esthetically Pleasing Typeface:

The Problem: Much the same as in the pretty picture. Typefaces, as we all know, carry a great deal of emotion in very obvious and very subtle ways. They are also design objects. Thus, the selection of a typeface for an ad is often based on design elements rather than on communication. Certain typefaces are cold and austere in their purity of form—the well-known Helvetica typefaces are the perfect example. Yet this very purity of form that transmits ''COLD'' to the general audience transmits ''PURE'' to the artist choosing it.

One Solution: Try to pick a typeface that transmits what you see as the appeal of what you are selling—excitement, movement, confrontation, joy, uniqueness. It should jump from the page along with the graphic image.

3. A Terrific Quote From A Terrific Review From A Well-Known Reviewer (Preferably The New York Times)

The Problem: Everyone knows the jokes concerning quotes in ads. Broadway producer David Merrick hiring someone named Clive Barnes to praise a show the real Barnes (who was, at the time, The New York Times' theater critic), had panned is my personal favorite. The trouble is, the general public knows the jokes, too. Add to this the difficulty that every ad contains a quote saying: ''ONE OF THE TEN BEST (DANCES, DRAMAS, OPERAS, COMEDIES, MOVIES) IN THE EN-TIRE HISTORY OF LIFE AS WE KNOW IT'' and you see the problem. Since everything can't be one of the TEN BEST (there are, after all, just ten numbers in ten), then which really is and which really isn't? This, too, is static.

One Solution: It is somehow hard not to use quotes. These are, after all, the ''experts'' and they've said wonderful things about us. The point is, don't use them as static—use them as reinforcement to describe, to ''pitch,'' to confirm the buyer's superb judgement. Communicate your own special message in some other way. I will discuss this topic in a separate section below.

4) Dates, time, programs, etc.: Yes.

Thus did Staley and I set out to express these thoughts, and more that were to come, in an advertising campaign that could at least begin to address the question of why I couldn't fill 1,561 seats for eighteen performances in the midst of a set of truly extraordinary reviews at lower prices than most other live attractions in New York City.

The next step was for Staley to see the Taylor Company in performance. (He, like so many others, had never seen us.) Luckily, the Company had a season at the Brooklyn Academy of Music, and Staley attended every performance. Following the first, and to my great relief, he came out of the theater bug-eyed and red-faced. He said, in what was almost a scream: ''I am your audience. I never knew it could be like this. Why didn't I know?'' And he went home and started to write an ad.

Before the actual writing, however, he needed to know more about dance and the dance audience. There was another problem to be overcome—how to appeal to a new and broader audience while not offending our traditional and dance-aware audience. As we already had a respectable-sized and loyal audience, this had to be taken into consideration.

We began by looking at the dance world in general, and then the particular place the Taylor Company occupied in that world—in advertising parlance, the ''positioning'' of the company.

Staley had me write what I subsequently called my term paper. He asked me to choose the five other dance companies that I considered our closest ''competition.'' What was their work like? What were their strengths and weaknesses? Who did I sense their audience was? What was their profile—demographically, by sex, by age, by income level. What was their advertising like? What were their sales results like? From this term paper, we determined that the classical ballet had come closest to ''commercial'' success. Both the major New York City companies, the New York City Ballet and American Ballet Theatre were, to our minds, the ''gold standard'' of the field. They played in very large, very impressive houses (the New

> "With few exceptions, the ad agency 'creative' people considered themselves failed artists and writers."

"All arts
advertising has
consisted of the
same elements:
a pretty picture, an
esthetically
pleasing
typeface...
this is static."

York State Theater and the Metropolitan Opera House, both shining white and impressive marble edifices in Lincoln Center), at somewhat higher prices for considerably longer seasons than ours. Corporate executives entertained clients at both. Because of movies and publicity and the romantic/classical ballet repertory, through superstars and through the built-in favoritism this country still holds towards European art forms, these huge ballet companies had established "respectability."

We, the moderns, on the other hand, although many of us had been around as long, did not have this visibility. Our seasons are considerably shorter, our theaters less impressive, and we are always off touring. Although our choreographers are often known, our traditions have not developed superstars in the Baryshnikov sense.

What we did have, however, was the conviction that we had an indigenous and uniquely American art form (at a time when the country was moving to the right politically), in many cases recognized and feted more abroad than at home (Mr. Taylor, and now Merce Cunningham have both been made chevaliers in France). And perhaps even more importantly, what we also had was an art that was accessible (by no means a dirty word), that could communicate to everyone, that could move audiences, that could excite them, and could make them laugh and cry. And there was also a huge audience already attending ballet and sensitized to the kind of communication that dance does so well.

Thus, Staley's job, as he set it up for himself, was to communicate this to the general public, with particular aim at the huge ballet audience, and to communicate this in a way that would jump off the page—overcoming the almost overwhelming static against which the ad would be situated. We also had to overcome what we both felt was the misconception in the general public's mind about what modern dance really was—not esoteric but accessible, not effete but athletic and virile, not always serious and obscure but also filled with joy and light.

C) The Campaign

We began by first reapportioning the advertising budget. In the past, newspaper ads had been relatively small in order to permit elaborate, four-color, coated-stock, direct-mail extravaganzas. Who did these impressive packages go to? To our traditional audience: our own house mailing list and lists swapped with other dance companies and cultural attractions. Sometimes we would be very daring and add a few thousand names from a particularly high-toned magazine. Yet we were spending all this money to impress all these people who had, presumably, already been impressed by the real thing—they had seen the work in live production. In a sense, they did not need to be sold—the experience with the work had done that for them.

Thus, the direct-mail budget was drastically reduced. A simple, word-processed letter would take the place of the elaborate direct-mail subscription packages of the past. The letter would provide a glimpse of the season to come—the premieres, the revivals, the repertory—and would remind the recipient of the wonderful time they had hopefully experienced. It would also provide a simple and convenient way to order tickets.

The rest of the budget would go to building an awareness and a presence, and to communicating a very special message. It would do this in the most natural outlet for this kind of message—the Arts and Leisure section of the Sunday *New York Times*—and it would do this in a unique way. It would also do it in a full page (permitted budgetarily by the reduction of direct-mail production costs), and it would be surrounded by as much white space as we could get.

D) The Message

In the section above about traditional arts advertising, what was described was what I call "Announcement Advertising." It does not sell. It does not tell the public *why* they should buy our product. What it does do is say, "Here we are. We are pretty and dignified. Take it or leave it."

We set out to do in our advertising what every other kind of advertising does except those for the arts—we tried to tell people *why* they should see us, what to expect of the experience, why we are better, different, worthwhile. It's important to know why you should buy a BMW rather than a Mercedes and what you will get for your money.

E) The Ad Itself:

For $21, you will understand sex, power, gravity, music, fear, humor and joy better than ever before.

In Moscow and Leningrad people start lining up at 3 AM in the morning, in lines 17 blocks long, in order to see the intensely American Paul Taylor Dance Company. These people aren't "art" snobs. They are housewives, soldiers, surgeons, teenagers.

Paul Taylor is a shy,
publicity-avoiding man who takes
those ingredients seen in great painting
and heard in great music
that can make crowds of people
become speechless and
exuberant.
He combines these forces
with the unexplainable
things that beautiful
glistening human bodies do
to our spirits
as they leap, touch, entwine,
make us laugh,
suddenly make us comprehend.

1 Tues. April 13/7:00 PM
   Gala opening night benefit
   Arden Court/Orbs●

2 Wed. April 14/8:00 PM
   Airs/Lost, Found & Lost†/
   Le Sacre du Printemps

3 Thurs. April 15/8:00 PM
   Profiles/3 Epitaphs/Orbs●

4 Fri. April 16/8:00 PM
   Airs/Lost, Found & Lost†/
   Le Sacre du Printemps

5 Sat. April 17/8:00 PM
   Esplanade/House of Cards*/
   Arden Court

6 Sun. April 18/2:30 PM
   Profiles/3 Epitaphs/Orbs●

7 Tues. April 20/8:00 PM
   (untitled new work)†/
   Private Domain/Cloven Kingdom

8 Wed. April 21/8:00 PM
   Esplanade/House of Cards*/
   Arden Court

9 Thurs. April 22/8:00 PM
   (untitled new work)†/
   Private Domain/Cloven Kingdom

10 Fri. April 23/8:00 PM
   Airs/Lost, Found & Lost†/
   Arden Court

11 Sat. April 24/8:00 PM
   Profiles/3 Epitaphs/Orbs●

12 Sun. April 25/2:30 PM
   Esplanade/House of Cards*/
   Arden Court

13 Tues. April 27/8:00 PM
   Profiles/3 Epitaphs/Orbs●

14 Wed. April 28/8:00 PM
   (untitled new work)†/
   Private Domain/Cloven Kingdom

15 Thurs. April 29/8:00 PM
   Airs/Lost, Found & Lost†/
   Le Sacre du Printemps

16 Fri. April 30/8:00 PM
   Esplanade/House of Cards*/
   Le Sacre du Printemps

17 Sat. May 1/8:00 PM
   (untitled new work)†/
   Private Domain/Cloven Kingdom

18 Sun. May 2/2:30 PM
   Airs/Lost, Found & Lost†/
   Le Sacre du Printemps

Program subject to change. †World Premiere *City Center Premiere ●Major Revival

Reserve early. Experience an American art form at its very height.

Discount deadline: March 19

SINGLE TICKET PRICES BELOW:	15% DISCOUNT FOR 2 PERFORMANCES:	15% DISCOUNT FOR 3 PERFORMANCES:
☐ Opening night* benefit $150 (No discount)		
☐ Orch $21	☐ $35.70 ($17.85 each)	☐ $53.55
☐ Mezz. A-C $30	☐ $51.00 ($25.50 each)	☐ $76.50
☐ Mezz. D-H $20	☐ $34.00 ($17.00 each)	☐ $51.00
☐ Mezz. J-L $15	☐ $25.50 ($12.75 each)	☐ $38.25
☐ Mezz. M-N $10	☐ $17.00 ($ 8.50 each)	☐ $25.50

*Call 966-6959 for information

Performance(s) I want to see _____
(Indicate by number, 1 through 18 from list above)

Number of tickets for each performance _____

Total price $ _____
Box office opening: Monday, March 29. Group discount 10%.
Call 581-7907

MAIL TO CITY CENTER,
131 W. 55th ST., NYC 10019

To charge subscriptions, call 581-7907 weekdays 10 AM-6 PM. To charge individual performance tickets, call Chargit (212) 944-9300

☐ Check enclosed, payable to City Center Subscriptions

☐ Charge to ☐ MasterCard ☐ Visa ☐ American Express
Card # _____ Expiration date _____
Signature required _____
Name _____
Address _____
City _____ State _____ Zip _____
Daytime phone _____ Evening phone _____

Beyond ballet. Beyond inhibition. Beyond language.
The Paul Taylor Dance Company

18 performances only. April 13-May 2/City Center

"The corporate funding officers all said the same thing: 'Oh, you're the company with those ads. It's about time you not-for-profits tried to sell yourselves. We thought they were terrific.' "

Let us look at this ad as a collection of separate elements:

1. The Headline: "For $21, you will understand sex, power, gravity, music, fear, humor, and joy better than ever before." A word about "sex"—this is an issue that the dance world does not often confront openly. On any rational level, part of the appeal of dance in live performance is unquestionably sexual. The dancer's superb body, in scanty and form-molding costumes specifically designed to accentuate the perfection of that superb body, with lighting specially designed again to reveal that body moving through space, is undeniably a powerful element in the subconscious appeal of dance, whether it is acknowledged or not. In the most crass Madison Avenue terms, "sex sells." The very word makes most readers pay attention. Placed in the upper right-hand corner of the page, where the reader's eye falls first, it is a gimmick, but to my mind a valid one, to make the ad read.

Staley's choice of the other words in the headline, all words that relate specifically to the work was, to my mind, inspired. With the opening "For $21," a certain wit and irony was injected that lightened the possible pretension of the headline. My own initial reaction was, "And for $22.50 you can sit at the right hand of God." It certainly jumped from the page.

2. The Sub-Headline: "Beyond ballet. Beyond inhibition. Beyond language."

- "Beyond ballet": Obviously, target number one was the ballet audience discussed above.
- "Beyond inhibition": Target number two again had to do with the subconscious appeal of the dance—those superb bodies doing things that we mere mortals cannot. I am constantly impressed, following a performance, watching people walk up the aisles dancing. Children are a particular delight in this regard because the inhibitions of being "grown up" and restrained have not yet been fully implanted. I remember in my own early days of watching dance, I would find myself, with great embarassment, trying to bourée up an aisle, or spin at a street corner. This element of the appeal of dance is visceral in its nature and thus unconscious.
- "Beyond language": dance is a non-verbal art. It communicates in other words and yet we say, "I was so happy, or I was so sad that words failed …"

3. The Body Text: "In Moscow and Leningrad, etc.": an attempt to address that still-existing prejudice about anything home grown being inferior to that which is imported. The facts were true and impressive—in 1976, the Taylor Company toured the USSR with the results mentioned. "Paul Taylor is…": an attempt to pin a personality (we live in an age of the celebrity) on the relatively little-known and intensely private man whose company this is. It was an attempt to counter the superstar syndrome, and to make something essentially faceless have a face.

4. The Drawings: As mentioned earlier, we felt that photographs do not work in newspaper reproduction and that they cannot possibly express the movement that is at the heart of dance. Thus, a commercial artist was engaged to sit in on rehearsals and to see every photograph we had. His mandate was to express the movement, to express the mystery, the athleticism, and the humor of what we were selling. The drawings that resulted felt somewhat classical in feeling, almost Leonardo-like, and fostered the impression, despite the movement they contained, of a permanence and stability to the institution. The typeface, a Times Roman, reinforced this impression, and somehow managed to tone down any potential misunderstanding of the headline. Additionally, and bear this in mind, it is easy to read and it reproduced well in newspaper printing, particularly in the *Times,* since it is an adaptation of their own typeface.

5. The Ordering Mechanism: I had felt for a long time (and this was confirmed by Staley after he had studied other arts advertising), that we were making it too complicated to buy our product. The huge ordering mechanisms we are all familiar with, involving boxes and calendars and seating locations, was familiar to those who were used to ordering tickets in advance, but off-putting to the general public. We gave ourselves the mandate of simplifying the ordering process as much as humanly possible. We eliminated the usual calendar format for performance

schedules. We eliminated the usual box format for seating locations. We numbered each of the performances (1 through 18); we made seat selection a check-off process; and we strove to make instructions as simple and wide open as possible. We were aiming for "Pick the nights you want, check the seats you want, and that's it." My own personal feeling is that we succeeded (in all fairness, others felt we had not) and we have simplified this system further still for upcoming campaigns. The subscription office at City Center had fewer problems with our orders than with any other company's.

The rest of the advertising campaign was constructed along traditional lines. We kept an advertising presence visible for six weeks following the first full-page ad (it was repeated the following Sunday, followed by smaller ads), and we ran day-of-performance ads, based on the "Beyonds" of the sub-head, for the "dailies."

F) The Results

I will discuss the results of the campaign in three components: advance sale results, day of performance buying, and long-term results.

1. Advance Sales: Tickets purchased through mail order, Chargit (a New York City telephone charge system for theater tickets), and at the box office prior to opening night, approximately doubled from the previous year. Total advance sales for the 1981 season were approximately $50,000, and slightly over $100,000 for the 1982 campaign. Subscription sales (available only through our direct mail campaign or through the two full-page New York Times ads) approximately tripled from slightly under $21,000 for 1981 to slightly over $56,000 for this campaign.

2. Day of Performance Buying: Overall sales for the season as a whole increased only marginally—from 76% of capacity for 1981, to 82% of capacity for 1982. Two works were premiered in the 1982 season, and both were very well received, but without the magic reaction that had been engendered by Arden Court of 1981. Arden Court itself, needless to say, was repeated. Performances in which it was included did marginally better than those without. Staley and I both feel that the dailies were not productive in the sense that the advance-sale advertising was. The dailies, of necessity, are smaller. They permit considerably less visual impact against the static of their placement. They must relay "Tonight at 8:00" information and that leaves precious little space for anything else. We even tried inserting some terrific quotes from some current terrific reviews from major reviewers, and this had no noticeable effect. Sales certainly held up, there was no decrease over previous years, but the dramatic response to the initial ads just did not happen. This is a subject to be addressed in subsequent campaigns.

3. Long-term results:

The power of a full-page advertisement in The New York Times, particularly boosted by the uniqueness of our message, has had substantial long-term ramifications. In the spring and summer of 1982, as a result of those forces drearily familiar to anyone in the arts reading this book, the Taylor Company had to hit the fund-raising trail very seriously. As I made the rounds of one corporate office after another begging for alms, the majority of corporate funding officers all had the same thing to say: "Oh, you're the company with those ads. It's about time you not-for-profits tried to sell yourselves. We thought they were terrific." Whether this got us one cent more in contributions than we would have gotten otherwise I cannot prove, but we had been noticed and we had been seen as trying to increase our earned income levels, and we met our goals for corporate contributions for the fiscal year.

The arts community, on the other hand, had a mixed reaction as did the members of our audience. Most managers and administrators were excited, as were some artistic directors of institutions other than my own. Some highly respected members of the community were deeply offended, the standard reaction being, "Paul Taylor doesn't have to be sold like (pause) this." Some audience members found the mention of "sex" in an arts advertisement to be reprehensible. Others felt the ads were patronizing. We received exactly sixteen letters protesting the campaign (Staley had predicted six), and one mailer that had carried the "For $21 line" on the envelope was ripped into tiny pieces and mailed to us in the business-reply envelope. I had two favorite reactions to the campaign. The first came from a man

I deeply admire and respect, involved in all the arts but particularly involved in dance who used the word "loathsome" in a tone of voice one would use if, at a fancy dinner party, a rotten and stinking mackerel was put on his plate. The second, from a prominent member of the funding community, asked if any of "its" money was involved in the campaign. When I said the campaign had been unusually productive, he replied, "Yes, but just who will you draw with these ads?" I must report that I saw not one little old man in a black raincoat salivating over our dancers at any performance. We tripled our subscriptions and we doubled our advance sales.

In Liberace's immortal phrase, we cried all the way to the bank.

OPERA: DEFINITIONS AND DIRECTIONS

(In the process of identifying contributors to this publication, it was very important to garner the participation of management people from primary performing-arts institutions. A telephone conversation with Gary Fifield, Managing Director of the Washington Opera, about this editorial endeavor so intrigued me that the only substantive approach to communicating the answers to the questions that we raised during our initial conversation was to do the same again. I engaged Gary in a discussion that would yield a transcribed dialogue between us rather than having him compose an essay or opinion paper on the subjects we investigated.)

JOSEPH MELILLO
I would like to begin our dialogue with a discussion on the art of opera. What is opera? How do you define it?

GARY FIFIELD
People have been trying to categorize opera for hundreds of years. Many people consider it solely a type of music, but it's not. It's *OPERA*. When *The Washington Post* started using an ABC listing, they insisted on including us under the music heading, but we finally got them to agree to put us under the separate category, "opera" when we advertise in the ABC's. The National Endowment for the Arts (NEA), too, attempted to find a definition while including opera in their music program several years ago. Eventually, opera was separated from the NEA Music Program, and now there is an Opera—Musical Theater Program.

To answer your question directly, I believe that opera is the culmination of almost all of the arts. Opera is singing and acting; it's frequently dancing; and it's pageantry, which relates directly to the visual arts. Simply stated, it's the last great magic show. I think that's why it's suddenly enjoying such a surge of popularity all over this country. Audiences for opera in the last ten years have grown by leaps and bounds. I think people are responding to opera differently than they used to, for any number of reasons. In some ways, it's a reaction to the "little box" (television), it's a reaction to certain trends in theater where relatively small, sparse productions proliferate. You see the popularity reflected on Broadway today with the return of the "extraordinary" musical. But to go back and answer your question, opera is its own unique self.

JM
Would you describe what your company believes its artistic purpose or mission to be?

GF
This company is unique in the United States. We use two theaters in the Kennedy Center—the Opera House, which has 2,200 seats, and is acoustically one of the best in the world. We also have the Terrace Theater, which has 475 seats and is a "jewel

Gary Fifield, Managing Director of The Washington Opera since 1976, was born in Los Angeles, California and attended the University of Missouri, where he majored in English Literature. Mr. Fifield became the Business Manager for the Kansas City Lyric Theater in Kansas City, Missouri, in 1962. From 1965 to 1969, he was Assistant to the General Director, Kurt Adler, of the San Francisco Opera Association. Upon moving to New York, Mr. Fifield became a free-lance consultant to various Broadway and off-Broadway productions, not-for-profit arts service organizations and costume and property studios. Mr. Fifield was Executive Director of Opportunity Resources for the Arts in New York, from 1972 to 1976. In addition to having been a member of the Board of Directors of the Cultural Alliance of Greater Washington and OPERA America, Mr. Fifield has been a frequent guest lecturer and participant in panels and conferences sponsored by the National Endowment for the Arts, Association of American Dance Companies, American Association of Museums, New York State Council on the Arts, and for numerous other arts-related institutions and committees.

"Audiences for opera are in some ways a reaction to small, sparse productions in the theatre."

box" of a theater. The Washington Opera is unique in that our audiences, during a continuous three-month season, go from one of these houses to the other. Now you ask, "What's the real difference between the two houses?" The spectacle, the choruses, and the dancers yield the grand opera experience—this is what we provide the public in the Opera House. But there are other works that are best seen in the Terrace Theater. Opera-goers are used to seeing *The Barber of Seville* produced in huge opera houses. Most people don't realize that the theater Rossini originally composed it for had only 800 seats. In a small theater, you tone down *The Barber of Seville,* play it with the size of orchestra it was originally scored for, and you must have—I know this term has become a cliché—*singing actors* in the title roles. While a gesture in the Opera House requires both hands stretched out as far as you can get them in order to communicate to the person sitting in the two thousandth seat in the third tier, in the Terrace Theater an artistic impact may be achieved with the arch of an eyebrow. The whole approach is very different. It's a theatrical approach. You have to avoid having fat ladies dying of consumption. You cannot cheat on costumes or scenery; it has to be a very elegant operation. But it's also a place where you can do extraordinary works, like *The Rake's Progress* or *Postcard from Morocco*—operas that have musical and theatrical values of equal importance.

To define our mission, we first have to realize that we exist in a special city, in a special building, and in a special combination of theaters. Our public is extraordinary. Subscribers include members of the international community, leaders from all over the country, and even members of the President's administration. We also have people from smaller cities and towns from all over the country. So in a sense, our mission is to use our two stage houses to properly produce the whole repertory of opera from the baroque to the contemporary. The big and the small, the various styles. Our recent *Tosca* had a very traditional production with an international cast. *Falstaff* had an entirely American cast in which ensemble performance was emphasized. In the Terrace Theater, we try to engage the most important of the younger American artists, the ones we believe are going to have major operatic careers. There again, we try to show an audience that works such as *The Barber of Seville* can be theatrical fun as well as musical fun and can be performed in an intimate context. We show them contemporary operas they don't get an opportunity to see, we include Gilbert and Sullivan works, and offer rarely produced Offenbach works. We try to remember that all of the production elements have to be given equal weight. We don't believe in "stand up and sing." We insist on three weeks of rehearsal, which is almost unheard of in this super jet age. We want ensemble performances set within the most appropriate theatrical setting. Great emphasis is placed on the scenery and costumes, because we consider them to be integral to the art form. We try to have as many rehearsals on the stage as we possibly can (which is a very expensive proposition), and we usually have two complete dress rehearsals with full orchestra.

JM
To relate this discussion of the "art" the Washington Opera is creating, to its management...as the managing director, would you clarify your relationship to the resident dramaturge and the general director of the company?

GF
It's very interlocked. One of the first things I learned in my career is that it comes down to how much art can you buy for a buck? It sounds horribly insensitive, but it's a fact of our lives that art and dollars go hand in hand. Although everyone might think of Frank Rizzo, whose title is dramaturg, as the art man and me (the managing director) as the dollar man, we have to work in tandem. Basically, Frank and Martin Feinstein, whose title is general director, develop concepts, which I usually know about because we meet almost every day. We talk about where we are in a project and what we think it will cost, and we solicit the opinions of other key staff people in order to substantiate our projections. But at an early stage, a key consideration is "can we cast a production the way we want it?" I think that's the same in any theater endeavor, so this is really when Frank and I begin working together. Frank does not negotiate contracts. He talks with the various managements all over the world. He

inquires if a certain artist is available and under what conditions. He discusses what we have in mind, and talks through the entire project so that the artist's representative can talk intelligently with the artist about the project. In this way, Frank begins putting together a cast. As he does so, he gets back to me with things I should be aware of in terms of the artist's desire to do the role, potential conflicts that are coming up, the speed with which I need to proceed. With this background, I then get on the phone and begin negotiating contracts. The same thing happens in terms of the designing and building of the scenery and costumes.

JM

I need to interrupt the flow of this discussion and ask a very basic question. Why are you a manager? What do you perceive your job to be as managing director of an opera company?

GF

Why am I a manager? I suppose it's because I discovered a long time ago that I couldn't sing or dance or act or paint pictures, and yet I always liked organizing things. And of course, I always loved the smell of it. It sounds corny, but there is a smell, and I like it, and I think I'm lucky in that I can earn my living doing something I like. Why opera? I suppose for me personally, because opera, when it works (and it doesn't always work), gives me some of the most extraordinary insights and the most amazing emotional experiences I've ever had. And it *is* complicated, it's *so damn* complicated. It takes so many hundreds of people doing so many things, and then in the course of only one day, any one of them can unravel the whole project. I love the complexity of it. What I see myself doing is really twofold—creating an organizational structure that allows the art and the artistic process to happen as smoothly as possible; and with my colleagues, forming a bridge that enables the public sitting in the theater and the artists on the stage to have that experience together.

Washington Opera. Noelle Rogers and Alan Kays in *Semele*. Photo: Richard Braaten.

JM

Do you have a management philosophy by which you create that organizational structure?

GF

I don't know if it's a philosophy, exactly. I try to hire people who know things I don't know. Over the years, I guess I've been a specialist in a lot of things. Now I feel that I've become a generalist. So I try to surround myself with department heads who are specialists. For example, I believe that these people who know a lot more than I do should be the ones to develop those areas of the budget they're going to be reasonable. Throughout the year, until that project is completed, the department head has to organize the people under him so that it can happen. By working this way, we force people to look closely at all the little things that usually fall between the cracks, because they each know their personal responsibilities. So if we're building new costumes for a show, the person in charge has to keep in mind the need for the necessary number of sewing machines, as well as the need for a certain fabric to get the look the designer wants. We expect a certain quality. The designer expects a certain quality. The department head has to determine how to deliver that quality for the amount of money that's budgeted.

I believe in leaving staff people alone. Again, because I trust in their expertise. I read an article in the *Harvard Business Review* years ago, entitled, "Who's Got the Monkey?" I used to let someone come to me with a problem and I'd say, "Okay. Let me think about it." But then suddenly, I thought, "who's working for whom, and who's doing my job while I'm doing that person's?" What I try to do now, when somebody comes to me with a problem, is ask them questions in such a way that *they* begin to realize that there are a number of ways to resolve the problem, and that they're the ones best qualified to figure out how to handle it.

JM

Now let's center our discussion on marketing. What do you define as "marketing?"

GF

I must confess I'm only beginning to discover what marketing means. I used to think it was just selling tickets. It's a lot more than that. The end result of good marketing is a healthy financial picture, both through *earned and contributed* income. We're seriously analyzing our own structure in that area. At the moment we have a director of marketing and public relations. We know that we've made wonderful progress over the last few years. But we know that the answer to our future in these troubled times is through involving more people with the company. This means adding more subscription series rather than more productions. I think the first thing you have to deal with is your visibility—positioning yourself in a market. And for us it's got to be a national positioning, because we have to go outside of Washington. It means working and strengthening our auxiliary organization, our Guild. It means attracting attention, and doing that as economically as possible. Postage is going through the ceiling. How long can we continue to rely on direct mail as we do now, to spend so large a percentage of our marketing budget on it? I'm not sure we can keep doing this kind of selling. What are the alternatives? Is it display advertising? Well, display advertising rates are going up almost as fast as postage. Is it collaboration with other organizations here in the city where there might be some crossover in markets, and yet where our products are so distinctly different that we eliminate competition? Is it telemarketing? I think these are issues that have to be explored.

JM

What do you think makes marketing different from the other sales programs or earned income concerns?

GF

I think marketing is hard facts. I think it's homework. Who do you think you are, and who does the public think you are? And how do you get that public image of your organization to the point where it affects your box office, your contributors? No matter how good your graphics, the public needs to have a sense of you and what you represent. I don't think graphics or a season brochure are the only elements that yield an audience. The need to have a sense of your value to the community is something that no brochure can really give.

Relating this to fund raising: I don't think individual donors are going to increase their contribution from fifty to one hundred dollars, unless they are informed. So you get out the message that one of the reasons you're a unique company in the United States is that you play in two theaters. That's where, in a traditional sense, promotion or press relations comes into the process. Where do most of those ticket buyers come from? We're later than a lot of companies in getting ourselves computerized. But finally, we can tie our subscribers into our contributors and we can start doing analyses of each one and their relationships to one another. I don't even know what the information is going to tell us about what we should do in the future, but we will at least have those tools to work with.

JM

You are communicating an interrelationship between marketing for earned income with marketing for contributed income. Is there an essential, cohesive element, function, or process?

GF

I think the same things that apply to the person who is going to buy your tickets apply to the one who is going to contribute. The systems you implement provide data which has two applications. "Who is who in connection to whom" has applications to fund raising as well as to ticket sales. We do a number of direct-mail solicitations, for example, and one is designed to go to *all* of our subscribers. That one campaign component, that visual image, I consider to be reflective of our marketing. That cohesive element linking contributed income and earned income is really the big picture, the unified approach. It's not the isolated, specialized things by themselves, but the compilation of all the elements, such as the process of selling tickets, raising money, Guild memberships, promoting events, the graphic look, the working with the printers, our personnel, etc. *They* are the *big picture, they* are *marketing.*

I want to elaborate on the direct-mail issue. The maintenance and buying of lists is essential. It's one thing for us to go to the computer and say, send this letter to all of our subscribers except those who contribute over $20,000 a year. What we want to exploit now is this image that the artistic product has given us and that the press has given us. If our lists aren't any damn good, if they aren't kept up to date, if we don't keep adding to them, if we're sending out mailings at the same time other organizations are, then we are not doing quality marketing. The mechanics of that type of fund raising is crucial. I think marketing is as crucial to that as it is to trying to find the subscribers and single-ticket buyers.

We don't have a marketing director at the moment. We play to near capacity houses, however. We have one secret weapon in the company that's unique to us, and that's Martin Feinstein. You have to remember Martin's background. Prior to joining the Washington Opera, he was Executive Director of the Kennedy Center, and before that, he was one of the top executives in the S. Hurok organization. Mr. Hurok, without acknowledging it, was one of the champion marketing experts of all time.

Martin is incredibly shrewd about this instinctively, and he's been doing marketing for many years in so many different contexts. We begin our renewal campaign so that the mailing arrives at the very end of one season for the following season. Our goal has always been to have the mailing out during the last week of performances. The renewals are returned in a matter of weeks after the final performance. By that time we can project what the box office will do in the upcoming season. I've resisted Martin on prices. We raised ticket prices over 40% between the 1980–81 season and the 1981–82 season. The house gross on a regular night (excluding the opening night) is now $75,000. In 1982–83 we raised ticket prices 20% and we're just about making it. We are, however, experiencing some resistance now at the top price.

JM
What's your top price?

GF
Top price in the orchestra is $40, and boxes are $50. But most boxes go on subscription plans. Then, in the process of preparing our budget, we use the percentage increase that we think we can implement. I bring this up because some of the draft presentations made to members of our executive committee result in their discussing ticket prices. They generally have agreed with Martin and me. Martin and I have agreed on what level prices should be, or he's convinced me. We then discuss this with our director of promotion and the development director. The development director is important to this process, because in 1982, we raised $150,000 through what we call "add-on contributions." We recommend to our subscribers (in fact, we even compute it for them on renewal forms) that they make a contribution equal to 25% of the cost of their tickets, which resulted in this amount.

JM
That's an extraordinary amount of money.

GF
It's been very successful for us, and our subscribers are not offended by it. There were a few who did object the first year we tried it, but those objections have subsided. The development director is important in our brainstorming sessions. We talk about the type of sales brochures we want. The most interesting example was in the 1980-81 season. We were introducing the integrated season between the two houses. We were also armed with the results of a consultants' study providing information on our low profile in the community. We decided to spend a lot of money that year on getting people to start thinking about the Washington Opera differently. That was a pretty extravagant brochure. A lot of the components were donated. It certainly had everybody talking about it and talking about us. The following year

"Postage is going through the ceiling. How long can we continue to rely on direct mail as we do now?"

we went back to a simpler mailing piece, since we thought we had accomplished what we needed in terms of image.

We work with an outside advertising agency for placement of ads and radio time. He and our director of publicity will come up with an idea of what the campaign should be. We send out a prospectus to our previous subscribers for renewals, and that usually brings in the first ticket sales, generally by the month of May.

The prospectus goes out before anything else. Also, as a part of that campaign, we will send two reminders. In the past, we have extended the deadline on the renewals, but we can't do that anymore, as it results in too big a work load for our ticket department.

The prospectus is a very inexpensive mailing describing the season and telling subscribers what they need to do to change seats or renew their seats (to those people that bring in the add-on contributions of $150,000 we talked about earlier). We time the arrival of our spring brochures accordingly, and start the process of finding new audiences. We also try to tie in our first major display ads. We've learned, traditionally at least, that Washington is very much like Paris or Rome. It empties in the summer months. And we use the summer to get caught up with everything that's come in through the spring campaign—both renewals and new orders. The Sunday after Labor Day, we begin our fall campaign, which is a second direct mail piece supported by display ads and radio spots. For two years now, we've been tracking everything that comes in and relating it to when we dropped something in the mail. What was the response rate, what date did ads appear, what was the reponse from it? This year we have two years worth of experience to evaluate. We're working on a chart to determine which of the direct-mail pieces dropped at which dates, and which had the greatest return. We are attempting to discern such specifics as: What is the relationship between the placement of display ads and the direct-mail returns? Can we tell anything from the timing of radio spots?

None of this is very original or creative. It takes a lot of planning and setting up of systems so that a very small staff in our ticket department can begin logging the source of the mail orders as they begin handling them. Our ticket department, by the way, will be under the supervision of the marketing director when that position is created.

Washington Opera. *Wiener Blut.*
Photo: Richard Braaten.

JM

You have explained to us that you are going to be structuring this management position with your organization. What type of individual is a marketing director? What qualities will you search for in this professional?

GF

A marketing director has to have two overall characteristics: One is an extraordinary sense of detail and an ability to follow through. When you stop and think about that Monday after the first big ad for new subscriptions resulting in a sudden load of 500 mail orders—each one having to be entered into a system—you need a viable, detailed system. Is the staff under the marketing director trained to do that properly? Have they been trained in a way that's going to allow that information to be collated with other data effectively? That type of streamlined attention to detail is terribly important. List maintenance and research are so crucial, and of course, detailed. To know how to do these things without bogging yourself down is a special talent.

The second quality a marketing director must possess is a very imaginative nature. Our computer will tell us a great deal about the relationship between our subscribers and our contributors. How do we use that information? Heretofore we only knew numbers. But interpreting that information requires a kind of sophistication that's related to detail — in short, imagination. An imaginative approach is knowing what's happening, what's working for other companies across the country, and how we can make some of these ideas work for us.

We have more performing-arts activities in this city per capita than any other city in the United States except New York, largely because of the Kennedy Center and the many visiting attractions it presents. Imagination is fundamental. First, you need the background and the skills, which include graphics, printing, mailing, direct mail—all of that. Do you make your direct-mail piece look different when everybody in the city is trying to begin their final campaign the day after Labor Day? What do you do artistically that makes *you* look different? How does your ad look? I think of the Metropolitan Opera when they did the incredible campaign all over New York a number of years ago, "Strike a blow for civilization." All kinds of people thought, "what is this all about?" But no one forgot that campaign.

In my first job, in Kansas City (before any of us knew about "marketing"), we had a number of billboards donated to us. An advertising man on our board came up with a design for them. I thought it came close to being ugly. He urged me to wait and see. What he went for was recognition factor, something that really did jump out at the viewer. I'm not sure I agreed with him aesthetically, but the point was that he knew what he was doing, and we sold a lot of tickets. That's the kind of imagination you look for in an individual.

JM

How will that individual fit into the organization that you've created? What will your personal relationship be with him—as well as the relationship between Martin Feinstein, the general director, and the dramaturge?

GF

The marketing director will be added to those reporting directly to Martin, who pays more attention to box office than anybody I've ever known. We have reports that arrive on our desks every morning beginning with the first day of the campaign that tell us just about anything we want to know, including how this day compares with the same day last year. Martin can walk into the box office and tell at a glance how many empty seats there are in the house. Given his own background, it makes absolute sense to have the marketing director report directly to him. But again, as it is with the publicity director and the development director, when a concept is being developed, I'll be asked to join in. I think it's as important for me to know these things as it is to know what's going on with the costume budget.

It's interesting that our development director is the one who gave form to the idea of a marketing department. Several months ago, we were both working on a Sunday evening and broke for dinner. She said we had to do something with our marketing. She demonstrated that she simply had to have help. I asked her to write me her ideas, specifically a job description of a marketing director, and then I asked our publicity director to do the same thing. The job descriptions were almost identical. I had asked them not to discuss it with each other, because I wanted as much of their input, independently conceived, as I could possibly get. I was amazed at how they both had come up with very much the same thing.

JM

To conclude, what would be your advice if I were sitting across this desk from you and said that I wanted to create an opera company. I've come to you because of your many years in the world of producing opera. What do you want to communicate to me about the supposed future of the opera world professionally?

GF

First of all, does the community you have selected want opera? And once you readily determine that they don't, please, go someplace else! If they do, then as your first resources, use those men and women who invited you there, or who indicated that they would give you a hand. The whole process is a system of concentric circles. From that first group, you've got to establish your board of trustees. Then they start bringing in their friends. They know something about their own community. Do you start with the people who usually have the money to buy tickets—professional people like doctors and lawyers? Is it a college town? Is there an orchestra? What has worked for other groups in town? Begin analyzing the community. *Know what your resources are.* Strive for excellence in everything. What are your orchestral resources? What are your choral resources? Have you engaged good people to train them? And then shoot for a scale that your resources can support.

And then, within that scale, try to make every element equally outstanding. This is really what it comes down to. I think the most important advice is to get them talk-

> "In 1982 we raised $150,000 through 'add-on contributions.'"

ing about you and the quality of what goes on your stage. And that's what has to be translated to the public, after all the homework and the analysis of your resources is done. If you're not putting the very best on your stage that you can, the most brilliant marketing strategy in the world is not going to help.

Patricia Cox

MARKETING THE PERFORMING ARTS: A PERSONAL VIEW

My personal reasons for being a marketing director for the arts are to communicate—to share this passion, this excitement, this terrific experience, with, if you'll pardon the hyperbole, the world! This feeling for the arts isn't the only qualification you need to be a professional marketing director, but it helps.

Marketing the Arts is More than Just Selling Tickets

I'm sure there are many philosophical arguments to prove that art exists in a vacuum, without an audience to perceive it, but I disagree. It seems to me that true art *is* the interaction between art and audience—the art of communicating a vision and the perception of it.

The marketing director is responsible for making that "holy flow" happen. In other words, for understanding what it is the artist is doing, and aptly communicating it in a motivational way to the outside world. First and foremost the marketing director must understand and share in the process of creating. Marketing directors have a major impact on the success or failure of any artistic moment; we should see ourselves, literally, as part of the art.

Too often, the marketing director is pigeon-holed and left on his own, almost in a vacuum, to deal with the specific tasks of advertising, publicity, or subscription sales, as if the product we were selling was a ticket.

In fact, in the performing arts, the artistic vision is the product. Whether it is a vision that encompasses an entire institution and the many events it produces, or a single concert, the artistic vision must be the starting point.

Unlike in the commercial theatre world, our bottom line is good art, not necessarily profit. Therefore, as marketing directors, we do not try to create a product to fit what we know about customer need. Rather, our job is to understand our art thoroughly, and understand the desires and needs of our customers thoroughly, so that we can effect an exchange of value between the two.

Frequently, artists will be suspicious and antagonistic towards the marketing director and his efforts because they have a negative attitude about the whole idea of selling their work. There are artists who believe that it is vulgar, cheap, insulting, or even destructive to the art. This opinion is, of course, based upon experiences with the stereotypical "Madison Avenue" type of marketing person, or a basic misunderstanding of the marketing process.

Our challenge as marketing directors in the performing arts is to find and persuade an audience for our artists—whatever they choose to do.

The first task of a good marketing director is often to educate the artists to this nurturing, positive definition of marketing, and to build a trusting relationship. Only then is it possible to work together to define their goals and begin the process of reaching out to the public.

The Marketing Director Has Power!

As the keeper and communicator of the flame, so to speak, the marketing director has a very powerful, influential position.

Patricia Cox was a founding member and Director of Audience Development for the Saint Nicholas Theatre in Chicago for five years. She also served as the Director of Development for the Academy Festival Theatre, and as Executive Director of the Chicago Alliance for the Performing Arts—a service organization with a membership of 150 theatre, music and dance companies in Chicago. Recently Ms. Cox has worked as the Marketing Director of the Manhattan Theatre Club in New York. She has also taught "Arts Marketing" for Columbia College in Chicago, and has lectured frequently on marketing and development in the arts at colleges and universities including Columbia University, New York University, and Adelphi University. She has served as a consultant for FEDAPT, ART/New York, the Illinois Arts Council, the Cleveland Foundation, and numerous arts organizations ranging from theatre and dance to literary magazines and arts service organizations. Currently, Ms. Cox is a freelance consultant in marketing, development, and performing arts management throughout the country.

Photo: Gerry Goodstein

"Marketing directors should see themselves, literally, as part of the art."

Anything and everything a potential audience (the community at large) hears, sees, feels, learns about an artist or a work of art before actually experiencing it will color the way they perceive the art.

I first felt the weight of this responsibility while building the St. Nicholas Theater in Chicago. We were rushing to finish an old warehouse to co-produce David Mamet's newest play, *American Buffalo,* with the Goodman Theatre. David was artistic director of St. Nicholas, and a firm believer in the theories of Constantine Stanislavsky. In fact, St. Nicholas was in some ways patterned after the Moscow Art Theatre and the Group Theatre. David felt that every aspect of the theater, from the color of the walls to the state of the restrooms to the personality and knowledge of the box-office staff to the discount flyers *had* to reflect his artistic goals.

We scoured and scrubbed and nailed and sweated to the cadence of *"It's got to be right—for Stanislavsky, for David, for THE ART!"* We were a little carried away, but by opening night that attention to detail paid off. The place was still no more than a fixed-up old industrial building, but it had somehow absorbed the "soul" of the artist—as had everyone who helped make it happen.

I didn't have the title of marketing director at that point, but my role was to drag out of David what he "really" meant and communicate it to the volunteers and outside world so that from the moment potential audience members saw our space or walked past our front sign, they were on the right track and could best perceive our art.

As the marketing director you powerfully influence—even control to a certain extent—the expectations and preconceptions a viewer brings to your art.

The Scope of the Job

Since the product the marketing director is involved in selling *is* the art and not just tickets, and since the way the art is presented to the public has a major impact on the way it is perceived, it stands to reason that someone—the marketing director— should be charged with coordinating *all* of the public-impact activities of the organization. This should include developing a coherent visual style and a verbal "party line" for the institution, as well as for any individual events it produces. The marketing director should serve as an "image consultant" for any other department involved in communicating with the outside world. Last but not least, the marketing director should make sure that the institutional goals as well as the individual vision are clearly understood internally among staff members, interns, board members, etc., for every event in the season. Clearly, this position extends beyond the traditional job description of the public relations director, the communications director, the audience development director, etc.

As marketing expert Philip Kotler states in his work, *Marketing for Nonprofit Organizations,*

> Marketing is the analysis, planning, implementation, and control of carefully formulated programs designed to bring about voluntary exchanges of values with target markets for the purpose of achieving organizational objectives. It relies heavily on designing the organization's offering in terms of the target markets' needs and desires, and on using effective pricing, communication, and distribution to inform, motivate, and service the markets.[1]

He also asserts that "marketing is oriented to results, and this requires a broad conception of all the factors influencing buying behavior."

In other words, marketing is a process of matching a product with a customer. The marketing director is responsible for integrating the public-oriented functions within a business in order to make the highest-priority potential customer realize they want what you've got, and to make this match in the most cost-effective way possible. To accomplish this, any good marketing director must follow a plan to:

1. identify the product
2. identify and prioritize the likely market segments
3. motivate the customer to take an action—to make the purchase
4. provide the means through which they can execute that action
5. maintain and expend their commitment to the product.

[1]Phillip Kotler, *Marketing for Nonprofit Institutions,* 1977, p. 5

Items 3, 4, and 5 really refer to the utilization of a set of tools called the "marketing mix," which includes the design of your offer, pricing, communication and distribution.

Specifically, I feel that the marketing director under this definition of integrated marketing is directly responsible for the planning and implementation of

1. public relations/publicity
2. advertising
3. single-ticket sales, group sales, special promotions, etc.
4. subscription
5. community development/outreach
6. budgeting—both income and expense for the department
7. department staffing.

and responsible for the public impact aspects of

1. the box office
2. the receptionist
3. the house-management staff
4. the volunteers

All of this boils down into three main areas of activity. The marketing director should

1. build an image for the arts
2. get the best, most appropriately prepared bodies into seats, and
3. bring in the most income possible for the smallet possible expense.

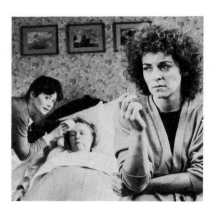

Manhattan Theatre Club. Suzanne Bertish, Fran Brill and Hope Cameron in *Skirmishes*. Photo: Gerry Goodstein.

All are essential to your art—the right preconceptions, the people to perceive it, and the dollars to actually create it.

Some marketing directors shrink from actually demanding that potential customers *do* anything. Discreet suggestions about attendance or contribution are made in low-key, tasteful brochures; ads without phone numbers or deadlines are spread about. Discount-and-deadline-oriented offers are eschewed for the "quality" approach. Hogwash, I say! As marketing director, your task is *not* to be nice. It is to, as appropriately but as persuasively as possible, *motivate* people to pay you money to experience your art. Your job is to know how to do this in a way that still reflects the heart and soul of your product.

Meetings…Meetings…Meetings…

Because the duties of the marketing director include the coordination of many activities and departments in an arts institution and public impact, the marketing director must develop a close working relationship with those other departments, and most importantly, with the artistic and managing directors.

The Artistic Director

In all performing arts organizations, it is difficult, often impossible, to have regular daily contact with the artistic director. Marketing directors are also presumed not to *need* this contact in order to perform. The artistic director is busy — very busy creating the art—so for the sake of efficiency, any business details that should be handled with the artistic director are transmitted through the managing director. This separates the marketing director from the source of the arts, to the detriment of both the artistic and marketing directors.

On the "vision" level, the marketing director really needs to hear what the artists are trying to create, what they perceive their vision to be from "the horse's mouth." No written document or second-hand report can communicate the nuance, the spirit, the passion and struggle behind it all. And the marketing director's visceral experience of that vision usually provides the extra spark, the drive that will allow him to really understand what makes the artist and his institution and art unique, what makes it worth experiencing as an audience member, what makes it worth

"Some marketing directors shrink from actually demanding that potential customers *do* anything."

the ticket price or the contribution. Marketing directors can create sales plans, brochures, and press releases while development directors can write proposals and pitch corporations for contributions without this artistic input, but close examination will reveal that these materials lack the truly individual stamp or impact that communicates the specialness of your artist.

The Marketing Director

The artist, too, can benefit from direct interaction with the marketing director. He has first-hand experiences with the way audiences are responding to the artistic director's choices—from copmplaints, lobby interaction, discussions and surveys. For example, the artistic staff at MTC (Manhattan Theatre Club) and most cultural organizations is very concerned with balancing a season's experience for our subscribers. Balance means weighing plays that are more challenging and difficult against more lighthearted, easier-to-take fare. This sometimes became, in the artistic staff's perception, a question of balancing quality with "what the subscribers will like." I was able to determine from talking with subscribers and from survey results, that the subscribers had chosen MTC primarily *because* of the challenging, stimulating work we do—and in many cases, they resented what they considered "fluff" in the season. This information was news to the artistic staff and helped to alleviate the feeling of distrust between the artists and the audience.

The marketing director can also help the artistic leaders to verbalize and "think through" what they are trying to do. The first time an artist is required to commit to a direction for any given year is either for the subscription brochure of a major grant application. With creative interaction, the marketing director can help the artistic director clarify his or her thinking and organize it for presentation to the outside world.

The marketing director should be interacting directly with the artistic director about copy, graphics, press releases, etc. The process of determmining the visual style of the organization as well as how to verbalize the "party line" is a long one, and probably never ending. In fact, preferably never ending. How to say it, how to show it, should always adhere to the main principles of the organization, but adjust as the artistic director and the art grow and change.

Exactly how he interprets the artustic vision and incorporates it in the tools of his marketing mix should be the result of a dialogue—a negotiation, if you will—between him and the artistic director. He must utilize all his skill and talent simultaneously to communicate truthfully about his art *and* to tell his audience what it needs to hear to buy a ticket.

The Marketing Director as Part of the Executive Management Team

The marketing director plays an important role as part of the Executive management team. He should be an active participant in long-range and short-range planning and be involved in discussions about,

1. How many events to produce in a season, what balance of subject matter, period, etc. needs to be achieved
2. what kind of packaging should be used—a subscription plan, single-ticket sales, passcards, low-prices student rush, etc.
3. what earned income level the institution must achieve, and whether this is possible given the kind of artistic vision and the conditions of the marketplace
4. what kind of audience mix should be sought
5. curtain times, length of runs, location of performances.

All of the above and more must be worked out in strategically scheduled meetings and should always reflect the artistic goals of the artist and organization while remaining sensitive to financial and administrative considerations.

For example, a theater like the Manhattan Theatre Club has an artistic vision that it makes it impossible to provide play titles and dates for its audience very far in advance. And yet, MTC does primarily new plays—so there is no guarantee of an audience unless the critical reviews are good. To protect the development of new work from the show-by-show vicissitudes of audience and press, MTC needed a committed and informed subscription audience. Consequently, a flexible passcard subscription system was developed, designed to serve the needs of the art *and* ensure maximum earned-income levels. This system is constantly "in the proces of refinement." Lynne Meadow, Artistic Director; Barry Grove, Managing Director; Connie Alexis, General Manager; and myself review together the goals and problems of the "monster" we have wrought, several times a year and often revamp accordingly.

Pricing is another important issue that has a great deal of impact on the way people perceive the art, and on the kind of people who become your audience, not to mention your ability to sell tickets.

Questions about pricing that need to be addressed by the marketing director, the managing director and the artistic director together: What do we need to achieve in earned income to be able to do the kind of work we want? How much money can we raise? How do ticket prices affect fund-raising ability—will individuals or foundations see you as insubstantial (not "major") if ticket prices are too low? Will we appear elitist if they are too high? Where are we in relation to the price levels of our direct competition—similar organizations—in relation to other comparable cultural activities, to sports events, movies, dinner out, and other entertainment options? What does a top price of $22.00 say to the general public, or to the press? Would it prevent the people we prefer as audience from attending? What expectations does it set up for people?

There is a great deal of difference, and I'm not just talking about number of seats, between a theatre experience on Broadway and at LaMama, or a dance concert at Lincoln Center or the Kitchen. At MTC, we are careful not to let prices reach the Broadway level, although demand seems strong enough to accommodate it. Our spaces are small, and less than luxurious or comfortable. We certainly wouldn't want our patrons to come in expecting lots of red velvet, chandeliers, and gold trim, only to be disappointed before the show even begins. The ticket price must not mislead the audience, preventing them from buying or undercutting earned-income potential.

If there is a separate development director in your organization, I would recommend that he participate in these discussions about pricing and income potential. There is a lot of crossover involved, and these departments should balance and coordinate their efforts.

The Managing Director

In addition to working with the managing director on the philosophy/policy level, the marketing director should have a very clear, very open day-to-day working relationship. In most cases, the marketing director reports to the managing director, who hired him and according to the book, has final say (with the artistic director) about what he does. However, for this relationship to be as productive as possible, I feel it should be more of a collaboration between professionals, then a honcho/minion type of relationship.

I really appreciate a managing director who serves as a sounding board, helping me think through new ideas and approaches, who can provide me with an overview of my activities in relation to the organization as a whole, who can help me develop priorities among my efforts over the long term and on a daily basis.

One of my favorite things about the performing arts is the way things change. Because we're involved in a "live" art form, every day is different. Dates change, titles change, plays change, performances change. It's exciting, vibrant, and crazy. I love it! But I rely on the managing director to have his finger on the pulse and to keep me informed—or at least alerted. I think it is best to work out together with the managing director the quarterly, yearly, and three-year goals of the department. After you have done the initial research into the nature of your product and the market place, you should present a marketing plan outlining the marketing mix you will employ — promotion , public relations, press, single-ticket sales, discount sales, subscriptions, groups, etc.—the schedule, the budget, the staffing necessary, the pricing, and the income you project. Each element should be discussed with the managing director, according to his comments, and finally agreed on. You are then free to implement the plan, basically on your own. I like to check in with the manag-

> "Information from the marketing department can help alleviate distrust between artists and audience."

ing director and artistic director at the crucial stages of any big project — the subscription campaign, the big ad announcing each show, a new discount program to reach special audiences, etc. This ensures you keep in touch with how well you are in sync with them and also prevents any misunderstandings. I do not suggest you wait until the final stages—last minute disagreements cause strain and force compromises that no one has time to think through.

I also keep the managing director apprised of schedule and budget changes, ticket sales (and my suggested responses) and solicit his advice on any problems that might occur. He needs this information to help me, and to keep the organization as a whole working.

Of course, there are always times when, as chief administrator of the organization, the managing director must make decisions without being able to consult the marketing director. That's the nature of the business. But as much as possible, the managing director and the marketing director should keep the channel of communication open and flowing in both directions. Personally, I find the most stimulating and productive environment in which to work is one that combines freedom with guidance.

The Development Director

The development department is essentially also a marketing department in that it must match a product—the art—to the needs of a selected market segment—corporations and foundations, federal, state, and local arts agencies as well as individuals (often the institution's customers) — for the purpose of stimulating a response, which is a contribution, not a ticket sale. The marketing mix is a bit different, but many of the tools, like direct mail, phone solicitation, the use of public relations to build awareness, etc., are the same. Very often, the market segments targeted by the two departments are also the same. Both departments are directly responsible for determining and communicating the larger artistic mission of the organization, as well as raising money or selling tickets. In many cases, performing arts institutions are set up so that the two departments are completely separate, and regretfully the result is all too often that one hand does not know what the other one is doing.

In order to achieve the best results, I believe the two departments should be looked at by executive management as two parts of an overall institutional marketing plan. If the management functions are not actually coordinated by a single person, it should be understood by all concerned that the plans of the individual departments need to be worked out together. This way, the efforts of each area will not conflict and compete, but can reinforce and enhance each other.

It is crucial that the marketing director establish a strong, intimate working relationship with the development director. If there is confusion about which department coordinates the public profile, or pursues community development or high level public relations, I suggest the two department heads clarify the situation between themselves. I strongly urge that the marketing director and development director meet regularly to share goals, plans, and schedules, and more informally, to exchange "professional" information, ideas, problems, and techniques. This can have tremendously positive results:

1. Your graphic and verbal image is reinforced by both departments, and this heightens the effect of both your efforts.
2. You can plan programs together to meet the income goals of the institution. MTC achieves a large percentage of its individual contributions each year from our subscription campaign. We are also developing a corporate contributions campaign that links employee ticket discounts, corporate performances, and priority subscription sales to corporate giving. There are endless possibilities for increased ticket sales *and* contributions through this kind of collaboration.
3. You'll save time and money, and sanity by planning schedules carefully. This will avoid mailing to the same people at the same time and driving suppliers like typesetters, printers, designers, and messengers crazy with simultaneous crises.

Manhattan Theatre Club. Michael Cristofer in *No End of Blame*. Photo: Gerry Goodstein.

4. You hone your professional skills. Both of you will be utilizing direct mail, phone solicitations, computer programs and time, printed materials of all kinds...and you can both improve your abilities by sharing what works and what doesn't.

5. Each of you can assist in making the other's department's projects a success. I help to publicize MTC's annual benefit—and the development director makes sure I get all the names of attendees for the subscription campaign.

The Board of Trustees

The marketing director should have some direct access to the board of trustees. At the very least, the marketing director should be presented and field questions about the marketing plan and budget for the year. If an oranization is just getting started or contemplating a major expansion, I recommend a marketing committee of the board be established to participate in policy setting and long-range planning, outreach into the community, and to provide technical assistance and professional resources in the marketing area. Even if a standing board committee is not required, I find it informative and stimulating to review marketing plans and materials with board members who are experts in the field.

The Business Office and the Box Office

The business office and the box office are extremely valuable source of information for the marketing director, and vice versa.

The marketing department and the business office should work closely together on monthly expense tracking, on income results per event, and relations to suppliers, always attempting to find the cheaper or more efficient way.

In many performing organizations, the business office and the marketing director share responsibility for supervising the box office—the business office takes care of the money and systems side, while the marketing director oversees all duties relating to dealing with the public. This requires that the business manager and marketing director act as a team, agreeing in advance on goals and priorities.

The marketing director should work with the box office to determine how to represent the overall goals of the organization and the ''party line'' on any individual event. The marketing director should also be involved in the treatment of customers. For example, policy or guidelines can be established that help the box office know when to bend a rule, or how to say ''no'' nicely in eighty-seven different languages, or how to turn people away from sell-outs without losing them as customers, or how to turn general inquiries into ticket sales, etc. Any time there is a discrepancy between system and audience needs, the problem becomes a shared concern of the business, box office and marketing departments.

Take the case of Mrs. Smith. She and her husband have been suddenly called to Europe and must exchange their tickets, *now*. There is a very reasonable box office rule which requires all exchanges to be processed after the run of the show begins. Tickets must be in hand before the exchange is made. Mrs. Smith, of course, has only one possible performance she can attend before the big trip, and as she lives in New Jersey, she can't possibly get us the ticket back in time to switch. As to waiting until the appropriate date to exchange—forget it! Normally, the box office would politely tell Mrs. Smith to suffer...they can't make exceptions for everyone who wants to break the rules. Understandably, they insist on some method to their daily madness.

If you have a good relationship, the box office can provide you with important feedback about audience problems and responses: their complaints, their likes and dislikes, their mood, and *where they heard about the show*. My favorite moment on any show is when the tide turns from ''advertising'' or ''a review,'' to, ''I heard about it from a friend.'' And the box office tells me the day it happens. I love them. At the very least, they should be capturing names, addresses, and phone numbers from every inquiry and reservation. If possible, they should be tracking what tool is pulling best—ads, reviews, radio, word-of-mouth, discount offers, etc., and how much the phone is ringing! And of course, they're the ones who let you in on the intangibles: how the audience feels, what their mood is.

Equally important is the house manager and staff. Their demeanor, ability to smoothly solve problems and represent the institution are crucial to making the most of your marketing efforts.

Portrait of a Marketing Director

The job description for a marketing director as I've outlined in this chapter is comprehensive, to say the least. To do it professionally, I feel the marketing director must possess a complex set of talents, skills and experiences. He or she must be a good manager, able to participate in top-level planning and run a multi-faceted department. The marketing director should also have excellent technical skills, including the ability to work with computers, statistical and financial analysis, large scale printing, telemarketing, etc. In addition, the marketing director must have excellent verbal communication skills, a strong sense of design, and the ability to direct writers and visual artists.

In terms of temperament, the marketing professional should be somewhere between a saint and a used-car salesman. I mean that he or she needs the insight and sensitivity required to draw from artists what they are trying to accomplish, the patience to deal with customer "input" and the aggressive single-mindedness required to close any sale. Ideally, the marketing director will be able to combine an obsessive concern with detail and deadline with flexibility and a sense of humor.

Finally, the marketing director must have the talent and the gift, to take in a huge amount of raw information—numbers, facts, opinions, and desires—and transform that input into a plan of action, one that sells tickets, raises money, builds awareness, is cost-effective and efficient. And it must be someone who does it all with the passion and creative force their art needs and deserves.

This Manhattan Theatre Club mailing piece functions as the MTC subscription office newsletter, which also incorporates a single ticket order form, a calendar of events for both stages and the cabaret, and a fund-raising appeal. Graphic design by Don Moffett/Design.

MTC Calendar

September—October—November 1983 Schedule

- DownStage—THE PHILANTHROPIST, September 27–November 13.
- Upstage—BLUE PLATE SPECIAL, October 18–November 20.

SUNDAY	MONDAY	TUESDAY	WEDNESDAY	THURSDAY	FRIDAY	SATURDAY
Sept 25	**Sept 26**	**Sept 27** DownStage 8:00	**Sept 28** DownStage 8:00	**Sept 29** DownStage 8:00	**Sept 30** DownStage 8:00	**Oct 1** DownStage 2:30 8:00
Oct 2 DownStage 2:30 8:00	**Oct 3**	**Oct 4** INVITATIONAL PERFORMANCE DownStage 6:45	**Oct 5** DownStage 8:00	**Oct 6** DownStage 8:00	**Oct 7** DownStage 8:00	**Oct 8** DownStage 2:30 8:00
Oct 9 DownStage 2:30 8:00	**Oct 10**	**Oct 11** DownStage 8:00	**Oct 12** DownStage 8:00	**Oct 13** DownStage 8:00	**Oct 14** DownStage 8:00	**Oct 15** DownStage 2:30 8:00
Oct 16 DownStage 2:30 8:00	**Oct 17**	**Oct 18** UpStage 7:30 DownStage 8:00	**Oct 19** UpStage 7:30 DownStage 8:00	**Oct 20** UpStage 7:30 DownStage 8:00	**Oct 21** UpStage 7:30 DownStage 8:00	**Oct 22** UpStage 3:00 7:30 DownStage 3:00 8:00
Oct 23 UpStage 3:00 7:30 DownStage 2:30 8:00	**Oct 24**	**Oct 25** UpStage 7:30 DownStage 8:00	**Oct 26** UpStage 7:30 DownStage 8:00	**Oct 27** UpStage 7:30 DownStage 8:00	**Oct 28** UpStage 7:30 DownStage 8:00	**Oct 29** UpStage 3:00 7:30 DownStage 2:30 8:00
Oct 30 UpStage 3:00 7:30 DownStage 2:30 8:00	**Oct 31**	**Nov 1** UpStage 7:30 DownStage 8:00	**Nov 2** UpStage 7:30 DownStage 8:00	**Nov 3** UpStage 7:30 DownStage 8:00	**Nov 4** UpStage 7:30 DownStage 8:00	**Nov 5** UpStage 3:00 7:30 DownStage 8:00
Nov 6 UpStage 3:00 7:30 DownStage 2:30 8:00	**Nov 7**	**Nov 8** UpStage 7:30 DownStage 8:00	**Nov 9** UpStage 7:30 DownStage 8:00	**Nov 10** UpStage 7:30 DownStage 8:00	**Nov 11** UpStage 7:30 DownStage 8:00	**Nov 12** UpStage 3:00 7:30 DownStage 2:30 8:00
Nov 13 UpStage 3:00 7:30 DownStage 2:30 8:00	**Nov 14**	**Nov 15** UpStage 7:30	**Nov 16** UpStage 7:30	**Nov 17** UpStage 7:30	**Nov 18** UpStage 7:30	**Nov 19** UpStage 3:00 7:30
Nov 20 UpStage 3:00 7:30						

detach here

Ordering Information
UpStage Series

SUBSCRIBER RESERVATION PERIOD
August 30–September 18

DEADLINE FOR GUARANTEED SEATING:
September 18

Week	Dates	How to get Tickets
Week 1	Aug. 30–Sept. 4	By Mail
Week 2	Sept. 6–Sept. 11	By Mail and in Person
Week 3	Sept. 13–Sept. 18	By Mail, In Person and By Phone

Exchanges will be processed after September 18 per availability.

SUBSCRIBER HOTLINE: 288-3141

BOX OFFICE HOURS
Aug. 30–Sept. 25 Tuesday–Saturday, 1:00 pm–6:00 pm
Closed Sunday and Monday
Starting Sept. 27 Tuesday–Sunday, 1:00 pm–8:00 pm
Closed Monday

BOX OFFICE TELEPHONE: 472-0600

HOW TO ORDER BY MAIL—
It's easier than it looks! Just complete boxes 1-5 below. Orders processed in order received. MAIL TODAY.

1. CALENDAR: UpStage Order Form

NAME _____
ADDRESS _____
_____ ZIP _____
PHONE: Day _____ Eve _____

For Office Use Only
D S _____
U S _____

2. UPSTAGE: BLUE PLATE SPECIAL

Please note: Some performances may sell out early. Please be sure to include TWO alternate dates. Please check if you prefer the best seats available chosen from any of the following dates: ____

Preferred Date _____ Time _____
1st Alternate _____ Time _____
2nd Alternate _____ Time _____

Subscriber Tickets _____ # Passes Enclosed _____

Don't forget your friends! Subscriber guest tickets are available at these discount prices!

Better seating is usually available for performances *early in the run* of each show. Beat the crowds.

Yes, I'll take _____ UpStage Guest Tickets @ $_____ = $_____

Performance Times/Ticket Prices OCTOBER 18–NOVEMBER 20	Non-subscriber Ticket Price	Subscriber Guest Ticket Price
Tues. Wed. Thurs eve. at 7:30	~~$19.00~~	$18.00
Fri, Sat, Sun eve. at 7:30	~~$20.00~~	$19.00
Sat & Sun mat at 3:00	~~$16.00~~	$15.00

3. DOWNSTAGE: THE PHILANTHROPIST

Please note: Some performances may sell out early. Please be sure to include TWO alternate dates. Please check if you prefer the best seats available chosen from any of the following dates: ____

Preferred Date _____ Time _____
1st Alternate _____ Time _____
2nd Alternate _____ Time _____

ATTENTION UPSTAGE ONLY SUBSCRIBERS:
You can order DownStage tickets NOW and get $1.00 off regular box box office prices for yourself and your friends! (per availability)

Count me in for # _____ DownStage Discount Tickets @ $_____ = $_____

Performance Times/Ticket Prices SEPTEMBER 27–NOVEMBER 13	Non-subscriber Ticket Price	Subscriber Guest Ticket Price
Tues. Wed. Thurs eve. at 8:00	~~$22.00~~	$21.00
Fri, Sat, Sun eve. at 8:00	~~$24.00~~	$23.00
Sat & Sun mat at 2:30	~~$22.00~~	$21.00

4. SPECIAL SEATING REQUIREMENTS
If you have sight or hearing difficulties or other physical disabilities:
_____ I require special seating. Please specify _____

5. TOTAL AMOUNT ENCLOSED = $_____ (For Discount and Guest Tickets)

6. ENCLOSE: stamped self-addressed envelope, order form, appropriate # of passcards, or a check for total amount due and mail. Make checks payable to the Manhattan Theatre Club. Please allow 2 weeks for processing your ticket order.

MAIL TO: Box Office, MTC
321 East 73 Street
New York, NY 10021

7. For information about how to order with friends or as a group, see your subscriber handbook or call 288-3141.

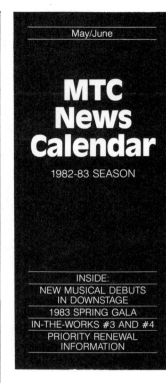

May/June

MTC News Calendar
1982-83 SEASON

INSIDE:
NEW MUSICAL DEBUTS IN DOWNSTAGE
1983 SPRING GALA
IN-THE-WORKS #3 AND #4
PRIORITY RENEWAL INFORMATION

MTC Newsletter:

BECOME AN MTC CONTRIBUTOR

YOUR GIFT to MTC helps shape the future of theatre in America. Rising costs combined with decreasing government support have created a significant deficit this year. Your support is the key to maintaining current programming and providing opportunities for the development of new plays and special projects.

Our thanks to all of you who have already made a contribution to the 1983/84 season. The year is getting off to a great start and we're glad you will be sharing it with us.

If you haven't yet made your gift, do it now to take advantage of the special benefits and privileges available only to contributors. Priority calendar mailings, preferred reservation privileges and a Ticket Reservation Hotline are only some of the unique ways we say "thank you" for your support. And, your gift is even more valuable because it can be used to match a National Endowment for the Arts Treasury Fund Grant.

Make a contribution, and add to your enjoyment of great theatre with special privileges all season long. For more information contact the Development Office at 288-2500.

JOIN THE FRIENDS OF MTC

The Friends are MTC's most ardent supporters. As an active volunteer group, these men and women from varying professions help us plan and give Opening Night parties, raise funds at the Phonathon, work on benefits and special events and much more.

Join us on SEPTEMBER 14, 1983 for the first Friends meeting of the season. You'll hear about the exciting projects planned for the year and meet other "theatre fans" who help MTC grow.

DownStage:
A WITTY BRITISH PLAY

The Philanthropist
by Christopher Hampton
directed by André Ernotte

SEPTEMBER 27–NOVEMBER 13

The Philanthropist is that very rare play—a truly witty high comedy, that exhilarates as it touches us, with its deft look at relationships among the over-educated.

Philip is a professor, a master of language. He could give you an anagram for "La Comedie Française" without batting an eye. But when it comes to sex, he discovers that people are more elusive than words.

When *The Philanthropist* was first staged at London's Royal Court Theatre in 1970, it heralded the arrival of a dazzling young playwright, Christopher Hampton. Since then, Mr. Hampton's plays have been produced around the world, and include *Savages*, *Treats*, and *Tales from Hollywood*, which is currently playing at the National Theatre in London.

André Ernotte is a director of international repute whose most recent works include *Christmas on Mars* at Playwrights Horizons and the world premiere of Tennessee Williams' last play, *A House Not Meant To Stand* at the Goodman Theatre. He previously directed *Crossing Niagara* at MTC.

Subscriber Notes:

1. Purchase tickets for your friends through this calendar —and save $1.00 off regular box office prices! We've extended the run of our DownStage shows, so there's more room for everyone. But MTC productions frequently sell-out, so order now!

2. Beat the crowds! Better seating is usually available for performances in the first two weeks of the run of each show.

Subscriber Discussion:

You're invited to join us for special subscriber discussions about *The Philanthropist* with members of our artistic staff on Friday, September 30 at 8 pm and on Saturday, October 1 at 2:30 pm.

UpStage:
NEW YORK PREMIERE

Blue Plate Special
Book by Tom Edwards
Music by Harris Wheeler
Lyrics by Mary L. Fisher
Directed by Art Wolff

OCTOBER 18–NOVEMBER 20

Will Connie Sue Day put back the pieces of her shattered career and regain her country singing star crown? Will Ricky Jim figure out why his vegetable garden is glowing green, and rescue little Joey from the Curse of the Damned? Will Della live down her scarlet past, and triumph in her anti-Nuke Campaign?

For the tongue-in-cheek answer to these and other pressing questions, tune in for *Blue Plate Special*, a heaping helping of Country & Western lunacy. Join us for this evening of pure soap-opera fun!

Tom Edwards, Harris Wheeler, and Mary L. Fisher have each worked extensively in the Atlanta area. *Blue Plate Special* marks their New York debut.

Art Wolff most recently directed the premiere of Shel Silverstein's *Wild Life* Off-Broadway and the premieres of *Hotline* by Elaine May and *Gorilla* by Shel Silverstein at the Goodman Theatre in Chicago.

Subscriber Notes:

1. Purchase tickets for your friends through this calendar —and save $1.00 off regular box office prices! MTC productions frequently sell-out, so order now!

2. Beat the crowds! Better seating is usually available for performances in the first two weeks of the run of each show.

Subscriber Discussion:

You're invited to join us for special subscriber discussions about *Blue Plate Special* with members of our artistic staff on Friday, October 21 at 7:30 pm and on Saturday, October 22 at 3 pm.

PART II:
Principles of Marketing

Douglas Eichten

THE MARKETING PLAN

Any of the following situations sound familiar?

- The managing director just came in and demanded a full-page ad in Sunday's paper, and the budget is already spent.
- The president of the board of trustees just asked why we don't have posters this year, and you are not sure.
- The artistic director asked if it would be all right for the scene designer to design the advertising.
- The receptionist wondered why we never buy spots on his favorite radio station.
- You told your boss you had learned some special methods of promotion in your last job that will solve all your new organization's problems, and they are not working.
- The chairperson of the board's finance committee asked how cost-effective direct mail is.

The above situations occur frequently in any organization and always will. However, what we all need is a way to answer those questions, to keep everyone happy and still fill all the seats.

We can only begin to find solutions to these situations when we initiate a comprehensive planning program for our organizations' entire marketing area. Without a written, well-organized plan, you are subject to judgment calls by your boss, second guessing by the board of trustees and constant controversy within the organization over the marketing activities.

Planning is always needed. It's easiest and most fun to plan when things are going well. A plan is developed and implemented, and we have a good time analyzing its success. It is also very easy to stick to the plan when it is working. Our great difficulty when times are tough is that we may not have a plan and, therefore, may have caused the problem we are in. Or, we may not have the confidence in our plan to stick with it long enough for it to work.

Planning in arts organizations became a bit of a fad in the late 1970s when corporate and government leaders recommended that arts managers turn to strategic planning. As selling tickets became more difficult in the early 1980s, many organizations abandoned the planning process in favor of the eternally popular method known as, "shooting from the hip." A plan, during difficult times, will not only protect you from those who feel they know far better than you how to promote your organization, but will also give you the confidence that you are, in fact, doing everything you can to make your campaign successful. Confidence greatly reduces stress and pressure and keeps you from "burning out" during difficult sales periods.

Planning in the marketing area organizes your thinking, maximizes the effectiveness of all of your resources, carefully outlines each employee's assignments, and identifies your problem areas and how you will deal with them. To be effective in all these areas the market plan should be available for distribution to the manage-

Doug Eichten is the Communications Director for The Guthrie Theater, Minneapolis. The three departments which he heads are Publicity, Advertising/Sales and the Box-Office. Before joining the Guthrie staff, Mr. Eichten was assistant to the business manager, Theatre Arts Department and assistant to the director, Concerts and Lectures Department, both at the University of Minnesota; publicity director, Carnival Theatre, Eugene, Oregon; and business and publicity manager, Theatre Department, Saint Mary's College, Winona, Minnesota. He has a Masters Degree in Arts Administration from the University of Minnesota, where he was awarded fellowships by the Bush Foundation and the McKnight Foundation. He has participated as a panelist and guest speaker at arts marketing seminars in New York City, Connecticut, Colorado, Utah, Wisconsin and Banff, Alberta and has assisted theaters as a consultant in Ohio, North Carolina, Wisconsin and Minnesota. Mr. Eichten is an adjunct professor at St. Cloud State University in Minnesota.

ment, to the board, and to the marketing staff. Everyone then knows what the marketing area is attempting to accomplish and how it will be done. A good, solid plan will give the board of trustees and the management the confidence that the appropriate planning and organization of resources have taken place and assure them that they do not have to intercede constantly with their own ideas. Without the plan, the marketing staff will receive constant advice, and in my experience, once that advice is given, action is expected.

You may have seen leather-bound market plans prepared by professional agencies and large corporations, and therefore, think that it would be difficult for a small arts organization to produce and use such a document. Market planning is right for any organization that is planning to sell something. The size of the organization is irrelevant when it comes to needing a plan. It makes no difference if the organization is staffed entirely by volunteers or has a marketing staff of twenty. It makes no difference whether there is no marketing budget or whether that budget is $750,000. Each organization needs a market plan to get the most out of their promotion efforts.

The plan is the responsibility of the person who communicates directly with the public. The plan that we will discuss in this chapter can certainly be prepared by board members, by a manager, by a marketing director, by a marketing staff, by volunteers — in fact, by anyone involved in the marketing process. The person responsible for this task can certainly turn to others for help. Depending upon the complexity of an organization's marketing efforts, a plan could be prepared in a week and at no direct cost to the organization. On the other hand, a complete market plan may take more than a month to prepare and may involve some direct expense. Without a doubt, the benefits of a market plan will always justify the time or money spent on developing the plan.

The Guthrie Theater. *Peer Gynt.*
Photo: Joe Giannetti.

Mission Statements/Organizational Goals/What We Want to Be

Before you can begin to work on a market plan, it is imperative that you know what your organization is trying to accomplish. The market plan will eventually deal with advertising, publicity, public relations, and other means by which your organization communicates to the public.

One would hope that the management of the organization and the board of trustees has already prepared a brief document—a "mission statement"—describing the organization, what it is and what it hopes to be. If one does not exist, it is now time to develop one. The organization needs to take a serious look at its reasons for existing, and it must determine where it wants to go, where it is now and how long it will take to reach its ultimate goals. To prepare for a market plan, we need to know where the organization feels it fits in its community and what groups of people it is trying to reach.

The mission statement as articulated by the artistic leadership and a complete set of organizational objectives for the short range and long range, should make up the first chapter of your market plan. At the time when the board of trustees and the management of the organization explain the mission and goals of the organization for this plan, they should also be asked to describe the mission and goals that they think are appropriate for the marketing area.

Situation Analysis

In Chapter Two of your market plan, you should undertake a total study of your community. That study must begin with a definition of your primary and secondary community boundaries. The primary community is generally the immediate area from which your organization attracts its audience. The secondary community will probably involve the rest of the city, county, state, and neighboring states. You may even consider the entire region or the nation as your secondary community. The market plan will focus on the primary community, but the question of how large your community really is relates back to the first chapter and the questions about what you want to be and whom you want to reach.

When focusing on your primary community, it is important that you thoroughly understand its makeup to be able to prepare a successful market plan. You need to study the problems and opportunities the community presents. Does it have a healthy economy? What is the competitive picture concerning other arts organizations? What other forms of entertainment are your competitors? What is the penetration of cable TV in your community? You need to get information on the expense and income budgets of your competition, which will tell you something about how realistic your own budgets will be in the coming season. The performance schedules of these other organizations will help you in defining your direct competition. The ticket prices will help you make a better pricing plan for your organization, and you can start by considering every organization that sells tickets as your competitor. You don't have to think of a competition as an enemy, but you must remember that you are competing for leisure dollars and time.

To further understand your community, you have to understand who lives there. A complete demographic picture of your primary community is essential to the market plan. The most recent census taken in your area will give you all the demographics you need. The 1980 census is available from city planners, the United States Census Bureau, and the public library. Census information is broken down by census tract so that no matter how small an area you have defined as your primary community, you should be able to get this demographic information. The primary elements that you will need to consider are age, sex, education, occupation, and income.

Chapter Two in your market plan should also include a thorough description of the community — its climate, the number of large corporations in the area, the number of corporations with home offices, a description of the neighborhoods that make up the community, information on military facilities, educational institutions, and the religious makeup of the community. Much of this information can be obtained from the public library, local advertising agencies, chambers of commerce, government planning offices, and state and local arts boards.

Now that you are certain of the mission of your organization and you have a complete description of your community, it's time to get a better understanding of your audience. Current operating organizations will obviously study those people who are now buying tickets. New organizations will have to turn their attention to the audiences of organizations with the same mission and objectives. Studying an audience can be quite difficult and expensive. Many organizations attempt to get an understanding of their audience by stationing someone in the lobby and taking a guess at people's interests by guessing their ages, noting the color of their hair, and figuring out their occupations by the clothes they wear. It doesn't work. No matter what the size of an organization, the audience is far more complex than any of us might guess. Sophisticated audience surveys can cost a great deal of money and leave many unanswered questions, possibly just developing the need for further research. However, there are methods by which an audience can be studied with reliability and little expense. You must begin by asking yourself why you want to conduct the research and how will the research be used. For the purpose of the market plan, the research should be conducted so that you can learn as much as possible about the people who currently buy tickets so that you can sell them more tickets and encourage people who do not now attend to change their ways.

The survey information will also be used to select the most effective marketing tools and the proper time to use them. These tools will get your message across to your audience. To learn as much as possible about your audience, you have to survey them as they attend performances. From time to time you may want to learn more about your season ticket buyers—you can use your mailing list to send them a written questionnaire.

But to understand "your audience" you need to survey them. You can either do this at the time they attend the performance or you can get the names and addresses of everyone at one performance and mail them a questionnaire. This latter method may not be successful since you are trying to judge changes in audience patterns by day of week or time of year.

Many organizations insert a questionnaire in a percentage of the house programs distributed for each performance. They then ask the individual to fill out the questionnaire sometime during or after the performance, and to leave it with an usher or mail it back to the organization. The problem with this method is that often, as few

"Without a written, well-organized plan, you are subject to judgement calls by your boss, second guessing by the board of trustees, and constant controversy."

"Start by considering every organization that sells tickets as your competitor."

as ten percent of the people who receive the questionnaire actually fill it out, and this may severely reduce the confidence level concerning the information received.

After randomly selecting respondents, attempt to get each of them to participate. The higher the percentage of people actually responding, the higher the confidence level. Some organizations have had good luck offering incentives to people to get them to return their questionnaires. The incentives may be money, coupons for drinks at the lobby bar, or reduced price on tickets to future performances. It is still necessary to make some checks on this information to ensure reliability. For example, you may ask patrons what price seat they sat in and whether they are a season ticket-holder or not. You should already know the percentage of people in each price range and the number of season ticket-holders at that performance, so that you can check what you know against the percentages of questionnaire respondents in the various price ranges and season-ticket versus single-ticket purchases. This comparison will give you a good idea of whether or not you have a representative sample.

If you do collect the names of everyone purchasing tickets for a performance, I would recommend that you randomly select as many people as possible and follow up the next day with a telephone survey. If a very high percentage of the people you call answer the questions of the survey, you actually need a very low percentage of the total audience to give you a reliable sample. If you can not get the names of everyone who attends your performance, you may station several employees at the doors where tickets are torn and ask every tenth or twentieth person if he would please give you his name and phone number for the purpose of a telephone survey that will take place the next day. To prepare the survey questions you must take into account what you really need to know that you can act on, not just what might be interesting to know, and also the type of questions that can be asked easily over the telephone in a short conversation.

A written questionnaire can generally ask more questions and request more detailed answers. Your choice between a written survey and a telephone survey must, of course, be decided once again on reliability, use of the information, time available, and budget. In each case, you must take into account the time that the individual has available to answer the questions and the "assist" you will need to provide. With both the written and the telephone survey, multiple-choice questions are essential. The "assist" is the selection of answers you provide. When in doubt about preparing a survey, it is wise to seek professional guidance. This can often be obtained for little or no money from advertising agencies and university research-marketing departments.

To help you determine what questions you will want to ask, think first of how you will use the information. Age can be very helpful if you are considering purchasing radio spots. Knowledge of the percentage of men and women in your audience will help you concentrate on the magazines and radio stations that can be of the most help to your campaigns. Education, occupation, income, and residence can be very helpful in the selection of mailing lists and telephone lists for direct mail and telemarketing campaigns. As you prepare questions for the survey, you will certainly want to involve other departments of the organization and possibly the management and board of trustees. However, you must be careful that the survey does not lose track of its objective—all information must be actionable. Length of the survey is also an extremely important consideration.

If a fairly large number of individuals has been surveyed, you will be able to do some cross-tabulations. By cross-tabulating the information, you will be able to develop profiles of various groups. For example, you could study the demographic differences between season ticket-holders and single-ticket buyers and Saturday matinee buyers. You do have to be careful, however, that you have surveyed enough people in each group to give you confidence in the information obtained from the cross-tabulations.

Once you have determined the basic demographics of your audience, you may want to study your audience's attitudes toward your organization. Without considerable professional assistance, it is dangerous to attempt to cull attitudes from phone or written questionnaires. Attitudes have to be studied in context of their importance to the person being surveyed and the level of the emotion involved. An important tool in studying audience attitudes is the focus group. A focus group is generally ten or twelve people randomly selected from the total group to be studied. The focus group is asked to meet at a "neutral" location where the members are brought together for a discussion. Often, these people are given an incentive in the form of money or a gift to make sure that they will actually attend.

It is imperative that the discussion be led by someone trained in group-discussion techniques. The staff of the organization should provide the group leader with specific guidelines as to what they hope to learn from the meeting. The discussion leader will keep the conversation on track and keep any one of the members from taking over the discussion. Taping the meeting is a good idea for later study, however, it is also important that the discussion leader prepare an analysis of the event. You should keep in mind that what is learned from the meeting cannot be projected on a percentage basis to the entire group you are studying. For example, if ten people are selected from a group of one hundred, and one of those selected has particulary strong opinions, you cannot conclude that one percent of the entire group feels the same as that individual. The purpose of the focus group is to discover attitudes that may not be known by the organization. This group gives the organization an opportunity to see how deeply people feel about certain issues.

Focus groups are often used to assist in writing advertising copy and to prepare the way for more in-depth research. To go more deeply into the audience attitudes and to be able to project that information to the entire audience, it would probably be necessary to conduct a series of in-home interviews, but that is an extremely expensive procedure. You may find that the focus groups give you all the information you need to continue the market plan. Throughout this entire process, be sure to get assistance from professionals in the research area so that you do not overreact to casual comments from audience members. An unbiased analysis of any of these findings is critical.

Assuming that you are developing a market plan for an artistic event, it will be necessary at this point in the plan to describe the artists and the program that make up the event. The event should be compared to previous events of its type and its advantages and disadvantages should be taken into consideration. The plan needs to examine the prices you have charged for this type of event in the past and to figure out how this program fits into the organizational objectives. This chapter of the plan should contain a complete description of the artists involved and the program to be presented.

The situation analysis should now turn to sales programs. You should take a comprehensive look at the sales programs that your organization has used in the past. An organization's past sales programs may include season tickets, group sales, student sales, corporate programs, other volume purchase-programs and, finally, full-price ticket plans. In addition to the sales programs used in the past, your plan must include an outline of the marketing tools used to promote those past events and sales programs. After detailing the cost of each of those marketing tools, it will now be possible to prepare a cost-benefit analysis of each of those sales programs. When considering the cost of a sales program, be sure to include the amount of staff expense used in promoting and servicing the program. A cost-benefit analysis is simply a determination of the cost needed to bring in each dollar of income produced by a sales program. This is not the time to decide whether or not each sales program was effective based on cost-analysis alone. Each sales program, in addition to income, needs to be analyzed in light of its objectives, its benefits, and its direct expenses.

The final element of your study of the situation analysis is an outline and description of last season's or previous performance's market plan. You should be concerned with what that plan was trying to accomplish, what its results were and what tasks were not accomplished. You want to see if there are any elements of that market plan that can be carried over to the new plan.

You now have a complete description of your organization's objectives, its community, its audience, the event it hopes to promote, the sales programs it has used in the past, an analysis of their results, and a description of the past market plan. You now have a solid base of information upon which to set marketing objectives for the new project, select sales programs for the new campaign, define a target audience, develop a strong message, and select the appropriate marketing tools to carry that message across.

Marketing Objectives

Now that you have a thorough understanding of your organization and your community, it is time to turn your attention to the marketing plan for the upcoming campaign. To prepare your strategy for the campaign, begin by setting marketing objectives. Objectives should be established in at least four major areas: audience maintenance, audience expansion, audience development, and audience enrichment.

Audience Maintenance

As you prepare for a new marketing campaign, one of the first groups that you will typically overlook is your current audience, on the assumption that they will use their past experiences when considering new events. Maybe you do not give them any attention at all, feeling that they are already with you.

A successful marketing campaign must be built on a very strong foundation, and that foundation is the current audience. The current audience ranges from those people who will attend anything you do to those folks who have attended their first event at your organization this past season. You should be concerned with not only making sure that they buy tickets again this season, but that they, in fact, increase the frequency of their attendance. You can best increase this frequency and maintain attendance by building a strong relationship with each member of the current audience. Your relationship with current customers can be strengthened by frequent communication, such as newsletters, letters to new buyers explaining your procedures, advance notice of special events, and letters to segments of the audience explaining your organization's hopes, dreams, and specific plans.

One of the major areas that will ensure audience maintenance is membership renewal, the purchase of season tickets for the upcoming productions. However, in addition to setting goals in the renewal campaign, you must be sure that you pay attention to goals aimed at increasing audience frequency of attendance. Once you have developed programs for maintaining your current audience, it is then important to set specific ticket goals for each program wherever possible. Specific ticket goals aid in better financial planning and make it possible to monitor and properly assess the success of each program.

Audience Expansion

You will also want to prepare strategy and set objectives and specific marketing goals in the area of audience expansion. Having set goals for renewing your current audience and increasing its frequency of attendance, you should turn your attention to the new people you can bring to the organization. To set objectives in the area of audience expansion, it is important to understand the concept of target marketing. When an organization either does not have a large enough audience or wishes to expand its audience, it often makes the mistake of seeking an audience that is quite different from the audience that currently attends. This is either because the marketing people feel that the current target audience has been saturated, or that there are segments of the community that do not now attend that they would really like to interest. For example, some organizations have found, after the completion of a very basic audience survey, that very few people from the automobile assembly plant attend their events. Even though the plant workers are extremely different demographically from the current audience, the organization sets out to build them into a new audience all in one season. Generally, these efforts end in dismal failure because of lack of time and funds to make an appropriate marketing effort.

Target Marketing

Someday, the employees of the assembly plant may indeed be part of your current audience. However, in the meantime, with limited funds and limited staff, you should be concerned with *target marketing,* an area governed by several principles. First of all, you must recognize that the number of new people attending your events each year is directly related to the efforts and funds you expend on attracting them. It is certainly true that audiences need exposure to a wide variety of cultural events

The Guthrie Theater. Gerry Bamman and John Lewin in *Peer Gynt*. Photo: Joe Giannetti.

to encourage them to increase their attendance. However, without the organization's efforts to attract them to their events, very few of these people will take that first plunge and attend for the first time.

The second principle of target marketing is very easily understood, and that is that your resources are limited. Because you do not have unlimited budgets or an unlimited staff to attract new audiences, you must focus your attention on those people who are most likely to attend but do not now attend your event.

The third principle is simply that those people who are most likely to attend your events are most similar to the people who now attend. By this I mean that they are approximately the same age, have reached the same educational levels, have the same types of occupations, and live in the same neighborhoods as your current audience.

To better understand the concept of target marketing, think of tossing a stone into a pool and watching the concentric circles that appear. The point at which the stone entered the water and the first circle emanated outward represents your current audience. The other rings formed closest to the center ring are those groups of people who are most like your current audience, demographically. As you move further away from the first ring representing your current audience, the groups of people become less like those who currently attend. Someday, we certainly hope that everyone who lives in the community will attend your organization's events. But to make the best use of your current funds and time, it is important that you begin work on those groups of people who are most like those who now attend. As you saturate each ring or group of people, you begin to move further out, concentrating your audience-expansion objectives on new groups. These objectives will relate to the organization that is seeking the new groups, how many will attend, and how you will attract them.

Audience Development

The third area of marketing objectives is audience development. In any experience, if people were not exposed to the professional arts while they were in high school and college, there is very little chance that they will attend these events after they leave school. In fact, the only hope you have to attract these people to the arts is to encourage someone who is a regular member of your audience to drag these folks with them.

Audience development must begin with a comprehensive school program. It is extremely important that your organization offer student matinees, tours, symposiums — any type of program that involves high school and college students. Often, students are brought to an event against their will, but having attended the event, they find it enjoyable and will begin, hopefully, a long relationship with the art form.

The second area of audience development concerns adult attendance. The student program is a long-range effort, but most organizations must develop new audiences more quickly. One important method of bringing adults to the theater, even when they have attended the arts previously, is through a good group-sales program. People who are very nervous or even frightened about attending a particular art event on their own may attend in a group, because there is safety in numbers. Corporate evenings at your event may attract many people who otherwise would not have attended, simply because the company is sponsoring the event and many of the person's friends and colleagues will also be there. A reception or other social event after the event can help guarantee a successful group outing. Having once attended with a group, individuals may very well attend on their own, if they found that experience enjoyable.

Audience Enrichment

The final area of marketing objectives is audience enrichment. It is important to set objectives that are concerned with making sure that everyone who attends your organization's event has an enjoyable experience. You should give consideration to convenient parking, to lighting in the area, to newsletters, to workshops and symposiums, to the program magazine handed out at the event, to the service the

"Once you have determined basic demographics, you may want to study your audience's attitudes toward your organization."

customers receive at the box office, the temperature in the auditorium, the attitude of ushers, the availability of restaurants, beverages, and chairs in the lobby, displays of design and past production photos. The important consideration is that the audience members enjoy attendance, that you have given enough information so that they understand what is going on onstage, that they know the location of all your facilities, and that the entire staff makes them feel welcome.

This chapter of your market plan should also review the overall attendance and revenue goals that the management of the organization has set for the current season and/or the separate event. These goals will be extremely important in your evaluation of sales programs and in the selection of marketing tools.

Sales Programs

The next major chapter in your market plan should cover the selection of sales programs. You must examine what you expect from each of these programs, the appropriate target audience for each, the message that you want to deliver to those target audiences and, finally, the marketing tools best suited to carrying that message across to your particular target audience. Other writers will cover each of these major topics in detail in other parts of this handbook. But it is important that you understand that each of these areas need to be fully outlined in your market plan.

Based on past history of your sales programs and your current income and ticket-sales goals, you should carefully select the sales programs that have the best opportunity of meeting revenue projections. Typically, a mix of programs will be necessary, since one single program hardly delivers enough audience to allow an organization to realize its goals completely. Each sales program should be assigned a sales goal so that it can be properly evaluated in terms of its benefits for the year's campaign. This will help you determine whether or not to repeat the effort in the coming seasons. Attention should be given to renewal objectives as well as the number of new buyers that the program can bring to the organization. Be realistic in your projections for new buyers. Overly optimistic sales projections may cause you to commit your time and efforts to programs with a marginal possibility for success, and therefore, little time will be left for other sales programs that could be far more beneficial.

Considerable attention in your market plan should be given to defining a target audience for each sales program and to developing message guidelines and selecting marketing tools to deliver this message. Marketing strategy for your new campaign should concentrate entirely upon a target audience, a message, and delivery tools for each sales program. You will have many options in each of these areas, and their advantages and disadvantages should be discussed in your market plan. Once you have determined what sales you can expect from each sales program and what it will cost to generate those sales, a cost-benefit analysis of each sales program can be prepared. Attention should be paid to the cost per dollar of income that indicates your return on your investment. Don't forget to include staff salaries when determining the expense of a sales program. After you have determined a cost-benefit analysis for each sales program, you can then determine which programs to emphasize and which programs to eliminate in the strategy for the new campaign. The most efficient method for selecting sales programs is to rank each program according to its benefits and costs, thereby establishing a priority ranking for each program.

It is now time to introduce the all important budget to your market plan. Give top priority to programs that produce the greatest number of sales for the least expenditure. If you prepare a list ranking each sales program in this manner and indicate along side it, the actual cost of the program, you can quickly draw a line at the point when you will run out of marketing funds and/or staff time. At this point, it will be very clear which programs just are not efficient enough to be included in the current campaign.

Monitoring System

The next chapter in your market plan should establish a system for monitoring the sales results and the expenses of each of your sales programs. The monitoring system should compare actual sales against goals. In order to develop such reports,

"If the 'word-of-mouth' created by early audiences is not strong and positive, there is very little that marketing can do."

it will be necessary to code messages as often as possible. For example, it is extremely important to code the various lists that you may purchase or swap for with other organizations to send out brochures and to attempt to understand which electronic media, be it publicity or advertising, is doing the best work for you. Every staff member and volunteer involved in the marketing program should make frequent reports on the results and evaluations of the marketing strategy and plans. The box office must also play a very important role in monitoring the results of all sales activity. At the completion of the campaign, you will have all the results you need to make your next market plan even more successful than the one you have just prepared.

The Final Chapter

The written market plan that you and your organization now possess should clearly:

- make better use of your organization's resources
- more efficiently assign and schedule employee and volunteer work
- coordinate and unify all marketing efforts
- facilitate an evaluation of all sales programs
- create a system for pointing out problem areas
- identify opportunities
- establish a progressive approach toward your organization's goals
- provide more effective media selection by eliminating major guesswork
- give you, your boss, and the board of trustees confidence that the organization has a well-thought-out plan with an excellent opportunity for success.

"What If"

One of the more frequent questions asked about the market plan is, "what if the plan is not working." One early warning signal that there is something wrong with a plan is a failure to reach satisfactory progress towards sales goals. You must be able to identify this lack of progress as early as possible and be careful not to overreact.

Your first reaction should be to have confidence in your plan. Take plenty of time to research properly what is actually causing the failure to reach the sales goal. You may have to do some informal research to determine the level of the public's awareness and the actual "word-of-mouth" on the event being promoted. You must determine whether you have underpromoted the event or whether it is just that people who have seen the event are not recommending it (or worse, bad-mouthing it) to friends, neighbors, and business associates. Underpromotion should be very unlikely given a well-prepared market plan. You should also be aware of the major role played by "word-of-mouth" created by the audiences early in the run of the production is not strong and positive, there is very little marketing effort that can overcome that situation. If you can determine that the actual promotion message is causing the audience to be disappointed in the event, then, of course, a correction should be made.

Also, all events do not appeal equally to all audiences. With your understanding of the event and the way you see audiences reacting to it, you should take another look at your target audience. You may have, for example, determined your target audience to be between 25 and 49 years of age, with heavy emphasis on those over 35. But checking the early sales for the event, you may now find that the event is actually attracting a much higher percentage of people *under* 35. At this point it is appropriate to shift the target and keep promoting.

Don't underestimate the pressure you will receive from the management and board of trustees and even the pressure from your own desires to abandon the plan and instead, buy as large an ad as possible in the newspaper with the largest circulation. Keep in mind that spending additional money will only help if you have underpromoted or misjudged your target audience. If additional spending is considered appropriate, be sure to determine whether the new efforts will sell enough tickets to pay for the additional expenditure and significantly contribute to the general budget of the event. Although the additional expenditure may sell some additional tickets, it may not sell enough, and just breaking even may not be acceptable. However, if the plan is not reaching its sales goals because of a less than satisfactory acceptance

"Overly optimistic sales projections may cause you to commit your time and efforts to marginal programs."

by the audience, then it is time to get on to the promotion of the next event. When in doubt, trust your market plan, and remember all the hard work you and others put into making it your guide to success.

Micheal House

THE MARKETING MIX

Micheal W. House is currently a Principal in Mallory Factor Incorporated where he heads the Advertising and Graphics Division. Previously he was Vice President for Marketing at the Brooklyn Academy of Music. Mr. House was Marketing Manager at the Hartford Stage Company, and Management and Marketing Consultant at the Performing Arts Center at Bath, in Bath, Maine. Other consultancies have been for the Harlequin Theatre in Atlanta and Washington D.C., The Atlanta Ballet, and Atlanta's Fox Theatre. Mr. House is a graduate of Kalamazoo College, and holds a MA in Arts Administration from the University of Michigan.

My mentor Sally Doud Way (a founding member of the American Conservatory Theater, the Long Wharf Theater and the Alliance Theater Company), taught me that there are basically three types of people who make up potential audiences. There are those who so love the theater that they will pay to see just about anything if it is on a stage. There are those who are not now, nor whom ever will be interested, no matter what you could possibly do to convince them. And, then there are those who are interested even though they don't know it yet.

It is our job as marketeers* to just say enough to let the first group know that the show is happening, to avoid the second completely, and to let the third understand what a wonderful time they're going to have.

She spelled out the most basic concept of marketing:

YOU CAN'T GET SOMEONE TO BUY SOMETHING
THEY DON'T PERCEIVE THEY NEED OR WANT.

Marketing is a system that allows an organization to focus its limited resources so that it can increase the probability of obtaining its goals.

The marketeer who works in the commercial sector believes that a product's potential for success increases if it is designed to appeal to specific consumer wants. This traditional marketing process begins with an evaluation of the needs, wants, and perceptions of the prospective market. The product is then developed based on that research. The means of presenting this product—how it is packaged, how much it costs, how it is best promoted, and how it is to be bought—is then conceptualized, tested, and finally taken into the marketplace.

The marketeer who works in the non-commercial, culture industry, on the other hand, begins with the product which he rarely selects or to which he even gives input. He *does* utilize, though, the methods and systems developed by his commercial sector counterpart to present this product to the selected markets. This "arts marketeer" begins his process by analyzing his product and determining how the marketplace perceives it, who would and could possibly buy the product, and what those people need to hear to make the purchase. He then packages the product, prices it, establishes the manner in which the tickets will be bought, and then promotes the product.

Some consider marketing "the science of the exchange process." Marketing begins with the model that an exchange will occur when each of two parties perceive that the other has something of value which will satisfy him. When the perceived satisfaction exceeds the cost and the hassle of the physical transference, the exchange occurs.

It is the job of the marketeer to *match up* these two parties.

To make the match, the marketeer must know quite a bit about both: what each wants, is able to do, and, most importantly, what exactly he can and can't do to in-

---

*The author has requested the use of the word "*marketeer*" as opposed to *marketer* which is used in all other sections.

> "People don't buy things or services, but rather purchase a perceived satisfaction."

fluence the outcome. The marketeer knows every exchange is controlled by four variables: the *Product,* the *Price,* the *Promotion,* and the *Placement.* These are called the Four P's.

As the law of gravity is basic to physics, the Four P's are basic to marketing. Whether you sell socks or Shakespeare, pots or Puccini, ties or toe-dancing, whenever an exchange happens, these four factors are present. What is great about all of this is that the Four P's can be controlled. They can be manipulated to your advantage, *if you plan* their use. That means you can partially control the future of your company.

This plan, the way in which the Four P's are to be combined is called the *market mix.* I am constantly amazed at the number of arts administrators, who wouldn't dream of making a cake without a recipe, but who merrily jump into creating a company without any plan or just a small part of one. They show less of a concern for their livelihood than their sweet tooth. Not only must the company establish its artistic goals and financial plan, but it must also establish solid, realistic planning for a way to present itself to the public and a way to earn every last red cent it needs.

Marketeers have even created a little jingle to help them remember how important this is: *The master marketeer manipulates the market mix to make the money mandated. You must plan the product, price, promotion and placement for present and potential purchases.*

The product is what the business offers in the exchange process. Although this appears to be a very straightforward idea, it is very much like a china doll—beautiful, fragile, difficult to make, and not to be played with by children.

People don't buy things or services, but rather purchase a perceived satisfaction. The consumer's primary motivation for buying a particular object or service is that he sees in it the capability of satisfying a complex matrix of his desires. These capabilities are called benefits.

The implication of this model is apparent. It is not what a thing is, but rather what you think it will do for you that determines whether you need it or no.

The successful, traditional marketeer will begin with the identification of market desires and then make a product to satisfy those real or imagined needs. But, for the arts marketeer this means taking a given product and then identifying what real or imagined needs it satisfies. To increase his product's potential for success, the arts marketeer structures the presentation of the product to emphasize the real benefits for which the selected markets are willing to make the exchange.

Visit the shampoo section of any drug store and you will find more than fifty different brands. If you look at their ingredients you will notice that they are all practically the same. But now look at them closely. They are all so drastically different in appeal—the bottles, the colors, the extra ingredients such as beer, honey, animal proteins, etc. Yet Brand X is much more successful than Brand Y. Why?

The answer is packaging.

What makes Brand X more successful than Y, although both are virtually the same product, is that X has successfully identified itself with the most important market desires one can obtain from the purchase of the product. The buyer is not only buying clean hair, but also sex appeal, health, or whatever. The marketeer has manipulated the product without changing the ingredients, only pointing out its virtues to the public by its successful package.

The concept of packaging is very important for the arts marketeer. It is usually the only way in which the product can be molded to match what is understood to be the real and imagined needs of the selected markets without putting a constraint on the artistic vision of the organization. Whether you are selling tragedy, tunes, or tutus, the final decision to buy a ticket depends, not on the virtue of the performance, but upon which of the leisure/entertainment options will best satisfy the customers' desires. Not idealistic, but practical.

In the not-for-profit arts world, packaging has mainly taken the form of subscription packages offering a litany of prescribed benefits. Even though each marketplace is different, their needs are different, and even though the style of work is different, we still see the same subscription campaign with the same benefits worded exactly the same way. What works in Chicago may not work in Chattanooga.

Let's compare two case studies of two similar packages at two different organizations in two different cities.

When the Hartford Stage Company was planning the subscription campaign for the move from its old, smaller theater to its new, larger one, little research had been done as to who the currrent subscribers were or why they subscribed. The research that had been done and reinforced by conversations with the board members, leaders in the community, and subscribers showed that the profile of Stage Company subscribers didn't vary drastically from the national profile of theatergoers. The profile described in studies done by the Ford Foundation, American Council for the Arts, and the Baumol-Bowen surveys, showed that the major indicators of attendance were a high-status job, high income, and a high education level. Also, it was found that people had a greater tendency to attend if their total evening was planned out for them.

The research also showed that while the Stage Company had been in existence for twelve years, it had a fairly low local profile.

Since the Stage Company was moving into a larger market as a relatively unknown product, they borrowed an old retail trick. They decided to decrease the risk of buying by increasing the perceived value of product without increasing the price tag. In other words, they increased the appeal of the product by making it responsive to more needs and desires of its market without making it more expensive.

What was devised was the NEW, FUN, AND EASY TOTAL ENTERTAIN-MENT PACKAGE, which gave each subscriber two dinners for the price of one (one per show), normal discount theater tickets, safe and convenient parking, plus the standard benefits: guaranteed seating, the same seat year after year (amazingly, a very important benefit), ticket exchange, no waiting in lines, free magazine/newsletter mailed to your home, priority notices, snow-exchange policy, etc. The theater had arranged for six complete evenings "out on the town," totally planned out and at a great savings. When you bought two subscriptions, you could realize savings equal to one subscription.

In that single campaign, with a small increase in ticket prices and $10,000 additional expenditure, subscriptions jumped from 7,500 to 17,000. One shouldn't be foolish enough to believe that packaging was responsible for the jump—they did have a brand new building and the first highly targeted and visible sales campaign they had ever mounted—but research showed that the package was responsible for directly motivating 20% of the new sales.

Packaging is the area where arts marketing can make the product responsive to the market. It creates tangible solutions to real needs. It is not sales gimmickery. Sales gimmickery can be very destructive to the main product — the arts — and ultimately to the marketing effort as well.

Gimmickery will:

1. Attract people who are not ready to attend, whose expectations will not be met, and who will be turned off, possibly forever.

2. The whole principle of using gimmickery creates a vicious spiral in which one must create bigger and better promotional packages annually to maintain or increase sales. This moves you away from concentrating on your core product and moves you towards ideas like going into the discount coupon business, with coupons valid for dining, bowling, flowers, records, books, and of course—stuck in the back of the booklet—the theater's skits, tunes, toe-dances, whatever.

A similar program the BAMpac, was introduced at the Brooklyn Academy of Music, but its incorporation was not based on any formal or informal research. It even went contrary to some older research which stated that the lack of restaurants in the immediate area was not a deterrent to attendance because restaurants and dining were not determinants of attendance. This packaging of BAM's programs had no significant influence on sales.

But one aspect of the BAMpac has become a central benefit in the minds of BAM subscribers — the transportation discount voucher. This voucher provided half-price parking in the well-lighted, adjacent parking lot or half-price on the BAMbus express from Manhattan, to BAM, and back to Manhattan. This benefit spoke directly to the darkest fears of an audience nervous about attending a performance in

"What works in Chicago may not work in Chattanooga."

"A case needs to be made for the virtues of the single-ticket campaign."

what many perceived to be a distant, depressed neighborhood. While this didn't generate new sales as the Total Entertainment Package did for the Hartford Stage Company, it at least inhibited negative arguments about attendance.

Each marketplace is different, and its needs are different. You will see many brochures in your career. Most of them will devote at least one panel to subscription benefits—some more, some less. Most will stir a sense of déjà vu, most you will wish you had a copyright on, and with most you will wonder: "Are all these benefits really necessary to make a sale? Has this organization listened to its market to see if that benefit is what it wants? Is this packaging effective? Have the benefits been emphasized according to ranking of importance to the marketplace, or, are these all of equal importance? HAVE I TOLD THEM THE MOTIVE (MADE THE CONNECTION BETWEEN NEED AND SATISFACTION)?"

I can't tell you how many times I have seen a subscription brochure that offers a discount (apparently an important motive for the sale, since it directly affects income), but the amount has not been stated anywhere.

Perhaps all that need be done is to add a benefit. Maybe nothing needs to be changed, or maybe the emphasis is misplaced. The marketeer realizes that the options are there to be creatively used. The market will help to make that decision—but you must *listen* to it.

For more than twenty years, subscription has reigned as the primary, and often the only method of selling tickets. The king is not dead, he just no longer has absolute power.

While there remain organizations with growing subscriptive bases, many theaters with previously strong subscriptions have seen that base erode, some faster than others. The sad thing about it is that many of those theaters have forgotten the old art of single-ticket campaigns and really haven't set out an effective campaign, let alone money to generate sales.

The reasons for subscriptive declines at this point can only be hypothesized, but I wonder if this trend isn't actually beneficial to the arts. We don't need to make a case for mounting subscription campaigns; the reasons have been well stated by others: cash flow, audience and income insurance against flops, the cost-effective nature of multiple sales, market incentives, and so forth. But perhaps a case needs to be made for the virtues of the single-ticket campaign. The primary benefit of a single-ticket campaign is its developmental nature.

As a product becomes more defined (and a subscription is a very defined product), the market becomes smaller. Subscription, by the nature of its marketplace appeal, eliminates many segments of the market. Campaigns developed to target specific markets for a single production provide the organization an opportunity to introduce another segment of consumers to their product. Those new consumers are then added to their organization's mailing list. Repeat contact with those people will help to provide repeat business.

This is not an academic activity. Many studies have shown how the neophyte can be developed into the perfect patron. The "perfect patron," the subscriber/contributor/volunteer, begins as a single-ticket buyer, and through repeat business, he develops over a two-to-three year period into a subscriber. After two or three years of subscribing, he develops into either a volunteer or contributor, and after two or three seasons of being a subscriber/volunteer or subscriber/contributor, he becomes a "perfect patron." If the consumer takes more than three years to reach a new plateau, he will never become a "perfect patron."

The single-ticket campaign, also, has the added benefit of keeping the institution in view of the public. This allows for a controlled growth and establishment of the organization's "image." In many ways, it softens or prepares the market for that Rite of Spring—the annual subscription renewal campaign.

Many organizations have a somewhat negative image of their products and justify a subscription as an insurance policy against their "turkeys." They run scared, sell themselves short, and minimize their potential to maximize their successes and income.

But maintaining a subscription orientation is a short-sighted, highly pressured procedure that can only satisfy the organization's short-run needs. There *is* life after subscription. By maintaining a balance between subscription and single-ticket sales programs and campaigns, the organization provides itself a means to control public perception and growth.

Most non-commercial organizations, I am convinced, rely on an Ouija board to set prices. Others have taken the name ''not-for-profit'' entirely too literally and believe that it is their unalienable right to lose money and mount huge deficits. I want to assure you that it is perfectly all right, and some say quite reasonable, for the ''not-for-profit organizations'' to establish responsible pricing practices for the product or services they produce so that they can earn money.

Pricing remains one of the more intriguing aspects of theoretical arts marketing and is one of the more difficult aspects to realize. Amazingly, the pricing principles of commercial and non-commercial organizations are not that different. Both utilize pricing to obtain a profit, although each defines ''profit'' differently. The commercial organization defines profit as cash dividends, whereas the non-commercial organization believes that its profit is the maximum use of and/or quality of its product or service.

In determining the principles leading to a pricing structure, the organization must take into account both the consumer and its own perspective. The consumer will engage in an exchange if he perceives that the amount of satisfaction or benefits to be obtained from the product exceeds its cost, and that cost is within his reach. The organization must determine its own objectives—how does it want to be compared (and it will be compared) to other organizations offering similar products, what is the current demand for the product, how much does the product actually cost to produce, and what can a pricing structure do for the organization?

The answer to the latter is central:

The purpose of pricing is to maximize income potential while at the same time stimulating sales and opening new markets.

For the non-commercial organization, ''maximizing income potential'' remains delimited by the organizational objective that sees profit as the maximum utilization of their high-quality product. Therefore, these groups look to exploit established markets and generate new demand. While pricing is not a determinant of purchase, its influence is strongly felt in the selection decision.

Pricing structures are generally recognized as capable of addressing one of four objectives:

1. generating a cash profit or profit maximization,
2. covering a portion or all of the costs or cost recovery,
3. stimulating the market to make additional purchases,
4. turning the market off.

Profit maximization is basically making the most amount of money possible. It is determining the highest price that can be charged without inversely affecting the cost of production or the level of demand. While commercial arts organizations rely on this pricing principle, the not-for-profit groups usually use it only as a subscription benefit.

It is interesting to note that the total costs of a product, direct and indirect, are born by the consumers of the product. The operation is not divided into producer and product, each with its own separate source of income.

When the two are separate, and pricing is based on making enough on ticket sales to cover the direct production expenses, it is called *cost recovery*. Most not-for-profits, given their markets and organizational objectives, can't expect to set a price structure that could match the total costs of their products, let alone generate a cash profit. Therefore, they select to recover a ''reasonable'' amount of the total cost. Often, the boundaries of what is ''reasonable'' are defined by available contributed income or quantifiable market demand.

When the organization's objective is to attract the greatest number of customers in the shortest period of time, it sets a low price. This approach is called *market stimulation*. Often, this pricing strategy is used for new products in order to stimulate the growth of the marketplace, or to capture a large share of the competition's audience. Like ''free trial'' promotions, this strategy minimizes the markets' perceived risk in purchasing an unknown product and gets customers to use it once—or with enough frequency to establish brand loyalty.

Utilization of low prices to stimulate a market can be successful if:

> ''Many organizations have a somewhat negative image of their products and justify subscription as insurance against 'turkeys.' ''

1. the market is price sensitive, that is, it reacts quickly and radically when prices change,

2. the cost of production decreases through high volume (this does not apply to theatre seats),

3. the low price would affect competition.

Know what you are doing when you decrease ticket prices to stimulate a market. Make sure you are not creating a vacuum that can never be filled either by earned or contributed dollars. And be aware that the level you set now will live with you for many years.

This is the principle behind the conceptualization of subscription (as opposed to a series ticket. The series ticket is just a convenient sales-package idea where price and price discount are low priorities for the buyer).

To repeat, the purpose of pricing is to maximize income potential, while at the same time, stimulating sales and opening new markets. Each individual consumer brings with him varying levels of perception, desires, and ability to the exchange arena, and these factors can be manipulated to achieve pricing's purpose.

Demand-oriented pricing structures are based on the varying intensities of a market segment's demand. A higher price is charged when demand is high and vice versa, irrespective of the cost of production. This pricing discrimination takes many forms:

1. Customer-based discrimination is illustrated by offering lower prices to large potential markets. Take, for example, Three S's: Students, Soldiers and Senior citizens. Markets like these requiring added stimulation to attend get lower prices.

2. Location-based discrimination is charging more for front center orchestra than rear balcony.

3. Time-based discrimination is charging less for Wednesday matinee than Saturday evening, if Wednesday matinee is a weaker seller.

4. Product-based discrimination is charging uniformly more for musicals than for dramas.

For demand-oriented price structures to work, certain questions must be answered.

• Can you segment the markets? Do they exhibit different intensities of demand? And can they be communicated with directly?

• Is there any chance that the low-priced seats will not undermine the higher? If there is a significantly lower attendance on Friday than Saturday, does lowering Friday's price then only rob from Saturday night, thus lowering income?

• Will the cost of segmenting and managing of all these differing prices exceed the extra income generated?

Most consumers develop strong ideas of a reasonable range for the price of a given product. Today, the reasonable range for a Broadway show is $17.50 to $45.00 or even $50.00. While $100 tickets still raise eyebrows, the consumer will make the purchase if the perception of satisfaction is high enough. That purchase will even be made at the sacrifice of other things. If a Broadway musical sets its top Saturday night price at $7.50, this would generate skepticism and questions of the quality.

There is a certain inevitable amount of circular reasoning involved in pricing decisions. As the marketing program is implemented, prices can be changed quickly to respond to consumer demand. But the pricing process must begin somewhere. Specifically, the base ticket price must be established as the marketing program is being formulated.

The marketeer has any number of choices in setting the base price. There is a continuum of possibilities ranging from highest price to lowest price, with the top price generating no demand and the lowest price not covering enough costs.

In the arts, we are still living with the social guilt of the Sixties, and usually set the base ticket price at levels which are absurdly low and which are not responsible to the operating budget.

One of the founding purposes of the National Endowment for the Arts was to make the arts affordable to all economic levels of the community. We have since found out that those people who weren't utilizing the arts prior to subsidized tickets,

> "People who weren't utilizing the arts prior to subsidized tickets weren't utilizing them after."

weren't utilizing them after — no matter how much audience development was sponsored.

Not-for-profit doesn't mean that you lose money or don't make money.

Price structures for the not-for-profit must be established upon the realities, behavior, and perceptions of the marketplace in conjunction with the objectives, realities, and true costs of the organization.

The number one problem that faces most arts organizations is that a very limited number of people know these organizations exist. They feel they have made the better mousetrap, and therefore, the world must know about it; or worse, everyone they know knows about it—two ''knows'' don't make it right. The next step these folks take to broaden their horizon is to try to get the world to buy their tickets.

Emerson said, ''If a man can build a better mousetrap, the world will beat a path to his door.''

Sorry, Ralph, you're wrong!

Unless I know about the mousetrap and understand that it can satisfy my needs, I'll stick to Decon.

Communication is the prerequisite of exchange. I must know your product exists before I can buy it.

Remember you can't get someone to buy something they don't perceive they need or want. All you can do is inform a person that a product exists and present it in a way that speaks directly to that person's wants and needs.

The objective of promotion is fourfold:

1. Inform the selected markets: WHO is selling, WHAT is being sold, WHEN it is, WHERE it is, and HOW to buy it.

2. Make the association between the desire for the product and satisfaction it can provide, or, state its unique position.

3. Enhance a positive public perception.

4. You must *penetrate* deeply into the selected market, *reach* as much as possible, and *surround* them with enough information and stimuli to motivate them to a purchase.

You must communicate to motivate a market to close a sale.

To obtain these objectives the marketeer lays out a detailed plan of attack. The plan

1. establishes the objectives and priorities of the promotional campaign

2. selects and defines the target market

3. defines the message that needs to be communicated and

4. selects the media that bests carries the message.

Before any promotional campaign, or for that matter, any plan, is designed, its objectives and priorities must be defined and *written down*. The objectives must be based upon the marketing objectives (which are based on the organization's objectives) and the realistic constraints of time, money, and personnel. You must define why the campaign is being undertaken, what can be expected of the campaign, and what it will do for the organization.

The reason for defining the objective is simple and practical: How else do you know when you're a success? The reason for writing it down is equally practical. Simply, this is the first step in controlling the roaring beast in front of you.

The average person in his lifetime consumes tons of food and gallons of liquid. Imagine sitting down at a table and finding that all the food and water you would ever consume had been placed in front of you. Then you are told you have to eat and drink every last bit of it at once. You would probably say you couldn't do it. But if you were told to divide it into the individual servings to be apportioned over your lifetime, the idea wouldn't seem so insurmountable.

That is the way you tackle the large problem facing you: Break it down into manageable size. To begin to take control of it, write it down. This is the most important step to learn in the most difficult process.

But you will also find that after this, the rest falls into place easily.

As you know, it takes two to tango and create an exchange. I will assume that you know all about yourself, but what about the other person? You need to know how to find that person, and how he lives, sees the world, and envisions himself.

> "Not everyone has the same degree of interest in your product, and therefore you should not have the same degree of interest in them."

"A person must be exposed to anywhere from 4 to 15 consecutive identical impressions before he will be aware of your product."

The market for a given product does not encompass everybody. The definition of the market is dependent upon the product. The more defined a product is, the smaller the market. As I stated at the very beginning, every product has a non-market, an actual market, and a potential market. Not everyone has the same degree of interest in your product, and therefore, you should not have the same degree of interest in them. An organization just can't operate with any efficiency if it treats the whole market as having equal levels of interest and ability to buy its product. This realization and separation is called *market segmentation.*

There is no one way to define the terms that permit the marketeer to segment the market. The main criterion is to look for those which will aid in making promotional-tool selections. Most media define their audience in geographic and demographic terms, stating how many of what type of people use their products. These terms have become popular because consumer interest is often highly associated with geo/demographic variables, and because they are easy to recognize and measure.

A third way to define a market segment is by lifestyle and personality profile. These are the most difficult variables to uncover accurately, but they are critical in truly understanding a market (and thus in better serving that market's needs). They are also indispensable in conceptualizing the creative strategy in a campaign. Their importance in determining the selecting the "editorial" context in which your message appears, is now becoming central in media selection.

As I stated earlier, the basic principle of marketing is to design and promote the offering in such a way so that the consumer will see it as the answer to his needs and desires and will buy it. You will never convince consumers that they have to have it, that it is their duty to support it, or it's high art so of course they'll want it. You must build awareness of your product, arouse interest in it, stimulate the consumers' senses and motivate them to buy it.

To build awareness, you need three things:

1. A repeated message increases knowledge and awareness. There must be considerable repetition to establish an awareness of a product. Depending on the source, a person must be exposed to consecutive, identical impressions anywhere from four to fifteen times before he will be aware of your product.

2. Once advertising stops, awareness will drop off. The elephant does forget.

3. The public's ability to retain your message is increased by clustering exposures—in other words, if you are running a radio campaign, the commercial will have a more lasting effect if fifteen spots are run in three days than if they are run over three weeks.

The next step is to arouse and motivate a person to action.

We become aroused or activated in three ways:

1. Internal need and drives (i.e., hunger and sex)

2. Stimulation of some type from an environmental element (i.e., burning your finger)

3. Through our fantasies

But arousal is not enough. The object is to motivate the consumer to do something (buy a ticket or give money). Our behavior is the result of a learned goal, a motive. For example, the Pepto-Bismol ad creates in us the feeling of indigestion and then, as in the case of Pavlov with his dogs, the ad teaches us that whenever we feel "sick to our tummy" we must think of Pepto-Bismol.

Action occurs when a consumer realizes that a need that has surfaced can be satisfied by something. We marketeers need to know how to stimulate that need and make it surface; we must make consumers aware of our offering, and tell them how to obtain it, and teach them that satisfaction can occur by exchange of their goods with our product.

Basic to the understanding of consumer motivation and behavior is the concept that we see and hear what we want to see and hear, remember what we want to remember, and forget the rest. We can't be motivated to do something without being aware of it.

Therefore, the most effective communication is that which is consistent with the needs, emotions, and feelings of those for whom it is intended.

The final step in creating the promotional campaign is planning the media mix or the selection of the communication tools that most effectively penetrate the targeted market.

There are as many tools at your disposal as your imagination will allow. They can range from door-to-door solicitation to direct mail, from Public Service Announcements to sophisticated television spots. No matter what you think up, it can be classified as either personal selling, advertising, publicity, or sales promotion. When the targeted markets have been selected and defined, and the message you want to convey has been conceptualized, the media-planning aspect can begin. Look at the various types of media available and select those that can best convey your message.

Let's suppose, for example, I had discovered that it was crucial to convey the colorful production values and the expert dancing of my ballet company. This would mean I should concentrate on those media which would provide me visual impact, preferably in color, and also with movement.

The second step would be to match the demographic profile of the targeted markets with the media with a similar audience profile. From this point on the procedure becomes tricky. I would recommend *Advertising Media Planning* by Jack Sissors, E. R. Petray, Crown Publishing Company, Rush St., Chicago, Ill. 60611, or better yet professional advertising people, and then figure out which of these provided the most cost-effectiveness.

The methodology of constructing the media mix has never been an exact science and the principles that guide the selection process change constantly. The guiding theory used to be establishing ''meaningful' levels of reach and frequency and then purchasing media that would obtain the desired goal.

Reach and frequency are terms of measurement that the media planner uses to estimate the efficiency of a plan. These measurements are based upon ratings and circulation figures. Reach is the number of people who have the *opportunity to see or hear* a given message. Frequency is how often that person would have the *opportunity to see or hear* the message.

The object is to ''buy the numbers,'' to get the highest reach with adequate frequency irrespective of the context in which the ad will appear. What results is arbitrariness and waste. Why should a man watch a TV spot where Jane Russell tells him about bras for full-busted women?

As communication costs have shot out of control, and as the advertisers have demanded a greater control of costs, planners have found an increased efficiency in a tighter, lower reach into more defined markets with greater frequency. In other words, the planners are looking into the context in which ads are placed to eliminate talking to most of the marginal and non-markets, concentrating instead on building awareness and motivation through greater repetition and more aggressive dynamic advertisements.

I cannot stress how important it is to lay out the promotional campaign in great detail. Remember that it is your map. It shows you how you are to get from Point A to your goals. It is not the Ten Commandments, engraved in stone. Even though a plan's key elements may have been tested, if the campaign just isn't working, change it. There is nothing wrong, shameful, or guilt-inducing about a promotional campaign going awry. The irresponsibility comes from not recognizing the problem and taking action to correct it. Don't panic. Take a deep breath, and fix it.

The fourth ''P'' of the market mix is—the placement—or where and how the purchase will be made and where it will be consumed.

Often, a sale isn't made because the customer couldn't get anyone to sell him a ticket, or buying a ticket became an event larger than the program he wanted to buy, or the consumer perceived that he needed a passport to get to the theater, or because the consumer thought that particular theater would really be a dreadful place to spend a couple of hours.

The profit sector often calls placement distribution, channel management, or, simply, physically getting the product out into the marketplace (or the market into the place). This aspect of the market mix is more central to understanding the marketing process in the economic sector than in the not-for-profit sector, and in particular, the culture industry.

The easier it is to buy and use something, the greater the likelihood that it will be bought.

For example, just think how much fun you would have (or really how often you would buy one) if every time you wanted to have a Coke, you had to trot on down to

> "There is nothing wrong if a promotional campaign goes awry. Irresponsibility comes from not recognizing the problem and taking action to correct it."

Atlanta, Georgia, where the main office and factory is. To meet Coke's organizational objective, which is "to put Coke within an arm's length of desire," Coke needed to establish a system of middlemen (agents who come between the consumer and producer to carry the producer's offering either one step closer to or to the consumer for consumption) and retail outlets that would carry their product.

The concept of the middleman is important for those arts organizations or artists who need an organization to "book" them (e.g., dance companies, a bus-and-truck show, etc.). These organizations must put together and manage a whole system, or utilize an already existing system, like a booking agency, to make the contacts (this is known as wholesaling). These people can sell their offering either to another wholesaler who will physically place the product in the marketplace and take on the agonies of working out the details of a bus-and-truck, or even of getting an actor from L.A. to Podunk, USA, for a run of a show, or they can sell it to a retail outlet like a theater, which will in turn sell it to the ultimate consumer—the ticket buyer.

But, more important to the not-for-profit cultural organization is the understanding that a theater is a retail outlet and as such, is subject to all the conditions of a retail outlet.

Philip Kotler, Northwestern University Marketing Professor, defines the term "atmospherics" to mean the conscious designing of space to create certain effects in buyers. The management of atmospherics can be a particularly important promotional tool for retailers. For example, "a restaurant may have a good, busy, or depressing atmosphere.

"The atmosphere of an organization is apprehended through four of the five senses: Visual—color, brightness, size and shape; aural—volume and pitch; olfactory—scent and freshness; tactile—softness, smoothness and temperature.

"Atmospherics should be carefully managed to reflect the tastes and desires of the target market segment."

Perhaps one of its most influential (and sometimes most frustrating) aspects for the theatre is its location and the services available for that site. For The Brooklyn Academy of Music, this is always a very important factor to consider when designing any strategy. The facility is located outside of the main residential area of its prime market, and people perceive its location to be unsafe and too far away. The Magic Theater, whose playwright-in-residence is Sam Shepard, is located in a National Urban Park—Fort Mason, San Francisco—which is located by the Marina. There was inadequate public transportation serving this area. The Magic's market was young vanguard, many of whom relied upon public transportation—transportation that was inconveniently located to the theater.

The marketeer must be aware of how easy it is (and is perceived to be) to get to the theater. If the audience arrives in cars, is there convenient, safe parking? Or, if public transportation is needed, how far away is the nearest stop, and when does the service end—after your curtain?

The distribution system for a theater is somewhat more complicated than the economic retail outlet, since a consumer doesn't directly purchase the product, but instead buys a "short-term, lease agreement"—the ticket. Therefore, the primary objective of the marketeer in making decisions about distribution is getting those tickets within an "arm's length of desire." This means, once again, knowing the market and its lifestyle patterns. Do your consumers use credit cards: Are they tourists? What department stores do they use? etc.

What are all the potential outlets and methods of making a sale? Their utilization will not increase potential sales, but will prevent a decrease in potential sales.

Of foremost importance is an efficient and sales-oriented box office. The box office should not be overlooked as a source of potential sales. As a matter of fact, the theater should view the box-office personnel as the salespeople of the theater. The box-office personnel are not reservation takers, but order getters and problem solvers. They should be trained to be more aggressive in getting people to buy even if they are only calling for information, they should redirect people to other seats for performances when a show is sold out, they should be helpful and have positive attitudes about every show—no matter what their personal opinion.

While sometimes offering examples relating to the arts, I hope I haven't made any grand sweeping statements which appear to say that there is only one way for the not-for-profit, cultural organization to sell itself. That is where many theaters fail in their sales efforts. They look at what other theaters do to promote themselves and copy it—and more often than not, they don't solve the problem they had set out to solve.

There is only one way to match a specific market with a specific product—and that is to stop, look, and listen.

You must *stop* rushing forward into unplanned and badly thought-out activities. You must *look* at the product you are offering and understand what it is, why anyone would want it, and why it is being made. You must *listen* to the market—how do they think, who are they, and what do they want. Once you know that, the rest comes easily.

Cora Cahan and Elizabeth Cashour

FINANCIAL NEEDS IN MARKETING

In early 1981, in a discussion with representatives of other dance companies about marketing for the Joyce Theater, phrases such as "determine the cost-to-income ratio," "realize the results may be skewed," and "always perform a test market analysis," introduced us to "MarketSpeak". Although our vocabulary continues to expand with each passing performance season, our basic approach to identifying and encouraging people to attend performances of the Feld Ballet (i.e., audience development) has been to follow four simple axioms:

1. "To have begun is half the battle; be bold and be sensible."

    —*Horace*

    (Use common sense, but don't be afraid to venture new ideas and take risks.)
2. "We haven't the money, so we've got to think."

    —*Lord Rutherford*

    (Hold fast to the bottom line of the marketing budget, unless costs can be cut.)
3. "To thine own self be true."

    —*Shakespeare*

    (Maintain a level of quality, creativity, and style that reflects the artistic point of view of the company.)
4. "Pray for good reviews."

    —*Any Honest Marketing Director*

The Feld Ballet, was only eight years old in 1982, when it began its New York City performing history anew with an inaugural season in its recently renovated 475-seat performance home, the Joyce Theater, at Nineteenth Street and Eighth Avenue. This engagement ended a four year hiatus, during which the company toured the United States and countries abroad. The four-week summer season was followed by another three-week engagement in October 1982. Both seasons introduced or re-introduced the Feld Ballet and the choreography of Eliot Feld to New York City audiences and critics, enabling us to reclaim some of our old audience while identifying a new one. However, the most straightforward approach to describing financial needs in our company's marketing will be to focus on the marketing campaign for the Feld Ballet's six-week, self-produced spring 1983 season at the Joyce Theater.

This spring season was special and unique in several ways:
1. The six-week engagement was the longest self-produced season the Feld Company had ever performed.
2. Marketing for the season included a full-fledged subscription campaign for the first time.
3. With the spring season, the Feld Ballet completed what had been designed as a blueprint performance year. This design included:

    a) a short, three- to four-week home season in the fall of each year, offer-

Cora Cahan's association with dance began as a child when she studied with several of the major teachers in the United States. Before becoming Executive Director of the Feld Ballet, she danced with both modern and classical ballet companies, as well as in plays and musicals at stock and resident theaters. Ms. Cahan has taught in college and university dance departments, public school systems, and at Jacob's Pillow. In addition to her involvement with the dance world, Ms. Cahan is married and has two children.

Photo: Lois Greenfield

Elizabeth Cashour joined the Feld Ballet in 1979 as Director of Development and Marketing. Previously she served for three years as the Acting Director for the Joyce Theatre Foundation where she helped engineer the four-million dollar fund raising campaign which renovated the dormant Elgin Theater to create the Joyce Theatre—New York's first theater designed specifically for the presentation of dance. Her other responsibilities have included Associate Administrative Director of AMAS Repertory Theatre in New York, Company manager for an Off Broadway musical, Theatre Program Assistant at the New York State Council on the Arts, and Box Office Manager for Baltimore's Center Stage. Ms. Cashour holds a BA degree from Loyola College, and has written short stories and plays.

Photo: Steve Saden

The Feld Ballet. Gloria Brisbin in *Anatomic Balm*. Photo: Lois Greenfield.

ing a limited repertory of eight to ten ballets, with a minimal marketing budget allocated for bolstering single-ticket sales, and a greater reliance on the Joyce Theater's own membership drive for advance ticket sales[1];

b) national and international touring interspersed throughout the year for a total of six to ten weeks, for which the company receives a fee. These performances are produced by a sponsor; and

c) an extended six-to-nine-week spring season in the Joyce Theater, presenting a repertory of fifteen to twenty ballets, and an increased marketing budget aimed at securing an audience armature — a steady framework of subscribers who purchase tickets to more than one performance of the Feld Ballet in advance.

The spring season is essential to the company's existence in that it provides a substantial portion of the dancers' contracted work-weeks. Yet, it also poses a great risk—audience interest in the Feld Ballet, particularly in its first spring season, must keep pace with this increase in performance.

The marketing team at the Feld Ballet consists of the executive director, the director of development and marketing, our advertising agent account executive (who has worked with the company for the past six years), and Eliot Feld, Artistic Director. It is very important to Eliot that the marketing of the company reflect its artistic point of view, even if to a somewhat limited extent, and his ideas and opinions are requisite to the conception and accomplishment of the campaign. The executive director and the marketing director work very closely together, meeting frequently to discuss marketing, promotion, and public relations in preparing the campaign. Each brings to these discussions questions about the company's marketing in relationship to the overall activities of the organization. The marketing director then researches these questions and backs up any assumptions that have been made with facts and statistics. She is aware of any changes in the general operating budget throughout the year, so that the marketing income and expense projections can be kept in line with the overall organizational financial picture.

During the summer and fall of 1982, discussions between the executive director and the marketing director, and often with Eliot Feld, began the long process of designing the marketing strategy for Spring 1983. First, we addressed the issue of what had to be accomplished through the campaign. We set ourselves the task of persuading, enticing, and thoroughly convincing *twice* as many people to attend the Feld Ballet during this season as had attended any single season in the past. Due to the sizeable financial expenditures projected for the season (dancers' salaries, theater rental, the cost of creating new ballets, *and* the marketing budget), a larger percentage of advance sales was also desirable. We reviewed the marketing tactics for previous Joyce Theater engagements, looked at the subscription and other ticket discounts of other performing-arts organizations, and turned a keen eye to interesting sales techniques in the commercial world (everything from book clubs and magazines to hamburgers). These provided us with the fuel for preliminary discussions. Next, we outlined the general means by which we would reach our goals:

1. A direct-mail subscription offering to selected mailing lists;
2. a direct-mail subscription offering to Joyce members in advance of the Feld Ballet's general mailing;
3. newspaper advertising to support the direct-mail subscription offering;
4. newspaper advertising to sell single tickets;
5. an increased effort in the area of group sales; and
6. publicity (by definition, favorable presentation in the news that is not paid for) handled by an outside press representative in conjunction with our own on-staff press coordinator. They would attempt to secure articles in the news (newspaper, radio, television) at particularly strategic points during the cam-

---

[1]The Joyce Theater instituted a membership campaign in the fall of 1982, offering discounts (agreed upon by each participating dance company) to all events in the theater. "First choice at the Joyce" enabled the member to select performances at a discount prior to a designated member deadline. With their Joyce membership card, they could also receive discounts at participating restaurants in the neighborhood. All solicitations for members and the entire fulfillment procedure were paid for and managed by the Joyce Theater. In return, dance companies paid a service charge of fifty cents per ticket for all tickets sold through the program.

paign (when the direct-mail piece is dropped, when the subscription advertisement appears in *The New York Times,* just prior to the company's opening, opening night, at the premiere of new ballets, as well as sustained publicity throughout the six-week run).

Having developed the general outline, the marketing director prepared research materials to aid in further discussions. This packet included detailed budgets from the first two seasons (showing side by side what had been projected and what had actually been spent), ticket-sales analyses for the first two seasons specifying sales in all price categories, a calendar of deadlines for the spring campaign, income projections for the spring season (featuring ideal, conservative, and best cases), and a preliminary marketing budget.

Even at this juncture, the marketing budget was based on as many hard facts as could be be assembled. Using the six ''general means'' outlined above, the following questions were asked in order to prepare the budget:

1. *Direct-mail subscription offering:* How many households should receive this offering? To answer this question, a general rule of thumb, substantiated and modified slightly by our past experience, was used.

   Rule of thumb—One percent of the households targeted to receive a direct-mail offering could be expected to respond, ordering an average of two tickets each.

   EXAMPLE: 100,000 pieces of mail are sent out by company X. It can reasonably be expected that 1,000 people will respond to this offering ordering two tickets (in the case of a single-ticket offer) or two subscriptions. Therefore, this direct-mail piece should sell 2,000 tickets (or, in the case of a two-performance subscription, 4,000 tickets).

A careful selection of mailing lists and names was compiled by the marketing director, who selected first from available dance patrons in the New York metropolitan area (by arranging list exchanges with other dance companies), general- arts patrons (first selecting subscribers to other arts organizations, and often if the subscription list was large enough, subscribers within zip codes which are particularly strong for the Feld Ballet) and then five to ten percent of the list was selected as a test audience. For this test purpose, the Feld Ballet made selections within our strongest zip code from *New York* magazine and *Ballet News* mailing lists. We believed that these two lists reached an audience that would be most receptive to a ticket offer from our organization.

Once the number of mailers was determined and the selection of lists was made, very specific questions were asked. We phoned our advertising agent, various printers, the post office, the mailing house and others with these questions. What computer charges would be incurred? What is the current bulk-rate postage? How expensive will it be to label and mail the piece? Current estimates were received for all services required. The nature of the direct-mail piece was then questioned. Would it be four-color or black & white? Would it need to be folded or binded? It was too early to project the exact nature of the piece, so informed assumptions had to be made. Scrutinizing the printing and production costs of prior mailers done by the Feld Ballet, as well as those done by other organizations, enabled us to determine a per piece cost (i.e., a direct-mail brochure costing $15,000 to print and produce 100,000 copies cost fifteen cents per piece).

2. *Direct mail subscription offering to Joyce members:* How many subscriptions could we expect to sell through the Joyce Theater's own membership? We projected a much higher return from this list, since the membership program was less than one year old, and since a large percentage of the members had bought tickets to the Feld Ballet in the fall. All of the members had bought at least one ticket to a dance event at the Joyce Theater.

3. *Newspaper advertising to support the direct mail subscription offering:* How well has newspaper advertising performed in the past in attracting subscribers? How can we determine the response rate (particularly in the case of *The New York Times,* which has a circulation in the New York metropolitan area of over 1.5 million)? Since we had no past history of placing subscription ads, we decided to budget conservatively and limit newspaper advertising for this purpose to one large ad in the Sunday *New York Times,* one week follow-

"We hope for full houses of paying customers, even if a great portion of the audience has purchased their tickets at a discount."

"We turned a keen eye to commercial sales techniques— everything from book clubs and magazines to hamburgers."

ing the mailing date for the brochure. (This was done so that the brochure and the ad would reinforce each other, and so that the targeted mailing list of patrons would receive the offer prior to the general public announcement in the newspaper).

4. *Newspaper advertising to sell single tickets:* How many ads would we need to place in advance of the engagement and throughout it? How large must these ads be to be effective? What other means of selling single tickets could be used to cut newspaper-advertising costs? Since the spring season would be twice as long as our previous run, a large increase in newspaper advertising was budgeted to maintain visibility. This was followed by a rate check at various newspapers to anticipate any increases in basic costs, and a formal schedule of ads, including dailies, was prepared.

5. *Group sales:* How could we increase group sales utilizing existing staff and materials so that the cost of acquiring these groups is simply the discount offered? Aggressive group-sales solicitation began immediately. The marketing director researched and identified groups in the New York City area that would be most interested in the Feld Ballet (high school and college dance programs, Jewish community groups, and organizations with a proven interest in cultural events, to name a few). Each group was sent a press kit, including the company's history, reviews, and photographs, with a cover letter explaining our group sales policy and rates. The marketing director contacted each of these group-sales candidates with specific programming and ticket information closer to the engagement.

6. *Publicty:* What is new and newsworthy this season to merit major press coverage? The marketing director, press representatives, and press coordinator met with the executive director and Eliot Feld to discuss the upcoming season. We decided that the creation of two new ballets and the revival of a work not seen since 1978, and the impact this major self-produced season would have on the company were worthy of publicity. We then discussed how we should best present ourselves to the press to insure maximum attention in all forms of the media.

Following the question and answer period, estimates were assembled, the preliminary budget was typed, and the most variable of all of the marketing analyses was prepared—the income projections for the spring season.

Which came first, the discount offer or the single-ticket price? In our case, the two were volleyed back and forth until the desirable discount and fair single-ticket price met center court. Should the single-ticket price be uniform for all seats in the house? For all performances? Should the subscription discount be greater than 25% (but less than 75%)? Variables were changed and interchanged, as "what if" income projections were run through the adding machine. We always determined the best and worst cases in each situation. After a series of discussions with the entire marketing team, the following conclusions were made:

1. A 40 to 50% discount would be offered to subscribers, since price incentive had been successful previously in acquiring first-time viewers. We also hoped to encourage the notion of "two performances for the price of one," thereby affording the subscriber the opportunity to enjoy a greater variety of a very diverse repertory. This more than generous discount was chosen after a very labored and serious discussion and an analysis of various subscription discounts. We decided to use the ticket discount as a marketing tool, projecting that a larger discount would secure a greater number of subscribers than might respond if the savings were less. Our hopes were to meet our income projections while playing to full houses of paying customers, even if a great portion (perhaps as much as 50%) of the audience had purchased their tickets at a discount.

2. A uniform ticket price for all seats and all performances was selected to present clear and precise options to the public. The seating configuration at the Joyce Theater is unique in that each seat is indeed equal (no sight-line problems, and no seat is more than fifty-five feet from the stage) so there is no need to devise a price scale for the house. An across-the-board pricing structure would also allow subscribers to choose their own date easily, rather than being forced to comply with series configurations or weekend-

only/weekday-only choices. The ticket buyer could purchase a subscription which conformed to a hectic schedule rather than vice versa. This became an added benefit and incentive to buy. The subscription offering was limited to the first four weeks of the run, since our research indicated historically, the earliest performances had been the most difficult to sell. The final weeks would then become vulnerable, but there would also be more time to react to audience and critical response with a new marketing strategy, should ticket sales be lagging behind projections. (But remember, we always pray for good reviews.)

Having reached these conclusions, we needed to decide the very important issue of how much the campaign should cost in relationship to a) the results projected, b) the other expenses for the seaon, and c) the company's general operating budget. First, each individual part of the marketing strategy was reviewed. For instance:

GIVEN: It costs $50,000 to create, print, and mail a brochure, through which we hope to sell 10,000 tickets. With the subscriber discount, the customer will pay $10.00 per ticket.

THEREFORE: We will spend $5.00 to make $10.00. (Or, reduced to a lower common denominator, we will spend fifty cents to make a dollar.)

Through this analysis, we were able to determine which part of the campaign was the most expensive, which section should, or could, be cut, and which could be increased, if necessary. To further compare the marketing budget to the income projected, we identified the total cost of producing the season and compared it to the new, though still conservative, income projections. A direct relationship between the season's expenses and income forecast was then drawn so that the company projected a break-even engagement. This reaffirmed the company's ability to offer the 40% discount on subscriptions and still maintain the desired balance between income and expenses.

Ten days before the quarterly board of trustees' meeting, the executive director and marketing director met with the comptroller to formally incorporate the new, detailed marketing budget into a revised general operating budget. We discussed the effect of the changes in marketing on the overall budget. Should we increase the amount of unearned income projected? Should we reduce other, often unrelated costs in the general operating budget to compensate for any overruns in the marketing budget? Should the marketing budget itself be cut? The symbiotic relationship between the marketing and operating budgets was drawn to create an equilibrium. The board then analyzed the marketing budget during their review of the revised general operating budget. After a discussion of the importance of this particular campaign to the company during this year and in future years, the board voted their approval. (They would be informed of any radical departures from the marketing budget as presented, and would receive a full report of the results following the spring campaign.)

With the board-approved budget in hand, creative discussions began about what *exactly* the direct-mail offering, the newspaper ads, and all of the other promotional materials would be. We discussed how publicity would enter into the strategy. As the creative portion of the marketing scheme took hold, we carefully proceeded, matching ideas to numbers, guided to a great extent by the "Yankee ingenuity" of our advertising account executive. Various price quotes or "a-best-possible-offer-given-the-circumstances" were always received before we proceeded with any design initiative. Often, our advertising agency solicited bids from as many as ten different printers before developing an idea further. Before the size of an ad was increased to boost sales, or matte stock was replaced by a glossier version, the costs were compared against the actual budget. The marketing director maintained a careful account of all the costs incurred throughout the campaign. She reported any major deviations from the budget to the executive director and in conclusion, prepared a final report of actual expenses against projected costs. In addition, no bills were paid by the comptroller until they had first been signed and approved by both the marketing director and the executive director.

Although alternative plans for our marketing strategy had not been outlined in detail, we had discussed elements of a second plan of attack. Our best defense, however, was in planning conservatively, so that any fortification necessary for Plan A could have been accomplished with implementation of an easily enacted, in-

> "A uniform ticket price for all seats and all performances presented the public with clear and precise options."

"Our best defense
has been planning
conservatively."

expensive Plan B. If and when Plan B had been called into action, time and money would have been both of the essence.

Throughout the spring season, the entire marketing team reviewed daily ticket reports and discussed appropriate responses. For instance, during the previous season, one particular ballet seemed to draw standing-room-only audiences. By responding to this enthusiasm immediately with the addition of that ballet to several remaining performances (and by immediately informing the public of this change in programming through our print advertising) the last week of the engagement was sold out in advance. This allowed us to drop some of the daily advertising we had projected. At the end of each week of performances, a detailed audience analysis was prepared to identify any problems and allow us to take any necessary alternate measures as quicky as possible. This analysis is also one of the first tools we will consult in planning our next marketing campaign for our next season.

It has been very important in developing the marketing for the Feld Ballet that discussions be open and ongoing. Ideas and questions are constantly brought to the fore by all members of the team, and thorough research, particularly on the part of the marketing director, is done expeditiously in response to these discussions. The marketing director must have a thorough understanding of the limits of the departmental budget and the manner in which the projections for income and expenses within this budget affect and are affected by the larger budgetary allocations for all aspects of the performance engagement and the general operating budget. Throughout the planning and implementation of the campaign, the following are of paramount importance: the tracking of marketing expenses to ensure that the organization remains on budget, the projection and tracking of income (particularly in determining ticket prices and a discounting structure in line with attendance goals), and an overall analysis of each component of the designed strategy (i.e., was the subscription successful? If so, what aspects of the campaign contributed to that success? How successful were single-ticket sales? What trends were established throughout the run?).

For now, we have begun the battle. We believe we are being sensible, and we hope that our marketing strategy will be bold.

PROTOTYPICAL MARKETING BUDGET (SEASON)

SINGLE TICKET ADVERTISING

1. Advertising agent's fee $_____

2. Art production for newspaper advertisements, handbills,
   posters and any miscellaneous   _____

3. Poster costs (number printed)   _____

4. Handbill costs (number printed)   _____

5. Weekly newspaper advertising for the run (small dailies only)   _____

6. Newspaper display advertising:
   (Individual listing of dates, sizes and costs for all newspaper display advertising)   _____

7. Miscellaneous costs   _____

    TOTAL SINGLE-TICKET ADVERTISING: $_____

SUBSCRIPTION CAMPAIGN ADVERTISING

1. Advertising agent's fee $_____

2. Direct-mail piece (Number of pieces)   _____

    Design   _____

    Production   _____

    Printing & folding   _____

    Purchase of mailing lists   _____

    Computer services   _____

    Mailing-house costs   _____

    Postage   _____

3. Newspaper advertising   _____

4. Miscellaneous costs   _____

          TOTAL SUBSCRIPTION COSTS: $_____

MISCELLANEOUS MARKETING COSTS

1. Group Sales Expenses $_____

2. Publicity expenses: $_____

    Press representatives fee   _____

    Photography   _____

    Press-kit materials   _____

3. Other: _____

          TOTAL MISCELLANEOUS COSTS: $_____

          TOTAL MARKETING BUDGET: $_____

                     + 15% CONTINGENCY* $_____

*When the very first marketing budget is done for the year, it is often advisable to cushion the projections
with a contingency of not more than 15%.

PROTOTYPICAL AUDIENCE ANALYSIS (Seasonal)

	First Week	Second Week	Third Week	Fourth Week	Total
Capacity (# performance X seats)					

PAID ADMISSIONS

	First Week	Second Week	Third Week	Fourth Week	Total
Full price	_____	_____	_____	_____	_____
Discounts offered (Listing of all discounts including standing room)	_____	_____	_____	_____	_____
Total discounts	_____	_____	_____	_____	_____
TOTAL PAID ADMISSIONS:	_____	_____	_____	_____	_____

UNPAID ADMISSIONS

	First Week	Second Week	Third Week	Fourth Week	Total
Press comps	_____	_____	_____	_____	_____
Complimentary tickets	_____	_____	_____	_____	_____
TOTAL UNPAID ADMISSIONS:	_____	_____	_____	_____	_____
TOTAL ADMISSIONS:	_____	_____	_____	_____	_____

% of total capacity:

	First Week	Second Week	Third Week	Fourth Week	Total
sold at full price	_____%	_____%	_____%	_____%	_____%
sold at discount (for each discount offered)	_____%	_____%	_____%	_____%	_____%
complimentary	_____%	_____%	_____%	_____%	_____%
press comps	_____%	_____%	_____%	_____%	_____%
deadwood	_____%	_____%	_____%	_____%	_____%
all paid admission	_____%	_____%	_____%	_____%	_____%
all in attendance (paid & unpaid)	_____%	_____%	_____%	_____%	_____%

PROTOTYPICAL INCOME PROJECTIONS—(SEASON)

TOTAL CAPACITY OF THE SEASON:_____

CASE I

TICKET TYPE	TICKET COST	PROJECTED # TO BE SOLD	INCOME
Subscription	_____	_____	_____
Group sales	_____	_____	_____
All other discount (list individually)	_____	_____	_____
Full price	_____	_____	_____
TOTALS	_____	_____	_____ **

*What percentage of capacity is this?_____%
**What percentage of maximum potential income is this?_____%

CASE II

(Following the pattern of Case I, variables are changed and interchanged through a variety of cases from *worst case* through *best case*.)

AUDIENCE ANALYSIS (WEEKLY)

Name of Company

Week #

Season (rates)

	Perf 1	Perf 2	Perf 3	Perf 4	Perf 5	Perf 6	Perf 7	Weekly Total	Total to date
Total capacity									
Full price sales									
Subscription									
Discounts: (list all discounts)									
Press comps									
Other comps									
Available/Deadwood									

Week's Percentages:

% of total capacity:
sold at full price:
sold on subscription:
sold at discount:
press comps:
other comps:
available/deadwood:

% of total capacity paid admissions:

% of capacity in attendance:

Average Percentages for the run to date:

% of total capacity:
sold at full price:
sold on subscription:
sold at discount:
press comps:
other comps:
available/deadwood:

% of total capacity paid admissions:

% of total capacity in attendance:

PROTOTYPICAL DIRECT MAIL REVIEW & COST ANALYSIS

MAILING LISTS USED (List below all those organizations with whom you have arranged mailing list exchanges or purchases)	# OF PIECES MAILED (After all lists have been merged/purged—not the number of names that have been entered into the computer)	ORDERS RECEIVED	RESPONSE RATE (Orders received divided by the number of pieces mailed)	# TICKETS ORDERED	COST Cost of the mailing divided by the total number of pieces mailed, multiplied by the number of pieces mailed to each individual list, plus any unique costs for the use of any list. EXAMPLE: It cost $15,000 to design, create and mail a brochure to 100,000 customers; therefore the per piece cost was 15¢. 5,000 of those customers came from List A. It also cost $200 to purchase the one time use of those names from List A. Therefore, List A cost (5,000 X .15) + $200 = $950	INCOME	AVERAGE ORDER (Total income from each list divided by the number of orders received)

TOTAL RESPONSES

Robert Schlosser

AUDIENCES

The audience! What would we do without it?

We assume that it cannot do without us, that we, in the world of dance, music, or theater, hold a valid and necessary place in the community. I think that assumption is correct.

The performing arts are an integral part of the sociological scheme of things because they speak directly to the human experience—the audience's experience—through works that strike an emotional chord, that make us laugh at our own foibles and follies, that teach us to be better people, that raise the level of society, and improve the quality of life.

Throughout this chapter, I will mostly use the words "theater" or "plays," because that is my context, and my typing fingers are conditioned to those words, and because they are less cumbersome than the entire phrase, "or dance company or opera or chamber ensemble, etc." So when you come to references that are theatrical, simply transpose up or down the scale to the key in which your particular performing-arts organization sings!

Let's assume, then, that your "theater" is artistically competent, and that the writing for its stage is truthful. (If it isn't, you should quit!) Your theater reflects the time in which it exists and the community it serves. Therefore, it must make every effort to reach as wide and diverse an audience as possible. It is a *responsibility* of your theater to do that.

This does not mean that your offerings should be everything to all people. The theater leads its audience; the audience does not lead the theater. That is the business of television, because television *is* a business and must sell the products of its sponsorship by giving its audience what it wants. A theater that allows its repertoire to be dictated by the audience should be put out of business as swiftly as possible.

Whether your theater is committed to a broad range of dramatic entertainment or a very specific repertoire, there are people out there who will respond to and thrive on what happens on your stage. The trick is to reach them, understand them, educate them, and make sure that there are as many different "faces" in your audience as there are in the community that is your theater's home.

Audiences! Who are they? Where do they come from? Are they happy? Will they stay? Do they participate? Can they contribute money? Do they have a sense of ownership? Are they loyal through thick and thin?

Finding answers to these questions is the responsibility of that area of the theater's administration that handles marketing or audience development — whatever you choose to call it—whether it be a separate department, part of press and promotion, or in general administration, depending upon the size of your organization. No matter where it is placed, marketing or audience development cannot be isolated from the rest of the operation. It is the hub of the organization —an integral part of the effort to put on plays. It must have a healthy connection to, if not a direct involvement in, the issues of demographics, education, public relations, production, design, performance, fund raising, contracts, advertising, scheduling, subscription, dramaturgy, casting—in short, all the aspects of running a theater.

Robert J. Schlosser began his theatre administration career as Subscription and Box-Office Manager for the San Francisco Actors' Workshop in 1962. In 1965, he accompanied Workshop directors, Jules Irving and Herbert Blau, to New York where they assumed leadership of The Repertory Theatre of Lincoln Center. As Audience Development Director of the RTLC, he pioneered programs for making a major, national theater accessible to a broad spectrum of the New York metropolitan community. In 1973, he was invited by Gordon Davidson to join the Mark Taper Forum as Audience Development Director where for the past ten years he has continued to break new ground in creating programs for potential audiences in the greater Los Angeles area. Mr. Schlosser is a Director of the Theatre Audience Project, an organization consisting of university literature and theatre department teachers; a member of the Coordinating Committee for The Shakespeare Year (1981-1982); the founder of Project D.A.T.E. (deaf audience theater experience); and a member of the Co-producers Committee for the 1984 Olympic Arts Festival.

"A theatre that allows its repertoire to be dictated by the audience should be put out of business as swiftly as possible."

The theater invests money and time to give the audience pleasure. It also invests artistic commitment. The audience invests money and time in the support of the theater. It also invests an emotional and intellectual commitment. Audience development directs the traffic on this two-way street that connects theater and audience, and keeps the movement going in both directions.

To ''direct the traffic'' most intelligently, you have to find out who your audience is.

You are new in town, about to unfold your tent, and you want people to come and see your wares. How do you go about targeting an audience? You have to know the territory. Go to the civic agencies (the Chamber of Commerce, board of education, information bureau, library), and research the community thoroughly. What is the population, the ethnic make-up, the number of educational institutions, the extent of tourism, the median income of each residential zip code? What is the square-mile area of the community? How sophisticated is the public transportation system? How far are people willing to travel to attend a cultural event? What kinds of entertainment does the community support? Who is your competition? What are the city's chief industries? Where is the center of town?

By finding the answers to these and other fundamental questions, you will begin to define your city geographically, demographically, and psychologically. You will know, therefore, where you potential audience is located, and how you should state your promotional message to reach them.

If you already have an established audience, one of the best ways to find out about them—though obviously not conclusive—is to go into the theater and look around during intermission. But in order to discover why that one Tuesday-night audience responds like pig farmers when, at every other performance during the run, people love the show, you need concrete evidence. You get that evidence through an audience survey or questionnaire.

The audience is held captive within your four walls for two to three hours. Why not take the opportunity to find out a few things about them?

Various types of questionnaires serve various needs. You can either get a handle on the potential success of a production from a preview audience, or learn everything there is to know about your subscribers and single-ticket buyers. If you are presenting an ongoing series of events for a special sector like gifted children or the deaf, for example, ask them their special needs. Surveying a non-subscription event will yield useful information for reaching a possible new audience in the future. If you have the time and a creative impulse, ask your subscribers what their favorite plays are of all those they have seen at your theater. (I guarantee you will be genuinely surprised by the results, and, if you examine the analysis carefully, you will gain invaluable information about your subscribers.)

For previews, a questionnaire can be used simply to find out if the audience likes the play. The level of enthusiasm can provide you with a sense of how word-of-mouth may affect advance ticket sales and can have practical influence on the amount—and therefore, the cost—of further advertising and promotion you may or may not need. You can include questions about what production values they admired most, thereby stimulating an awareness of those theatrical elements that they might have been taking for granted. If you have a bent for the insidious, ask a question that you don't necessarily need to know the answer to, one that will prepare an audience for a play that dramatizes a difficult subject.

Recently at the Mark Taper Forum in Los Angeles, for example, we presented an original adaptation of Franz Kafka's *Metamorphosis* by the English theater artist, Steven Berkoff. Because of the highly expressionistic style of the production, we included the following question, hoping to suggest subliminally that the original story was, indeed, in the play if only the audience would wait for it to emerge:

Since Franz Kafka wrote *Metamorphosis* in 1912, each generation has seen its particular society or period of history reflected in some way by Gregor's predicament. What is it in Steven Berkoff's dramatization that has a particular meaning for you, in the context of today's world?

To get to know your audience, a well-planned, comprehensive survey can tell you all you need to know. If your house capacity is around one-hundred or less, use a homemade survey and analyze the results yourself. If your theater is more substantial in size, you must use a sophisitcated market-research survey if the analysis is to be taken seriously. I strongly urge you to use an outside market-research agency. Is there one represented your board of trustees who will donate his services, or, if not, can your board members promote such a service through their professional contacts?

If you are fortunate to have an in-house computer or access to computer services, investigate the idea of programming it for the survey analysis. If you are about to acquire a computer system, make sure that its initial programming includes marketing analysis capability. Adding programs later on is costly.

What do you want to find out about your audience through the market-research survey? Answers to the following will provide you with a fairly decent notion of who comes to your theater:

- Do you subscribe? Did you ever?
- Why do you subscribe (provide the possible reasons) (day of week, reviews, plays, cost/saving, seat location, etc.)?
- Do you buy additional non-subscription events?
- How far in advance do you plan a theater outing?
- When, in advance, did you purchase tickets?
- How did you get tickets (subscription, mail order, phone charge, friend)?
- How did you get here (car, cab, bus, etc.)?
- How many people in your party?
- Do you ever bring your children?
- What newspapers and magazines do you read?
- What radio stations do you listen to at what time of day?
- What influenced your decision (reviews, newspaper article, radio or TV interview, word-of-mouth, interest in a specific playwright, director or performer)?
- How often do you watch television, what programs, what time of day or evening?
- Do you subscribe to cable and what channels do you watch?
- What is your sex and marital status?
- What is your education, employment, age, annual income?
- What credit cards do you use?
- What is your zip code?

"Define your city geographically, demographically, psychologically."

The demographic survey is useless if it doesn't reach a segment of your audience that represents who *really* comes to your theater. Choose a period of time that reflects the profile of at least 10% of your audience. If you are all ready to go and the production bombs, shelve the survey until you have a production that is selling well, so that the mix of subscribers and single-ticket buyers is at an optimum level. You might want to survey segments of the audience at wide intervals over your season to observe any change of pattern. In other words, is there any difference between those people who attend in the fall and the audience you perform for in the spring?

What do you do with the results of your survey? They should tell you who is not coming to your theater and, therefore, who you should set your sights on. They will probably confirm what you already suspect—that you have a healthy variety of people with particular profiles. Now you will know in clearer detail where they come from. You can now focus heavily on those areas to attract more of the same high responders.

Demographic surveys can be dangerous, however, if you allow the statistics to become a fixation. They are a guide, not an end to themselves. Don't spend valuable time over-scrutinizing the analysis when you ought to be out there doing something with what you've learned.

There are more methods for getting an audience to your theater than you will probably have time to put into operation. Consequently, you must choose the most effective, fundamental tactics your budget will allow. If you haven't the funds to support a basic promotion campaign, I suggest you keep your tent folded until you can raise enough money to buy paper, a printing service, and postage, at least.

"The use of non-selective direct mail services is becoming a thing of the past."

Give yourself as much lead time as the customary and universal chaos of your organization will allow. Establish goals and objectives, and be realistic about them. How many performances are in your program of events? How many ticket buyers do you need to provide both the income you've budgeted and a decent audience for your performers? Plan your strategy in detail, on a day-by-day schedule. Set deadlines that are reasonable and reachable, and be conscientious about meeting them.

Arm yourself with the tools of the trade—a postal-regulations guide, membership in your community's convention service or visitors bureau, publications by FEDAPT and Theatre Communications Group, local corporations directory, subscriptions to marketing periodicals, and Danny Newman's *Subscribe Now!* (see Bibliography).

Most performing-arts groups present a series of events that form a package, so I strongly recommend subscription as the foundation of your audience-building effort. If your programming is of a nature that renders a subscription plan irrelevant, I urge you to consider establishing some sort of support membership —a body of people who are "The Friends Of Your Dance Company" or "The Patrons of Your City's Chamber-Music Society" — who can be called upon as audience whenever your company performs. Offer them a membership pass or card that recognizes them as a special audience and guarantees a ticket discount, priority seating, and perhaps a reception with the artists. This type of solid, loyal audience is a nucleus that will assure you of advance and renewable income and a base on which to build a larger audience each time you offer a public performance.

While you are plotting your campaign, consider the possibility that not everyone *should* attend the theater. My father, for example, was a good, sensible man who didn't give a hoot about the theater. He came to see plays at theaters where I worked two or three times over the years simply because he felt it was his duty (affably performed, I must say) to support his son's line of work—whatever it was. But he neither gained from, nor gave anything to, the theatrical experience. Sitting in a dark place watching make-believe struck him as slightly silly and wasteful of his time. Should the promotional dollar be spent pursuing someone like my father?

Consider, as well, that your theater may not be everyone's cup of tea. There is always the patron who walks out after five minutes before he has had any real reason for disliking the play. Are you *not* going to produce that play about prison life because there may be a man in the audience who objects to the word, "damn," used in *any* context? If your theater is striving to reach the highest and the most adventurous artistic objectives (and I hope it is), you don't want the auditorium filled with an audience that adamantly refuses you the right to risk and failure. This is not to say you can't turn an audience around, and I will elaborate on that possibility later in the chapter. Simply be certain you are directing your promotional effort toward the responsive ticket buyer.

How to formulate a subscription campaign, the single most important effort in audience development, and how to solicit the individual ticket buyer, are covered superbly elsewhere in this book. Nevertheless, I wish to add a word about direct mail: It remains the most cost-effective means to reach a potential audience, despite the decline of responsiveness to direct mail over the past few years. This decline has forced a reevaluation of the way lists are used and selected. The wisdom of exchanging mailing lists with other arts organizations, however, remains solid. They come rent-free, for one thing, and you can assume that the prospect's interest in another arts program will bode well for his responsiveness to yours.

The use of non-selective, direct-mail house services, on the other hand, is becoming a thing of the past. Under that system, names were selected only according to what the median income was in a certain zip-code area. A proportionate number of people in the higher-income brackets was also selected. There was no measure of the level of responsiveness from these individuals. Just because they earned higher incomes did not necessarily mean that they were interested in the arts or were even responsive to mail solicitation.

More favorably prominent on the scene now are the lists services that can provide names and addresses of individuals who have proved themselves both culturally oriented *and* highly responsive to mail solicitation. These services can provide national or local service and can zero in on specific areas of your community.

Because of their sophisticated computer capability, the various lists you select can be merged to eliminate duplication and consequently will reduce mailing costs.

No matter whom you mail to, it is imperative that you code the solicitation so that, as you target your market, you know what list source it represents when the order returns. If the solicitation is a self-mailing brochure, the order coupon should be on the back of the address panel. This allows you flexibility in coding either the coupon or the address label by letter, number, symbol, or color.

Coding is some recognizable method by which you can tell one list from another. Let us say you are sending brochures to 100,000 names that you have compiled from your own mailing list and lists of other arts organizations. For the sake of example, each list consists of 25,000 names. You give each list a letter—A, B, C, D, etc. Some place on the coupon printing plate, out of the way but somewhere accessible to you, is engraved the four-letter series, "ABCD," which the printer runs for the first 25,000. That first batch off the press is your "D" list. Before the next run, the printer removes the "D" from the plate, leaving, "ABC." The next 25,000, therefore, is your "C" list, and so forth. If you have a number of very small lists, the printer will go bonkers if he has to stop the press for every 500 brochures. This frequent halting of the press is also expensive, because a printer's time is costly, so you may want to apply your code to the mailing label on the address panel.

Labels borrowed or rented usually come with their own coding. If they do not, you may have to rely on a different typeface peculiar to the lender's label and different from your own list. For your own use and for lending to other organizations, it is important to apply codes to your lists as a matter of everyday maintenance.

If your array of variously obtained mailing lists offers no distinguishable characteristics (which is highly unlikely), think about using colors, either for the name and address type or for the label itself. Should your mailing be a large one, comprised of several different lists, and you have run out of colors, use a combination of the above codes. It doesn't matter what method of coding you use so long as it is the most inexpensive.

Assuming that your direct-mail campaigns are successful, and you actually have an audience for your season—what do you do with them now? Remember your role as director of traffic on that two-way street?

A strong, ongoing relationship with an audience is very important, and can be established by means as seemingly inconsequential as the language you use on your brochures and flyers. It can also be generated by the approach to your subscribers in written communications throughout the season, or by the creation of programs that will involve them more deeply in your theater's activities. Every phone call, whether it be a ticket transaction, an information inquiry, or a complaint should be personal in tone—not just friendly or cordial. These people are your *family;* treat them accordingly.

Answer *every* patron letter personally and invite ongoing correspondence. Given the current image of the modern world as a giant computer, your audience may be surprised—and certainly grateful—to learn that human beings run the place. Grasp any opportunity—curtain speeches, post-play discussions, lobby receptions—to let them know that your theater is anxious to participate with them in a dialogue. The beauty of these ploys is that they cost you *nothing*, except, perhaps, a little stagefright, if you are not used to standing up in front of an audience. Refreshments for the more sociable activities can be the pot-luck contribution of your volunteers.

Publish a subscriber newsletter that lets the audience in on your theater's plans and expectations. This *does* cost money, obviously, so again, try your board of trustees. Is there a printer among them? Approach the local restaurants. They may have gained significant business from your audience (or want to), and will pay for your newsletter through advertising.

The subscriber newsletter has countless uses. The average audience is ravenously curious about what goes on behind the scenes, what the invisible people who are not performers look like, or why an event was chosen to be a part of the season or series. You have the opportunity to show your audience how much goes into putting on a play through photographs of the costume and scene shops, designers in a huddle with the director, and rehearsals. Publish letters from subscribers indicating that not everyone in the audience is of one mind about a play,

Mark Taper Forum. Keene Curtis, Rene Auberjonois and James R. Winker in *The Misanthrope*.

"The subscriber newsletter has countless uses... the audience is ravenously curious about what goes on behind the scenes."

that a variety of reactions is not only possible but valid. Background material on the current or upcoming attraction that may not fit or be appropriate to your playbill is also useful to educate the subscriber further. It can always be useful to you as a chance to prepare the audience for a "difficult" or less accessible event.

Publish a subscriber newsletter that lets the audience in on your theater's plans and expectations. This *does* cost money, obviously, so again, try you board of trustees. Is there a printer among them? Approach the local restaurants. They may have gained significant business from your audience (or want to), and will pay for your newsletter through advertising.

The subscriber newsletter has countless uses. The average audience is ravenously curious about what goes on behind the scenes, what the invisible people who are not performers look like, or why an event was chosen to be a part of the season or series. You have the opportunity to show your audience how much goes into putting on a play through photographs of the costume and scene shops, designers in a huddle with the director, and rehearsals. Publish letters from subscribers indicating that not everyone in the audience is of one mind about a play, that a variety of reactions is not only possible but valid. Background material on the current or upcoming attraction that may not fit or be appropriate to your playbill is also useful to educate the subscriber further. It can also be useful to you as a chance to prepare the audience for a "difficult" or less accessible event.

The more informed and educated an audience becomes about your organization, the more they will support your theater in its most adventurous moments. Conversely, a sophisticated audience will provide a challenge to the artists to produce the best possible work and maintain the highest theatrical standards.

The need for a healthy relationship with your audience grows more acute as that audience widens to embrace people who may never have been to the theater before.

Now, I'm going to risk a bolt of lightning from that great subscription god in the sky by saying: Not every seat in your theater *should* be subscribed! If it were, what would you do with people who *cannot* subscribe for any number of very legitimate reasons? Turn them away? How can you claim that you serve the entire community if you slam the door on that community by offering no alternatives to subscription?

You want to attract as wide a range of people as possible. To embrace that breadth of audience, there must be a program for everyone—students, the poor, the aged and handicapped, the uneducated and uninformed, the transient, the spontanenous and the ethnic, the emotionally fragile, the elite, the outsiders as well as the insiders. You must be able to say, "No one has an excuse for not being able to attend my theater."

In terms of numbers, students and other groups constitute the most substantial market. They are also the most accessible, and you may eventually be able to convert them into subscribers.

Students are an *essential* part of a theater's audience. They are both your theater-goer of today and your audience of tomorrow. Enticing students out of the movie house and into your auditorium isn't easy. You must provide attractive programs —not just one, but several. The price for each of them should not exceed the price of a movie ticket.

The student "rush" is now a classic policy—unsold tickets are made available from half-hour to curtain to students with full-time enrollment identification. Students can be reached through their teachers who may be eager for field trips, who are teaching a play (or directing a musical) that is part of your season, or who are enlightened enough to believe that a trip to the theater is an educational experience. These students come in groups. A promise of a post-play discussion with the cast is an effective additional inducement.

The best investment for both you and the student is a special-student subscription. Guarantee the same privileges you offer a "regular" subscriber at an unbeatable price. Scratch a student and you'll find a bargain hunter who will look at an offer of, say, five plays for $20.00 or $25.00 as a steal!

An effective method of selling student subscriptions, widely used by resident theaters in the United States, is through college or university campus representatives. The idea is to recruit student salesmen on campuses who, because they are in the very midst of the market, can more effectively spread the word and establish themelves in the field as contacts for the theater. If a student subscription policy demands verification, in person, of the full-time student status (which it should), the campus rep can act as the theater's agent and save the student subscriber a trip to the theater.

The theater provides the reps with promotional materials and the incentive of a free subscription for an established quota sold (at the Taper, the quota is ten subscriptions). The campus rep can be recruited by a help-wanted type-line in the first student subscription ad in the campus newspaper or through theater, humanities, or other departments, through the student asociation office, the campus bookstore, etc. And certainly, there can be more than one rep on each campus. Once the rep is set up for business, his name and phone number should be included in all student newspaper advertising. The cost of a student subscription campaign is relatively low. Campus newspaper advertising rates are inexpensive, flyers can be simple because the ticket-price message is strong, and regular campaign posters are easily adapted to the student market by sniping them. (A "snipe" is a strip of paper—similar in dimension to a bumper sticker—that you apply to the printed poster where it will not interfere with the design and advertising message. It is commonly used to declare that an event is "SOLD OUT." The student snipe should say something like, "FOR STUDENTS ONLY: 5 EVENTS FOR AS LITTLE AS $20.00!") The investment is probably the soundest aspect of a subscription campaign except renewal. The student might, indeed, be acquiring the subscribing habit that will last the rest of his theatergoing life.

In audience promotion, group sales is second in importance only to subscription. People in numbers who meet regularly for any reason are a potential market. Out there in your community are women's clubs, fraternal organizations, social clubs, professional societies, political associations, ethnic organizations, senior citizens' clubs, corporation employees. And at some point they may have reason to come to your theater. It is up to you to give them that reason. Once they attend as a group, they are a stronger prospect for subscription, either as a group or as individuals.

Assembling a group mailing list is not as horrendous a task as you might suspect. The telephone book can supply you with the names of schools and a tremendous variety of organizations. Don't be afraid of the telephone. It is your most effective tool for gathering information, and it can make your group list comprehensive. If you are starting from scratch, endeavor to obtain the group lists of other local performing-arts organizations.

You may encounter resistance from them. Maybe they don't wish to share the spoils, and there will be nothing that you can do to pry their list out of them. (Try every ruse you can think of anyway!) They may loosen up once you have established yourself with a list of your own that you can wave in front of them for bartering purposes.

With no list resources at hand, go to the Yellow Pages—as simple-minded as it sounds—and extract the names and addresses of any groups that look social or in any way of related interest to what you are doing. Once you begin attracting a group audience, your list will grow automatically, but you should never stop searching out organizations to add to it. Enrich your group mailing list with corporate contacts. Simply call the corporation and find out if it has an active employee recreation program.

Code your lists so that you can send your mailing to a limited group market for a special event. Keep it clean—i.e., remove the names of people who have moved away, changed address, or died—and monitor your list for duplication. Waste of printed matter and postage is sinfully expensive.

The group market is plentiful with particular audiences for whom an individual play may have special appeal. Is there a substantial British community in your city that should be contacted regarding your production of *Major Barbara?* With *The Tenth Man* coming up in your season, have you solicited the local Jewish organizations?

In accommodating a sale, keep the processing system as simple for the group representative as it is for you. He may never have tried to arrange a theater party before. Use whatever formula works best. It doesn't have to be complicated to be efficient. Essentially, you need to agree on an available date, reserve the tickets, establish a payment date, and dispatch the tickets when they are paid for. A *simple* contract keeps everything clear for both parties. A deposit or interim, partial

"The price for student admissions should not exceed the price of a movie ticket."

Mark Taper Forum. Edward James Olmos, Rachel Levario and Mike Gomez in Zoot Suit.

payment is an extra and unnecessary step, if you establish a payment due-date that is sufficiently in advance of the performance so that you can sell the ticket if the group should cancel. I'd suggest a lead period of two weeks for up to one-hundred tickets, and a month for more. I have also never understood the need for stratifying the group rates; i.e., a 10% discount for forty-nine or less; 15% for fifty to ninety-nine, etc. A class, club, or women's organization is of a certain size. A further saving on a discounted ticket price will not increase their membership or your group sale.

Does your theater have a racially mixed audience? If not, and you want that situation changed, you can do that by reexamining the kinds of plays you are producing and by instituting *strong* programs aimed at attracting a diverse audience. There is no formula, no how-to handbook to be found, no secret to be discovered about how to create programs that reach out to special constituencies or that make your theater accessible to everyone. When you can embrace that idea, the release of your imagination will be extraordinary, and you will realize that you are free to do just about anything.

Ask yourself, "Is there something about the play we are doing that may attract or appeal to an untapped part of my community?" If you are producing a play by the South African playwright, Athol Fugard, contact college and university African studies and political-science department instructors. Just because they are educated doesn't mean they have cultivated a theatergoing habit. For *Raisin in The Sun,* invite the ministers from the large churches in the black community to a performance early in the run. I can almost guarantee your production will be the subject of their sermon the following Sunday.

Special audiences won't come to you just because you trot out your usual bag of tricks—running ads and sending flyers. You must literally go into the community. Talk to the heads of organizations or institutions; introduce yourself to the leadership of the Chinese community and ask if you may address their merchants' association; go to the fiestas and Holy Day parades in the Hispanic community and pass out flyers translated into Spanish.

Bear in mind that you can venture out into the field anyway, regardless of particularly "special" sectors of the community. Promotional inducements to buy tickets can be effective to a lesser or greater degree in a market that is already inclined to attend your theater. There are still potential audiences who won't respond because they don't know anything about you or because they have a resistance to your theater, owing to a variety of false assumptions. Conventional advertising will not attract their attention, nor will walking up and down in front of their houses stark naked wearing a sandwich board.

A slide show is a simple, practical and less embarrassing alternative. Many theaters have production slides that can be interestingly arranged to provide a clear presentation showing what the institution is all about. If you do not presently have them, make certain from now on that whoever shoots your productions takes at least one roll of colored slides. He should also photograph non-performance activities like people lined up at the box office, post-play discussions, special events, audiences having a good time. You want your slide-show audience to see that other people just like themselves come to your theater and enjoy the experience.

If the projection equipment includes an audio tape, a carefully prepared voiceover can highlight your theater's most prominent attributes and slant the point of view toward the community's interest. Without an audio tape, a *well-trained* operator would bear the responsibility of "live" narration. In either event, the person who presents the slide show must have a thorough orientation on the artistic, administrative, and financial structure of the theater in order to respond intelligently to both sophisticated and uniformed questions following the presentation.

You can take a slide show almost anywhere, providing you can find a darkened room. Therefore, the diversity of possible audiences is limitless. Merchant association meetings, recreation centers, women's clubs, educational institutions, ethnic societies, luncheons and dinners, all are excellent arenas for a slide show, and will afford you opportunities to inform an area of the community heretofore untapped. A pleasant aspect of this form of audience conscience-raising is that many of these groups are hungry for featured events at their meetings and will welcome a slide-show presentation, especially if they have no guest speaker, or if the guest speaker is not particularly exciting.

If your theater has an organized volunteer contingent, enlist those members who are adept at public speaking to assume the slide-show outreach responsibility. It is important, once again, that these volunteers be thoroughly trained about the ins and outs of your theater.

Another way of delving into the community is with a performance. Well-planned, modern shopping centers are beginning to flourish all over the country. Administrators of these centers are very hospitable to cultural events performed in their malls, because they believe that the entertainment will contribute to increased sales. Do you have a children's play, a lunchtime theater program, a cabaret, any program about an hour in length? Take it to a shopping center.

It might be more helpful, rather than discussing audience expansion in general terms, to illustrate various methods through specific examples. The following are a few of the programs currently operating at the Mark Taper Forum in Los Angeles, which carry forward the fundamental intention of educating and nurturing the audience. By "education," I don't mean teaching the audience what to think or provide facts, or, for example, plumb the depths of Freudian implications in *Mourning Becomes Electra*. We want to educate them on how to *be* an audience, to open up to the experience of the theater, to sit forward, engaged in what is happening on the stage rather than to lie back and passively allow it to happen. (Television has taught us all some very bad habits.)

OPERATION DISCOVERY: For every subscription event, 1,000 tickets (2% of our capacity) are held back from general sales for distribution in the community through public-service agencies. Charge for the tickets is nominal. The agency is sent an announcement and description of the event, along with the available dates and whom to contact at the theater to make the reservation. A maximum of twenty-five tickets per order allows us to accommodate as many different agencies as possible. The minimum is ten. The objective of the program is to encourage attendance by individuals who would never come to the theater for reasons of financial or sociological circumstances. There are currently eighty-seven agencies on our list and the range includes senior-citizen centers, homes for wayward adolescents, unwed mother hospices, parole agencies, mental health clinics, probation departments, family counselors, and drug and alcohol rehabilitation agencies.

HOT-TIX: For every performance—except Saturday evenings—10% of the house is held back from general sale until the day of the performance, when they are available from 4:30 to 6:30 p.m. at a discount of $4.00 off the regular ticket price (from noon to 1:00 p.m. for matinees). The program is intended to attract audiences who cannot afford a subscription but *can* manage individual events at discount prices, who prefer spontaneous theatergoing and would *never* subscribe (until we convert them!), who move into town mid-season after subscriptions are no longer available (and may encounter a sold-out production), and who are visitors and tourists (again, faced with a sell-out). During the several years since the program's inauguration, we have had no indication that HOT-TIX undercuts subscription.

THEATER ARTS WORKSHOP: Annually, we invite students and their teachers from high-school theater departments to the Taper on a Saturday morning for a three-hour program that is meant to provide them with a glimpse of life in the professional theater. In most communities, young people attend movies regularly and the theater seldom, if at all. This problem is particularly acute in Los Angeles, where the existence of the film and television industries cast a dark unattractive shadow over the other performing arts. The objective of our workshop, therefore, is to stimulate an interest in live theater and to obliterate the mythology that young potential actors are assured a dazzling career in movies and TV only if they are good-looking and can memorize lines. The concept that substantial training in the theater is essential to becoming a good actor in *any* performance media appears to be unknown to many high-school theater departments.

The Theater Arts Workshop takes place in the theater. It is sponsored by the Junior Chamber of Commerce, which means that it is totally subsidized. We are

> "Educate them on how to *be* an audience, to sit forward, engaged, rather than to lie back passively and let it happen. Television has taught us bad habits."

"Do you have a children's play, a lunchtime theater program, a cabaret, any program about an hour in length? Take it to a shopping center."

able to pay the artists a modest fee and provide a printed program. The coordination of the event and control of expenses is intrinsically very simple. I act as producer and bring together the workshop components from on-staff resources and our current production. The Chamber is advised up front of the cost of the necessary union stagehands, the nominal remuneration for the participants, and the cost of designing and printing the program. Our in-house graphics department waives a design fee and is able to produce a simple but attractive program at a very low cost.

The workshop includes an hour with our casting director who describes the nuts and bolts of auditioning, the interview, picture and resume, and choice of audition material; an hour with a director who uses the students to demonstate the diversity of possibilities in interpreting a scene; and an hour of question-and-answer with professional actors from our current production. Actors with strong professional experience and expertise can, within an hour, miraculously sweep aside misconceptions about the profession. Since we make arrangements for the students to see the production prior to attending the workshop, the credentials of the actor are firmly established by the time they appear for the Q. and A. The more recognizable the actor, the more dramatic the conversation.

The most vivid example occurred a few seasons ago when we presented Jack Lemmon, Walter Matthau, and Maureen Stapleton, who were appearing on our stage in *Juno And The Peacock.* The youngsters were giddy with anticipation about talking to three such celebrated actors, but, as the ''movie stars'' described the hard knocks they had suffered, the years of struggle and perserverance they spent in the live theater before ever appearing in films, and the fundamenal necessity of solid theater training, their young faces sobered discernably. (The workshop is evaluated every year with questionnaires.)

OPEN FORUMS: The post-play discussion is the easiest and most obvious means of direct contact with large groups of your audience. It affords you the opportunity to hear a variety of responses to your work, and, if you listen carefully, you can discover what the audience members bring to the experience.

Over a period of time, an audience will define itself, and therefore, will enable the theater to measure and weigh the responses. At the Mark Taper Forum, four subscription evenings are designated in subscription advertisements as ''Open Forum'' series. They are moderated by the literary manager and are separate from other special programs that also involve post-play discussions. Subscribers choose these series because they *want* to talk with the company about the play afterward. The majority of each of these four audience-groups has attended these Tuesday evening series for several seasons. Each audience has emerged as slightly different from the others in its collective personality. If there is anything to be learned by this, it is to resist broad generalizations about who your audience is and what it thinks. Good theater attracts a range of different kinds of people who bring with them a myriad of sensibilities.

TEACHERS INSTITUTE: Every summer, we offer a two-day workshop on the theater for primary- and secondary-school teachers as part of a two-week institute on the performing arts sponsored by the educational wing of the Los Angeles Music Center. Participants number approximately 150, and during the two days we aim to demonstrate various theatrical functions.

The objective is two-fold. Rather than provide specific tools for the teachers to use in the classroom (theater-games-to-teach-Johnny-math), our hope is to awaken creative impulses that will make the participants more imaginative and stimulating teachers. We also hope to break down barriers that prevent people from seeing that the theater is an essential part of the educational process — as well as make the teachers themselves a better audience. Components of the session are of a both lecture-demonstration and participatory nature and include improvisation, techniques of playwrighting, sign language, make-up, performance discipline, scene work, and the attendance of a play with a preparatory seminar.

ALUMNI PROJECTS: One of the major and most successful efforts to ''educate'' an audience is through an association with college and university alumni organizations. At present, there are three alumni projects at the Taper. The largest, which has provided the model for the other two, is with the University of California at Santa Barbara. Promoted by the UCSB Alumni Association and composed of both alumni and students, the group takes an entire preview matinee house on subscription. For an hour prior to the performance, they meet in a large rehearsal room for a workshop/seminar conducted by an unusually dynamic professor of literature from the University, Dr. Homer Swander. His objective in the workshop is to provide a "context" for seeing the play, to create a receptivity in the theatergoer, to stimulate a readiness for the event. His method varies depending upon the play. Rarely does he deliver a straight lecture, but, instead, he gets the audience on its feet, actively participating. This might involve reading a scene from the play, improvising, singing, telling jokes, or relating personal experiences, or all of those things.

For example, in dealing with a play about deafness, he forced the group to sit in utter silence for an hour and asked them to communicate with each other non-verbally. And for a play on feminism, he placed the men on one side of the room with the women on the other and asked that they hurl insults at each other. The result of this kind of preparation are audiences who go into the theater with an almost electric anticipation, and its responses to the productions over the year have been consistently and markedly more finely tuned than any other audiences during the run.

Following the performance, the alumni remain in the auditorium for a discussion with the performers and, since the play is in previews, also with the director, designers and playwright (who is usually both alive and present, since most of our work consists of new plays). After the discussion, the audience brings the entire company back to the rehearsal room for a pot-luck supper—food that *they* bring themselves. Usually, these dishes are used to entice an actor or director or playwright to sit at a particular table, and therefore, the cooking competition is fierce.

The supper affords small groups the opportunity for one-on-one informal discussions with individual artists over fried chicken and potato salad. The artists are delighted with the project, and the audience thrives on what it recognizes as a rare opportunity to investigate a play and the creation of its production thoroughly.

Over the years, these alumni have learned how to be an audience in a very special way. Recently, I asked an actor friend to join us for the pot-luck segment of the project. As usual, throughout the supper various audience members came over to chat about the production, and after a while my friend turned to me and asked, "Who *are* these people?" I explained that they belonged to a general type of audience with the normal diversity of occupations and interests.

"That's impossible!" he exclaimed. "They all sound like they're in the profession. Their questions and observations are much too sophisticated and informed for the layman." And, of course, he was right.

PROJECT D.A.T.E. (Deaf Audience Theater Experience): In December, 1978, we began a project for deaf audiences. We are very proud that this project has become a model for other theaters throughout the country. Guided by the advice of two prominent deaf actors, we began to educate ourselves about the world of the deaf. It quickly became clear to us that we had an obvious responsibility to try to make our theater accessible to the deaf, particularly when we discovered that, while the deaf and hard of hearing constitute a 10% of the overall U.S. population, they comprise an astounding 19.6% of the population of the Los Angeles area.

During the 1978–79 season, we invited members of the deaf community to performances, experimented with workshops and techniques of interpreting, and developed a system of preparation that would make a play for a hearing audience accessible to a deaf one. Thanks to a modest grant from the National Endowment for the Arts, we hired a deaf person as the project's coordinator. He amassed a mailing list and established solid relationships with deaf-advocacy agencies, educational institutions, and public-service organizations in the deaf community. Having a deaf person actually running the program also enhanced the Taper's credibility among the deaf.

Concurrent with bringing to the staff a deaf person, the Taper's hearing staff began taking weekly sign language classes during their lunch hours. The box office and front of house staff were instructed in signing sufficiently to accommodate deaf ticket buyers.

"It should not shock you that the majority of people in your city do not go to the theatre, and never will."

By the beginning of the following season, a scheduled number of performances were offered to the deaf on a subscription basis, and 231 people responded. The general format that evolved from that initial season is as follows:

Summaries of the play are forwarded to the ticket holder in advance. Scripts are sent to a dozen libraries in the area that have special services for the deaf, so that if a deaf patron wants the ultimate literal preparation, he may read the entire script before coming to the theater. Before the performance, a workshop is held in the theater, conducted by a deaf scholar who lectures on various aspects of the play. We also bring in designers or a stage manager who discusses the physical values of the production (the deaf obviously possess a heightened visual sensibility). The performance is simultaneously interpreted in sign language by two certified interpreters. Afterward, the deaf audience remains in the house for a discussion with the actors.

Perhaps the most significant and far-reaching single event that has occurred since the inauguration of Project D.A.T.E. is the world premiere production of *Children of a Lesser God,* a play about a deaf woman in a hearing society. Although Project D.A.T.E. was not responsible for the creation of this extraordinary play, it certainly helped to ensure its popularity. The work that the program had already accomplished in creating a deaf audience and in establishing contacts with deaf actors in Southern California contributed immensely to an ideal atmosphere for the play's development at our theater and for its support in the community.

In an early stage of its writing, the play was sent by its author, Mark Medoff, to Gordon Davidson, Artistic Director of the Mark Taper Forum who immediately recognized the play's potential. Upon visiting Los Angeles for a reading of the play, Mr. Medoff met with the deaf consultants on Project D.A.T.E. for advice and information on deaf culture that he could bring to his rewrite of the play. Based on its successful development, Mr. Davidson decided to include *Children Of A Lesser God* as the second production of the 1979–1980 season.

This was a signal to the project staff to promote the work in the deaf community, where we knew the play would obviously have a very special meaning. Teams of the staff went out into the community to make contact with every institution who had any conceivable relationship with the deaf. It was no surprise that the response was overwhelming, and that the run of the play was sold out almost immediately after opening.

The above are some of the ongoing programs that form a cornerstone on which our audience is built. A variety of smaller projects provide the mortar, such as daytime theater visits for high-school students at which we define the working operations of a professional resident theater, drama workshops for emotionally disturbed people, and the establishment of a committee of minority leaders who inform their communities about our work.

If you have thrown up your hands at this point because you think you haven't enough staff to develop an audience, you should know that all of the activities described in this chapter—from subscription-campaign strategy to specialized community programs—are coordinated at the Mark Taper Forum by two people: the audience development director and his assistant. This is *not* wizardry. It is a simple matter of defining and laying out a basic strategy and adding elements to it that will broaden in scope as time and energy allow. Again, most of the special programs that deepen the audience-development effort do not cost much, if anything at all. Only the imagination is taxed.

While there are always new, undiscovered audiences and new ways to reach them, it should not come as a shock to you that the majority of people in your city do not go to the theater, and never will. There is nothing you can do about that, no matter how dynamic your marketing or audience development operation is. What you *can* do is make sure there are many different faces in your audience and that they adequately represent your community.

Mark Taper Forum. Phyllis Frelich and John Rubinstein in *Children of a Lesser God.*

Harry Clark

MEDIA: PRINT AND ELECTRONIC

I. Some Communication Principles About Advertising

A. How Any Form of Communication Works

Advertising is a "performing art." One might argue the degree to which it is a genuine "art," but unquestionably, we are bombarded with advertising "performances" daily on television screens, on magazine pages, on billboards, and through the radios. Because of its pervasiveness, advertising is subject to a tremendous amount of consumer scrutiny and criticism; the song "I Can Do That" from *A Chorus Line* accurately describes the way most people feel about the advertisements and commercials they see.

And, indeed, with the amount of mediocre advertising we see, it is not unfair to say that many people could create better advertisements or commercials. Why is advertising so often off the mark? What is it that makes people feel mildly compromised or even somewhat affronted by so much of the advertising they see?

It is certainly not because advertisers wish to insult consumers. On the contrary, millions of dollars are spent in researching advertising communication to make sure that the ads achieve some agreed-upon goals. The problem lies not in intentions but more in the goals themselves and in advertiser's possible misunderstanding of what advertising can, in fact, do.

If it were just a simple matter of ordering people to buy the product, then we would see a tremendous amount of advertising with the headline, "Buy my product." The simple fact is that when told to do so, millions of people *don't* go out and buy the product. They simply ignore the advertising. Nonetheless, it is surprising how much advertising uses "buy my product" diction. We have all seen the claims "the biggest," "the best," "the fastest growing"—all different ways of saying "buy my product"—and yet, millions of Americans ignore these advertisements.

What the advertiser does not do in these kinds of claims is allow room for the reader or viewer to respond to the advertising. Each person responds to every piece of communication in an individual manner. Right now, you are responding to the words on this page in a variety of possible ways: "Will he ever get on with it?" or, "How many more pages do I have to read?" or, "What was it that I had to buy on my way home?" or, "How will I get everything done by the weekend?" You respond daily to thousands of different kinds of communications — not just from advertising or books, but from all sorts of sources. When the people around you peremptorily order you to do something, how do you feel? You are apt to resent their tone. The first thing you need to do is to work off that resentment before you can begin to do anything productively. The same resentment occurs when you see advertisements that tell you to "do something." You first need to work off your resentment to that advertiser before your attitudes will begin to shift and allow you to think, feel, or react positively to the advertisement as its sponsor might have intended.

So, in considering any form of communication, you must first consider the

Harold F. Clark, Jr. is Managing Director of Lansdowne Advertising, a Division of the J. Walter Thompson Company. He personally is responsible for all clients, from Christian Dior to Ty-D-Bol. Prior to Lansdowne, Mr. Clark was Group Account Director on Burger King. He joined the Company's International Department in 1959, as an International Account Representative in the New York Office. He was transferred to Frankfurt in 1965 where he began his assignment as an Account Supervisor, and was promoted to Director of the German Company in 1969 and Managing Director of JWT—Frankfurt in 1970. On his return to New York in January, 1974, he was named a Senior Vice President in charge of coordination of all administrative matters with JWT office manager. In September, 1974 his responsibilities were expanded to include company-wide personnel policies and training programs and all internal and external communications. Mr. Clark has a B.A. from Amherst College, an M.A. from Stanford University and a Ph.D. from Columbia University. He has been involved in the theatre both as an actor and a director. His wife, Julie Denny, is an actress. The Clarks live in Princeton, New Jersey with their two sons.

responses you wish to evoke. What do you want people to think? What do you want their attitudes to be? Do you want them to shift or change attitudes? Once you know how you want people to respond, it's easier to begin to determine what the language and images should be to evoke that response.

B. How Advertising Works

You will note that nowhere here do I imply that advertising makes people buy anything. It doesn't, and it can't. Advertising works to modify, change, reinforce, or supplement existing attitudes that a person has about a brand or a service. Once the attitudes have shifted, then the person may draw upon those attitudes and undertake a specific course of action. He will never be inclined to purchase a product or a service unless he has positive attitudes toward it. Advertising can help contribute to the positive attitudes; but that's all it can do. It does not function as a door-to-door salesman who, with the actual brush in his hand, can complete the sale to the doubting housewife.

Some advertising comes very close to being this direct. But the only advertisement which, in fact, can evoke an immediate direct response would be one with the headline "watch this space." A reader can do that and fulfill the promise of the headline without moving out of his chair, getting a pencil, or exerting any major effort. Anything else beyond that headline requires a different kind of response, one that involves the recipient thinking about doing something. Attitudes, feelings, and beliefs must somehow be affected before he undertakes any specific action.

The next most direct kind of advertising, that which is called "direct response," is advertising that provides a telephone number one can call to get more information. "I'll do that right now," might be the response. The recipient notes down the telephone number or, indeed, makes an immediate telephone call . "Operators are standing by" says the advertiser, and the success of the commercial depends greatly on the number of telephone calls that are received within a short period of time after it is run.

Somewhat less direct are advertisements that contain a coupon suggesting how to write away for more information. "Tell me more" might be the response to such coupon advertising. Respondents tear it out and send it in to receive more information.

A variant of this kind of advertising, of course, is subscription advertising, where one orders the product or service by sending in the coupon with payment. This is the function of most performing-arts subscription advertising, and its success is measured by the number of responses it generates. Note, however, that this does not guarantee a direct sale. The subscription manager is not standing at the front door with a bag of tickets in his hand. The advertising has to evoke the response, "what a good idea—I think I'll do that" before the coupon is torn out and sent in.

A great deal of advertising presents new facts or information about a product or service to evoke the advertising response "I didn't know that." Information about a new season is similar to product improvement in this regard. It is presenting new information to people who are already generally familiar with the product or service.

Other kinds of advertising are even less direct. Advertising can be used to reinforce values, to intensify attitudes, or to reconfirm beliefs.

Finally, much advertising, of course, is designed to change or modify attitudes. "I didn't know that" or "that reminds me" might be the responses of this sort of advertising.

C. When Do You Need Advertising Communication?

By "advertising," we mean any paid form of commercial message that is received in the household. This can come in the form of newspaper advertisements, television commercials, but also from direct-mail pieces or other subscription announcements, you might choose to use.

What you, the advertiser need to do first is to decide what you want to use advertising for. Do you even need it? So much advertising serves no useful purpose and appears to be used only for the sake of advertising. Everyone else does it, so why shouldn't we? It is important to know exactly why you want to advertise, and what you intend to achieve by it before undertaking it at all. It can be an expensive and wasteful process unless you know at the outset exactly what attitudes you intend to modify or change.

In the performing arts, most advertising is the "what a good idea" or "I'll do that right now" variety. It is designed to encourage people to send back the order form for a subscription series.

But is it conceived and laid out in such a manner that the response, "I'll do that right now" is easy and inviting? If your headline is simply, "Send in your money for 1984 subscription right now," will you simply be talking to yourselves? Is this not just a form of "buy my product" advertising, allowing no room for a consumer response?

Finally, it is important to know when advertising designed to modify attitudes should be used. There may be existing attitudes among your potential target group that need to be addressed and changed before your customers will be apt to send back an order form. In order to know when this sort of advertising should be used, it is critical to know as much about the target groups for your advertising as possible.

II. Advertising Target Groups

To whom is your advertising directed? Who are they? Where are they? In addressing these questions, we frequently tend to focus only on the demographics of our target groups. We know where they live, we have a reasonable idea of their household income, we know how many children they have, and whether or not they may have attended college. This is important information for planning media, and one needs to have it. But it does not really help much in the creative process.

To help decide what kind of advertising you need, you must know what these people are really like. What are their attitudes to your performing-arts center? What did they think of last year's program? What kinds of performances do they like? Or want? What is the competition? When they do not come to a performance, what else are they doing? Are they watching television? Are they going to the movies? Are they reading? What is the competitive framework, and how do you really fit into it?

What is the difference between the audience for your music series, dance series and play series? Generally, they are not the same. But what are their specific differences? Even if you cannot determine exactly what their differences are, you can at least posit them in some intelligent manner. You can construct hypotheses about these audiences which, because they are based on experience and good sound judgment, are apt to be true. Take the time to write down these hypotheses. Look at them frequently, and review them with your colleagues. Is there general agreement about them? Are they specific enough? Do they really get to the core of the relevant attitudes that might affect the reasons why people do something?

Obviously these are questions which you can research—if you can afford it. You need to do more than the program-stuffer kind of research. Program-stuffer research is useful to a point but, after all, it only talks to ticket buyers. How do you get to non-ticket buyers? What do they think? Why don't they buy? Have they ever bought? What made them stop? What are their dissatisfactions and objections?

Outside research can be used to learn more about non-buyers. It is an expensive tool, but one worth exploring—especially if there are serious signs of audience erosion over a long period of time. If, despite the best artistic judgment, you are not generating audiences, it may be worth a few thousand dollars to learn more about why.

There are other outside resources you can use to help analyze problems. One of these resources is an advertising agency.

III. Do You Need an Advertising Agency?

Advertising agencies come with some given strengths and weaknesses. It makes sense to know what these strengths and weaknesses are before making the decision to employ an agency.

Most agencies are systematic and experienced in marshalling creative resources to solve specific problems. They tend to attract good creative people who enjoy an

> "When told to do so, millions of people *don't* go out and buy the product. They simply ignore the advertising."

"Advertising works
to modify, change,
reinforce or
supplement
existing attitudes."

opportunity to apply their creative abilities to a number of different kinds of accounts. Agencies attract the better creative people simply because they *do* provide this opportunity to work on many different kinds of projects, and they also keep them busy most of the time. To use creative people "in house," you really need to have enough work to offer them so that there is not a costly "down time" when they are not busy. Because agencies can provide full-time employment, they can afford to pay creative people better salaries—another reason why such talent tends to end up in advertising agencies and not on the staffs of marketing departments in client organizations.

Advertising agencies almost invariably buy media less expensively than anybody else. This is a simple result of the fact that they buy more media for more clients. They are in the marketplace more frequently and get in faster than clients can. They are aware of media opportunities and availabilities and ultimately have more clout, so that they can negotiate better rates. Clients tend not to want to believe that this is true of most agencies. It is frequently, and erroneously, felt that a client could save the 15% in media costs (agency commissions) by placing media directly. Time and time again, agencies have demonstrated their ability to out-perform individual advertisers to such a degree that they more than make up the 15% difference in costs.

Agencies are also trained to meet deadlines and to know how to find the best suppliers in the shortest and most economical manner. They are generally pretty good at production.

The weakness of advertising agencies, from the point of view of most performing-arts centers, is that they are expensive. Agencies seldom are in a *pro bono* mode where they are willing to contribute creative time and talent without compensation. And they shouldn't be expected to. Agencies work on a fixed margin, the agency commission, and over the last ten years, they have faced the reality of costs rising at a faster rate than advertising budgets. The already small profit margin has been squeezed even harder. Occasionally one reads about large agencies going bankrupt. This is almost invariably the result of agency costs increasing faster than client billings to cover these costs.

This squeeze leads to a second area of concern with advertising agencies, particularly larger advertising agencies. Unless an advertiser is large enough to command the best resources of the agency, he may be relegated to newer, younger, less experienced, and less expensive people. Smaller advertisers may not command the full attention of senior agency principals. Less experienced people can be costly because they need more time to solve a client's problem. This is not always the case with larger advertising agencies, but it is a danger which you should watch out for.

Agency billing structures can be very complicated. Again, the larger agencies have needed to create billing structures that serve the requirements of their large clients. These structures may seem slow and cumbersome for small clients who must have faster and more personal billing turn-around time.

If you elect to use an agency, there are some simple do's and don'ts which would help make your relationship with that agency easier and more productive.

First, be sure that you give an agency a full brief of the problems and the goals you have set. There is no reason not to be totally candid with an agency. By withholding specific information from them, you only make their job more difficult and the likelihood of their not responding with appropriate advertising recommendations greater.

Agree on an advertising strategy with your agency first. Do not let them go to work developing prototype ideas and layouts until there is total agreement on the strategy. Figure out what the advertising is intended to do, who the target group is, what the responses are that the advertising should evoke, and how the creative decisions are to be made.

This last point is very critical. How do you intend to make an advertising decision? Who will make it? Does the agency have access to that person? Does the agency know in advance by what standards its work will be judged? The range of possible advertising judgments is staggering. There are those people who judge only on the basis of research results (these judgments tend to lead to much of the very dreary advertising that permeates television screens). On the other extreme are advertising judgments which are made capriciously, e.g., those campaigns that are viewed by the wife of the president who decides whether or not she likes it (the "I can do that" school of advertising). It may even be decided by a numerologist on the basis of the number of letters in the headline.

All of this suggests that you should respect your agency for what they do know how to do. They want your business. They want to maintain their relationship with you, and they are not going to recommend something that is totally frivolous or "off the wall." Listen to their reasons for their recommendations, and give them an honest hearing.

On the other hand, don't let them be self-indulgent. There is, alas, advertising that is done for the sake of advertising. It appeals only to the advertising community, and it tends to be an "in-joke." This kind of work is easy to spot. It tends to be very "cute," filled with arcane humor or obscure references. When an advertising agency begins to drift in that direction, it is time to bring them sharply and firmly back to the strategy and to the responses of the target group who seldom are other members of the advertising community.

It is important to keep advertising fresh. Make certain your agency is coming up with new and original ideas. Particularly in the performing arts, advertising tends to be derivative. Someone sees something that another performing-arts center has used successfully and picks it up without really understanding why it worked. Without a doubt, much advertising can be syndicated, but only when the target audience and response factors are similar. Do your homework first, and then see if the advertising meets your specific needs and objectives.

Keep control of your costs. Work out a timetable with the advertising agency and make sure both you and they stick to it. Learn to "read" very rough layouts and avoid the costly steps that agencies must undertake to produce "finished layouts." These seldom add to the fundamental creative idea in any productive way and steal valuable time in the creative department of an agency.

While on the subject of costs, a final note: Pay your bills promptly. Do not undertake a greater financial exposure with an advertising agency—or, indeed, anyone —than you can meet on a timely basis. As I mentioned above, agencies work on a very small margin, have a critical cash flow, and need to be recompensed in an orderly fashion. Performing-arts centers are notorious in dragging suppliers—often with very good reason. They themselves do not have the required cash flow to pay bills promptly. In this instance, discuss this problem candidly with your agency upfront, and work out some means by which they can expect their payments in a manner that is appropriate for them and possible for you. Nothing destroys the delicate fabric of profitability in an advertising agency faster than the need to go to the bank to borrow money to cover what it has committed in behalf of its clients.

Beyond all of these "plumbing details," an advertising agency is most helpful because it can contribute to the creative process. In helping this creative process along, it is important for you to get to know the creative people, how they think and work. Buy them a drink. Invite them to a performance. Make them feel that they are part of your operation. The more that they know and understand about how you work, the better their creative work will be.

IV. The Creative Process

The most mysterious part of an advertising agency's life is the creative process. They don't keep it mysterious in order to shut the clients out of it. It is genuinely an area where there are no rules. No one can provide an adequate, and generally accepted description of how it works.

There is no simple formula to create effective advertising. What you can do is to be as explicit as possible about what you want to achieve with the advertising. The more precise the definition of your goals, the easier it is for the creative juices to flow. You can watch this process work in the dialogue between directors and scene designers; the most imaginative set designs come about when the director has been very explicit in defining the effects he wishes to achieve. It is similar with advertising. The most important contribution you can make to the creative process is the accuracy and completeness of your briefing and strategy statement.

Beyond that, it is important to give the creative process time and to let it be nurtured. You need to have a "fingertip" feeling of when to push and shove and when to stay away. You need to develop a sense of trust with the agency. You trust that what they are doing is in your best behalf, and that there are areas of expertise that they genuinely know more about than you do. They know more about producing commercials—they should, they do more of them. Show them that you trust their judgment in this process and don't try to second guess them in areas where you are paying them for their know-how.

On the other hand, you need to be honest in the creative process. If an idea is bad, then say so. But say it with grace. Advertising professionals can deal with criticism; they cannot handle abuse. It is up to you to learn to feel the distinction between professional criticism and personal abuse.

It can take weeks to develop a creative idea and minutes to destroy it. In those few minutes, not only is the creative idea destroyed but also that sense of trust you have tried to build up. Take time for the review of an agency's work, and avoid snap judgments. If something immediately and clearly is off-strategy, if it is inappropriate or unaffordable, there is no harm in making these judgments quickly. Conversely, if you come across an idea you love spontaneously and enthusiastically, there is also no reason not to say so. But most advertising recommendations fall somewhere between these two extremes. Take time to reflect and consider. Let the creative process grow in you as it has grown in the agency.

One final, and very personal note, about the whole advertising process and the use of an advertising agency. Laughter is a key ingredient in the whole process. It is, after all, only an ad.

V. The Role of Media[1]

A. Media Planning

Media planning is obviously part of the whole marketing-planning process. A media plan is nothing more than an interpretation of a marketing plan and a creative strategy into an actionable document for a given period of time. Before a media plan can be implemented, you need to know very clearly what the specific goals are: Where are we? Where do we want to be? How do we get there? These are all the questions you must ask in putting together the background of a marketing plan and then determining what the specific goals and strategies of that plan might be.

Critical in the media-planning process is the budget-setting level. How much is enough? We will get into this issue when we discuss reach and frequency of media. The other question, which is more difficult to answer, is "how much is too little?" In all advertising, if you can't afford to do enough, don't try to do it at all. Much advertising is wasted because not enough people have sufficient opportunity to see and respond to the advertising in the way that you intend. It is better not to even undergo the process. Much of what follows below will help determine whether or not you have the funds to afford the kind of advertising which will reach your target audience effectively.

The best conceived marketing strategies and creative executions are of little use unless they are directed at the correct target audience in media which will deliver prospects when and where desired.

The overall objective for a media plan is to deliver target prospects with the least amount of waste, as efficiently as possible. This is accomplished within the framework of a media budget. This budget represents the parameters within which

---

[1]Much of what follows has been provided by and with permission of the J. Walter Thompson Company, New York. I gratefully acknowledge my debt to them.

the plan is constructed, and is a practical constraint on the amount of media that can be purchased.

Necessary for the development of a viable media plan are several marketing and creative considerations. Let's outline these briefly.

B. Marketing and Creative Input

While all of the following may not be necessary, depending on circumstances, most will have an influence on the development of the media plan.

* *Marketing Objectives/Strategies*
  —Sales and subscription goals: What is the current goal? How is the advertising going to contribute to achieving that goal? What percentage of your subscription goal do you expect to generate from advertising?
  —Product changes: innovations, star packages, etc.
  —Promotions: discount rates
* *Current Year's Advertising Program*
  —Results: consideration for changing the strategy
          Why change?
  —Problems/opportunities
* *Role of Advertising* (What are we trying to accomplish?)
  —Elicit a direct response? (coupon, write-in, etc.)
  —Increase awareness and trial?
  —Maintain current position?
  —Change attitudes?
* *Source of Business*
  —Hold the current audience?
  —Get current audience to come more often?
  —Attract audience from competition?

Out of these considerations you can then describe the:

* *Target Market*
  —Audience characteristics (users, non-users/heavy users):
      demographics; ethnicity; lifestyle
  —Purchase influence/decision maker
  —Special market segments (college, clubs, etc.)
* *Seasonality* (timing)
  —Subscription patterns
  —Influencing factors (holidays, promotions)
  —Spending considerations:
      lead into peak seasons; meet new program or season introductions; quarterly spending constraints
* *Creative Considerations That Are Critical for Media Planning*
  —Creative strategy statement
  —Creative needs and requirements
  —Creative Units (lengths, sizes)

Communications Characteristics of the Advertising	Qualitative/Environmental Needs
intrusiveness	prestige
demonstration	authority/believability
visualization	humor
sound	emotional response
explanation	use of music
permanence	information/service oriented
color	lifestyle related

"Demographics are important for planning media. But it does not really help much in the creative process."

C. Media Objectives

The purpose of media objectives is making media exposure patterns conform to the marketing and creative needs received earlier.

They set forth within a given budget:

— Whom we wish to reach (market target)
— Where we want to say it (geography)
— When it should be said (seasonality)
— What we plan to say (creative execution)
— How often it should be said (reach, frequency, and continuity)
— Other considerations (promotions and testing)

To fulfill a set of media objectives, some media will work better than others. Before discussing media objectives, let's talk about some basic terms (a lengthier list is in the Appendix).

Audience

Magazine Total Audience	Television Viewing Audience
FORMULA	FORMULA
Circulation	TV Households
× Readers Per Copy (RPC)	× Viewers Per Household (VPA)
= TOTAL AUDIENCE	= TOTAL VIEWERS
EXAMPLE	EXAMPLE
Better Homes and Gardens	"Happy Days" on ABC Network
× RPC Adults	× VPH Adults
= TOTAL ADULTS	= TOTAL ADULTS VIEWING "HAPPY DAYS"
8,030M	16,870M
× 2.60	× 1.247
= 20,878M	= 21,037M

SOURCE: For *Better Homes and Gardens,* SMRB, 1981
For "Happy Days," NTI, 3/22-4/4/82
(Note: Here, and throughout, costs are cited as of a given time; they will undoubtedly be subject to change.)

Home Using Television (HUT)

Homes Using Television is the percentage of all television homes having their sets turned on at a particular time.

Example:
If 48,900M homes out of a total of 81,500M TV households have their sets turned on during the prime time (8–11 p.m. EST) period, the HUT level for prime time is 60%.

$$\frac{6 \text{ TV HOMES}}{10 \text{ TV HOMES}} = 60\%$$

When the same calculation is done with people, it is referred to as People Using Television or PUT.

Rating

A rating is a percent. Ten percent of the total TV homes equal a rating of 10.

Example: 2 TV homes out of 10 TV homes are viewing a particular program. Therefore the program has a rating of 20.

$$\frac{2 \text{ TV HOMES}}{10 \text{ TV HOMES}} = 20\%$$

(Source: SMRB, 1981)

Ratings are also available by various demographics; for example:

Teens 12–17
Adults 18–24
Men 18–24
Women 18–24
etc.

The same is also true of radio, where household ratings are not available.

Share

Share refers to a household rating's percent of the Homes Using Television at a particular time.

For example, from 8:00 to 8:30 p.m. during the week of November 26, 1982, the three television networks and local independents had the following HH ratings, HUT, and Shares:

	HH Rating		Share	
ABC	15.4		25%	
CBS	21.4	45.4	35	74 Network Share
NBC	8.6		14	
Local Inds.	16.1		26	
HUT =	61.5		100	

GRP's——Gross Rating Points

GRP's are the sum of all ratings.
For example, in April, 1982:

	Adult 18–49 Ratings
"Sixty Minutes"	14.4
"One Day at a Time"	11.1
"The Jeffersons"	14.6
"M*A*S*H"	13.6
GRP's	53.7

(Source: NAD, 4/82)

Since GRP's are the sum of all ratings, and ratings are percentages, this concept can also be applied to media other than television.

For example	%A18–49 Audience (Ratings)	×	# of Insertions	=	Sum of Ratings (GRP's)
Better Homes & Gardens	13.1%		5		65.5%

or

	A18–49 Rating
Better Homes & Gardens	13.1%
Reader's Digest	21.8
TV Guide	28.7
GRP's	63.6%

(Source; SMRB, 1981)

Cost Per Rating Point

This term refers to the cost of buying one rating point in a medium. The relationship varies by daypart; for example, the estimated network television costs for the 1982–83 broadcast season (mid–September, 1982 to mid–September, 1983).

Network TV Daypart	Cost/Rating Point Adults 18–49	
	CPRP	Index
Sports (primarily weekend)	$7,598	100
Prime (8:00 p.m.–11:00 p.m.)	6,777	89
Early Evening News (6:00 p.m.–7:00 p.m.)	6,729	89
Late Night (11:30 p.m.–1:00 a.m.)	5,547	73
Day (10:00 a.m.–4:30 p.m.)	4,373	58

(Source: JWT estimates)

Costs per rating point (CPRP) vary by daypart due to audience size; program content; commercial clutter; and whether it attracts men, women, children or all three.

CPRP will also vary on a quarterly basis. There are also CPRP's for local (spot) television and network and spot radio.

Cost Per Thousand

This is the standard media criterion of efficiency.

The cost of any media unit is divided by the estimated target audience, in thousands. This audience is always expressed in terms of standard units such as Homes, Men, Women, etc.

For example, in Detroit in May, 1981, a typical prime-time thirty-second spot (:30) television announcement cost $2,300 and delivered 244M Adults 18–49.

$$\frac{\$2,300 \text{ — cost for :30}}{244M \text{ — adult 18–49 viewers}} = \frac{\$9.43}{\text{Cost Per Thousand}}$$

Cost per thousand is best used to evaluate options between media of the same kind; i.e., *The Detroit Free Press* vs. *The Detroit News* or one radio station vs. another.

The use of this relationship is somewhat distorted when we try to compare two different media such as a prime network TV :30 to a newspaper insertion or two different creative units, such as a :60 vs. a :10 TV commercial.

Now that we've defined some basic terms, let's talk about some essential media planning concepts.

D. Media Planning Concepts

Reach and Average Frequency

— REACH
Percent of different individuals in the target group exposed at least once in a period of time (usually four weeks) to the advertising vehicle used.

—AVERAGE FREQUENCY
Average number of times people are reached by the media vehicle.

Reach × Avg. Frequency = GRP

$$\frac{\text{GRP}}{\text{Reach}} = \text{Avg. Frequency}$$

$$\frac{\text{GRP}}{\text{Avg. Frequency}} = \text{Reach}$$

A Theoretical Example of How Reach and Frequency are Computed

INDIVIDUALS	WEEK 1	WEEK 2	WEEK 3	WEEK 4
A		X		
B	X	X		
C	X		X	X
D	X	X		X
E	X	X	X	X
F				
G			X	
H	X	X	X	X
I				
J				
CUMULATIVE REACH	50	60	70	70
AVERAGE FREQUENCY	1.0	1.7	2.0	2.6
CUMULATIVE GRP's	50	100	140	180

(See below for explanation.)

As shown, the universe equals ten people, A thru J. During week one, persons B, C, D, E and H were reached. Since they represent fifty percent of the people in the universe, the reach is a fifty and the frequency a 1.0, since they have been reached only once.

During week two, an additional person, A, was also reached. The percent of the people reached therefore equals sixty and the average frequency is a 1.7 (100 GRP's divided by the sixty reach). In actuality, person B, D, E, and H were each reached twice and A and C only once, the average of this is also 1.7.

During week three, an additional person, G was also reached, and the average reach increased to 70%. As 140 GRP's will have run by week three, the average frequency is now 2.0.

In week four, no additional people were reached; however, C, D, E, and H were exposed again. Forty additional GRP's were therefore added, and the average frequency increased from 2.0 to 2.6 (GRP's, 180 divided by reach, 70, equals frequency, 2.6).

Effective Reach

Effective reach can be defined as the percent of a target audience exposed to a product's message often enough to produce a positive change in either:
   —awareness
   —attitude
   —or purchase of the product
It is comprised of two numbers:
(1) the predetermined number of exposures that should bring about a positive change, and
(2) the percent reach that is sought or affordable at that level. In setting an effective reach goal, it is necessary to make judgements concerning the relative value of each exposure to determine whether a consumer will be effectively reached.

Some eighteen different studies/articles between 1963 and 1980 have attempted to assess the value of various numbers of exposures on a consumer. Although no definitive answers have emerged, the data suggest:

- A single exposure has little or no effect on most prospects.
- Two exposures is an effective level for an average brand.
- Three or more exposures generally appears to be necessary for awareness breakthrough.
- Frequency levels are measures of affect on the target; reach is a by-product of achieving a frequency goal.

"Over 99% of all U.S. homes have at least one radio in working order. The average household has 5.5 sets."

Continuity

Continuity refers to the number of weeks that advertising appears over the course of a year. Continuity is essential to remind prospects about a service or product often and to predispose them whenever they are in the market.

How often?

How many of the target audience do we want to reach and how frequently?

This is dependent on your advertising budget and the interaction of reach, frequency, continuity, and the creative units employed.

For example, if more reach is desired, unless the budget is increased to provide for more GRP's, frequency will decline. Or, if fifty-two weeks of advertising is desired rather than, say, forty, reach and/or frequency will decline because the weight is more spread out over time. And since :60's cost twice the amount of :30's, if :60's are used, GRP's will be cut in half.

Look at the four elements as a pie. As one of the elements increases, its slice becomes larger, and some or all of the other elements decrease in size. Your advertising budget forms the parameters within which these elements operate.

E. Media plan elements

The objective of any media plan is to deliver advertising messages to the right people at the right time as efficiently as possible.

Media selection is an art and not a science, so let's review the dimensions of each medium, and the advantages and disadvantages of each.

There are eight basic media available to you for your use:

- Television (network and local)
- Cable Television (network and local)
- Radio (network and local)
- Magazines
- Newspapers
- Sunday supplements, Sunday comics, and free-standing inserts
- Out-of-home advertising
- Direct response

They can be used alone or in combination. Let's look at each.

Television—Dimensions

- Television ownership has reached a virtual saturation point, with 98% of all U.S. households now TV-equipped.
- Color TV ownership continues to grow. Penetration increased to 85% in 1980.
- Multiple set ownership now accounts for 51% of all TV households.
- The average household views television over forty-six hours per week.
- Viewing varies by household size with 3+ member households spending fifty-seven hours weekly viewing while 1 member households view only thirty-one hours.
- There are now over 750 commercial television stations in America (and 271 public stations).
- Cable penetration is estimated at 30% and growing.

Television Characteristics

—STRENGTHS

- Near universal ownership and usage enables the advertiser to reach large audiences.
- Delivers an enormous audience at any given moment. To illustrate, national tune-in levels range from 18% of households at 9 a.m. to peak of 65% at 9:00 p.m.

- Strong impact through the combined elements of sight, sound, motion, and color.
- Spot TV can be brought on a local market basis.
- The medium is intrusive by nature and demands the viewer's attention.
- Specific dayparts can be selected to reach different audiences.

—WEAKNESSES

- High cost.
- As a mass medium, TV is less efficient than other media options as a means of reaching narrowly defined, demographic audience targets.
- High cost of producing a commercial relative to other media.

Cable Television—Dimensions

- 30% of all television households are now wired for basic cable with rapid increases predicted. Included in this are 17% which also have pay cable (Home Box Office, Cinemax, etc.). Served by 4000+ local systems.
- Several full time basic systems in operation, among them are:
  USA Network
  Cable News Network
  Christian Broadcasting Network
  ESPN—Entertainment and Sports Network
  MTV—The Music Channel
  Satellite Program Network (incldg. TeleFrance)
  Spanish International Network
  WTBS—The Superstation
- Diverse programming: sports, health, movies, rock music, news, foreign language, how-to shows.
- As cable continues to grow, broadcast-network shares and ratings will continue to decline.
- As with broadcast television, time can be purchased on local originating systems (where available), locally within nationally televised programs, or nationally within a program.

Cable Television Characteristics

—STRENGTHS

- The same strengths apply to cable or to broadcast television except that:
  —The number of homes wired for cable varies considerably from market to market.
  —The out-of-pocket costs are lower than for broadcast television because fewer homes are reached, and audiences are smaller.

Additionally,

- Because of the multiplicity of cable systems within an area, it is possible to purchase time on a system that covers a particular trading area with little or no waste.
- Programming may be available that is compatible with your needs and performing-arts series.
- Long (:60, :90) commercial units are available and suitable for lengthy copy extension.
- Narrowcasting (programming intended for a selective audience) makes it possible to focus in on specific demographic targets.
- Low cost makes it possible to build frequency (and some reach) against audience segments that are relatively light television viewers (e.g., upscale adults with an interest in cultural events).
- Broadcast networks will increasingly lose viewers (particularly upscale people) to cable. Buying cable will help compensate for some of this loss.
- Franchise can be built for program sponsorships, multi-year price protection, and/or product exclusivity.

"Develop your strategy first. Do not let your agency develop ideas and layouts until there is total agreement."

—WEAKNESSES

- Only 30% of all U.S. TV households are currently wired for cable.
- Ratings and audience-composition data are virtually non-existant.
- Audiences are probably very small (but costs are also low).
- Programs are repeated more often than on broadcast television.
- The percent of homes wired for cable varies considerably from market to market.
- Not all national cable networks are available in every market, and coverage within a market can vary network to network.

Radio—Dimensions

- Over 99% of all U.S. homes have at least one radio in working order. The average household has 5.5 sets.
- 95% of all cars are equipped with radios—up 182% since 1960.
- Transistor set sales up 77% since 1960. Seventy-five percent of teenagers, 53% of adult women and 55% of adult men own transistor radios for their personal use. There are now 116% more radios than people in the United States.
- Radio reaches 95% of all people in a single week and 81% in one day.
- There are now over 7,800 radio stations in America.
- About 40% of the stations are FM.

Radio Characteristics

—STRENGTHS

- Radio time can be purchased nationally on a network basis, regionally or locally.
- The wide variety of radio-station formats makes it possible to reach almost any specific demographic target.
- Both low unit-cost and very cost-efficient.
- The medium is immediate in delivering prospects when you want to reach them.
- Long commercial units can be purchased locally.
- Locally many stations provide merchandising; e.g., counter-cards, remote broadcasts, contests, and premiums.
- Station personalities can be used to lend credibility and persuasiveness to the advertising message.

—WEAKNESSES

- Expensive to build reach because of the high degree of audience segmentation. People tend to be loyal listeners to only a few radio stations. Time on many stations may therefore have to be purchased to achieve reach.
- Radio is primarily a background medium. People are usually engaged in some other activity while the radio is on and/or they aren't actively concentrating.
- Because the medium is audio only, it is difficult to convey a demonstration or a visual excerpt.

Magazines—Dimensions

- The average-issue circulation of all ABC (Audit Bureau of Circulation) audited magazines (431) in the past year was over 306 millon.
- Approximately 6.4 million issues are sold annually — an average of over eighty per U.S. household.
- There are over 1,120 consumer-oriented magazines published in the U.S.
- The trend in publishing has been the demise of mass-circulation magazines and the emergence of publications appealing to very specialized reader

tastes. Some of the more significant new magazines introduced in the past few years which appeal to the more specialized reading preferences are:

Omni	*Country Living*	*Money*
People	*Ms.*	*Self*
Savvy	*Working Woman*	*Discover*

- Approximately 66% of all magazines are purchased through home subscriptions with the remaining 34% from the newsstand.

Magazines

—ADVANTAGES

- Affords a high degree of audience selectivity through title selection.
- Excellent four-color reproduction.
- Possibility to select magazines with editorial content that provides a complementary environment for the product and lends prestige to the advertising.
- Good for communicating details.
- High degree of authority and believability.

—DISADVANTAGES

- Demonstration and dramatization are difficult to portray.
- National magazines with metropolitan editions are limited.
- Generally high premium paid for advertising space in metropolitan editions when compared to most other local media options.
- Lengthy closing dates (six to eight weeks), which means material must be prepared well in advance, and cannot be altered after the closing dates.
- Unlike the brodcast media and newspapers, reach builds over time. Therefore, responsiveness to the advertising is more gradual and coupon-redemption is slower.
- The positioning of the advertisement may be opposite other advertising.

Newspapers

—ADVANTAGES

- Immediate readership.
- Read for retail advertising.
- Coupon capability and very fast redemption. Therefore, excellent for promotions.
- Newsworthy editorial environment suitable for performing arts.
- High degree of local household penetration.
- Slight upscale market.
- Communication of subscription details.

—DISADVANTAGES

- As a mass medium, newspapers are relatively inefficient in reaching selective target audiences.
- Variable color reproduction.
- Heavy clutter, therefore positioning and the size of the advertisement are important.
- Visual only.
- Short issue-life.

Sunday Supplements, Sunday Comics, and Free-Standing Inserts (FSI's)

—ADVANTAGES

- The advantages previously enumerated for newspapers are the same for these media, distributed by Sunday newspapers. Additionally:

"Direct marketing is expected to rise considerably in the 1980s, due to cable and 'two-way' television…"

- Color reproduction is available.
- Readership is very high — supplements by adults, Sunday comics by the family, and FSI's by adults clipping coupons.
- All three media, particularly supplements and FSI's have high and rapid coupon-redemption rates.
- Cartoon panel advertising can be created for Sunday comics, thereby inviting readership.

—DISADVANTAGES

- Reproduction in Sunday comics is less than desirable.
- Sunday comics and supplements require a high out-of-pocket cost.
- Cost-efficiency is relatively high, due to limited pass-along audience.
- Supplements are not available in all markets, and FSI's may not be available when desired.
- Lengthy closing dates — six to eight weeks.
- Generally have much wider distribution than daily newspapers, therefore geographic waste may be greater.

Out-of-Home Media

- Twenty-four- or thirty-sheet posted boards on highways.
- Painted displays.
- Painted displays with embellishments (for example, a board the shape of the product, special lighting, or movement of a piece on the display).
- Transit advertising inside and outside of buses and subways.
- Displays at airports, bus terminals, etc.
- Small posters at train stations or posted on the sides of buildings.
- Neon spectaculars, à la Times Square.

—ADVANTAGES

- Very high reach and frequency among people who pass the display each day.
- Market-to-market flexibility.
- Possible to pinpoint coverage by section of a city (e.g., selective placement of panels in close proximity to high traffic areas, near theme parks, etc.)
- Very low CPM's (cost per thousands) against total potential audience impressions.
- Excellent means of reinforcing message.

—WEAKNESSES

- Background in nature; many other elements compete for the traveller's attention.
- Length of message must be short; therefore, a supplementary rather than a primary medium.
- Availability of desirable locations may be restricted by zoning regulations.
- Cannot deliver highly defined demographic target audiences efficiently because the medium is mass in structure.

Direct Marketing—Dimensions[2]

- Direct marketing is any form of advertising that elicits a direct, measurable response.
- Direct marketing today is a 100-billion dollar business.
- It is expected to rise considerably in the 1980's due to technology such as cable television, "two-way" television (which allows viewers to order products and services directly from their homes), electronic transfer of

> "It makes no sense to use a number of different media when you are not able to have a dominant position in any one of them."

---

[2]Material in this section supplied through the courtesy of David Soskin, President, Soskin-Thompson, a direct-marketing agency.

funds, electronic mail, and even more sophisticated computer and telephone systems.
- Direct marketing can be used effectively to accomplish a variety of marketing objectives:
    —It can sell products or services directly.
    —It can generate interest.
    —It can produce qualified sales leads.
    —It can generate traffic.
- Direct response advertising uses virtually every advertising medium:
    —Direct mail (letters, brochures, catalogs, couponing and sampling, billing enclosures).
    —Print
    —Television
    —Point of sale
    —The telephone
    —Outdoor
- Direct marketing is therefore a communications medium that cuts across other possible media.
- Every direct response advertisement is testable and measurable. Every direct response advertisement is therefore accountable.

—STRENGTHS

- Audiences are pinpointed in very refined ways.
- Testable at every stage.
- Selectivity.
- The message is not limited to the specific amount of space.
- It takes many forms, from a personal letter to a product sample.
- Through the use of the computer, mathematical models can be constructed to predict results.
- The computer can also be used to keep track of customers by name, address, zip code, telephone number, type of purchase, frequency, and amount of purchase.

—WEAKNESSES

- On a mass basis, direct response can be costly.
- It is a market that is being rapidly cluttered.
- Delivery vehicles differ, and what works in one magazine or newspaper or via direct mail does not necessarily work in another medium.
- The timing can be critical.

While it is difficult to decide what media to use for a campaign, placing them in perspective to achieve certain objectives may help. I've tried to do this below:

COMPARISON OF NATIONAL MEDIA CHARACTERISTICS

CHARACTERISTICS	TELEVISION		MAGAZINES (4/C PGS.)	NETWORK RADIO	SUN. SUPPS. SUN. COMICS FSI'S	NEWSPAPERS (1,000 LI.)	OUTDOOR
	BROADCAST	CABLE					
1. Reach/Frequency	Balanced	Balanced	Balanced	Frequency Emphasis	Reach Emphasis	Reach Emphasis	Both High
2. National Coverage	Yes	No	Yes	Yes	Almost	No	No
3. Full TV Market Coverage	Yes	Variable	Yes	Variable	Metro-Concentration	Metro-Concentration	Metro-Concentration
4. Speed of Audience Accumulation	Fast	Fast	Slow	Moderate	Very Fast	Very Fast	Fast
5. Repeat Exposure	No	No	Potentially	No	Unlikely	Unlikely	Yes
6. Current Prospect Selectivity Among Ad-Noters	Limited	Limited	Yes	Limited	Yes	Yes	Limited
7. New Prospect Development Opportunity	Best	Good	Good	Fair	Fair	Fair	Limited
8. Media Environment Clutter	Yes	Yes	Yes	Yes	Less	Yes	Sometimes
9. Media Environment Authority/ Believability	Fair	Better	Excellent	Probably	Probably	Good	NA
10. Copy-Delivery Capability	Short	Longer	Excellent	Short	Good	Good	Extremely Short
11. Color	Yes	Yes	Yes	No	Yes	No	Yes
12. Demonstration	Excellent	Excellent	Limited	No	Limited	Limited	Very Limited
13. Dramatization	Excellent	Excellent	Difficult	Limited	Difficult	Difficult	No
14. Intrusiveness	Yes	Yes	No	Limited	No	No	No
15. Cost-Efficiency Mass Audience Selective Audience	Good Poor	OK Good	Good Good	Good Good	Good Poor	Good Poor	Good Poor

F. In Summary

Media are selected to best accomplish the marketing and creative objectives. Criteria used in evaluating media alternatives to achieve these objectives are:

- Meeting creative needs:
  —Demonstration, explanation, color, coupon capability, etc.
  —Length or size of advertising units
- Effectiveness of message delivery:
  —Ability of the medium to direct the message to the proper target
  —Value of the media environment and message exposure in creating attention, comprehension, memorability, and motivation
- Efficiency in delivering the target audience
- Timing in relation to:
  —Seasonal media opportunities
  —New season introductions or promotions
  —Immediacy of audience delivery
  —Seasonal sales patterns (or days of week)
- Weight levels
  —Gross rating-point delivery
  —Reach and frequency or effective reach
  —Sporadic versus continuity
- Geographic coverage
- Flexibility
  —Lead time
  —Cancellation timing

Some Concluding Thoughts

Media planning and buying tend to be complicated matters—or at least the words and abbreviations used to describe the media would seem to make it so. It is not just the fact that media people are trying to make it look complicated; this is a critically expensive part of your overall marketing budget and needs to be as accurate as possible, despite its many different facets and ramifications. You will want to become as familiar with these terms and techniques as possible, because they will help you make judgments.

One of the advantages of an advertising agency is that its account executives can help you through the morass of media diction. They are familiar with it and are genuinely skilled in producing the most effective media planning to meet your needs.

But even here, there are several final caveats. Often there is a tendency to mix and match a number of different media within one overall marketing schedule. This tactic must be undertaken with considerable caution. It makes no sense to use a number of different media when you are not able to have a dominant position in any one of them. Be certain that you have enough of a presence in the first medium before moving on to the next, however seductive the allure of that next medium might be.

Print (newspapers and direct mail) is frequently the first medium used for the performing arts. Yet, the allure of television stands out clearly. We tend to look with yearning towards those performing-arts centers or companies that seem to be able to afford additional advertising weight in television. Before you seriously consider adding television to your schedule, however, be certain that you do not have to decimate your print schedule in order to afford it. Do a sufficient job in one medium before moving onto the next.

It is very important to be seen and noted. If you cannot afford to pay the price of a ticket all the way to Europe, it is better not to plan the trip than to buy a ticket that will only take you three-quarters of the distance. Likewise, it is better to forego advertising altogether than to undertake a program that does not permit you to be seen and noted in any one medium.

Finally, in making evaluations about media programs, the most important factor is your own judgment. Look at the various media options. Read the magazines, watch the programs, look at other advertisers, become intimately familiar with the editorial environment, and make certain that it is appropriate and relevant to your

"It can take weeks to develop a creative idea and a minute to destroy it. Avoid snap judgements."

"Too many head-lines are like a room full of people all shouting at once—nobody is heard."

purposes. There are reasons why fashion advertisers do not run advertisements in *Popular Mechanics*. You don't need sophisticated media experience to make that determination. Use good, sound common sense throughout your media planning, and you will discover that much of it is good, commercial sense.

This brings us full circle back to the nature of advertising and some of its general principles.[3]

In planning media as well as in creating advertising, remember that there is always an individual reader or viewer. That is why the greatest copywriters have so frequently reported that when they sit down to write, they have tried to think of one person to whom they are writing. In that sense, every advertisement should be thought of as a personal letter. And the language of most good advertisements is very human, the language of one person talking to another.

Sometimes advertising writers seem to forget and substitute something that can only be described as "advertising-ese"—diction never heard anywhere else on earth. A good test for advertising copy is to read it aloud. If you ear rejects the words or the flow, there is probably something wrong.

And remember, the consumer is not a moron. He is your husband. She is your wife. There is no future to be gained in advertising *down* to someone whom the advertising implicitly disparages.

The greater the news, the less the need for razzle-dazzle technique. If you had to announce that a cure for cancer had been discovered, you would make certain that the communication did not get in the way of the news; the presentation would be as stark and simple as possible. Since most news is of lesser importance, the fresh use of language and visual layout is all the more critical.

The headline of an advertisement normally performs the function of a traffic sign; it is designed to make the reader stop, look, and listen. If it doesn't do one of those things, something else needs to take its place—namely the visual. The headline may be long and informative, but if it gets too long it will defeat its basic purpose, which is to flag the reader's attention. It may, on the other hand, be as short as a single word working in close conjunction with an illustration for an almost poster effect.

The issue of long versus short body-copy has only one resolution: the copy must be long enough to get the job done—and that may be very long indeed. Today, although short copy is more often preferred, there are many highly visible examples of long copy.

Words, pictures, typography should all work together towards a single end. They should function as interactive parts of a single, harmonious unit. One of the most famous headlines from Stanley Resor, the man who built J. Walter Thompson, was "He who chaseth two rabbits catcheth none." Under that headline he wrote, "If you try to cover too much ground at once, you will miss your objective. A headline flashes to the reader the main point you want to make. But *several* headlines, scattered over the same layout, merely cancel each other out. They are like a room full of people all shouting at once—nobody is heard." This injunction applies to all of the ingredients of an advertisement.

Advertising tone is a major element in creating an appropriate advertising personality. And a well-chosen, well-executed advertising personality will build brand personality over time. It is not simply a matter of words, pictures, or typography. All of these contribute to the personality of an advertisement, just as the personality of a man is defined by a composite of what he wears, how he talks, what he says, how he moves, who he is. Every advertisement has a personality, if only by default. An accidental or ill-chosen personality is damaging to the personality of the brand it represents, but a strong, positive advertising personality will help build a strong and enduring brand personality.

And what is true of a brand is true for a performing-arts center or company. Decide what personality you wish to project and make certain that everything you do evokes a consistent, desired response to that personality. You will be doing your job professionally and successfully.

---

[3]Borrowed liberally from "Some Things We Have Learned," J. Walter Thompson (published privately).

Television

Network TV

Television networks are interconnected groups of stations (about 200 on each network) which receive programs from the originating point via AT&T lines.
There are three major TV networks:
—ABC (American Broadcasting Company)
—CBS (Columbia Broadcasting System)
—NBC (National Broadcasting Company)

Spot TV

The use of stations in selected markets for the purpose of spending in line with sales. The local stations used can be either independently owned or affiliated with a network.

Prime Time

The TV daypart that encompasses the 8–11 p.m. (EST) Mon–Fri. and 7–11 p.m. (EST) Sun. time period. Prime time is usually the most expensive of all dayparts because this time period reaches the largest audience. In addition, there is less commercial clutter and higher viewer attention and ad recall than other dayparts.

Fringe Time

The daypart runs from about 5 p.m.–7:30 p.m. (EST) (early fringe) and from 11 p.m.–1 a.m. (EST) (late fringe). In general, programming consists of news, movies, talk shows, and re-runs. Viewership is lower than prime, and consequently it is a less expensive daypart to purchase.

Daytime

Running from about 10 a.m. to around 5 p.m. (EST), this daypart is used by many advertisers to reach women, who comprise the bulk of the audience. Programming generally consists of game shows, soap operas, and movies. This daypart contains the highest degree of commercial clutter.

VHF
(Very High Frequency)

Television Channels 2–13. There are over 500 VHF stations in the U.S. VHF stations generally have the greatest range of coverage.

UHF
(Ultra High Frequency)

Television Channels 14 and above. There are over 200 UHF stations in the U.S. UHF stations generally cover a smaller area than their VHF counterparts.

Cable Television

Signals are fed into homes with cable. Currently 30% of all U.S. TV households wired for cable, rapid growth predicted. Several cable networks televising special interest programs are in existence.

"As a mass medium, TV is less efficient than other media options in reaching narrow targets."

Commercial Lengths

TV commercials generally occur in three lengths; 60-seconds, 30-seconds, or 10-seconds. The cost of a commercial is dependent upon its length. The cost relationshp of the various lengths are as follows:

Length	Cost Relationship
:60	100
:30	50
:10	25

Other than unusual circumstances (i.e., newsbreaks), 10-second announcements are not available on network TV.

Radio

AM (Amplitude Modulation)

This refers to the standard broadcast transmission system by the majority of licensed stations. AM stations generally have the largest audiences, partially due to their wide-ranging signal. Only rarely is stereo broadcasting possible via AM, although strides are currently being made in this area.

FM (Frequency Modulation)

A broadcast band used by many stations. FM reception contains no static, and stereo broadcasting is common. FM signals are not as wide-ranging as AM signals.

Coverage

The geographic boundaries to which a station's signal extends.

Merchandising/Promotion

Radio, moreso than other media, can provide additional impact on the local level via merchandising and promotional opportunities. These include contests, gifts, etc.

Daypart

Radio can offer a high degree of demographic selectivity by time period.
Early and afternoon drivetime (6–10 a.m., 4–7 p.m.—delivers the largest adult audience of any daypart.
Housewife or daytime (10 a.m.–3 p.m.)—selective in reaching women.
Evening (7 p.m.–Midnight)—slightly more male than female-oriented. Highest percent composition of teens.

Format

In general, listeners are loyal to a station because of its particular format. Radio advertisers, therefore, pay close attention to a station's programming format when purchasing this medium.

Magazines

Circulation

The average number of copies of a magazine distributed in an average issue, within a specified area (i.e., Total U.S., New York ADI, Worldwide).

Readers Per Copy

Average number of readers of one copy of a magazine. This may be expressed in terms of *total* readers within the household who purchase the magazine (primary readers).

Audience

The total number of readers within a specific group (i.e., total adults, women 18 to 49). The audience is computed by the following formula:

Circulation × Readers Per Copy = Audience
for example:

	Circulation ×	Total Adult RPC	= Total Adults
Reader's Digest	18,359	2.15	39,472M

Audience Duplication

An expression of the number of people exposed to *more than one* magazine. For example, a portion of the readers of *McCall's* and *Good Housekeeping* read both magazines.

Sunday Supplements

Sunday Supplements are the magazine-like additions to the local Sunday newspaper. Directed to a general audience, they are unique in that their distribution and growth potential are controlled by another medium—the Sunday newspaper.

They generally have a high degree of household coverage within an ADI, for example:

Sunday Supplement	% Households Reach
Columbus Ohio Dispatch, Citizen Jrnl.	52%
Des Moines Register Tribune	58
Hartford Courant	59
Milwaukee Journal Sentinel	61

(Source: Circulation, 81/82)

Newspapers

Newspapers are a local medium, because of their universal appeal, they provide coverage of almost all U.S. homes.

NUMBER AND TOTAL CIRCULATION OF U.S. DAILY AND SUNDAY NEWSPAPERS

	Number Of Papers	Total Circulation (000)
Daily Newspapers	1730*	61,432
Morning	407	30,541
Evening	1353	30,891
Sunday Newspapers	757	55,127

*Circulation for thirty "All Day" newspapers are evenly divided between morning and evening figures.

(Source: Editor & Publisher Yearbook 1982)

A national advertiser will use a newspaper to:
—Support new product introductions with immediate and broad market coverage.
—Deliver local advertising that requires specific printed information (i.e., price advertising).
—Provide local dealer support.
—Provide advertising that requires a reader response (i.e., coupons).

Newspaper Creative Developments

Color is now available in over 90% of all daily newspapers, though the medium remains essentially a black & white vehicle. The basic means of achieving color advertising in newspapers are:

ROP Color—Printed on standard news stock paper.

Hi-Fi—This technique utilizes a continuous roll of newsprint with the ad on one side while the reverse side carries editorial. Superior paper stock is used to guarantee good color reproduction, but the paper feed is continuous.

Spectacolor—As with Hi-Fi, editorial is on the reverse side of the ad. This technique is the highest quality of print reproduction available in newspapers and is generally comparable to magazine color.

Preprinted inserts—are advertisements that are inserted between the sections of a newspaper. They range in size from a single card insert to multiple-page booklets. They are very expensive.

Flexform utilizes free-form ads that are floated within a page and surrounded by editorial. They can be produced in color or black & white.

Outdoor

The nation's highway and road system can be used to expose an increasingly mobile public to outdoor advertising. In addition to reaching people in their automobiles, outdoor permits exposure in specific areas such as shopping centers, airports and stadiums.

Showing

The standard measure of coverage. A #100 showing (or 100 GRP's per day) is the number of panels necessary to provide daily exposure that is equal to the population of the market.

Posters

The most popular outdoor form is the 24-sheet poster, approximately 9′ × 20′. Standard variations are the 30-sheet poster (10′ × 22′) and bleed posters.

Junior Posters

Available in urban markets and is about 6′ × 12′. The structure is usually positioned at eye level and often on the sides of buildings.

Three-Sheet Posters

Vertical in appearance (8.5′ × 5′), these posters are essentially a point-of-purchase medium located on walls or buildings near retail outlets.

Painted Displays

Large and dramatic, hand-painted and about 14′ × 48′, these boards are usually located on high-traffic arterials or intersections.

They can be sold on an individual basis or in a *rotary plan* which extends market coverage by permitting the dispaly to be moved every 30 to 90 days. Usually sold on a 1 to 3 year contract basis rather than a monthly basis as for posters. The price usually includes two or three re-paints per year.

PART III:
General Application of the Marketing Principles

Michalann Hobson

MAKING THE MARKETING PLAN AND MIX WORK

WARNING: Making a brochure without the clear understanding of the mission and goals and the previous sales history of an organization, and its target audience is dangerous to the organization and should be unlawful.

It is no accident that this chapter is not first in the book. If you are reading it first, it is a big mistake.

Yes, this is the part about the tools, which you will note in Doug Eichten's planning guide (in the appendix) does not come until Section IV near the end. Again, no accident. Choosing the right tools is totally dependent upon the prior research and knowledge which he and Micheal House have outlined.

The tools should be thought of as weapons which can be harmful if not used properly. Each one sends out a message, in most cases a combination of a verbal and visual message. As such, they have the power to create an image of the organization, second only in importance to that which occurs onstage.

Considered and careful use of the tools is vital. Few of us have set a goal of promoting dishonestly to our audiences; few are out to set up a bad image for the artists whom we are supporting, and yet many have carelessly produced countless promotional materials that do not accurately reflect their organizations.

There are also *no magic formulas!* There is no such thing as the *right* combination of tools. What worked for someone else will not necessarily work for you, even if your programming is similar. Your artists, historical reference, and individual communities provide their own unique context.

And so it becomes a problem of *selectivity* and *timing*, only an accumulated knowledge of your product and marketplaces and an organized framework within which to manipulate the various sales methods will give you a sense of those. (It's "guts ball," but not Russian roulette with a bunch of campaign tools.)

The tools chosen must be inextricably linked to the target audience and ticket-sales plans/packages. To maintain this relationship, I have prepared a guideline that sets up various target audiences (groupings of potential buyers) and *access* to them and then related the *possible ticket plans/packages* to the *tools* that might be applicable to each group. It is intended that the following questions be considered as an overlay to the guideline:

Michalann (Micki) Hobson has been working on a project basis since 1978 as an Arts Management specialist in the areas of marketing and development campaigns, strategic planning, budgeting, product development, management training, and conference planning. Ms. Hobson was the Communications Director for the McCarter Theatre (Princeton), Michael Kahn, Producing Director, for 6 years and Public Relations Director for the Alliance Theatre (Atlanta), Fred Chappel, Artistic Director, for three years. Ms. Hobson has conducted numerous marketing seminars and workshops for FEDAPT, NYSCA the Alliance of Resident Theatres/New York, the Yale School of Drama, City University of New York, Southeastern Theatre Conference, among others. Ms. Hobson has worked with more than 75 performing arts organizations, including theater, dance and opera companies, symphony orchestras and presenting organizations in twenty-two states (from Alaska to Florida), and Canada.

Who do you have *now*?
Who do you *not* have?   ] TARGET AUDIENCE
Who do you *want*?

Where can they be reached?   ] ACCESS

What would appeal most to them?
(do they need additional perks?)] TICKET PLAN/PACKAGE

What should you use to get them
to buy this plan?   ] TOOLS/SALES METHODS

TARGET AUDIENCE	ACCESS	SALES METHODS/ TOOLS	POSSIBLE TICKET PLANS/PACKAGES
Current Attendees Past Attendees	Your own mailing list (track *ALL* subscribers and *ALL* single ticket buyers to *ALL* events)	Direct mail (personalized when possible) —letterpacks —brochures —newsletters —telegram reminders Telephone Lobby displays Program stuffers Tours Seminars Parties & other special events	• SEASON TICKETS • SINGLE TICKETS • SPECIAL DISCOUNTS FOR FAMILY AND FRIENDS (Prime groups to receive additional information via newsletters, seminars, in-depth profiles, guides, etc.)
Friends & Family of Current & Past Attendees	Use incentives to obtain their names such as sweepstakes drawing. Captive Audience		
Patrons of Other Arts Organizations in Community And Surrounding Area	Their mailing lists Captive audience	same as above (special letters addressed to this group acknowledging that they are members of particular arts organizations increases returns)	• SEASON TICKETS • SINGLE TICKETS (also good group to receive newsletters because of pre-disposition to the arts)
High School Teachers College Faculty	Unions (residence addresses) Schools (campus addresses) School publications Discipline associations Book fairs	Direct Mail Mail drops Ads & feature stories Personal contact Displays	• SPECIAL DISCOUNTS ON SEASON TICKETS FOR UNION MEMBERS ONLY (given to Union members in exchange for list) Imprint brochure with Union tie-in. • GROUP DISCOUNTS TO INDIVIDUAL PRODUCTIONS
College Alumni Associations	Alumni assoc. lists Alumni assoc. meetings Monthly publications	Direct mail (piggy-back) Speakers Ads & feature stories	• SEASON TICKETS • GROUP DISCOUNTS (Tie-in with other events already happening on campus) Parties, seminars, tours
Men & Women	Home	Phone Direct mail †Door-to-door †Coffees & cocktail parties Newspaper Radio TV ††(See Danny Newman, *Subscribe Now* for details)	• SEASON TICKETS • SINGLE TICKETS

Segment	Outlets	Methods	Offers / Tactics
Families	via "women" (see above categories)	same as above	• FAMILY PLANS with discounts for kids—balloons, contests, etc. to get their attention as well (see below)
Kids	Schools Youth centers Churches McDonalds Baskin-Robbins Sat. A.M. TV	Bulk distribution Bulk distribution Bulk distribution Special tie-ins Special tie-ins PSA's	• FAMILY PLANS special Sat. Matinee programs, workshops, tours, games. tie-ins which link kids programs to adult programs (let kids sell to their parents—gimmicks that require each to participate: balloons w/free give-away chits inside; lobby display of childrens art; contests; banners made by an art class, etc.)
Long Distance Commuters	Residences Radio Train/Bus Stations…	Direct Mail PSA's/promotions/buys Hand distribution Brochure/Flyer display holders Posters/3 Sheets Ads in train/bus schedules	• MINI-SERIES SUBSCRIPTION (3 or 4 productions) • INTRODUCTORY OFFERS good discount restaurant tie-ins w/discounts parking ease give bad weather protection (easy exchange at last minute)
Tourists	Information bureaus Chamber of commerce State department of commerce/tourism Hotel associations Restaurant associations Transportion centers, rail/bus/boat/car Shopping areas/gas stations, etc.	Displays Personal contact Special tie-ins w/ restaurants & hotels (Note: Summer theaters will be doing more than the above with billboards, bumper stickers, etc.)	• SINGLE TICKETS Special flyer with *maps*, schedule, prices, charge information, large phone number, emphasis on ease of ordering. Highlight production photos more than "words"—Slick & glitzy…This group will be judging it all by this ONE piece most of the time.
Newcomers	Real-estate agents Newcomers clubs	Bulk distribution through outlets	• SINGLE TICKETS with introductory discount offer (Some newcomers clubs will allow a letter to be included with flyer or brochure)
Hotel/Motel Employees *Restaurant Employees* *Cab Drivers* ("They spread the word for you")	Hotel associations Restaurant associations Unions Convention coordinators	Personal contact Personal contact (see Teachers Union) (Note: Prime purpose is to acquaint employees with your institution so that they will be excited about it and "sell" for you)	• SPECIAL DISCOUNTS OR PASSES in return for: —tent card placement —subscriber discounts to restaurant —displays Tours, parties after previews, meet cast, etc. to assure their involvement.
20's to 30's Singles	Apartment complexes (Recreational director) Ad agencies Singles clubs	Personal contact (Form a club just for them—a "Guild" of sorts—with social and volunteer (sales and production oriented perks.) Feature stories in apt.-complex newsletter speakers at their meetings "gimmicks" of all kinds!	• SEASON TICKETS • GROUP DISCOUNTS special flyer/brochure re their "Guild" and its benefits.

TARGET AUDIENCE	ACCESS	SALES METHODS/ TOOLS	POSSIBLE TICKET PLANS/PACKAGES
Corporate & Business Employees	Directors of personnel or recreation Small business owners Chamber of Commerce Local business association	Personal contact Mini previews at corp. or malls (lunchtime) Displays Articles in corporate newsletter Speakers at meetings (Note: All corporate materials should be simple, easy to follow, with clear explanation of benefits and *uncomplicated* price structures.)	• CORPORATE COUPON PLAN (discount coupons sold in minimum of 25 to business to be resold to employees or as gifts from business to clients—redeemed at discretion of coupon holder) can be used in any multiples to any program as listed on coupon. extreme limitations should not be put on this plan... prime benefit is to get them there at least once, with the best experience possible before and after! • GROUP SALES DISCOUNT on single tickets • BLOCKS OF SEASON TICKETS purchased by corporation or: —part of retirement plan —payroll deduction plan • DISCOUNT PASSES OR FREE in return for poster displays (usually used for small bus.) Tours, parties, meet the cast, corporate "evenings" etc.
Patrons of Sports Events	on site at games	Announcement at halftime Acting company in parades Pennants w/campaign slogan program stuffer combination promotions with teams—gimmick heaven! (Get team members to come to a production—announce to audience that they are there, etc.)	• SEASON TICKETS • SINGLE TICKETS INSTITUTIONAL IMAGE BUILDING special discount chits to be redeemed on either season or single tickets—given in return for permission to hand-out at game.
Senior Citizens	Senior-citizens centers State agencies Retirement associations	Mail drops Personal contact	• SINGLE TICKET DISCOUNTS • GROUP DISCOUNTS • PASSES (in exchange for volunteer services) —matinees—especially Sundays —buses—accommodate transportation problem when possible Tours, seminars, study guides, etc. Special flyer describing senior-citizen discounts or paragraph in group sales brochure

Market	Method	Source / Place	Offers / Notes
Disadvantaged	Personal contact	HAI (Hospital Audiences Inc.) Half-way houses State agencies Local arts council	• FREE or VERY LOW PRICES (50¢) to previews or more difficult performances to sell Set up with agency for short notice patrons as well as advance notice. Patron can be given opportunity to make advance reservations and then check day of performance for final availability. Add to the experience of groups brought through agencies—tours, etc.
Movie goers	Movie trailers	Movie theatres	• SEASON TICKETS • SINGLE TICKETS
Professionals Doctors Lawyers Dentists Bankers	Direct Mail (personalized—have members write each other) Piggy-back with their mailings; newsletters & periodicals	Professional associations AMA, hospitals BAR ADA Banks	• SEASON TICKETS • SINGLE TICKETS (Have special "lawyers-night" type parties with a production)
Students High School	Mail drops Workshops in school Speakers Personal contacts	School Drama, music & arts clubs PTA Teachers of individual discipline applicable to a particular production	• GROUP DISCOUNTS (1 chaperone free for every 20 students) SPECIAL PRICES/SPECIAL TIMES (matinees must be scheduled to accommodate bus needs of area) Tours, study guides, seminars & post-performance discussions
College	Campus hall Displays Ads & feature stories Leaflet Leaflet Displays, program stuffers, movie trailers Personal contact—special social tie-ins	Dormitories Student Centers Publications Communal eating areas Classroom (esp. Eng. & Drama) Other events attending (captive audience) Fraternities/Sororities	• COUPON BOOKS • RUSH TICKETS • 50% DISCOUNT ON SUBSCRIPTIONS • STUDENT DISCOUNT ON SINGLE TICKETS (Simple flyer explaining the student offer or offers—direct copy to students, FUN, emphasize flexibility, savings, easy to order, large phone #)
Government State Local Federal Arts Agencies/Commissions	Direct mail	Their lists	• FREE TICKETS (special block of seats for them for a program early in season Tour facility Tie-in with "meet the cast" party Invitations with good advance notice Announce to the audience that they are there Get pictures with cast

TARGET AUDIENCE	ACCESS	SALES METHODS/ TOOLS	POSSIBLE TICKET PLANS/PACKAGES
Women	A. MALLS DEPT. STORES BOUTIQUES FOOD STORES	Displays Piggy-back ads Direct mail— (bill stuffers) Shopping-bag stuffers	• SEASON TICKETS • SINGLE TICKETS WITH SPECIAL DISCOUNT OFFERS **Malls:** —costume/fashion show combinations using actors as models —craft shows—making props —discount chits tie-in to theme used for the month by mall —ticket drawing —mini performances **Dept. Stores:** —$5.00 gift certificate from store with each subscription purchased—theater pays store for each certificate issued **Food stores:** —special discount offer in bag stuffer—limit for period of time which coincides with something store itself may be offering.... tie-in sales gimmick when possible.
	B. CLUBS —civic —social —religious BUSINESS ASSOCIATIONS	Personal contact Speakers at meetings	• SEASON TICKETS $5.00 rebate to club for each subscription sold by club • GROUP DISCOUNTS Dinner/Theatre PL packages plus tours & seminars
	C. BEAUTY PARLORS DOCTORS OFFICES (Any other "waiting room" situations)	Scrapbooks	• SEASON TICKETS • SINGLE TICKETS Place brochures in pockets at end of scrapbook; convert to single ticket flyers after subscription campaign

The Planning & Mixing Guidelines—Notes

This guideline should never be considered complete or final. It is just the beginning; a reference and reminder. It should be added to; subtracted from; manipulated over and over; by YOU. (Burning it is also an option.)

Target Audience & Access

The groupings of potential targets under this heading on the guideline are in *no* particular order, with the exception of the first category, which should be set in stone in that position:

The *Current Attendees; Past Attendees; Friends And Families of Current & Past Attendees* are the primary targets for ANY arts organization. You will therefore need to know *who* they are for solicitation. A simple concept; no marketing courses needed to understand it. And yet, how many times do we cave into the excuse that the box office cannot get *All* the names and addresses, especially when performance time nears. I submit that getting the additional personnel needed to retrieve this data (and it does not always require more) is much less costly than the list-buying that goes on year after year to reach "arts oriented potentials." We keep passing up the very patrons at our doors.

In addition to the name, address, and phone of your customers, you need the event, date and number of tickets purchased for every sale. These should be obtained at the point of purchase to eliminate any guesses. You are recording actual behavior, building a "mini-bio" on all partons. (No more guest books in the lobby, cards inserted in the program, or asking if someone wants to be on the mailing list.) You will then be able to add any contribution history, volunteer activity, etc. This can be done with simple manual systems; it does *not* require a computer. None of the more sophisticated marketing methods will be useful to anyone, regardless of the cost of software or hardware, if the raw data is not collected first.

And if word-of-mouth is the way good news travels, don't forget the people who call in for information. They must also be added to the mailing list with a date of entry and the type of event (if requested) they are interested in seeing.

Your own mailing list is your prime resource, but it is worthless unless updated and cleaned out continually (through address correction requests on the mailing pieces). It is less effective without the additional data outlined above.

Possible Ticket Plans/Packages

The plans and packages, a combination of program, pricing, and scheduling, are simplified on the guideline from the following more detailed choices:

Season Tickets

- Packaging all or most of the productions, usually with
  —additional benefits or perks
  —some or all performances *without* discount
  —some or all performances *with* discount
  —student discount
  —senior-citizen discount
  —preview
  —gift
- Partial or "mini" season-ticket package:
  —Commuter specials for long-distance customers
  —"Spring" packages; grouping last several productions
- Family packages for full or partial seasons, including special prices for children
- Passes:
  —Admission to all or selected events, first-come-first
  —served basis; can be linked to tax-deductible contribution
  —costing more than full price.

Single Tickets

- Full price
- Discounted by putting on "advance sale"
- Voucher plans Example: TDF in NYC; MAT in Minn.
- Discount Chits:
  —Can be of any value for any performance—dollar-off coupons/
  —two-fers, etc., distributed to selected targets by mail, hand
  —distribution, etc.
- Rush tickets (discount offer for day of or hour prior to curtain)
- Half-price ticket booths (initiated by the TDF "TKTS" booth in NYC)

Many cities are now offering this service to arts organizations, Arts councils/consortia can cooperate in forming this most advantageous method of dispersing unsold tickets at the last minute.

- Very low priced tickets, such as 50¢ for disadvantaged
- Gift certificates
- Coupon books, especially for college students, flexible use; can be redeemed under a variety of stipulations;

Free

- Tickets distributed to underprivileged through such organizations as Hospital Audiences. If your community does not have such an outlet, one can be formed through the arts council or a consortium.
- Promotional tie-ins/give-aways
- Introductory offers to carefully selected targets.

NOTE: At any time the potential buyer/or recipient of a free ticket is a newcomer to your organization, don't give them the worst seats in the house. This is *not* the way to convince them that they should return. Give them the best experience possible.

Selecting the Appropriate Mix of Plans/Packages:

It is at this point that the question of subscriptions/season tickets finally comes up! Packaging a series of events and placing them on sale by subscription not only assumes that a subscription base for the institution is warranted, it also means that the institution will provide money for the campaign, staff to execute the various elements of the campaign, for the box office personnel to handle the increased clerical demands, extra benefits for the subscriber beyond tickets, and manpower with which to obtain those extra benefits, and will continue servicing the subscribers with additional materials to further involve them in the process and enlist their participation in future seasons (maintenance).

Subscription campaigns and subscriber services are an investment. They cannot be dealt with halfway and still be expected to reach the big numbers for which they are so famous and pay off in future seasons. They are also no guarantee. Careful projections (new and renewal) should be made, and expenses should not all go into one basket, especially the subscription basket, until a secure base is evident and other sales programs have also been tested.

Plan ahead for the still unsold ticket:

Choose from the several methods listed above: Rush tickets, half-price ticket booths, give-aways to the disadvantaged, or selected new targets. The objective should be to fill the remaining seats with the next line of "potential" for *your* institution or provide a community service with them. This objective will vary from year to year, and yours will be different from that of other arts organizations in your area or another region. Choose carefully, and don't wait until the last minute to decide which plans to use.

Sales Methods/Tools

At the risk of repeating the obvious: to choose the right tools to carry the message about your sales plan/package to a specific target audience, you must understand what messages can or cannot be conveyed, the frequency of use required for effective results, and the extent and limitations of each tool.

The Message Match Up

To expand on this concept, I have prepared a chart including five general message categories:
1.) Describe the product
2.) What's in it for the buyer?
3.) Answer their questions
4.) Tell them what to do and how; request action
5.) Provide support testimonial and match it with some of the basic tools/sales methods to evaluate the levels of communication reached and the obvious visual and verbal potential of each.

If, for example, you have decided that the benefits (beyond the product itself) of a particular package are the most important items to attract a particular target, you should read across the chart (horizontally). It will quickly become apparent which tools will best serve this purpose.

The Target Audience Match Up

Your target audiences should be divided into two groups, those who are current customers (renewals) and those who are prospective buyers (new). You should be speaking to each target directly and specifically. Some general marketing concepts to keep in mind:

Current customers (renewals) are more responsive to mail and can withstand a higher frequency of contact with more copy and greater design variety than

Prospective buyers (new) for whom the goal is to build an identity and credibility, using design continuity extensively with less copy.

Letterpacks vs. Brochures

A letterpack will involve the receiver more fully, it can say more, it can be personalized, and the response can be made easy with personalized order forms and return envelopes. Letterpacks generally yield a higher return than brochures. Because they are more expensive, it is imperative that you send them to the prime targets, without duplications; a return to the argument for maintaining your mailing list with a complete listing of all buyers and interested prospects.

CAMPAIGN ANALYSIS FORM

_____ Source Code

_____ Source Name

_____ Dates Mailed

_____ Quantity/Circulation

COST ALLOCATIONS: Accounting Ref. #:

_____ Creative Concept/Design   _____

_____ Photography   _____

_____ Type/Stats   _____

_____ Paste-Up/Mechanical   _____

_____ Printing   _____

_____ List Rental/Labels   _____

_____ Addressing (sort, tie, bundle)   _____

_____ Postage (@ $_____)   _____

_____ Advertising Space/Time (net)   _____

Enclosures:

_____ _____ _____

_____ _____ _____

_____ _____ _____

_____ _____ _____

_____ _____ _____

_____ Total Distribution

_____ Total Sold

_____ % Return

_____ Cost per _____

_____ Cost per dollar of income

_____

_____

The Front Line of Sales

Although a great deal of emphasis has recently been placed on organization and business management of the arts, there are two aspects of marketing lessons learned from the profit sector that seem to elude many. One is the efficacy of data retrieval just discussed, the other is the front line of sales.

In the case of the arts, this means the box office. Poor servicing of the buyer does not, unfortunately, ensure doom in the not-for-profit arts, and so we find some of the lowest paid personnel, working in small, unmanageable quarters. Often, they are using unwieldy or ineffective accounting systems, they have too few phones, windows, and staff for the volume, with little or no information about the product. And then we say to them, _sell!_—convert single-ticket buyers into subscribers, be kind and pleasant at all times, account for every penny, retrieve data, and never put the phones on hold. Unfortunately, we fail to give these people a hit every time out!

This must be part of the on-going planning. It is the job of the marketing personnel to work closely with the box-office personnel in every area of the sales. They must see order forms, price grids and ordering directions _before_ they are printed and mailed, they must be trained to be the best salespeople possible, they must be fully acquainted with the product, and their environment must be the most efficient and cheerful possible.

This Is A People business, Folks!

All of the slickest tools and methods are no substitute for common sense and instinct, which are basic. And they are _free_! Listen to yourself—develop your own sensibilities, your own subjective views and ideas. Talk with the people inside your organization—your artists, your production personnel, your box office and your partons. Make *person-to-person* contacts in your community, know your customers' needs and desires. Trade information with other colleagues, work with the knowledge you get from the shared information. Play with your own data—3x5 mailing list cards; zip analysis, printouts, coding charts—make the information your own. It's a slow build, but it lasts.

As you plan the groups to go after and the tools and methods you will use, keep in mind that we do have audience-development responsibilities. The artist is only one aspect of the creative process—the spectator by his active response completes the cycle. We run the risk of losing the original concept of helping audiences grow, differentiate, and evolve if we think only in terms of corralling ticket buyers.

The fight is no longer to recognize the need for sound "marketing" programs in the arts, thanks to the many foundations, service organizations and innovative individuals in the profession. What we do have to fight for and remember is what we are marketing. We must learn new methods, reevaluate the old, select carefully, and plan in detail. At the same time, we must *not* relinquish the unique identity of our own institution, our own special product, our own artists. A great deal can be lost if the process becomes more important than the product.

The Planning Schedule

It is *not* yet time to sit down with your designer and make your brochure!

It is now time to get out a blank calendar—a full 12-month one please—and begin to plot the *timing* of the use of the various tools which you have selected. Having no schedule or only a poorly executed one can minimize the effect of precious dollars and available manpower.

Your schedule should also include time for research into the use of various tools such as telemarketing; continuing meetings with the artistic personnel; meetings with designers; education of box-office personnel as to content, plan, production, data retrieval; and the full plan for ordering of materials. (A "Materials Planning Chart" page 17 will assist in bulk ordering of paper supplies. This is much less expensive than ordering them as you need them.)

Plot every element of the campaign right on through the final performance. Do not take it one step at a time. This produces *crisis campaign management,* and it makes everybody nervous. If you are running a subscription campaign, it does not stop there. The plan must continue through all single ticket sales efforts...and they need to be on the calendar as well as in the budget!

The calendar will become a yardstick (like the budget) as to what you can and cannot do. There are limitations, and you must be prepared for them in advance. There are no tricks for this, no charts, no graphs—you JUST DO IT.

The Final Guideline:

If you can't do it well; don't do it.

Plan only those things which you can complete, and complete well in their entirety, including a tasteful and correct representation of your organization, whether through the mail, on the phone, or in person.

What To Do With Them Once You've Got 'Em

No less important than getting an audience is *keeping* it. This is a job that requires careful maintenance.

Maintenance must begin the moment the purchase begins. Cheerful and informed personnel at the box-office are the partons' first contact with your theater. If the buyer is purchasing a single ticket, he can be told in person and/or informed by mail of other events and/or other ticket purchase plans which your organization might be offering. If the buyer is purchasing a subscription, you should begin a full plan of maintaining contact for the year.

The *first* year a patron becomes a subscriber is the *most critical.* He should receive many more contacts by mail than those subscribers who have been coming for several years. A sample plan might be:

- Immediate acknowledgement of the order(confirmation) within twenty-four to forty-eight hours.
—A second excuse to mail within 3 to 4 weeks of receipt of the order — background on the theater; newsletter; or other such perk.
- Further information on the productions; an announcement card of a special event; and invitation to a tour or seminar or some other personal touch three to four weeks after the second mailing.
- A subscriber handbook or coupon book detailing all of the benefits you have advertised with their subscription, mailed with their tickets. Another letter and any special-event notice which might be appropriate, mailed approximately four to six weeks prior to opening of first production.
- Another newsletter; program; profiles of the company — some in-depth materials which further involve the patron, mailed after the first production.
—Post-card announcements for special events, reminders for subscription events with single-ticket offers for friends, etc.
—A special treat such as a poster, calendar, or souvenir program.

Subscribers who have been coming for more than one year can receive fewer mailings, but must not be forgotten. Suggest that they get those marked with a bullet above and any new posters or souvenir programs they might not have received in prior years.

Subscription Brochure Checklist

Outside Mailing Panel

- ( ) Name, return address
- ( ) Bulk-rate indicia
- ( ) Address correction request optional
- ( ) Sell line; photographs; quotes

Interior (options)

- ( ) Play Titles and blurbs
- ( ) Quotes (Message from producer/artistic director, etc. or quotes to cover such)
- ( ) Production photographs
- ( ) Company photographs
- ( ) Photographers credit lines
- ( ) Map and directions to the theater
- ( ) Discount (with deadline clearly delineated)
- ( ) Benefits of subscribing with short blurbs describing each
- ( ) Titles and casting are subject to change (disclaimer)

"Bottom Line Material"
**These items should be near each other and on the same side of the brochure.

- ( ) **PRICE GRID (make any discounts clear)
- ( ) **SCHEDULE GRID (note any performances sold out with an * or write "Sold Out" across grid)
- ( ) **HOW TO ORDER instructions
- ( ) ORDER FORM (heavy dotted line around order form with the words "Order Form" prominent)
    —Name, address, city, state, zip lines
    —Daytime phone line/evening phone line
    —Order spaces and total column
    —Contribution line
    —Payment block
      Make checks payable to _____
      Charge acct. # lines or boxes with expiration date line and signature line if required by bank

—Request for stamped self-addressed envelope
—Coding box (for office use only)
—any qualifiers or ID's required for special discount offers
( ) Subscription office telephone number
   PLUS ... CODE EVERYTHING IN THE CODING BOX! (by hand if necessary!)

Subscription-Based Audience

PROS:

- Money up front
- Bodies to fill the seats of non-hits as well as hits
- Builds a body of people who may likely become further involved with the organization through volunteering; contributing; serving on the board
- a leverage for foundation and corporate support which requires a "display" of community desire/need/involvement
- initial high cost for procurement; renewal gradually less and less expensive

CONS:

- inherent costs (money and manpower) usually not considered when evaluating the basically low cost of renewal such as:

  —Processing:
  strip tickets more expensive than regular tickets
  forms and other supplies
  personnel
  space/utilities
  phone (separate hotlines etc.)
  data retrieval

  —Benefits:
  manpower to obtain them (restaurant deals; etc.)
  expense in handbooks, coupon books etc. to display the benefits
  manpower to carry out some of the perks (tours, parties, etc.)
  some benefits selected can require an actual purchase such as totes, cookbooks etc.; and priority discounts on special events are also actual costs as is the discount itself (if offered) on the subscription

  —Analysis/Maintenance:
  must be ongoing year to year; keeping careful records of all purchases/trends
  First-year subscribers must receive additional maintenance being contacted more often throughout the year
  All subscribers must receive in-depth communications regarding the organization

  —Personal contact:
  needed to keep renewal rates high; prevent attrition; requires manpower (paid or volunteer)

- Can ultimately provide a "sterile," homogeneous audience base if great care is not taken to solicit a "mix"
- If discounting subscription tickets, the best seats on prime times are being sold to the most likely buyer for the least amount of money. They then must be re-solicited for a contribution to make up the difference.

  To balance this, a careful analysis of the discount (section by section/performance by performance) can determine whether or not the discount is necessary. In many cases, first choice of seating and performance time may be enough for the subscribing patron.

THE TOOLS	Direct Mail		Telephone	Broadcast Media		Print Ads
	BROCHURE/FLYER	LETTERPACK		RADIO	*TV	NEWSPAPER & MAGAZINE
THE MESSAGE	(CONVICTION)		(PURCHASE)	(COMPREHENSION)		(COMPREHENSION)
1. *Describe Product*	Visual &Verbal	more detail available	*only verbal*	Verbal (audio: words, sound, music)	Verbal & Visual	Verbal & Visual (less effective than direct mail)
2. *What's In It For the Buyer (Benies)*	Visual & Verbal	more detail available	full explanation available— *no visual*	minimal detail available		similar to brochure, less effective
3. *Answer Their Questions*	Visual & Verbal	more detail available	most efficient possible	very little potential		very little potential unless very large ad
4. *Tell Them What To Do and How*	Visual & Verbal	can be *fully* personalized	limited to changes for immediate action	minimal potential		similar to brochure, less effective
5. *Provide Support Testimonial*	Visual & Verbal	more extensive	limited compared to direct mail because *full* testimonies cannot be read	little or none with the exception of singular quotes		

*local cable affiliates may offer greater coverage depending on the area

THE TOOLS	Posters	Billboards Transit Ads	Tent Cards Bookmarks Placemats	In-House Publications (newsletters/programs/magazines/study guides/in-depth profiles)	Publicity (print and broadcast media, both news and feature stories)
THE MESSAGE	(COMPREHENSION)	(AWARENESS)	(COMPREHENSION)	(CONVICTION)	(CONVICTION)
1. **Describe Product**	choice of visual or verbal—limited to one short and simple message		can be detailed reminder/usually heavy verbal	Visual & Verbal	Visual & Verbal Extensive potential
2. **Same as #2 Above**	minimal, if any		minimal	extensive potential	Extensive potential to answer needs by describing arts experience. Minimal in describing tangible benies connected to the sale
3. **Same as #3 Above**	very minimal		very minimal, if any	detail available, limitations similar to letterpacks	High Potential answering questions related to arts experience. Minimal in answering specific questions related to sale
4. **Same as #4 Above**	very minimal		minimal	not personalized, but can be detailed fully	Minimal
5. **Same as #5 Above**				can be detailed as extensively as desired	Extensive potential (especially reviews) but mostly beyond marketer's control

The Money & Manpower Match Up

One of the most important references for "tool study" is Danny Newman, the father of subscription campaign methods. His tireless pursuit across the country, developing a seemingly endless list of sales techniques has given us untold choices and examples. They are not detailed here, as they are available in his own publication, *Subscribe Now.* The Scale & Zeal chart that follows is my breakdown of Danny's tools. I divide them between those which basically require money and those which require manpower to be used effectively. Selection among these must be directly related to the needs of the target audience *and* to the ability of your organization *at the time* to carry them out.

Scale & Zeal Chart

This chart summarizes many of the subscription campaign methods developed by Danny Newman, TCG, and Ford Foundation Subscription Consultant. I have chosen to present them in this skeletal form in order to indicate a mass saturation and personalized sales differential, as well as to reflect an *expense* and *manpower* division.

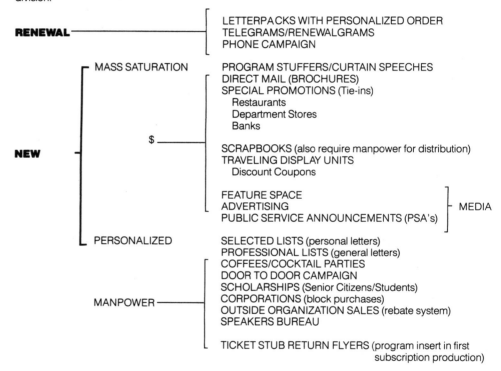

Money (Mass Saturation)

The tools that fall into these categories basically have been used for mass saturation and inherent in them is *cost*. In some cases the items can be promoted (obtained for free) but in general, they must be budgeted. Keep in mind that repeat mailings of brochures to large numbers is an integral part of these campaigns, but they are expensive and must be planned carefully.

Manpower (Personalization)

One of the most important of Danny's campaign innovations was the personalization of so many of his techniques. Those organizations that have been successful with his methods were relentless in the use of these particular tools. They recruited countless volunteers to carry them out. These volunteers provided a very special one-to-one contact with the patrons, and they were free. It will be an accident of history if the brochure becomes the monument to his success, a centerpiece perhaps, but not the driving force.

The importance of personalization is also apparent in the newer phenomenon of *telemarketing*. (One would think the phone had just been invented yesterday!) The big difference in this "personalized" tool is that it moves out of the manpower category into the money one. Red flag material—all costs must be evaluated. In addition to the phone manager's fees and solicitation commissions, there are hidden expenses, such as additional space requirements, phone equipment (set-up and maintenance), clerical assistance, list procurement, staff time, office supplies, and utilities. Budgeting must also account for the significant attrition rate, often quite a bit higher than that of other sales methods. Consideration should also be given to the product you are selling compared to that offered by groups that have been successful using this method. Because this tool does have a high "purchase" communication value, it should be considered seriously, but evaluated carefully.

All of these direct-mail contacts are to enhance the patron's knowledge of the organization, not to solicit for further funds. The latter can be carefully planned within the above program, but not in replacement of it. *Involve* them first (throughout the year); *solicit* second; *renew* third.

Data Retrieval And Analysis

Probably the most often avoided aspect of the marketing plan (even though everyone seems to love to use those words now) is the tracking of each tool and results for a cost-benefit analysis. If, for example, a direct-mail piece is not coded for each list purchased, the returns cannot be analyzed demographically, the worth of the list cannot be evaluated, and the cost per ticket sold is lost. The fact that coding and tracking costs a certain minimal amount is never a legitimate excuse for not doing it. If each full campaign is to be a test in itself, and if this is the most expensive and lengthy method of testing, we must pay for additional coding and track *everything*.

As the coded forms are returned, they can be charted by day of return, zip code, series (performance day), new versus renewal, and source (the piece itself). These charts can be drawn up by hand in any number of ways. Just get the information and put it down. I have provided a sample of a source coding chart (See Campaign Analysis Form, page 20); which will give an accurate, detailed analysis of the entire campaign when the information is all combined.

All of these direct-mail contacts are to enhance the patron's knowledge of the organization, not to solicit for further funds. The latter can be carefully planned within the above program, but not in replacement of it. *Involve* them first (throughout the year), *solicit* second; *renew* third.

Data Retrieval And Analysis

Probably the most often avoided aspect of the marketing plan (even though everyone seems to love to use those words now) is the tracking of each tool and results for a cost/benefit analysis. If, for example, a direct-mail piece is not coded for each list purchased, the returns cannot be analyzed demographically, the worth of the list cannot be evaluated, and the cost per ticket sold is lost. The fact that coding and tracking costs a certain minimal amount is never a legitimate excuse for not doing it. If each full campaign is to be a test in itself, and if this is the most expensive and lengthy method of testing, we must pay for additional coding and track *everything*.

As the coded forms are returned, they can be charted by day of return, zip code, series (performance day), new versus renewal, and source (the price itself). These charts can be drawn up by hand in any number of ways. Just get the information and put it down. I have provided a sample of a source coding chart (See Campaign Analysis Form, page 20); which will give an accurate, detailed analysis of the entire campaign when the information is all combined.

MATERIALS PLANNING CHART

LIST TO BE USED	QUANTITY	SOURCE OF LISTS	WHO WILL MAIL (MAILING HOUSE, BANK TRANSFER CO., ETC.)	LIST DATES			CLASS OF MAIL			ENVELOPE PRINTING					ENCLOSURES						CODE	OTHER
				ORDERED	RECEIVED	TO BE MAILED	1st CLASS	3rd CLASS	BULK	STOCK ORDERED	1st CLASS	BULK RATE INDICIA	RET. ADDRESS	SLOGAN	RET. ENV.	RET. ORDER FORM	SCHEDULE/ PRICE GRID	FLYER/ BROCHURE	PERSONAL LETTER			

SUBSCRIPTION PRELIMINARY COUNT

Month _____

SUNDAY	MONDAY	TUESDAY	WEDNESDAY	THURSDAY	FRIDAY	SATURDAY
OLD___ NEW___ HOUSEHOLDS___ CUM___	OLD___ NEW___ HOUSEHOLDS___ CUM___	OLD___ NEW___ HOUSEHOLDS___ CUM___	OLD___ NEW___ HOUSEHOLDS___ CUM___	OLD___ NEW___ HOUSEHOLDS___ CUM___	OLD___ NEW___ HOUSEHOLDS___ CUM___	OLD___ NEW___ HOUSEHOLDS___ CUM___
OLD___ NEW___ HOUSEHOLDS___ CUM___	OLD___ NEW___ HOUSEHOLDS___ CUM___	OLD___ NEW___ HOUSEHOLDS___ CUM___	OLD___ NEW___ HOUSEHOLDS___ CUM___	OLD___ NEW___ HOUSEHOLDS___ CUM___	OLD___ NEW___ HOUSEHOLDS___ CUM___	OLD___ NEW___ HOUSEHOLDS___ CUM___
OLD___ NEW___ HOUSEHOLDS___ CUM___	OLD___ NEW___ HOUSEHOLDS___ CUM___	OLD___ NEW___ HOUSEHOLDS___ CUM___	OLD___ NEW___ HOUSEHOLDS___ CUM___	OLD___ NEW___ HOUSEHOLDS___ CUM___	OLD___ NEW___ HOUSEHOLDS___ CUM___	OLD___ NEW___ HOUSEHOLDS___ CUM___
OLD___ NEW___ HOUSEHOLDS___ CUM___	OLD___ NEW___ HOUSEHOLDS___ CUM___	OLD___ NEW___ HOUSEHOLDS___ CUM___	OLD___ NEW___ HOUSEHOLDS___ CUM___	OLD___ NEW___ HOUSEHOLDS___ CUM___	OLD___ NEW___ HOUSEHOLDS___ CUM___	OLD___ NEW___ HOUSEHOLDS___ CUM___
OLD___ NEW___ HOUSEHOLDS___ CUM___	OLD___ NEW___ HOUSEHOLDS___ CUM___	OLD___ NEW___ HOUSEHOLDS___ CUM___	OLD___ NEW___ HOUSEHOLDS___ CUM___	OLD___ NEW___ HOUSEHOLDS___ CUM___	OLD___ NEW___ HOUSEHOLDS___ CUM___	

Week of: _____

Weekly Subscription Tally

								RUNNING TOTAL
CODE								
BALANCE								
RENEWAL								
BALANCE								
NEW								
BALANCE								
THIS WEEK TOTAL								
TOTAL								

SEASON SUBSCRIPTION ANALYSIS

PIECE (CODE OR COMB. CODE)											TOTALS
RENEWAL											
NEW											
TOTAL											
TOTAL DISTRIB.											
% RETURN											
COST OF PIECE (TOTAL)											
COST PER PIECE RETURNED											

WEEKLY SALES REPORT—SUBSCRIPTION SERIES COUNT

_____ **Season**

Page _____

SERIES										TOTAL
THIS WEEK										
TOTAL TO DATE										
%										
*FINAL TOTAL ___										
%										
*FINAL TOTAL ___										
%										

Divide this area to your *actual* number of subscription performances (series)

*Previous seasons

Michael Prewitt

PRODUCTION

You want to put people in seats—to sell out the house for a play, a ballet, an opera, a symphony. On any given night, you've got sixty-four TV channels, the bestseller list, King Tut or his current blockbuster equivalent at the museum, a special issue of the latest *Now* magazine—all of these to compete with.

How do you cut through all their high-priced promotion to speak with a simple, strong voice that will move *your* audience from hearth and home to your drafty—or stuffy—theater? Not an easy mission.

The first task is to get back to basics. You are selling a product. You have an audience—a market—to sell to. And you have in your tool kit various marketing activities that can connect your product with its market.

Michael Prewitt is Creative Head of DANA, an advertising agency in Princeton, New Jersey. DANA's clients include American Bell, Western Electric, Dow Jones, Mellon Bank and Pilobolus.

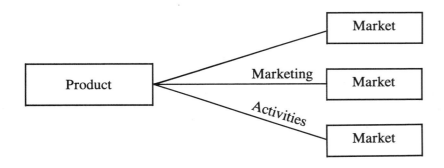

How do you put together those three elements to produce the result you want—putting people in seats?

This chapter (along with a dramatic interlude) is about putting people in seats. It's about the processes you use (or could use) to make your job as successful (and painless) as possible.

"Hey, Lady, Here's Your Creative"

Curtain rises on a cold, damp office in the basement of the New Repertory Theater. The office is filled with desks, their unanswered phones ringing incessantly. Piles of last year's subscription brochures lie around, yellowing posters of past productions are taped to the wall, two weeks accumulation of styrofoam coffee cups and this week's *Variety* are also in evidence. This is the war room, the place where the work gets done.

Enter Bill, the ad agency rep. He is in his early thirties, wearing New Balance running shoes, tan corduroys, and an oxford-cloth shirt with a string tie. He's got a portfolio under his arm. Madison Avenue not only runs the length of Manhattan, it threads its way through nearly every town in America.

Enter New Rep's marketing director. She is ageless, with unlimited energy and sporadically intense concentration. She makes her way through this engine room of an office like Katharine Hepburn in *The Desk Set*.

MARKETING DIRECTOR: Well, what have you got to show me?

BILL: We've been working night and day on this piece since you hired us. I've got the boards here in my portfolio, and I thought I'd run them by you before we go to press. Do you have a few minutes.

M.D.: A few minutes? I thought you folks would bring me some rough concepts and then we'd talk about the direction of the campaign.

BILL: Well, we went to the library and took out all the plays. We've got a first-class research group, remember. Then the creative team got hot, and we came up with this concept for the plays in the season. We figured it's the Eighties, so what the hell, computer graphics seem to say it all. We got this graphics shop downtown with a real knack for interpreting the classics on a computer screen. They did *Hamlet*—and we were knocked out. I mean, we went nuts when we saw the stuff. So we rolled out the concept for all six plays. Wait till you see this art.

M.D. But I haven't even briefed you on the company and our marketing problems.

BILL: But we're more of a creative boutique. We believe in The Big Idea. Research, analysis, demos—that's for the big, gray agencies. Haven't you read your David Ogilvy?

M.D.: So let me see these big ideas. But what if they're not right for us? What if we have to make changes?

BILL: Changes? You haven't even seen this dynamite stuff and you're talking changes. Don't worry—we abide by the industry standards. You know, AA's and all that…We've got you covered.

THE END

What follows could be your antidote for situations like the preceding one.

Putting Together the Marketing Team

As marketing director, you have clients you have to respond to. An artist, a managing director, a board member on the "marketing committee," the board chairman, and God knows who else. From the outset, be careful to identify all the interested parties and to involve them at the right time. (The last thing you want is an interested party coming out of the woodwork, just as your job is about to be produced.)

Now, the good news: You can have control over the other member of your marketing team: your agency. (You could hire a single, free-lance designer and writer, a design firm, or a full-service advertising agency. But to simplify things, let's call this member of the team, The agency.)

You and Your Agency

Choosing—Which One?

Here's where you get to be client. In exchange for dollars, a few cups of coffee, and some comps on opening night, you get to sit back and watch creative geniuses at work. If only it were that simple! Good marketing (especially good creative marketing), is a collaborative process that naturally begins with selecting the right agency for you and your product.

The first criterion is *chemistry*. After all, you and your agency are about to bring some new ideas and images into the world. The partnership had better be one of trust, respect—even caring. Visit the agency's shop and meet the people who wil be working on your business. Ask to see how they've solved other marketing problems. Don't get caught up in finding a firm that *specializes* in the arts. You're looking for people who can wrestle with your product and distill your message down to a simple promise, then take that message to the right people. That task *doesn't* require in-depth knowledge of Wagner's Ring Cycle or years of work with the local summer-stock company. Arts advertising and design are really disciplines that don't require specialization. A good agency will quickly get up to speed on the con-

"You will profit from the fresh perspective that an agency will bring to your marketing activities."

ventional marketing activities in your category.

There are two major reasons why you shouldn't limit your agency to arts specialists:

1. Good agencies routinely handle a variety of marketing problems for an array of clients. Agencies can rarely afford the luxury of specializing on a stable of clients, all from the same industry. Clients are naturally sensitive to conflict-of-interest issues. If an agency is working for one bank, it is usually locked out of seeking other bank clients. Consequently, agencies have been forced to develop methods of getting up to speed quickly on the effective marketing activities in any given business category.

2. You will profit from the fresh perspective that an agency will bring to your marketing activities. From the agency perspective, marketing the arts is, first and foremost, a marketing problem.

Once you've broadened your horizons to the widest range of possible choices, try to narrow the field by defining just what you need (and can afford) in an agency. Most agency services fall under the following categories:

Account Management. Usually the marketing function. These people help the client decide how to position their product, what markets to go after, and what marketing activities to employ. Your budget and level of experience will determine whether you need this function.

Research. The market-research function will help you narrow your position, refine your targets, rank and test the effectiveness of your marketing activities. Again, your experience and budget will determine if you need this agency service.

Media. Media people have become more and more important as the variety of marketing activities available has grown. They can help you decide how much of your budget should go into TV, radio, direct response, print, etc. They'll also help you decide on the schedule of these activities. Beyond media planning, an agency is set up to buy the space, time, mailing effort, etc.

Creative. Even if you can't afford or don't need the other agency services, you've come to the agency for its creative services. One agency I worked for used to describe itself as, "Nothing but Ideas." In a way, that's true. Copywriters, designers, art directors, illustrators, photographers—they're all in the business of ideas. You need them.

> "Why reinvent the wheel? If something has worked for the competition or your cohorts in another city, why shouldn't you use it?"

In selecting an agency, it's important to set up a competitive situation—it's good for all concerned. Try to find at least two agencies to choose from. An agency will work harder on its presentation and proposals if they know there is a choice involved. You will benefit from seeing different perspectives brought to the table.

In fairness to the agencies, don't ask for chapter and verse on how they'd solve your problems. You don't need that to make your choice. And, as you'll find out below, the best creative work, will happen *after* you hire the agency anyway.

Here are some of the questions you should ask the agencies who are competing for your account:

- How have they solved other marketing problems or developed other creative concepts?
- What were the results of these campaigns?
- How would they structure a relationship with you?
- What would they charge for their services and how would they bill?
- Who would be working on your business?

Once you've chosen the competitors, make sure you've cleaned up the selection process. Have you asked each agency to present the same things? Have you involved the right people from your organization in the choice?

One final words about chemistry. Imagine that you've hired one of the agencies you've looked at. Imagine that you come back from lunch and there is one of those pink "while-you-were-out" slips on your desk. Beyond all the hype and awards and clients lists of the agency, do you look forward to returning the call? If you do, that's good chemistry.

"Try to distill your message to the fewest possible words and a visual image."

Prepping the Agency

Nobody is going to come up with your company's campaign from a dream in the middle of the night. You've got to work hard to prepare your agency for their job. (The harder you work for them, the harder they'll work for you.)

First, show them what you've done in the past, both creative and media, what has worked and what hasn't. Beyond specifics, what has your company's image been? How has this image affected sales? Do you want to build on the image or alter it? Start by immersing the agency in your history.

Second, what are your competitors and counterparts doing? If you don't have a file of competitive work, build one. Why reinvent the wheel? If something has worked for the competition or for your cohorts in another city, why *shouldn't* you use it? Once you have these materials on hand, sit down with your agency and do a competitive analysis—products, markets, marketing activities.

Third, do some opinion research. What do ticket buyers—and non-buyers—think of your product? Pricing? Length of run? Variety of your offerings?

With these facts in front of you and your agency, you'll all be better prepared for the concept-development stage of the work.

Concept Development

The concept meeting is a time to get everybody together to think out the direction of the campaign. You and the agency can structure the discussion with a presentation of your analysis, or you can use the meeting as an open-ended discussion to draw out additional ideas and perspectives from your artist, managing director, board members, etc. In either case, the meeting or meetings should cover:

- The product—position, cost, benefits
- The market
- Marketing activities

Try to keep the discussion as open as possible. This is your chance to let everybody have his say.

Insist that the agency be secretary for this meeting. Collect all the ideas generated during the meeting in a systematic way. Once you have collected all these ideas, ask the agency to do a *design brief.* A design brief is a distillation of the best thinking of your marketing team into a statement that the agency can use as the cornerstone of its work. A few years ago, a rental car company distilled its marketing situation to a few simple words in a design brief: In "renting cars, we are number two. We have to try harder." Out of that design brief came a somewhat memorable advertising campaign.

The other advantage of the concept meeting is, frankly, a political one. You have done your best to involve everybody concerned in the process. Once you've collected and distilled everybody's thoughts in a brief, you have a mandate for your work with the agency. If all goes well, you can avoid the design-by-committee stuff that kills so much creative work.

Try to discipline the agency into putting its design brief on a single sheet of paper. Make the direction as simple as possible. Circulate the design brief, and get all the players to sign off on it. Now you're ready to go to work.

Roughs

Good agency work is a process of refining. Don't ask for finished work at the beginning. There are lots of creative ways to show a concept without taking the final photographs or typesetting the rough copy. Be sure you let the agency know that you want to see *rough layouts.* This stage is critical for review and approval. Without going to extreme effort and expense, the agency can present a concept, a direction to you and your team. If there are problems or major revisions, you haven't incurred any huge costs. (On the subject of costs, put the burden on your agency to define what each stage of the process will cost. That way, you can hold them to their rules and avoid the nasty surprise of costly revisions.)

For example, let's say the agency sets the type on the brochure, and it doesn't fit. If they've accepted your copy, then it's likely to be their problem and their expense to reset the copy or shorten the text. If, on the other hand, you change the copy by changing one of your programs, then it's your change and your expense. By spelling out who is responsible for changes up front, nobody will be surprised when the final bill is submitted.

Comprehensive Layouts

Another vague term from those wonderful folks in the ad biz. A *comp.* (comprehensive layout) is as close to the finished product as can be realized without going into full production.

This stage in the process should get a thorough review from all concerned parties. From now on, things start to get expensive, and everybody should know this. "Speak now, or forever..." should be the password.

Proofs

One of the great ironies of our business is that just when you're called on to be your most precise and nit-picky, you're also involved in the hysteria of deadlines —insertion closings, press dates, printing schedules. It's a wonder that anything gets "spellt" correctly.

A proof is the great safety net of the creative world. Suddenly there appears on your desk an innocent-looking piece of blueprint paper called a blue line, a blue proof, a brown print, or some such jargon. Beware! Take a deep breath. Take a run around the block. If you sign that proof, and there is a typo in the headline like,

> *"A Steetcar Named Desire* Opens New Season,"

you bought it. All 750,000 copies of your brochure are yours for the rest of your life.

Whatever the job costs, you have to pay it. If your artistic director demands a reprint, then you have to print the job again. If the press is busy and can't do the job till next month, then...

I don't need to go on.

A proof is one of the holy of holies in our business. If you're not in a frame of mind to review it, checking all the type for accuracy, making sure the right captions are under the right pictures, seeing that page four comes before page five, then find your most compulsive colleague, lock him in a room and tell him there's a bottle of Chateau Margaux '61 in it for him if he gets it right (or at least a nice cold beer).

The agency also has some responsibility here. Make sure they give you enough time in the production schedule to proof the job thoroughly. The last thing you need is a crazed messenger on his way to the printer or video house telling you to sign on the line in the next ten minutes or you'll blow the deadline.

Production Quality Check

Visit the production house (printer, video, radio, etc.) with your agency when they're ready to roll. Insist that you sign a copy of your work when you're satisfied that they've achieved the best possible quality. Then insist that all the copies look like the one you signed.

Creative Guideposts

1. The Billboard Communication Technique.

We are all bombarded with thousands of messages every day. Your message is going to compete with all of these other messages, most of which will be seen or heard many more times than yours. Think of it this way. You're driving on a superhighway. You see a billboard for a couple of seconds, then it's gone.

Try to distill your message to the fewest possible words and a visual image. Maybe just the words. If you haven't gotten the audience's attention and made your point in the time it takes to pass a billboard, you're finished.

"Copywriters, designers, art directors, illustrators, photographers— they're all in the business of ideas. You need them."

2. One simple message, over and over

Distill your message down for effective billboard communication, then repeat it over and over again. Brochures, ads, TV, radio, the mail—use the same simple message until you're sick of it. That way more people will see it—and remember it—for the first time.

3. Family Resemblance

Make all your messages look, sound, feel alike. If you use Times Roman Bold type and a cartoon to announce *Hamlet,* then use Times Roman Bold type and a cartoon to announce *Nicholas Nickleby.*

4. Good Old Black & White

Edward Steichen said, "The possibilities of the Kodak box camera have never been fully explored." It's the same for good old black & white. Besides being cheaper (no small benefit), black & white gives you the impact of graphic communications at its most basic. In a world that insists on using color for more and more messages, your message will stand out and have even greater impact. This point has the greatest application to newsprint. Most newspaper ads take on a mottled gray look. Create an ad with heavy white or black; and you're sure to dominate a page (the logo for the Broadway production of *Equus* comes to mind as a memorable graphic which never failed to attract the eye to its space).

The simple, strong outline of the horse head became an icon for theatergoers. In the end, it's not just black or white that works, but *how* you use them. Strong black or strong white normally forces the design to its simplest form.

5. Photography

Studies show that people want to see what goes on in the entertainment they're about to pay good money for. Unlike a Coke or a pair of Levi's, which they've experienced before, a creative work could be something weird, something dirty, or, God forbid, something boring. The best way to advertise a creative work is within a photograph. *Show* what the audience will really *see.*

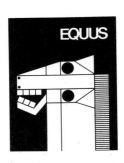

**Poster design for *Equus.* Copyright ©
Gilbert Lesser.**

6. Good creative must be on strategy: what you set out for it to do.

a) To put people in seats.
b) To position the product.
c) To position the organization.
d) To celebrate the performing arts (oh, come on).

7. The Offer

Avedon and Shakespeare together couldn't sell a campaign based on a bad offer.

Administrative Guideposts

Purchase Orders

Make the agency write your purchase orders for you. Make them as specific as the tightest contract.

On Time, On Budget

As the project manager, you have the responsibility of seeing that your jobs come in on time and on budget. Every creative job offers its own set of surprises. Some must be absorbed by the agency. Other surprises call for a conference with your agency to determine whether the additional effort—and cost—is worth it. The surprise will probably come right in the middle of the creative process, when the clock is ticking and the deadline is foremost in everybody's mind. In deciding whether to spend the extra dollars on Ansel Adams or to go with the local budding photographer (at one-third the price) keep in mind the overall impact of your piece on the audience. Sometimes the extra expense can be justified. If so, make sure you justify it with the people responsible for paying the bills. Nobody likes to okay a budget overrun after the fact.

Being on time is an art in itself. The production process outlined above is a complex undertaking. Roughs, comps, illustrations, type, proofing, blue proof, etc. etc.

Get out your calendar during the calm days at the beginning of the project. Build in some slippage days right from the start. If you need the finished job on the 25th, tell the agency you need it on the 20th. If the typesetter gets sick, or the proof gets lost in the mail, or *Carmina Burana* has to be substituted for *Swan Lake* at the last minute, you'll still make the deadline—and everybody will look good.

Barter

You have a product that is valuable to your suppliers. Barter can be an excellent way to help lower your costs. Promotion for a play, a ballet, or a symphony can be a lot more exciting as a portfolio piece than the current plumbing catalog or automobile commercial. Use your wits to see if your suppliers could take part of their payment in the form of tickets for your performances or as a mention in your playbill as one of your patrons.

Summary

Here's a list of eight reminders from this chapter:

1. Go out of your way to involve *all* the interested parties at the critical points in the marketing and creative process. Make a list: check it twice.

2. In selecting an agency, *chemistry* is the first criterion. Try to set up a competitive presentation as one of the bases for awarding the business.

3. The harder you work in preparing your agency for this job, the more they'll do for you.

4. Ask the agency to do a *design brief* which distills your strategy down to its simplest form. Use the design brief as a way to keep interested parties involved. The design brief will give the creative solution a rationale.

5. Get the agency to spell out its creative process — roughs, comprehensive layouts, proofs—and the costs of changes at each stage.

6. Good creative for arts marketing is a simple ''billboard'' message, used over and over. Black & white is the arts' most powerful (and cheapest) medium.

7. Good creative can't compensate for a bad offer.

8. Creative work always contains surprises. Protect yourself with extra time and money to allow for these surprises.

David J. Skal

DESIGNING PROMOTIONAL MATERIALS THAT WORK

For better or worse, our society is becoming a visual culture. We read less and less, watch television more and more. Verbal skills have declined even among the educated—remedial reading courses are offered at major universities everywhere. Sensory stimulation—the design, the look, the *feel*—seems to take precedence over rational communication in almost every marketing situation. The communications industry is becoming (to some) alarmingly sophisticated in its use of computer graphics and other forms of visual exotica. The resulting environment has been justifiably described as an "electronic blizzard," and, like it or not, this is the context in which your promotional materials must compete. To put it in slogan form, without the look, there is no hook.

"Hold on, you say. We're a not-for-profit *arts* group. We only deal with *direct mail*. We don't have any *money*. So what does this electornic blizzard have to do with us? Just tell us how to design our subscription brochure. It's already two weeks late.!"

Okay, okay, I *know* you're in a hurry. And I appreciate the pressure you're under. And I do intend to tell you what I know about designing effective brochures. But first I'd like you to spend a few minutes with me away from your desk, away from your deadlines, to examine just what it is we expect and what we *should* expect from this mysterious process called "graphic design." (You do have the time. The reason your brochure is late is because your artistic director hasn't picked his season yet. So, relax.)

To me, design is the most crucial and most often ignored element of arts promotion. Think about it—all your plannning, all your budget, all your copy, all your organization's projected income finally hangs on one thing; that is, the potential audience member's split-second reaction to a two-dimensional arrangement of ink on paper, a split second in which a hundred little conclusions are reached. Is this important? Is this professional? Is this interesting? Does this remind me of anything? Is this going to be difficult to read? Is this something for rich people? Does this have anything to do with me? Is this feminine? Is this masculine? Is this *too* masculine/feminine? How do I feel about my masculinity/femininity?

And so on. All of this happens before any of the *content* of the brochure or advertisement has been consciously absorbed. And it is here that graphic design becomes your critical element. Design is, very simply, the means by which you get your message off the paper and into the head of your audience where it can do its work.

While it is not an exact science, good design can be analyzed. It can often be best defined by what it is not. It is not decoration or embellishment. It is not merely "tasteful arrangement." It has, objectively speaking, almost nothing to do with the aesthetic standards applied to choreography, costume design, or interior decoration—and you should not lead your artistic director or board president's wife to believe it does.

One definition of design may be stated as follows: the forceful presentation of an

David J. Skal is a Manhattan-based writer, designer and marketing consultant who has created brochures, advertising campaigns and publications for a wide range of cultural organizations, including the New York City Opera, the 92nd Street Y, FEDAPT, the American Council for the Arts, ASCAP, the Lincoln Center Theater Company, Theatre Development Fund, and many others. As publications director of Theatre Communications Group (TCG), he produced the widely acclaimed anthology *Graphic Communications for the Performing Arts*, two editions of *Theatre Profiles* and founded the monthly feature journal *Theatre Communications*. Mr. Skal has held positions with arts organizations across the country, including the Hartford Stage Company, the American Conservatory Theatre and the National Endowment for the Arts. Also well-known as a writer of fiction, his futuristic novels and short stories have appeared widely, both in the United States and in translation.

Photo: Gerry Goodstein

"The arts have an obligation to set certain aesthetic standards, not only in performance, but in *all* their communications."

intended message, engineered for maximum impact, absorption, and retention.

When scanning the entertainment pages or the pile of junk mail (and that's exactly what your mailing piece is considered until it proves itself to be different), the general public makes no distinction between the ''commercial'' and the ''not-for-profit.'' Either a piece commands attention or it doesn't. And, no doubt about it, visual expectations are very high. When you buy into the communications environment, either via the mails or via the airways, don't expect anyone to make special allowances for a slipshod presentation. Nobody cares that you ''didn't have time to design anything.'' Nobody cares how much trouble the artistic director gave you over photo selection. *Nobody cares* about anything except the *impact* of the finished piece. And it's your job to navigate the promotional concept and keep it intact past all the personalities, politics, and budget restrictions. If not...well, you lose. And so does your organization.

Communications design in the 1980s is, now more than ever, a professional's game, so I'm not going to spend any time here telling you how to ''do it yourself.'' You have too many other things to do. But you *can* become sensitized to the design process, learn to tell good design from bad, understand the basics of typography, and learn how to get the best work out of a design professional. Like any other creative endeavor, graphic design requires innate talent, some special technical training, and, perhaps most important, a certain detachment and objectivity—the ability to see your organization from the outside.

If all these things are being expected of you and you hold a staff position, then you're being dreadfully overworked. Sadly, too many communications and marketing directors *are* expected to be graphic designers and production artists in addition to shouldering their considerable responsibilities in the areas of press relations, budgeting, media planning, etc., etc. In many ways, this is a good example of the inattention design receives in our culture. It becomes an afterthought, a decoration(if it can be afforded), rather than something central and dynamic and indispensable.

So your first hurdle may well be convincing your employer that you need a budget for design. There are several strategies you may employ. First (especially if you are dealing with an artistic director), there is the argument that the arts have an obligation to set certain aesthetic standards, not only in performance, but in *all* their communications. Most people form their first impressions of your organization exclusively from these secondary means. What are the arts *about* if not some form of heightened, eloquent expression?

Second, there is the financial argument. Obviously, strong, coordinated design will create benefits: An immediately recognizable ''style'' for your organization will require less maintenance (i.e., promotional expenditures and valuable staff time) than a scattershot approach. Be sure to bring along several good examples of design work from other arts organizations, along with their attendance figures. It helps if these examples are no more complex from a strict production standpoint (paper, colors of ink) than your own.

If all else fails, you may resort to the ''I'm overworked and need help'' approach. It may help to describe the situation in terms your artistic or managing directors will readily understand—i.e., a director is not expected to act and design the scenery and costumes, even though he is responsible for the supervision of these activities. A managing director is responsible for the smooth physical and financial operation of the company, but not without the help of bookkeepers, a board of trustees, janitors, etc. Should you, then, in the absolutely crucial slot of communications/marketing officer, be expected to do your job without benefit of basic professional services?

The best argument of all, however, is a favorable reaction to good design by a funding source, your board, or the press. Getting the first professionally designed project off the ground will be difficult, but few organizations will be willing to retreat to an amateur posture once the benefits of good design have been made clear.

(Good design, however, does not necessarily equal good marketing. I am assuming throughout this chapter that all other components of your marketing strategy are first-rate. Good design can't help a bad marketing concept, but bad design can certainly hamper good marketing.)

Now you need to find a designer. What do you look for? It's sometimes difficult to know, since the qualifications of a "graphic designer" are at least as nebulous as those of an "actor." Training is important, but experience is more important. I personally view myself as a "creative director," since I write and design, as well as hire and oversee other creative people. Many designers, especially those with experience in larger studios, are adept at contributing not only to the presentation, but also to the content of your campaign. Others are specialists — they have terrific visual taste but will work strictly with what you give them. Other people who call themselves "graphic designers" aren't much more than paste-up artists. They know how to fit type and piece together a mechanical, and that's about it. The term "graphic designer" can apply to anything from the sophisticated efforts of a professional design studio to the disappointing work of free-lance hacks.

The best way to judge a designer's credentials is by a careful review of his portfolio. Ideally, it will contain a range of work, containing both finished, printed samples and perliminary sketches. A good designer will be able to talk about his work in terms of *problems* and *solutions*. (What problems did each assignment pose? How did the designer solve them?) The portfolio should also display the designer's ability to deal with both typography and image. Don't make the mistake of hiring a designer who is primarily an illustrator or printmaker. Be sure the work in the portfolio bears some technical resemblance to the kind of work your own organization plans.

Don't hire a designer who seems in any way defensive about his work, or gives you any clues whatsoever that he may be difficult or inflexible. A good designer should be able to deal with concept changes.

Now that you have your designer, how do you best approach your problem? Before designing specific promotions, you should consider a top-to-bottom overhaul of your organization's institutional identity. Assemble samples of all printed materials from the last two years. Are your identity graphics fairly consistent, or do they change radically with each new printed piece? Do you have a logo? Do you have more than one logo? Do you have a consistently identifiable typeface that you use in most of your printed materials? Do you use standard advertising formats?

Chances are, what you have before you is a grab bag, which means that design coordination is in order. The following is a checklist of elements that should be included in any institutional graphics program:

- Logo
- Letterhead
- Envelope
- Business card
- News release paper
- Advertising formats in all applicable sizes
- Mailing label
- Building or box-office signs
- Type standards for brochures and publications

While it appears at the top of the list, I don't want to put undue emphasis on logos. Sometimes just a type face will do. Sometimes the old logo just needs a slight reworking, a new context. Too often, the logo becomes the overwhelming focus rather than an integral part of a larger system. *Coordination* of printed materials is what makes your design efforts click—not just a new logo.

You're now ready to prepare what we might call the "design brief" for your designer, which should consist of:

1. All printed samples above
2. A general description of the kind of image your organization is seeking. Austere and institutional? Friendly and informal? Avant-garde or experimental?
3. A checklist of all pertinent applications and physical restrictions.

For instance, if your new logo or letterhead will be printed in two colors, will it also work in black & white? Will it ever need to "read" on television? What is the smallest size it will ever appear? The largest?

> "Good design can't help a bad marketing concept, but bad design can certainly hamper good marketing."

also work in black & white? Will it ever need to "read" on television? What is the smallest size it will ever appear? The largest?

It's always important to look at preliminary sketches, and you should not skip this step, even in the interest of meeting a deadline. Changes are far too costly and time-consuming once finished artwork is underway. Make sure you have seen and approved roughs before mechanicals are executed.

Don't ask your designer to make presentations to large groups of people, be they staff, board members, or whomever. *You* should be the primary point of contact in your organization for the designer, and he should regard all your approvals as final. It's your final responsibility to deal with personalities and internal politics, not the designer's. In this same regard, limit the number of people you show work to for approval. The more criticism you ask for, the more criticism you'll get. Even when dealing with those people whose approval is essential, don't ask for suggestions unnecessarily. Remember, your employer is expecting *you* to solve problems. If you seem unsure or tentative in your recommendations, it's only natural that he will also become nervous, and then critical, and then even impossible to get anything past. Submit presentations in as finished a form as possible. The more "real" any project seems at the outset, the fewer "suggestions" you'll get, and the faster you can move towards its implementation.

By way of illustration, I'd like to tell you about a case history of an identity project I recently completed for the 92nd Street YMHA in Manhattan. The Y is a very large organization—almost a city within a city, home to everything from chamber music concerts to racquetball games. None of the existing promotional materials or advertising for these diverse activities had much to do with each other, although they worked well enough to reach specialized constituencies. Still, they failed to create a broad-based public image for the Y—exactly the kind of recognition they needed to reach new audiences and encourage corporate contributions.

In analyzing the Y's problem, I found that they were suffering from acute "alphabet-soup syndrome." Like many groups, they had fallen into the common trap of selecting new typefaces for each new brochure or ad, and, as a result, sacrificing all visual continuity.

I looked for a solution within the problem itself, and found it in a restricted use of typography. I decided to use Times New Roman for everything—headlines, text, even their new logo would be a minimalist celebration of a distinctive typeface. Below you can see the results, which have been working well for over a year:

> "Too often, the logo becomes the overwhelming focus rather than an integral part of a larger system."

People in Performance.

Where Else?

Where else can you enjoy lieder singers one night and Tin Pan Alley the next? Where else can you sample, *under one roof,* world class musicians, superstar vocalists, internationally-acclaimed mimes, and one of Manhattan's most unique and exciting theatre companies? Where else can you find so many *exclusive* New York recitals, experience so many moods, such an abundance of talent, all in an acoustically superb, living-room-comfortable ambience that has made the 92nd Street Y one of the country's leading centers for the performing arts?

Where else?

Nowhere Else.

KAUFMANN CONCERT HALL

"Audiences. . .should be beating down the doors to get in." New York Magazine.

Claire Bloom
Alicia de Larrocha
Yo-Yo Ma
Shirley Verrett
Tennessee Williams
Isaac Bashevis Singer
Mary McCarthy
Robert Penn Warren
Felix Rohatyn
Elie Wiesel
William F. Buckley, Jr.
...and You!

People at the 92nd Street Y.

92 Y St

Times New Roman

72 point Times New Roman (Foundry)

ABCDEFGHIJ
KLMNOPQRS
TUVWXYZ&
abcdefghijklmn
opqrstuvwxyz
1234567890$

"Communications design in the 1980s is more than ever a professional's game."

The benefits may at first seem paradoxical. If you restrict type, won't everything look the same? Well, to some extent, yes…but isn't a family resemblance a positive thing? The design focus must shift away from type into the much more interesting areas of copy concepts, color, photos, and illustration. And this feeling of ''sameness'' often exists only within your organization. The general public doesn't live with your graphic day in and day out, as you do.

Type suppliers and manufacturers perpetuate visual pollution through the constant introduction of new, mediocre typefaces. These people feed on the common delusion that ''more must be more,'' when in fact, there are only a handful of typeface families really good for your purposes and versatile enough to fit almost any mood or occasion.

The classic serif faces include Bodoni, Garamond, Century, Times and Baskerville, and similar styles. The classic san-serif faces are Helvetica, Futura, Franklin Gothic, Univers, etc. These are usually available in various weights and sizes, condensed and expanded versions, and italic versions. They work equally well as display and body faces. They've stood the test of time. Properly utilized, they'll never let you down.

Typography is probably the single most important element in designing graphics, and yet, again paradoxically, when done right, it seems to be effortless, even invisible. To help you achieve greater proficiency in spotting potential trouble spots, the following is a checklist of the most common pitfalls in typography:

Mixing too many faces. Stick to the classics. Never mix two different serif faces, or two different san-serif faces. Under some circumstances, it may be effective to mix a serif face with a san-serif face, especially if it's done in a very bold mannner, but this is tricky. Your results will usually be much classier if you don't mix faces. Period.

Too many sizes and weights of type. Try to use as few variations within a type family as possible. Use boldface sparingly—even headlines can look better in text weight. Variations within a few point sizes are unnecessary and distracting. Keep size variations to 50% or 100% increments (e.g., 8 pt, 18 pt, 36 pt.) Before you (or your designer) specify a size or weight change, ask yourself if you've tried everything. Color? Capitals? Bullets? If it still doesn't work, then consider a change in size or weight.

Too much type on the page. The use of white space in graphic design is not wasteful, nor is it a plot by designers and paper companies to inflate your production budget. Neutral space is an important factor in keeping your design project readable; it adds rhythm, contrast, focus. It keeps your copy from appearing in intimidating gray blocks. In short, neutral space lets your design ''breathe'' and allows the reader to absorb your message easily. (It also eliminates layout headaches when you have to add copy at the last moment.)

It's important to remember that the best design can't help poorly organized copy. If you're having trouble specifying type, take a good look at your written material. It is logically organized? Is it clear which elements are the most important? The second? The third? Much bad design results from nervous decisions arising from insecurity about priorities. (''Maybe that headline should be bigger…is this prominent enough? Maybe we should use boldface…and maybe a point size larger…what about a different typeface?)

These kinds of last minute jitters have loused up more good designs than I care to think about. It's much less likely to happen when the client organization has planned its goals carefully. There's a long tradition of what I call ''know-nothing design'' in the arts—everything has the same shrill, demanding tone, saying, in effect, ''We don't really know *what* we're doing, or *why* it works, but if we hammer home *everything* that has worked for everybody else, and if we do it *all at once,* then it has to work.'' This is very much like the common American belief that English can be understood anywhere if only its spoken loudly enough.

We are fortunately beginning to emerge from this period of know-nothing design, and performing-arts groups are setting their standards higher. They're beginning to draw their inspiration not from other organization's brochures, but from the larger world of marketing communications. If you're not doing this now, you should be. Instead of looking down the road at the XYZ Repertory Theater's latest campaign, start looking at what American Express, Mobile, and Exxon are doing. Since you're undoubtedly aiming a large part of your efforts at an upscale audience, start looking at advertising graphics in places like *The New Yorker* and *Vanity Fair*. Look at department-store catalogues. Look at paperback covers. Look at movie posters and record albums. Pay particular attention to the new visual standards being created by computers and video. Keep a clipping file handy for your meetings with designers. Remember: Major corporations have spent a bundle learning what kind of graphic configurations are likely to attract many of the same people you're trying to attract. And this research and development is yours for the taking...if you pay attention.

While I don't expect all not-for-profit arts administrators to become graphic designers and art directors, I certainly anticipate an increased sensitivity toward design from those administrators who intend to remain in the game beyond the 1980's. It's about time that design in the arts involved more than just sets and costumes. "Supermarket graphics" are no longer a viable medium for the effective promotion of the arts...they're no longer viable for supermarkets. In the final analysis, people seek out the performing arts for deep aesthetic and spiritual reasons. Aesthetics are also the *raison d'être* of graphics, and there's a powerful, still largely untapped connection between the performing arts and the design arts for those who care to use it.

William Rudman

ESSENTIALS OF EFFECTIVE PUBLIC RELATIONS

Not long ago, as part of a consultancy, I attended a theater company's first performance in its gorgeous new home. "Gala," a word used carelessly these days, really did apply to this evening. The production was top flight; the inevitable curtain speeches from board president, artistic director, and manager were not only heartfelt but lively; and the community, which had embraced the company in an $8-million fund-raising bear hug, couldn't get enough of the actors, designers, technicians, women's committee — anybody even remotely connected with what they saw on stage. Thrilling!

The next morning I was to have breakfast with the company's manager and a representative from a large local foundation—an important funder—whom I'd met at the cast party. I spotted the man on the street, reintroduced myself, and walked with him to the office. We were bleary-eyed from the opening-night revelry, but that didn't keep the funder from asking, as we faced a glass door with the company's name on it, "Is it me, or are some of those letters crooked?"

I said I was in no condition to judge, but the guy was right, and you didn't need a ruler to settle the question.

The meeting went smoothly enough, the man departed, and at the end of the day's work, on the way out of the office, I mentioned to the manager that he had a crooked sign. "Give me a break," he snapped. "We've mounted the best production of *The Rose Tattoo* anybody's seen in years and this bozo is worried about a bloody sign? He's got nothing better to do?"

The manager, like his current production, was stellar, and I could easily forgive him a moment's lapse into defensiveness. But about that sign, he was dead wrong. Those recalcitrant Helvetica letters *stood for* his institution, just as the play stood for it, and just as any number of crucial but seemingly trivial things, ranging from a balanced budget to enough paper towels in the washroom, stood for it.

They add up to *Image*—the total impression someone has of your organization—and image is to be reckoned with. The way our institutions are perceived has much to do with how many tickets we sell, and to whom, and how many contributions we receive, and from whom. Image leads to our survival and growth, or to our failure.

The cliché, is true then—everything is public relations. But we'd better define this frequently misused term. Public relations is not the same thing as publicity; it is an organization's entire approach to communications, *one part of which* is publicity. The International Public Relations Association puts it this way (emphasis mine): "Public relations is a management function of a *continuing and planned character,* through which...institutions seek to win and retain the understanding, sympathy and support of those with whom they are or may be concerned."

That is one tall order. Although handling the public relations for an arts group, and hence bearing responsibility for shaping image—for "winning and retaining" support—can be great fun, it is also damn hard work.

Why? The not-for-profit performing arts concept is still a young idea, the subtleties of which are often lost on otherwise enlightened people. Zelda Fichandler, the founder of Washington, D.C.'s Arena Stage, has observed that in

Bill Rudman is communications officer for the Cleveland Foundation, the oldest and one of the largest community foundations in America. During his tenure at Susan Bloch and Company, the Manhattan-based public relations and publicity firm, his assignments included publicity for several dance companies on Broadway and numerous Off Broadway theater productions. Mr. Rudman has directed arts marketing campaigns as a staff member of Cleveland's Great Lakes Shakespeare Festival and New Hampshire's American Stage Festival, and has consulted for professional theaters and dance companies throughout much of the nation. He is also a radio producer/ host, and is producing the original cast album of Geraldine Fitzgerald's one-woman show, *Streetsongs.*

the early years of the resident theater movement, the phenomenon was most often labeled ''whaddaya-call-it theater.'' Let us not delude ourselves; despite the so-called ''democratization of culture'' in the last twenty or so years, public ignorance and confusion about what it is we do on our not-for-profit stages and how and why we do it are rampant. An important part of the public-relations job is to identify and address misunderstandings every day, not just during the annual sustaining drive, when we somewhat glibly inform our audience that they only paid for Act One of *On Golden Pond* or *Swan Lake*.

Ironically, much of the time our institutions' image problems are self-inflicted. ''What muddies the water,'' say Brad Morison and Kay Fliehr, pioneer marketers of the Guthrie Theater in their book *In Search of an Audience,* ''is that many organizations have not clearly defined what they want to be, nor do they come to understand who they really are. In such cases, it is inevitable that the public's image will be confused, and steps taken to improve it will be difficult.''

Robert Crawford, in his valuable book *In Art We Trust* (FEDAPT, 1981), talks in some detail about the Board/Staff Retreat process as one means of setting an institution on the right track. Suffice it to note here that those of us charged with telling an institution's story cannot do so, as Morison and Fliehr suggest, until board, artists, and staff have reached a consensus on our organization's mission; until together we have turned that mission into long- and short-term plans for meeting specific goals; and until we have taken a clear-headed, hard-nosed look at what the institution is all about right now.

Dialogue With Your Institution's Publics

This book is replete with warnings that we are not marketing toothpaste—that it is not our job to custom-design a product, but rather to find an audience for an artist, and to find ways to interpret that artist's work to the public. True enough, but that does not absolve us from getting in touch with the needs of our supporters, both actual and potential, and from trying to meet those needs in any way short of altering the product.

And the fact is, we have many publics. The needs of our subscribers are in many ways different from those of our single-ticket buyers, which are different from those of contributors, which are different from those of the press and government officials and corporations and volunteers and foundations and non-attendees and... you name it. A solid group-sales strategy for marketing a Clifford Odets play might well target the local chapters of both the AAUW (American Association of University Women) and the UAW (United Auto Workers). But you can bet that if you get both groups into your theater, they'll be there for dramatically disparate reasons.

You owe it to yourself to find out what those reasons are. I think there's something to be learned from the film studios and their megabuck drum-beating. There were *three* different advertising campaigns for *Annie Hall* and *six* for *Moonraker,* with each message conceived to speak to the needs of a different target audience.

By dint of working twenty-four hours a day at our institutions, we lull ourselves into thinking we know exactly how we're perceived by our various publics—and what those publics are looking for in us—and we speak to them accordingly. But much of the time it's a monologue: we're not really listening. A particularly ear-opening technique to correct that mistake is to engage an opinion-research firm (many will do it free for an arts group) to conduct a series of interviews called ''focus groups.'' These can be handled in many ways. Usually an objective discussion-leader interviews a number of groups, each containing members from one of our publics (a group of subscribers, for example, or a group of non-attendees). Depending on the goals of the research, the participants in each focus group may or may not share certain demographic characteristics, such as an age range or income level.

What emerge from the sessions are attitudes. The objective is to learn what people know about your organization, what they like, what they don't like. The challenge for you as communicator, of course, is to develop messages that speak to as many needs as possible but to do it without tampering with the integrity of your artists and their art.

You might then try your hand at writing what the corporate types call a "positioning statement." Positioning your institution means finding a unique shelf for it in the consumer marketplace. The process takes into account the needs of prospective customers: it is a plan to show the consumer "what's in it for him."

Example: The Atlanta Ballet. Several years ago, when I walked through the door for my first consultancy with America's oldest resident ballet company, I found manager Ken Hertz fast approaching apoplexy. The most potent message his staff had been able to come up with for the Company's critical direct-mail piece was a cutesy *Nutcracker* toy drum major assuring the reader, "I Never Met a Subscriber I Didn't Like." Clearly, the message had nothing to do with either artistic director Robert Barnett's approach to dance or the needs of prospective season ticket-buyers.

Eventually the ad agency of Ogilvy and Mather donated some time to the ballet company and, after doing a fair amount of research they produced a positioning statement that informed the entire year's marketing and public relations effort.

This is a good illustration, I think, because there's nothing magical about it; any one of us could have written it, provided we'd taken a comprehensive look at the company and its market. To wit: "The Atlanta Ballet should focus on its entertainment appeal. We want to make Atlanta Ballet-fans of people who may never have seen a dance performance—people who have the money and the interest to discover new kinds of entertainment. Our positioning should be: The Atlanta Ballet is entertainment everyone can enjoy."

By way of contrast, the next season's theme was: "What makes the Atlanta Ballet the most exciting show in town? It's athletic! funny! sensuous! chilling! The Atlanta Ballet is different." The subscription audience quickly doubled, but it's important to ask why. The repositioning was not an attempt to turn the company into the Rockettes, to alter or misrepresent the product. On the contrary, the new language worked because it changed Atlanta's perception about what was already onstage. The repositioning addressed the company's eclectic repertoire and Artistic Director Bobby Barnett's perspective on dance, while putting the company in the marketplace aggressively and distinctively.

> "You must deal with words before you dream up fancy logos and glitzy brochures."

Writing: The Key

Much of public-relations work—speaking and listening to publics in countless dialogues—requires some skill at and confidence in writing. If I have any secret to sell about the job description, it's that you can't begin to shape an image unless you can face a blank sheet of paper without *angst*.

You must deal with those blank sheets before you dream up fancy logos, glitzy brochures and four-color photo collages. They are to be filled with a language you develop for your institution over time, a tone and a way of talking about your company that speak to your mission, your product, and the needs of your various publics.

The pitfall is to be vague and nebulous. I used to tell students enrolled in a course I taught with the late, very gifted New York press agent Susan Bloch that anyone whose brochure copy screamed "Subscribe Now!" automatically failed the course. "Subscribe Now!" was pretty heady stuff when the season-ticket world was young; twenty years later it offers few insights about your institution and answers few of your publics' needs.

If you spend enough time at it, and push yourself to go deeper than "Celebrate!" or "Subscribe Now!" the discipline of writing will force you to organize, isolate, and choose priorities about what makes your organization special and what it offers the buyer. That is the key, because people buy and support the specific, the distinctive. Elements of the language you create should refer back to the positioning statement—indeed, all the way back to the mission statement—and inform the press release, the brochure, the print ad, the telephone solicitation, the public-service announcement, the membership letter, and so on.

"Brochure
copy screaming
'Subscribe Now!'
offers few if any
insights about your
institution, and
answers few if any
of your public's
needs."

In everything you write:
- Make the message brief and easy to understand. An old public relations man I know calls this the KISS principle—''Keep It Simple, Stupid.''
- Assign priorities among the points you're making and rank them in the text. In general, the most important ideas and sales points go at the top of the message. As journalists say, it's a matter of what you ''lead'' with.
- Try to be compelling, Webster defines *compel* as, ''to urge with force,'' which is the essence of good promotional writing. All the tools of rhetoric come into play here. Don't be afraid to convince! That does not mean shouting or hype, by the way. In press-release writing, as we will see, persuasion is aided by the implied credibility that comes from journalistic style and form.
- Retain a distinctive tone. Much of what you're marketing has to do with an experience. That's an intangible; it suggests personal and emotional involvement. Describe the experience and make it special. Bold, active verbs help to create a distinctive tone. So do the right adjectives—but don't always rely on quality indicators such as ''great,'' ''fabulous'' and ''sensational'' (these are verboten in press releases). With the help of Roget's Thesaurus, search for adjectives that suggest the *texture* of the art and the institution. Your language, no less than the work onstage, should give your institution a signature.

A few examples of these tips in action: From our born-again ballet company, an excerpt from ''The ABC's of the Atlanta Ballet, Or twenty-six Reasons to Buy Season Tickets.'' The language attempts to speak to the needs of the target market, people who, as Ogilvy and Mather broadly characterized them, ''have the money and the interest to discover new forms of entertainment.'' Research turned up intimidation as a resistance factor. The copywriter deals with it simply and with humor:

Q is for Quatre. French for ''four.'' As in *pas de quatre.* Literally, ''step for four,'' but it really means dance for four! A good example of what people mean when they say, ''But I don't understand ballet.'' Not to worry—ballet is not a spoken language! It's totally unnecessary to count in French to have a terrific time.

And to return to the company's campaign headline: ''It's athletic! funny! sensuous! chilling!''

Here is a blurb for a production of *The Playboy of the Western World* at the old Repertory Theater of Lincoln Center. It's by Susan Bloch, and one of the finest I've ever come across (emphasis mine):

A moonstruck dreamer starving for his place in the sun finds it, by chance, in a town hungry for heroes at any cost. Synge's folk tale for all time *slyly* captures the fire and joy of the Irish mystique as it *compassionately* satirizes the contradictions of a world gone topsy-turvy. *Primitive, lyrical, romantic,* and *cynical,* this masterful play of great wisdom and gorgeous language will be staged by John Hirsch.

What does she lead with? An image (''A moonstruck dreamer starving for his place in the sun'') that neatly, poetically, and compellingly gives us the essence of the play's conflict. The italicized adjectives (and two adverbs), when juxtaposed, begin to unravel the mysteries of a complex piece of theater. And in the rhetoric of one marvelous, economical parallelism (''great wisdom and gorgeous language''), she markets what is distinctive about all of Irish drama! Certainly we know what kind of evening we can expect.

Finally, a classic from a subscription brochure for Robert Kalfin's Chelsea Theater Center, that gloriously unpredictable company which in the 1960s and 1970s gave birth to such productions as *Candide, Yentl, Strider,* the Brecht-Weill *Happy End* and LeRoi Jones's *Slaveship.* Here the copywriter captures that rarest of birds: a controlling metaphor (''the Ultimate Voyage'') that sums up and makes special an entire institution and mission:

On the brink of the new season, Chelsea offers once again the Ultimate Voyage for the theatergoer. A Chelsea subscription is, as it has been for the past twelve years, your passport to a most exhilarating theatrical odyssey. The Chelsea experience will be as provocative, frisky, perplexing, magical, tumultuous, playful, play-filled, and entertaining as ever. Any island cruiser can offer a week of moonlit nights and summer romance. Chelsea often inspires serious seductions and permanent passions. Not your ordinary boat, the stalwart Chelsea and her crew ignore sharks, blackouts, tropical storms and fads to travel the most exotic routes, bringing you—says Clive Barnes—the "most adventurous theater fare in the nation."

Which reminds me: unless we're representing the Moscow Art Theater it is not a sin to be playful from time to time in our public relations! The light touch, in the arts as in life, is likely to win friends and influence target markets.

In the shaping of institutional image through language I believe, one mistake is repeatedly made. That is to place an overriding emphasis in our messages on commitment and outreach to the community. We do this at the expense of art. Occasionally there are good reasons for it—sometimes an arts institution's mission can't be separated from what has been referred to as a *"marriage"* to the community it serves. This is often true of smaller organizations, especially those nestled in rural areas without many cultural resources. It is often also true of inner-city groups that offer supporters more direct participation by filling a quasi-settlement-house function.

But in general, there ought to be *some* artistic perspective providing motor energy for a professional institution, and it is that perspective that should become the centerpiece of the public relations effort. Cleveland Ballet's Artistic Director, Ian Horvath, likes to say that "Cleveland is almost as important as 'ballet' in our name." The point is, *almost*. While it's terribly important that our publics know about and support our seminars in high schools and our work with senior citizens and the handicapped, it is even more important for them to know why the work onstage is, in and of itself, an artistic statement eminently worth making.

Let us not forget art for art's sake.

Publicity: What It Can and Cannot Do

In *Subscribe Now!,* the indefatigable Danny Newman states it perfectly. We can mount the most intricate and aggressive publicity campaign in the world, he says, but in the larger campaign "battle," publicity is only "artillery." It may weaken or stun the "enemy" (a.k.a. the prospective ticket buyer), but only the "infantry" of actual points of sale, such as a brochure or a telephone call, can march in for the kill.

So why do so many of us forget Newman's sage counsel? Why do so many of us insist on waging the bulk of our marketing battle with such limited weaponry? Maybe for a couple of reasons: One is the glamour of the publicity craft (at least in comparison to devising demographic strategies) and its fast payoff. I mean, it's *fun* to talk to editors and go along to the interview with the actor or the prima ballerina and see the results just a day or a week later. Nearly instant gratification!

The second reason is the pressure we get from the artists we work with (understandable) and the managers we report to (no excuse—they should know better) that we're not doing our job unless the institution is in the paper every day, with three photos on Sunday. The artists we learn to deal with; what they want most is the assurance that we're supporting their work. As for the managers, we must educate them.

All of this is not to say that publicity is a waste of time. Far from it. Publicity is a vital part of any arts group's public relations program. It is a necessary part of long-term image-building, and in the short term, it can help sell tickets to one attraction or to an entire season.

But let us yell and stamp our feet, if necessary, until our managers realize that more important than getting in the paper every day is saying the right things when we do get in.

And saying them at the right time. A publicity campaign, like all marketing efforts, demands timing. You may not be able to control the release date of all the feature stories you place, but you can probably control more than you think: at the very least, the release of most news stories. A publicity campaign should have a shape—a beginning, a middle and an end—in which various "publicity breaks" bounce off the other marketing components: the brochure, the radio spot, the telemarketing, the coffee parties, and so on.

When the timing is right, you create what is called "synergy," in which the whole of the marketing effort becomes greater than the sum of its parts. The prospective customer turns helpless in the face of all the "impressions" bombarding him (some of them subliminally), and because of this, you sell a ticket. When the timing is wrong—when, for instance, you shoot off all your publicity guns at once—you dissipate the impact.

Preparing Publicity Material

What about saying the right thing in publicity materials? All the writing pointers we've discussed above apply, along with a few more that I'll toss in because here the list of our publics includes reporters and editors.

The press release is, as it has always been, the basic, agreed-upon tool used to communicate with the media. But don't let its official posture impress you into thinking that your message is more important than it is. Nothing galls me more to see press releases from arts organizations with the word **NEWS** at the top in fuchsia, followed by three exclamation points.

At the risk of heresy, I will suggest that most of us working for arts groups have little news to trumpet. There are exceptions, of course: WE make news when we announce a season or a guest artist, or when a new development affects the future of our institution. But most of the time our press releases merely pass on information about what's on our stages. So don't permit your releases to shout. And don't feel you must mail one out every week. Send releases only when you have something to say, and you'll find that more attention will be paid them. (Likewise, avoid press conferences for anything but the biggest stories.)

Just as you need not be a graduate of Pratt Institute to learn how to recognize and inspire good graphic design for your institution, you needn't have attended Columbia's School of Journalism to learn how to write good press releases. Read newspaper stories and listen to TV and radio reports for their structure and rhythm. A few tips:

• Learn to write "journalistically." The less editing your material requires, the greater chance you have of seeing some form of it in print. Even if the release is not used (at large papers, where space is tight, rejection is likely), a clear, crisp journalistic style and respect for accuracy will earn you points in the city room. Media folks tend to distrust slick public relations people who are always selling something. Dispel those qualms by absolute professionalism, not only in your personal bearing but also in your writing. Don't be a "flack"; be a reporter.

• Put the nuts and bolts (the who? what? where? when? why?) of your story up front in the first couple of paragraphs—in the first sentence if you can manage it. The most important information is imparted first; if an editor must cut, he should be able to cut from the bottom.

• Don't let your first sentence or two—your lead—get cutesy. And don't hype it. Keep it factual. Let the editor jazz it up should he decide to print some form of the release.

• Compress your thoughts. Economy of language wins respect. Don't write: "The Mayfield Players Theater was founded ten years ago and plans to celebrate its anniversary by presenting five local premieres," when you can state the same idea this way: "To mark its 10th anniversary, Mayfield Players Theater will present five local premieres." Every word should count.

• Ape the spelling and punctuation of the major paper in town. If that paper spells theater with an "er," so do you. If it does not use "Mr." or "Mrs." neither do you. If it places quotation marks around performing arts works rather than italicizing them, so do you.

• Be careful! Arts releases walk a tightrope. They should be factual, but they also should contain enough color to describe the art and offer a glimpse of what makes your institution distinctive.

To demonstrate these points, two examples:

Titus Andronicus, Shakespeare's electrifying drama of power play in Imperial Rome, will have its local premiere Thursday, January 20, at the Great Lakes Shakespeare Festival. Curtain time is 8:00 p.m.

Shakespeare unleashes a feverish parade of revenge and double revenge in *Titus Andronicus,* with traces of paganism and scathing conspiracy. Rome is in the process of selecting a new emperor and the pace is set for a tale of power. The two candidates for the throne are the two sons of the late emperor — Saturninus, the elder and Bassianus, the younger. The victorious general, Andronicus, publicly declares his support for Saturninus and finds himself a pawn between the power factions.

Often described as Shakespeare's most climatic play, *Titus Andronicus* was inspired by Thomas Kyd's The Spanish Tragedy which enjoyed surprising audience appeal during the late sixteenth century. It was first produced in America in 1924, and is perhaps the most rarely seen of Shakespeare's canon …

What's wrong here? Admittedly, the writer has done some research, albeit undigested, and does attempt journalistic style. But therre's too much plot, too much color (words and phrases like "feverish parade," "electrifying," and "scathing" are very purple prose), and the syntax is weak (what does "traces of paganism" mean? or "revenge and double revenge"? or "most climatic"?).

The most serious sin, however, is more subtle. The biggest challenge for an arts release is to make a case, for the significance of mounting the work in the first place. Not only does this *Titus* release fail to offer any compelling reasons for producing a difficult play; it nearly makes a case against attempting the production. Even the opportunity to create a little healthy controversy is botched. *Titus* is, as the writer declares, one of the Bard's rarely seen works. But if many scholars consider it bottom-drawer Shakespeare, what is there about this production that could change our perception of the play? What has the director found in it?

In neglecting the *Why?* of the story, the writer of the release has failed that director. The release is devoid of a public relations approach or "set up" for what is onstage. Audiences who read about the show prior to the opening are given no reason to order tickets. Even if the release does not get published, it can harm the production, because critics may rely on it for preparation. And what feature writer will want to do a piece on a show which, thanks to its advance material, has "flop" written all over it?

The difference between the *Titus* release and that accorded Chelsea Theater's New York premiere of the Max Frisch work *Biography: A Game* should be apparent.

FOR RELEASE: SATURDAY, MARCH 31 or
SUNDAY, APRIL 1, please

"BIOGRAPHY: A GAME" WILL RECEIVE NEW YORK PREMIERE THURSDAY, APRIL 5 AT THE CHELSEA THEATER CENTER

On Thursday, April 5 at 8:00 p.m., the Chelsea Theater Center will present the New York premiere of Max Frisch's *Biography: A Game* at the Westside Theater.

In this thought-provoking comedy, the famed Swiss playwright offers his central character, Kurmann, an exhilarating, seductive and terrifying opportunity—the chance to relive his life in any way he chooses. Like all of Frisch's work, *Biography* is marked by both compassion for, and impatience with, man and the choices he makes.

So audacious is *Biography* in style and technique that it has been hailed throughout Europe as a fresh theatrical form since its 1968 world premiere in Zurich, and the play ranks eighth among theater works most frequently produced in the German-speaking world. The comedy reaffirms Frisch's status as one of the major literary figures of our time.

Born in Zurich in 1911, the playwright and novelist was, until recently, a

"There were three different advertising campaigns for *Annie Hall* and six for *Moonraker,* each conceived to speak to the needs of a different target audience."

practicing architect whose first major building and writing projects were accomplished in the same year, 1943. His plays are anthologized in most collections of modern drama and include *The Firebugs, Andorra* and *The Chinese Wall.*

The Chelsea premiere, the first local major production of a major work by Frisch since 1963, has been mounted on the expansive, newly designed upstairs stage of the Westside Theater, with a company of twenty actors performing forty roles.

The play is directed by Arne Zaslove, the founder and artistic director of Seattle's Floating Theater Company, who staged Chelsea's acclaimed production of Tankred Dorst's *Ice Age* in 1975. Zaslove's New York productions include last season's world premiere of Chekhov's *Tatyana Regina* for the Judson Poet's Theater.

The central role of Kurmann is played by George Morfogen, whose Chelsea appearances include major roles in *The Prince of Homburg, Ice Age* and *Total Eclipse.* Pamela Burrell plays the liberated and fashionable Antoinette—the woman in Kurmann's life—and Paul Sparer is the Recorder, who offers the rules of *Biography's* game.

The company also features Charles Berendt, Roger Alan Brown, James Carruthers, Roger DeKoven, Igors Gavon, Elaine Grollman, Skip Lawing, and Charles White. Sets have been designed by Robert Ellsworth, costumes by Elizabeth P. Palmer, and lighting by Robert Graham Small. Production stage manager is Zoya Wyeth.

Biography: A Game will continue through April 29 on the following schedule: Tuesday through Saturday evenings at 8 p.m., with Wednesday and Saturday matinees at 2 p.m. and Sunday matinees at 3 p.m. Tickets are scaled at $10 for Tuesday through Thursday evenings and Wednesday and Saturday matinees, and $12 for Friday and Saturday evenings and Sunday matinees. Tickets may be charged on any major credit card by telephoning CHARGIT at (212) 239-7177.

The Westside Theater, located at 407 West 43rd Street, has been Chelsea's base of operation since its consolidation in Manhattan last summer.

The Chelsea's two-play spring season will conclude with the American premiere of Mark Rozovsky's *Strider: The Story of a Horse,* a theatrical adaptation of the famous Tolstoy short story, to be directed by Robert Kalfin with noted choreographer Patricia Birch. The play will run from May 31–June 24.

FOR INFORMATION, CONTACT
Bill Rudman, 212/873-0706
###

This release tries just as hard to prepare the media for an experience inside the theater as it does to get printed. I don't bother with plot details, just the play's central conflict. I research. The facts are offered in punchy, journalistic style. Paragraphs are short; few are longer than two sentences. I do not hype (adjectives are carefully chosen for textural value), though I do place the play in the context of Frisch's other works and, indeed, of contemporary world theater. Little known facts, such as Frisch's second career as an architect, add interest and may plant seeds for later feature stories.

You can assemble other material to support the press release. "Press packets," for example, are collections of additional information including biographies of artists, a perspective on your institution, or a listing of your resident choreographer's repertoire. "Feature bios" of artists contained in the packets are useful. Written in journalistic feature style, with plenty of quotes, these special stories can either be picked up by the media and run more or less as is, or used to supply the press with angles for their own interviews. Producing a lively feature bio that leads to publicity, of course, depends on *your* skill as an interviewer: You've got to find out and be able to articulate what is most intriguing about your artists if you're going to persuade anyone else to take interest. (Sample lead: "I love waking up in the morning looking forward to doing and risking," says the noted stage and film actress Geraldine Fitzgerald, whose risky new career as a singer has blossomed from a small cabaret act to a full theatrical evening, a one-woman show called *Streetsongs*.)

And, oh, you will be such a hero if your packets contain good photographs! Three objectives, I think, should guide your work in this area:

• No matter what art form you promote, find a photographer sensitive to what Elia Kazan termed "the precision of the living moment." Only when your photos shimmer with life do you have a chance of evoking art's excitement and mystery. Study the work of the masters. An hour spent with photographers Fred Fehl (in the book *On Broadway*) or Martha Swope (in *Baryshnikov at Work*) can be an inspiring tutorial.

• Choose photographs which represent the most compelling qualities of a production, which communicate its essence, and support what you've already written about it. Again, you must not fail the artistic director, the performing artists or the institution by inadequately preparing the arts-goer for what is onstage. You are interpreting the product. To do that, you should guide the photographer, selecting the moments he will shoot, making the final selections from the contact sheets, and even suggesting croppings.

• Make sure you have a decent chance of getting your photos printed. Find out what the local publications are looking for. Some, for example, will not accept shots with black backgrounds; other editors are fond of special composition.

Are press packets read cover to cover by the media? Rarely. But the materials are perused, and will get used if you resist the temptation to make them gestures of unbridled institutional egotism. Every piece in a packet should really mean something, should possess some journalistic currency. A good packet also suggests that you take your institution seriously, and that it deserves to be taken seriously by others.

Selling the Story Idea

If all you do is mail out information and photos, however well-crafted, they may be, do not expect to win significant air time or newspaper space. The best publicity breaks come when you single out editors and reporters and "pitch" them with ideas. Entertainment and society ("living section") stories are not the beginning and the end. The entire newspaper—or TV/radio station—is your oyster, especially for features.

In selecting what you're going to pitch, be hard on yourself: your goal is to sell tickets, so instead of trotting out the same tired actress who every year talks about "how wonderful it is" to be a part of a resident theater, look for the artists who have something fresh to say. In a very real way, you are an editor. If you pitch for a feature, you are saying you have a good story, one that merits attention and space. So make sure it does.

Piquing an editor's interest—and later the interest of his readers—depends on your creativity. During its first season, for example, the Guthrie Theater made the Minneapolis sports page with a story on *As You Like It*'s first-act wrestling scene, staged by a professional wrestler. I used to pitch to a religion editor who loved the offbeat angles I tossed his way, on *Our Town*'s moral issues, for instance. And what about a feature in the business section that profiles your board's corporate leaders and, between the lines, your institution's exemplary fiscal management?

How do you pitch? Understand that press people are bombarded with story ideas every day. That means you mustn't waste their time, and that your idea should be distinctive enough to appear to be wheat compared with everyone else's chaff. Target the editor or reporter most likely to go for the idea (and consequently the publication that is most appropriate for the "message"), boil the story down to its most noteworthy form, and hit—either with a phone call or, if you feel more comfortable, a memo. Here's a succinct example of the latter:

Once again the Irish have invaded the otherwise tranquil shores of Susan Bloch and Co.—this time in the person of Ron Hutchinson, the thirty-two-year-old author of *Says I, Says He . . . Say He,* the comedy which will receive its American premiere via the Phoenix Theatre on February 19, with a cast headed by Brian Dennehy and Joe Grifasi.

Hutchinson's work is muscular, entertaining, and explicit (critics' com-

"The best publicity breaks come when you single out particular editors and reporters and 'pitch' them with ideas."

parisons to Behan are frequent), and the play tackles the Irish problem and the Irish mystique with high spirits and hard-hitting satire. The author is currently playwright-in-residence at the Royal Shakespeare Company.

Hutchinson has just arrived in Manhattan and has much to say about his country, his comedy—even American actors. He's a fascinating man with a professional history that includes work as a fish-gutter, carpet-fitter, furniture-shifter and dole clerk.

How about a conversation? I'll call you soon to gauge your interest.

Specificity rules. There are five or six things here that a journalist can grab hold of as handles for the proposed interview. This is the opposite of the all too frequent, deadly pitch that goes, "We're opening our season next week, and I was wondering if there's anything you can do for us." Stitch this on a sampler: "My business as a publicist is to do for the press."

If the journalist buys the idea, you arrange all the details, and with his permission, try to be present for whatever you set up. That's particularly important in interviews with artists, who need the protection that comes from your familiarity with, and overview of, the institution. You're a resource the artist can call on for help. And whenever anyone from your company is to be asked questions by a member of the press, it is your duty to offer some preparation for the interview. Who is the journalist? What does he usually write about? What is he likely to ask?

Feature stories are not the only way to publicize your organization through the media. Among the often overlooked opportunities are:

• Listings—statistics show these are read, six-point type and all, and all you have to do is meet the deadlines.

• Column items—the writers of tidbit or gossip columns are eccentric about what they will take, and they usually demand "exclusives" (nobody else gets the item). With those caveats in mind, go to it! Millions of Americans glance at the front page and then go straight to their favorite gossip columnist.

• Editorials—a natural for a developing institution. But you can go to the well only so many times. Save this for when the message really counts, and be sure you have strong, substantive written material to back up your idea.

Working with the Visual Media

The decision to pitch a story to the visual media—photographers and television reporters—carries with it a new imperative: The word must become subservient to the almighty picture. Many of us deplore television's tendency to reduce America's most serious and pressing issues, as one commentator has put it, to "ninety-second mini-dramas." But the best advice is probably to learn to live with TV, and to learn its techniques, rules, and rhythms well enough so that you do not lose control of your institution, your artists, and your story when the videotape rolls.

The enemy of the visual media people is, of course, the "talking head," a person speaking on camera unaided by the so-called "sizzle" of action and movement. Christ Himself could arrive tomorrow and the evening news would ask Him two questions, then cut to fourteen capital cities around the world, not so much for reaction as for pretty pictures.

For television stories, then, keep your institution's message bare-bones simple. When you prepare your artistic director, board president or whomever is answering a TV reporter's questions (this goes for radio, too), instruct the spokesperson to respond with very short answers, phrased in very short sentences. When you invite visual media into your institution, scout out the most interesting backgrounds for the interview(s) in advance. If your company is in rehearsal, and there are opportunities for footage, so much the better; do not hesitate to suggest. The television camera is a hungry animal, gobbling up color and activity with the voraciousness of Pac Man. When the animal is not fed, it vents its anger in the form of disappointingly brief stories, or no stories at all. So milk your institution for all the visual interest it contains.

The visual media can be used to great advantage with stunts. You can create stunts as attention-getters; these upbeat gimmicks are limited only by your flair and imagination.

> "A publicity campaign should have a shape—a beginning, a middle, and an end."

Nobody applauds a stunt louder than the press, provided you do your part to make it work. Understand when you elect to go for one, however, that you are more than the idea person and the writer; you are Michael Bennett — director and choreographer — and you are totally responsible for everything coming off as planned. If you blow it, you will see how rapidly you get tagged as the publicist who called wolf. Also keep in mind that the stunts that help sell tickets do in fact bear some relation to your specific production or your institution. So keep the gimicks organic.

Here are two examples. The first is a Susan Bloch stunt, only a few years old and already assured a place in the press agents' hall of fame. In 1976, Susan was about to open the Australian Ballet on Broadway. Despite the presence of a star—Margot Fonteyn dancing the title role in *The Merry Widow*—the company was not well known in America and consequently ticket sales were dangerously slow.

Susan hand-delivered this "photo tip" just a day before the opening. Note that the tongue-in-cheek tone works because the release is written in factual, upright journalistic style:

Today, kangaroo expatriate from Down Under, Sydney Melbourne III, arrives in New York City from Pittsburgh in time for the premiere of the Australian Ballet's new version of *The Merry Widow* scheduled for tomorrow evening at the Uris Theater.

Seized by irresistible nostalgia, Melbourne ordered his secretary to telephone the Ballet's manager to inform the company that he would like to view the dancers of his native land and to request opening-night tickets. They were promptly reserved and held for him at the Uris box-office, to be picked up in advance.

The box-office manager was assured that Melbourne's private secretary would drive Sydney to the theater at 1 p.m. today in his personal hansom cab to purchase the ticket.

Sydney, on loan from the zoo, appeared as announced in full regalia. So did an army of photographers and TV reporters. The *Daily News* society columnist picked up the stunt and for two weeks charted the kangaroo's alleged goings-on among New York's social elite. Business, as they say, boomed.

If you think this all smacks of tackiness, I disagree. So did the Australian Ballet leadership, who adored the stunt. Sydney, after all, was positioned as an aristocrat! (A word to the aspiring publicist: Very little is predictable in this life, but animals, children, and pretty faces are best bets to get in the papers and on television. Thus it will ever be.)

And this is a stunt from my scrapbook, staged in 1980 for Cleveland's Great Lakes Shakespeare Festival. The company was about to welcome its one millionth theatergoer through its doors without much ado. For shame! A chance like this is any self-respecting publicist's dream! This photo tip also has a respectably journalistic structure, with a lead and all the other accoutrements. Unlike a formal press release, it comes right out and hypes, promising, a "media event," as the voguish parlance would have it.

FOR IMMEDIATE RELEASE, PLEASE

TO: NEWS ASSIGNMENT PRODUCERS AND EDITORS/ PHOTO EDITORS

RE: 1,000,000TH THEATERGOER TO SEE GREAT LAKES SHAKESPEARE FESTIVAL PRODUCTION ON FRIDAY, SEPT. 5 (8 p.m.) AT LAKEWOOD CIVIC AUDITORIUM

Vincent Dowling, Red Carpet, Trumpet Fanfare and 30-member Cast of Shakespeare's *Titus Andronicus* to Herald Arrival of Mr. or Ms. One Million

"The Broadway press agent has no evolving institution at stake; thus he simply does not use words and phrases such as 'mission,' 'long-range planning,' and 'artistic process.' "

On Friday, September 5 at approximately 8 p.m., Cleveland theatrical history will be made when the Great Lakes Shakespeare Festival's one millionth playgoer walks down a special red carpet at Lakewood Civic Auditorium for GLSF's spectacular production of Shakespeare's *Titus Andronicus*.

The unsuspecting Mr. or Ms. One Million will be greeted by Vincent Dowling, Festival artistic director, who will serve as "ticket taker" and perform the suspenseful final countdown at the door. A live trumpet fanfare will signal this milestone in GLSF's nineteen-year history.

Dowling will personally usher the one millionth playgoer into the theater, where the talented 30-member cast of *Titus Andronicus* will make a special pre-show appearance in costume to cheer the audience. Proclamations and letters of commendation in honor of the Festival will be presented by State Representatives Patrick A. Sweeney and Francine M. Panehal, Cleveland Mayor George Voinovich and Lakewood Mayor Anthony C. Sinagra.

The lucky playgoer will be awarded a theater weekend for two in New York City, among other tokens of the Festival's gratitude. Now begins the era of the Second Million.

Titus Andronicus, Shakespeare's harrowing tale of violence in ancient Rome, is the 109th play produced by GLSF, Ohio's only professional classical theater. Since its founding in 1962, the Festival has produced thirty-four of the Bard's thirty-seven plays, along with dozens of works by such masters of world drama as G.B. Shaw, Eugene O'Neill, Tennessee Williams, Molière and Oscar Wilde.

GLSF's one millon theatergoers include more than 250,000 Cleveland area students and the statewide audience which is visited annually during the Festival's fall tour.

The Festival has been awarded a $400,000 challenge grant by the National Endowment for the Arts and the Cleveland Foundation, based on the excellence of its programming, its statewide and regional importance, and the viability of its long-range plan.

The current seven-play season runs through September 28 at Lakewood Civic Auditorium with all plays now in the repertoire, including Shakespeare's *Henry IV, Part 1, Comedy of Errors* and *Titus Andronicus*; Anton Chekhov's *The Boor*; Brandon Thomas's *Charley's Aunt*; Eugene O'Neill's *Hughie* and James A. Brown's *My Lady Luck* (world premiere). Phone reservations may be made by calling 521-0090.

OPPORTUNITIES ABOUND FOR LIVELY PHOTOGRAPHS AND TELEVISION FOOTAGE. We hope you can send a representative to cover this colorful celebration on Cleveland's cultural scene.

WHERE: Lakewood Civic Auditorium, Franklin Blvd. at Bunts Road (parking across the street).

WHEN: 8:00 p.m.—theatergoers begin filing into theater; Vincent Dowling on hand as "ticket taker" to identify the one-millionth playgoer.

Approx. 8:15—live trumpet fanfare signals Mr. or Ms. One Million; Dowling presents champagne, flowers, etc.

Approx. 8:30—Dowling ushers 1,000,000th theatergoer into Lakewood Civic Auditorium, followed by ceremony on stage, including proclamations and salute by thirty-member *Titus Andronicus* cast.

Approx. 8:40—play begins.

ASK FOR: BILL RUDMAN, 228-1225

NOTE: *Titus Andronicus* is pronounced TÍE-TUS   AN-DRÁHN-IH-CUS

###

Several things to note about this one: Everything is spelled out, down to the minute. By implication, I assure those covering (or thinking about covering it) the stunt that their hands will be held—I have not missed a detail. I also tell the story in a "visual" way, with a parade of irresistible, photogenic and theatrical doings. What I am selling is in fact an easily edited ninety-second mini-drama with a beginning, a middle, and an end—with enormous human interest. I make points about the institution and the play as I go. Among the many things I do not assume is that the *TV* reporter will know how to pronounce the title of the play. And I follow up with phone calls.

As exhilarating as it was to see this stunt work without a hitch—and to see the story turn up on all the TV stations and newspapers—the most gratifying part was the reaction of a usually jaded colleague. "Rudman," said this TV reporter, shaking his head in disbelief, "you are *shameless!*"

The Publicity Hustle

Those of us who ply our trade in the not-for-profit arena tend to get a bit snooty about commercial publicists. The stereotype of the fast-talking, cigar-chomping Broadway press agent, concerned only about getting his star's picture in Sunday's *Times* or the item in Liz Smith's *New York Daily News* column persists and is disparaged.

But having worked both sides of the publicity street, I cry, "Unfair!" It is true, of course, that the transient nature of most commercial engagements frees their public relations people of responsibilities the not-for-profit folks feel (or should feel) keenly. The Broadway press agent has no evolving institution at stake; thus you will not find words and phrases such as "mission," "long-range planning," "accountability" and "artistic process" in his lexicon.

There is much to be learned, however, from his hustle. While the rest of us occasionally get sidetracked by a starry-eyed devotion to art that borders on pretension, the commercial publicist, in his single-minded devotion to collecting column inches, is apt to be more enterprising and energetic. Members of the not-for-profit fraternity may dismiss him as crass, but I ask you—what is crass about creating honest hoopla that attracts people's attention (and consequently helps sell tickets) —unless that hoopla misrepresents or undermines what is on stage? The late, titanic Broadway press agent Bill Doll, who handled Mike Todd's PR for twenty years along with hundreds of Broadway shows and the Ringling Bros. and Barnum & Bailey Circus, once told me about a party he threw at Madison Square Garden. The nationally televised bash celebrated the international success of Todd's movie *Around the World in Eighty Days*. "Everybody was there," said Doll. His face beamed when he added, "To rent a tux, you had to go to New Jersey."

Such spirit, pride, and style are in short supply in the public relations offices of our so-called "arts" institutions.

If you remain unconvinced that the best commercial press agents are creative, very bright, accurate, honest and humane, with an abiding respect and love for their craft and the arts they promote so tirelessly, read Harvey Sabinson's delightful *Darling, You Were Wonderful!* And if you want evidence that the best ones are brilliant journalists in their own right, with a historian's far-reaching perspective, study the late Richard Maney's elegant, urbane memoir, *Fanfare*.

Role models, these, and wonderful showmen. Their *chutzpah* need not be incompatible with art.

Working with the Press

We've discussed some of the skills that lead to good press relations. But what about personality? It seems to me the only crucial matter is to be yourself. Press people spot phonies easily; they have little patience with feigned anything. They respect a working professional who maintains honesty, integrity, and a sense of humor.

It also doesn't hurt your relationship with the press if you are somewhat compulsive in your attention to detail. A few winters ago I spent an afternoon on Central Park's frigid Great Lawn working with press to cover a public art installation. The piece on view was a mammoth white sculpture made of Styrofoam.

Finally, the last of the photographers and reporters departed. After hanging around for a while to make sure no one else was coming, I started the hike up to the street. Then I remembered the *New York Times* reporter was working on deadline,

"Very little in life is predictable, but animals, children and pretty faces are best bets to get in the papers and on television. Thus it will ever be."

"Find a photographer sensitive to what Elia Kazan termed 'the precision of the living moment.'"

and that I should check in with her—compulsively—one last time.

I called her from a booth on the edge of the Great Lawn, and my heart and soul sank when she answered her phone with, "Oh, I'm glad you called. Could you find out how much the Styrofoam would weigh if it were marble?"

It was 4:40 p.m., any marble stores in Manhattan would surely close in twenty minutes, and the last place I wanted to be was the middle of Central Park, freezing my fanny off making telephone calls.

I did it, of course, because I had to. (The fifth marble man I called—the first who believed I was for real—computed the answer.) I was the one who had persuaded the woman to cover the event; it was my business to help her. And it's no good your arguing, "Well, after all, that was *The New York Times*." I would have done it, and so would any other competent public relations professional, for the *Asbury Park Press*.

A few miscellaneous suggestions on dealing with members of the Fourth Estate:

• Don't be afraid to tell a journalist you don't know an answer to a question, and you'll have to check on it. All that says about you is that you respect the facts enough to want to get them right.

• The rules of the journalist/publicist relationship are tricky; they make little sense to the uninitiated. If you're new at it, be prepared to make mistakes. You'll find that the toughest newspaperman—the guy who turns red, screams, and starts to throw his desk at you when you mess it up—is the guy who later takes pride in admitting to having taught you everything you know.

• Don't limit your contact with media people to those mornings when you're peddling something. What about dropping a reporter a complimentary note on a piece he wrote on somebody else's company? Or offering a writer a story idea that has nothing to do with your institution?

It is with critics, of course, that we feel most vulnerable. We can prepare first-rate material and enjoy a fine relationship of mutual respect, but if the show doesn't work for the guy on the aisle, it doesn't work, and he is paid to tell us so. You have two choices: you can spend the three weeks prior to an opening night agonizing over what you said in the press invitations and whether you assigned the critics the right seats and whether you should chat with them between Acts I and II—or you can spend those same weeks doing the other 99 percent of your job.

Don't neglect critics. On the contrary, one of your long-term goals is to help them (and all your publics) gain a sense of your institution's mission and development. No doubt you feel a bit self-righteous about that. As *New York Post* critic Clive Barnes observes: "Because of our lack of princes and their courts, we in America are having to build our institutions the hard way. Generosity is called for. This does not mean that critics should overpraise. Simply what it means is that critics should be loving toward the inherent possibilities of their own cultural community."

But don't be defeated if your town lacks for the moment, even one writer with such a worldly and sensitive outlook. It'll happen when it happens.

In the meantime, you have work to do. Your work as a public relations officer is all about listening closely, thinking clearly, writing well, and communicating persuasively. Most important, your work is about communicating the joy and lasting value of art in a society that seems most intent on consuming video games and Betamaxes.

There is a certain nobility in that. The former *New York Times* critic and author Brooks Atkinson once wrote that the public relations person "who can write and who also has artistic and intellectual understanding is a gift from the gods." But don't let it go to your head. Like most challenging jobs, this one asks you to roll up your sleeves and get on with it.

Are all your signs straight?

Charles Ziff

COMPUTERS AND TEST MARKETING

Computers

Computers are *very* potent tools. They can simplify or complicate, clarify or confuse, facilitate or impair the marketing of artistic work with remarkable ease. Thus, they are tools that should be used selectively and approached with care.

Computer systems can assist the marketing process in several key areas:
1. Keeping records of those who purchase tickets and recording the purchases they make.
2. Keeping track of tickets or subscriptions for sale, and of how many of them have been sold.
3. Accounting for income received from the sale of tickets, subscriptions, and related items.
4. Analyzing the results of marketing activities, or making projections based on past experience.

While the most sophisticated computer marketing or box-office systems tend to approach the four areas listed above on an integrated basis, you are best advised to compare your needs to a computer system's capabilities by examining each area separately. That examination requires two steps: First, deciding what you need; and second, comparing your needs to a proposed system's capabilities.

Deciding what you need will be the more difficult and time consuming of the two steps. While only you can fully outline your organization's requirements, here are some specific capabilities you should consider:

Customer Records

1. Record names, addresses with zip codes, and telephone numbers.
2. Identify special types of customers—such as corporations, schools, VIPs, handicapped individuals, etc.
3. Record secondary, temporary or seasonal addresses.
4. Keep track of relationships among customers—such as those who share subscriptions.
5. Record text or statistical notations about customers.
6. Screen against or remove duplicate records.
7. Record purchases or donations made by customers.
8. Print a customer directory.
9. Print mailing labels, or encode mailing lists on magnetic tape.
10. Print customized form letters to names on your customer list.
11. Remove inactive customers.

Ticket Sales

1. Develop an inventory of seats for each hall.
2. Record the purchaser of each seat.
3. Print a seating chart that mirrors the architectural arrangement of seats in the

Charles Ziff is President of Ziff Marketing, which specializes in offering marketing and computer guidance to arts organizations across the country. The firm's clients include major institutions in the theatre, music and dance fields. Mr. Ziff also serves as principal project consultant on the development of the Arts Income Management System, a package of computer programs designed to assist arts organizations in marketing, development and income accounting. Prior to founding his own firm, Mr. Ziff served as Marketing Specialist in the Office on the Arts of the Ford Foundation. He also served as Vice President for Promotion at the Brooklyn Academy of Music. It was at BAM that Mr. Ziff pioneered the application of direct mail test marketing to the performing arts. Mr. Ziff was the Managing Director of the Nikolais-Louis Foundation for Dance, and prior to that position he served as an Associate Producer for station WOR in New York City. Mr. Ziff has taught arts administration at the New York University and City University of New York. He is a graduate of Wesleyan University, a trustee of the Association of Theatrical Press Agents and Managers, and the Brooklyn Civic Council. He lives in Colebrook, Connecticut.

hall, and indicate which seats are sold and which are still available.

4. Print a report that lists each seat, indicates if it has been purchased, and if so, by whom.
5. Develop a schedule of performances and/or subscription series for each hall.
6. Print a schedule of performances.
7. Scale the house for each performance and/or series, allowing for full-price sales and sales at various discount rates.
8. Designate house seats, press seats and the like for each performance.
9. Record the seat locations of seats sold to each customer.
10. Print subscription-renewal invoices.
11. Include suggested contributions on suscription invoices.
12. Print tickets, individually or in series. Or alternatively, print forms designed to facilitate filling ticket orders by hand.
13. Print ticket mailing materials such as envelopes or mailing forms.
14. Print reports summarizing sales activities by performance, by series, by discount rate, or by price category within a hall.
15. Print a list of customers who have purchased tickets or subscriptions for a performance, series, or season.

Income Accounting

1. Record payments received from customers.
2. Issue refunds to customers.
3. Process payments made by credit card and print credit card charge forms or encode charge records on magnetic tape.
4. Print an audit trail of payments received and refunds issued.
5. Summarize receipts for posting to a receipts journal.
6. Print a box-office statement for each performance.

Analysis and Projection

1. Analyze customers by zip code.
2. Analyze sales activities by source, comparing the productivity of advertising mediums, mailing lists, etc.
3. Analyze sales activities over time to compare current progress to previous experiences.
4. Project income potential for future events based on sales records from past events.

Before shopping for a computer system, you should understand several basic terms:

Hardware—the computer equipment itself.

Operating System—a package of programs usually supplied with the hardware, which enables the hardware to operate and execute application programs.

Software or Application Programs—specific lists of instructions that direct the computer to perform specific tasks, such as printing subscription invoices, computing a box-office statement, editing the text of a letter, or the like.

Central Processing Unit—the "Brain" of the computer that interprets application programs and manipulates data as the programs direct.

Disk Drive or Tape Drive—a device for recording or reading information stored on magnetic tapes or disks. These tapes or disks may contain application programs, operating-system programs, or data such as mailing lists, sales figures, and the like.

CRT (Cathode Ray Tube) or *VDT (Video Display Terminal)*—a device for entering data into the computer on a typewriter-like keyboard and displaying data on a television-like screen.

Printer—a typewriter-like device for printing data on paper.

Microcomputer—the smallest type of computer, generally about the size of a bread box and equipped with one VDT, one or two small disk drives, and a small printer. Such systems can cost from $2,000 to $20,000.

> "Test marketing provides an opportunity to catch errors or imperfections in brochures before hundreds of thousands of them have been printed."

Minicomputer — a medium-sized computer, generally about the size of a refrigerator, able to support several VDTs which may execute different programs simultaneously. It also has one or more full sized tape or disk drives and one or more printers. Such systems can cost from $20,000 to $150,000.

Mainframe Computer — a large computer, often housed in several cabinets, each the size of a refrigerator, able to support many VDTs, printers, tape or disk drives. It is capable of executing many programs for different users simultaneously. Such systems, which are rarely used by individual arts organizations, cost in excess of $150,000.

Computer systems may be acquired or used under a variety of arrangements, each of which offers advantages and disadvantages. As the cost of equipment has declined due to technological advances, most arts organizations interested in computerization have opted to acquire micro- or minicomputer systems of their own. Such systems may be installed as "turnkey systems" in which hardware and pre-designed application software are acquired from a single source; assembled by selecting application software from one source and compatible hardware from another; or commissioned by creating custom software designed to operate on equipment acquired as development of the software begins.

If acquisition of equipment is impractical or beyond your means, you can also computerize through service bureaus that maintain their own computers and process work for you. You might also consider time-sharing systems, in which VDTs and printers on your premises are connected by telephone lines to a computer maintained elsewhere. While these arrangements eliminate some of the responsibilities inherent in owning and maintaining your own system, they offer less control over the accuracy of your data and over the responsiveness of the system to your needs. Since service bureaus and time-sharing companies are usually able to offer price quotations based upon estimated work volumes, it is possible to compare the cost of using them against the cost of leasing or purchasing your own equipment.

No matter how careful you are in defining your needs, and in comparison-shopping for hardware and software, it is safe to say you will not anticipate every requirement you have now or may have in the future. The development of a computer system is therefore most realistically viewed as an evolutionary process — the system will grow and change as your needs and experience dictate.

> "Surely, testing is preferable to endless speculation over the effect of price, design, copy, or mailing list."

Test Marketing

Marketing the arts requires decision-making—on pricing, offer construction, copy, design, and the target for each offer. The decisions you make, generally based on recent experience and tempered by professional judgement, can sometimes have a more profound effect on income and attendance than the nature of your organization's artistic work.

In a sense, many marketing approaches evolve by trial and error. If a mailing list generates a low return, we do not use it again. If we raise prices and attendance falls, we do not continue to raise prices. If we place a naked lady on the brochure cover and sales skyrocket, we place more naked ladies on more brochure covers.

While experience and judgement are often sufficient bases for making marketing choices, situations occasionally arise where the choices seem so perplexing or the consequences of making an error so great that it seems worthwhile to make an effort to predict the outcome *before* a decision is made. Test marketing makes such predictions by letting a representative sampling of consumers respond to a proposed offering. Their reaction is used to gauge the responses likely to come from the larger public destined to receive the final offering.

Any part of a marketing effort can be tested, but the most frequent subjects of testing are price (if someone will pay $9.50 for a ticket, will they pay $10.50?), offer construction (will a fixed subscription sell as well as a make-your-own plan?), copy and design (will a bold headline stressing subscription savings outperform a more modulated statement about artistic content?), or mailing lists (will a demographically selected list costing $50 per thousand names outperform a list you can borrow from the local art museum for free?).

The most practical test-marketing technique for most arts organizations involves the use of randomly selected names from one or more mailing lists. In the same way that Gallup or Harris can evaluate the opinions of millions of Americans by interviewing several thousand people, so can you estimate the effect of alternative marketing approaches on all prospective ticket buyers by making a test offer to relatively few.

Sample Selection

The technique for selecting test respondents is called "nth name" selection. Suppose we have a mailing list composed of fifteen names:

1. Able	6. Frankie	11. Kenney
2. Baker	7. Georgie	12. Larry
3. Charlie	8. Harry	13. Michael
4. Danny	9. Isadora	14. Nancy
5. Edie	10. Jane	15. Olivia

If we wish to select three names at random from this list, we can divide the total number of names on the list, fifteen, by the number of names we want (three), to yield an "nth name" value of five. Selecting every fifth name from the list will give us a randomly distributed selection of three: Able, Frankie, and Kenny. If we want two equal samplings of three names in which no name is used more than once, we can compose a second sample composed of Baker, Georgie and Larry. If we wished to select 500 names from a mailing list of 30,000, we would divide 30,000 by 500, and select every sixtieth name.

The size of the sample we need is determined by the rate of response we anticipate, and the accuracy of the predictions we wish to make. This is true regardless of the size of the list from which the sample is drawn. Sample sizes may be computed by an equation, or may be drawn from the following table:

Anticipated Response	Sample Size	Margin of Error of Prediction
½%	19,100	.1%
1%	9,500	.2%
1%	4,225	.3%
2%	4,700	.4%
5%	1,800	1.0%
10%	860	2.0%
30%	400	4.5%
50%	380	5.0%
70%	320	5.0%
90%	140	5.0%

If you are adventuresome and wish to compute your own sample sizes, here is the equation:

$$N = \frac{(R)\ (1-R)\ (3.84)}{E^2}$$

N = the sample size you are solving for

R = the anticipated rate of response as a decimal (for example a 70% response would be .7)

E = the margin of error you are willing to accept in the prediction (for example, 2% expressed as .02)

Price, Offer, Copy and Design Testing

Price, offer, copy and design testing all work on the same basis: Two or more versions of an offering are prepared where all components are identical except the one to be tested. For example, you might have two identical subscription brochures in which only the prices are different, or one brochure that accentuates subscription savings and privileges, and one that concentrates on describing the works to be performed. Each version is then mailed with coded order blanks, to nth name samples of equal size, drawn from the same mailing list or lists. The offer is not identified in any way as a test, and actual orders are received and tabulated.

As orders are received, the productivity of one version can be compared with that of the others. The income and attendance figures generated by each sample are multiplied by the value of "n" to predict the actual income or number of orders that would be generated if the offer were mailed to the entire list. For example, testing two versions of a brochure featuring alternate prices, mailed to 400 name samples, drawn from a list of 15,000 subscribers, might produce results like this:

16,000 names/400 name sample = "n" value of 40

Version	Sample Income	Sample Attendance	Predicted Income	Predicted Attendance
High Price	$635	65	$25,400	2,600
Low Price	$540	78	$21,600	3,120

Management could then weigh the advantages of $3,800 in additional income, which would be generated at the higher price, against 520 additional attendances, which would be generated at the lower price.

In copy and design testing, all test orders can subsequently be filled without adjustment. In cases of offer or price testing, some adjustments must be made before orders produced by the losing version can be fulfilled. If the losing version carries a higher price, partial refunds must be issued as these orders are fulfilled. A brief note explaining the reason for the adjustment should accompany the refund. If the losing version carries a lower price, it is generally best to fill these orders at the lower price and record an adjusting notation for the performances involved on the box-office or subscription statement.

List Testing

List testing requires a simpler procedure. Here, nth name samples are selected from a variety of mailing lists under consideration. A single version of the offer is sent simultaneously to all of the list samples with order blanks coded by list. Then, the income and attendance generated by each list is multiplied by the value of "n" to determine the return that would be generated by using the entire list. For example, a performing ensemble who wishes to sell 2,400 new subscriptions next season selects samples of 5,000 names each, drawn from five prospective lists. The resulting prediction might look like this:

List	Size of List	Value of "n"	Sample Orders	Predicted Orders	Percent Response
ABC Theater	50,000	10	65	650	1.3%
XYZ Opera	100,000	20	32	640	0.6%
PQR Museum	80,000	16	36	576	0.7%
DEF Symphony	140,000	28	21	588	0.4%
MNO Ballet	65,000	13	11	143	0.2%
Total	435,000		145	2,597	0.6%

In this example, the MNO Ballet list might be discarded, due to its low percent response. Since it accounts for only 143 orders, the remaining four lists should still produce a sufficient number of orders to reach the 2,400 subscription goal.

Side Effects

Test marketing produces a number of side effects—some good and some bad. The good side effects include:

"Many marketing approaches evolve by trial and error. If a mailing list generates a low return, we do not use it again. If we place a naked lady on the brochure and sales skyrocket…"

- An opportunity to catch errors or imperfections in brochures before hundreds of thousands of them have been printed. (We have all heard of the infirm, elderly person whose telephone number was mis-printed as the charge-by-phone number in the opera company's season brochure.)
- The ability to estimate how orders will distribute themselves among subscription series or performance schedules.
- The ability to catch confusing aspects of order forms or instructions before thousands of improperly filled-out blanks arrive in the mail.
- The ability to predict what the income from a sales effort is likely to be.

The bad side effects include:

- Variations between predicted and actual responses, which can occur due to the elapsed time between sample and actual mailings.
- The inability to predict accurately how various offers will perform in media other than direct mail.
- The extra effort required to process order adjustments necessary for price or offer testing.
- Occasional consumer confusion, which may be prompted by test offers with varying prices or offers mailed in advance of public announcement of events.

Tips for Testing on a Tight Budget

If your budget for testing is limited, keep these thoughts in mind: Generally, test offers produce orders of sufficient value to cover the cost of the text. This is particularly true if materials are designed to limit the variations in copy, offer design, or prices to one side of a brochure, one color in the printing process, or one component of a direct-mail package.

In the case of list testing, tests may be conducted as part of your ongoing mailing program rather than done as a seperate mailing. Simply substitute smaller samples from many trial lists for a portion of the least productive list you usually use. Results of these list trials may then be used to alter your selection of mailing lists in a subsequent campaign.

Despite its limitations, testing proves its value time and time again. It separates brilliant copy and design ideas from creative disasters, prudent price adjustments from foolish ones, and great mailing-list finds from red herrings. It is surely preferable to endless speculation over what the effect of a price change, design or copy alteration, or mailing-list substitution might be.

Mark Arnold

TELEPHONE CAMPAIGNS[1]

The subscriber has become the *sine qua non* of the arts in America. He provides the income to launch our programs, fills our seats for every performance, allows us diversity in programming selections, and he regularly returns from season to season. He is the foundation that supports our theaters, and without him, our stability would be seriously jeopardized.

How do we find this crucial subscriber and build the audience support that ensures our survival? We mail 500,000 brochures. They go to magazine readers, civic groups, select zip/income households, or to anyone who might read them. Direct mail has been the primary sales thrust for building our audiences, and yet, when we look closely at the mail, we have to question its effectiveness.

Consider some statistics: How many subscribers attended your last season? What is the population of your community? How many brochures were mailed in your last subscription campaign? Your subscription base is a fairly accurate indication of your market saturation, or the percentage of your population that regularly attends the theater (1% is a realistic average). Yet, in many cases, brochures are mailed to more than 10% of the population, so it is conceivable that 90% of those who receive our brochures have no real interest in what we offer. We'll call this campaign where we spray our communities with brochures, hoping that a modest 1% return rate will hold, the *shotgun* technique. It's taking a gamble on low returns, and is not a very reliable way to sell subscriptions. What we need is a *rifle* technique. We've got to take aim at the prime market rather than skim the total market with our brochures. We've got to define the market, gain access to it, and then sell, sell, sell!

With large mailing lists, we lose selectivity and rely too heavily on low-return odds. Instead, we can really *sell* the theatergoing market with assertive, one-on-one phone contact. We reach the people *most likely* to subscribe, and *turn every objection into a subscription advantage*. We've all heard this resistance a thousand times:

> "I'm not really interested in subscribing. Besides, with my travel schedule I'd probably miss half of the shows."

But how often do we take the time to answer the complaint personally?

> "Well, Mr. Jones, I can understand that, but when you think about it, we're giving you six plays for the price of four. Even if you miss one, it's still a bargain. But the fact is, you won't miss any. If the date's not convenient, just call us, and we'll change it. It's that simple. Do you usually go out on week nights, or would weekends be better?"

People like to be sold. They will buy happily when you have won their confidence. Of course they set up resistances, but when you're willing to overcome

Mark Arnold is Director of Marketing Services for S.R.O. Consultants, Inc., a national performing arts marketing firm that has mounted campaigns to substantially increase the subscription base for major theaters, symphonies, dance companies and sports organizations throughout the country. Prior to joining S.R.O., Mr. Arnold was Marketing Director for Atlanta's Alliance Theatre Company. He is the author of Dialing for Dollars, published by Theatre Communications Group as the first volume of its Performing Arts Ideabook Series. His brochure concepts are used as a guide in TCG's Graphic Communications for the Performing Arts. Arnold has been a consultant to theater companies throughout the country and has conducted marketing seminars for TCG, ACUCAA, The Southern Arts Federation and The Georgia Theatre Conference.

Photo: Charles M. Raf

---

[1]Portions of the material in this section first appeared in *Dialing For Dollars* by Mark Arnold, published by Theater Communications Group a part of its *Performing Arts Ideabooks* series.

"Ninety percent of the people who receive our brochures may have no real interest in what we offer."

them, you can sell almost anything to anyone. The phone provides you with an ideal opportunity to convey the many benefits of your subscription offerings. Because you want to give your prospects the chance to ask questions, you must become active listeners. Then you can transform objections into positive subscription advantages and encourage the prospect to formulate his own clear decision about the value of what you're offering. Of course, you're right there to close the sale, leading the prospect through the process of subscribing.

Those who are effective over the phone are professionals who have earned a living previously at this kind of work. If they can sell magazines, they can sell subscriptions. Volunteers do little more than clean our lists, isolating those who already wish to subscribe from a large pool of names. In this respect, they may be helpful in canvassing the first round of renewals, or in a fund-raising drive directed at previous donors. But volunteers are rarely effective in convincing the uninitiated to make the choice to subscribe or donate. Simply stated, they're *not trained* in sales (and resist such training due to other commitments). They also get depressed by turndowns. One might make twelve calls before closing a sale. Professionals are undaunted by this, and won't lose their motivation. (Each "no" statistically brings them closer to a "yes" and they know it.)

Talented salespersons must also be rewarded for their work; you must provide them the chance to earn a good salary.

The Economics

Based on the experience of many arts groups, a 1% sales rate from direct-mail brochures is about the best you can expect. Given this 1%, you need 100 brochures to sell a single subscription. With postage hovering at 5¢, printing at 5–10¢ (let's call it 7¢), mailing and list costs at 8¢—each brochure costs us 20¢, and each subscription costs $20.00, or 40% of a $50.00 income average.

That same subscription can be reliably sold over the phone for $17.00, or 34% of income. We'll cover the $17.00 shortly, but first let's look at the economics of the run of a campaign. On the average, a salesperson can complete seven calls per hour ("complete" means actual sales messages delivered, excluding no answers, wrong numbers, or quick hang-ups). Salespersons work a four-hour shift (the maximum for this type of work). With ten salespeople, that's 280 calls per night, or 1,400 calls during a five-evening work week.

Depending on the quality of your lists, your sales return rate will fall in the range of 8%–12%. Assuming an average return rate of 10%, you can sell 140 subscriptions on 1,400 weekly calls, or 3,500 subscriptions over a twenty-five-week campaign.

At a cost of $17.00 per subscription, your 3,500 subscribers will cost you $59,500, or again, 34% of our $175,000 income (a $50.00 subscription average). Looking at the mail and that 1% return, you'd need 350,000 brochures to bring you 3,500 subscribers. At a cost of 20¢ each, they'd require $70,000 or 40% of your income. You're saving $3.00 on each subscription sold, or $10,500 over the run of the campaign. And, with the phone, you only pay against real-income returns, which greatly reduces the risk on your expenditure.

$17,00 Per Subscription Sold

A competent salesperson should be well-paid. Given part-time work and seasonal employment, you should provide the opportunity for your sales staff to earn $6.00 an hour, or $120.00 over a twenty-hour calling period.

With seven calls per hour over a twenty-hour week with a 10% sales rate, the staff should sell fourteen subscriptions per week. If you divide their weekly pay ($120.00) by your weekly sales (14) yhou have a per subscription pay rate of $8.57 (let's round it off to $8.50).

A reliable and experienced campaign manager should earn $3.50 per subscription sold, or $490.00 on 140 weekly sales. Add to that the cost of phones, lists, ads, additional brochure mailings, sales incentives, and other materials, for another $5.00 per subscription sold. With the above $8.50, this brings you to a total cost of $17.00 per subscription sold, or 34% of a $50.00 income. Payroll can be structured as follows:

Straight Commission

Pay against earnings, with no risk—$8.50 per subscription sold, or $119.00 per week for fourteen subscriptions.

Escalating Commission

Still pay against income return, with an incentive to reach higher sales levels: $7.50 per subscription on the first ten sales each week, and $10.00 per subscription on additional weekly sales. Total of $115.00 for fourteen subscriptions.

Base Salary & Commission

When required by law, as in some states, you must guarantee $70 per week (a $3.50 hourly wage) against a straight or escalating commission. But, with a guarantee, your staff has to producce a minimum of nine sales (to cover $70.00 at $8.50 per subscription). To protect yourself, you must establish minimum weekly sales requirements. If the minimum is not met by individual salespersons, then find replacements. You'll experience high turnover in the early weeks of the campaign, but through this effort, you will develop a very strong sales team.

(The above illustration is presented as a guide to estimating costs. Figures are based on an average of several campaigns in different markets. Variables such as number of staff, their sales success, quality of lists, and your phone company's rate structure may alter the actual costs of your campaign.)

Staffing the Campaign

The manager is crucial to the success of a campaign. He must be a teacher, motivator, artistic director, salesman and bookkeeper all in one. He will train new salespersons as they join the campaign, will ensure that sales efforts are honest and effective, will work to improve the techniques of less experienced staff, and will report to theater management on weekly sales, payroll, and earnings. The manager should be experienced in sales (preferably telephone sales) and may be located through classified advertising.

Sales staff must have the following qualities—enthusiasm, a pleasant and articulate manner, an outgoing and energetic personality, sales experience, and a positive attitude about the product. Initial interviews should be conducted over the telephone (here's a telephone sales effort you can judge) and candidates can be rated on each of the above qualities. Invite high scorers to start on the campaign, and test them over the first few weeks, (with backups on hold to replace ineffective staff). People with extroverted personalities may be found among the following groups:

> actors and actresses
> airline and travel-agency personnel
> hotel personnel
> waiters and waitresses
> schoolteachers (summer work)
> homemakers
> the handicapped

Staff may also be recruited through classified advertising.

EXAMPLE:

TELEPHONE SALES. If you have a pleasant voice, enthusiasm, and sales experience, the U.S. Theater Company needs you to sell subscriptions to its upcoming season. Part-time work with full-time pay. Call...

Calling All Theatergoers

At the top of your telephone roster should be last season's non-renewing subscribers. After the mail notices, curtain speeches, and program-stuffers, there will still be many patrons who keep putting off their renewal. A direct call can remind them of seat-reservation deadlines and reinforce the many benefits they enjoy as subscribers.

Then, you *must* reach all those who purchased single tickets last year. With advance credit card reservations, you can easily secure their names, addresses, and telephone numbers. It's imperative that all this information be stored. These people are your best prospects, because they've already been to the theater. Your job now is to convince them of the savings and convenience they pass up by not subscribing.

Other cultural attendance lists, club-membership rosters, and purchased lists (key zip/income demographics, magazine subscribers, new homeowners, etc.) can next be canvassed. Many of these are available with both labels and separate telephone numbers, or, you can hire minimum wage help to look up telephone numbers (don't waste the valuable time of sales staff—they should be selling).

City directories, which list telephone numbers by street addresses, should be purchased. You can track streets where many current subscribers live, and deliver your sales pitch to their neighbors. These directories are available from R.L. Polk, and Cole Publications, for about $125.00 per city:

R.L. Polk
777 Third Avenue
New York, N.Y. 10017
(212) 826-0600

Cole Publications
529 Fifth Avenue
New York, N.Y. 10017
(212) 867-5640

One very important resource for new prospects is existing prospects. When closing a sale, ask the subscriber for the names and telephone numbers of friends who might be interested in subscribing on the same night (perhaps with adjoining seats), and tell them, "I'd be delighted to organize a theater party for you!"

A television or radio campaign might also be employed to generate leads. Listeners will be encouraged to phone in to receive literature. While it's in the mail, you can look up the telephone numbers for a follow-up call to close the sale. A special promotion or prize drawing can also be used to generate leads.

Developing a Sales Script

Let's restate our reasons for making the call:

- To provide valuable information a prospect will be glad to hear.
- To point out the advantages of subscribing.
- To answer questions prospects might have about our offer.
- To transform objections into positive subscription advantages.
- To convince patrons to make a decision to purchase a subscription.
- To take orders over the telephone.

In any sales effort, think *benefits,* not *features.* A benefit refers to an advantage the *subscriber* will receive. A feature refers to *you,* the producing organization. On the telephone, you must take the perspective away from yourself and what makes your theater wonderful, and aim it towards the subscriber and how he'll benefit by becoming a regular member of the audience. Here are some examples:

Feature: we produce wonderful plays.
Benefit: you'll enjoy our wonderful productions.
Feature: our subscriptions are discounted 33%.
Benefit: you'll save 33% off the regular ticket price.

It is also important that you use the patron's name repeatedly. These are sweet words to him. In the opening of your sales pitch, you want to highlight the benefits of becoming a subscriber. Here is an example:

Hello, Mr./Mrs. _____. My name is _____, and I'm with the U.S. Theater Company. We're calling all the people who enjoy coming to our plays to let you know about the benefits of becoming a subscriber (pause). Have you attended any of our recent performances (converse).

Well, Mr./Mrs. _____, we've got six great plays running from September to May, and as a subscriber you'll save 33% off the regular box-office price. That's six great plays for the price of four, and two plays absolutely free! Why, even if you miss one, it's still a bargain, but the fact is, you won't miss any. If the date's not convenient, just call us, and we'll change it—it's that simple (pause).

Plus, you'll have a guaranteed reserved seat, and you'll never stand in line. We know you're going to have a fantastic time, and you can put this subscription on one of your credit cards. Do you usually go out during the week, or would weekends be better?

In the last sentence, you present what's called a "soft-choice close." The patron is not asked whether or not he'd like to subscribe (the positive choice is implied), but simply, which night of the week would be best. An alternate close would be, "You can charge this to any of five credit cards, which would be best for you?" or "I've got good seats in section A or B, which would you prefer?"

Following the opening, the patron might ask for information on the season, might order a subscription, or might respond with any number of reasons he does not wish to subscribe. Your job now is to overcome his objections. In our script, you need to prepare yourselves for typical objections, and develop the techniques to overcome them.

First, you must cancel out the stated objection, and then come back at the patron with other subscription benefits. You don't want to disagree with the patron (the customer *is* always right), but you must acknowledge his hesitation, state the benefit that cancels out the objection, and then discuss other benefits that make subscribing even more attractive. Here is a list of typical objections, with suggested copy to overcome them:

Not Interested

A) Tell me, Mr./Mrs. _____, when was the last time you enjoyed a really top notch performance? You know you deserve *first class* entertainment. Let me tell you about the great plays you'll see next season...

B) You know, Mr./Mrs. _____, I'm sure you attend other events like concerts or movies. Live theater is so fresh and exciting, and when you think about it, the theater is not any more expensive than the other events you go to...(describe additional benefits).

Will Buy Single Tickets

I see, Mr./Mrs. _____, which plays do you want to see most? I see...excellent choices. Last year we sold out on many performances, and I'm sure that tickets to _____ will be the first to go (pause). And when you think about it...(repeat other benefits).

Please Send a Brochure

We sent them out recently, and I know you were on the list. I'm sorry if it didn't reach you, but you were chosen as a VIP to be called. Think of me as your "Talking Brochure." I have all the latest information here in front of me, and I can answer all your questions here on the phone...(repeat other benefits).

Will Think About It/Discuss With Spouse

Well, Mr./Mrs. _____, of course I can call you back, but is there anything I haven't explained clearly to you? Orders are coming in every day, and while you're thinking, many of the better seats will be sold. So now is the time to order, while I have you on the telephone.

NOTE: Some theaters have actually assigned seats over the telephone. It's an added benefit that works well to close sales.

"People like to be sold. They will buy happily when you have won their confidence."

"The manager is crucial to the campaign's success. He must be a teacher, motivator, artistic director, salesman and bookkeeper all in one."

Can't Afford It

Well, Mr./Mrs. _____, I can understand that, but when you think about it, you'll enjoy a whole season's entertainment for as little as $35, plus, you're getting two plays for free! And these days, savings are an important consideration...(repeat other benefits)

Can't Plan That Far Ahead

(Describe your convenient exchange policy, then repeat benefits.)

Staff Training

While your sales staff may never have been to your theater, it's important that they know it well. At your first training session, provide a report on the theater that the staff can read at home. Include history, producing philosophy, primary artists, audience growth, the importance of subscription and subscriber benefits, the upcoming season, and the structure and goals of your phone campaign.

On a second sheet, provide important facts about the theater that will help salespersons while on the telephone—the theater itself, the artists, review quotes, awards, growth, parking, public transportation, restaurants, exchange policy, box-office hours, handicapped access, etc.

At your first meeting, discuss the importance of subscription and the goals of your telephone campaign. Detail the subscription offer and the many benefits of subscribing. Continue with a summary of the upcoming season and the excitement that surround the productions (provide them with an information sheet on the season). Describe the basic mechanics of the telephone campaign—who they're calling and why, and how they should work to overcome typical objections. Review the sales script step by step, and ask the staff to familiarize themselves with it.

At your next meeting, arrange for staff to pretend they're telephoning each other, with one person delivering the sales pitch and another responding with typical objections. Discuss the results, and remind the staff not to give up too easily, but instead, to keep coming back with new subscriber benefits.

You're ready to go, but don't forget that you must work continuously with staff during the course of the campaign. Some experienced salespersons will pick up an effective technique immediately; others will need advice and encouragement. In the early weeks, discuss call-results among the staff (what's working and what's not), and arrange for less experienced staff to learn from the more experienced. Be sure that sales pitches don't veer from what you really can offer. Misrepresentation should be grounds for immediate dismissal.

In addition to a subscription price schedule and order form, you'll need a call record sheet to track the campaign. Each salesperson should complete it each night, listing the prospect called, telephone number, and result of the call—i.e., new sale, renewal, wrong number, no answer, brochure sent, discussing with spouse, not interested, call-back date. The manager should track a sheet for each salesperson, recording sales, earnings, and commissions due. From this sheet, the manager can prepare a weekly summary of the campaign results and a weekly payroll sheet.

Many patrons won't purchase on the first call, but can be sold on the second or third attempt. Don't give up on the first turndown, but wait a few weeks, and pass names to new salespersons.

NEVER GIVE SALESPERSONS ACCESS TO PATRON CREDIT-CARD NUMBERS!

This may result in an unauthorized charge, where a staff person fabricates an order. Credit-card numbers must *only* be obtained from patrons during the course of a sale.

The ideal sales environment will allow for privacy without isolation. It's important that the manager be able to monitor pitches without traveling great distances. If four salespesons are placed around a large table, they'll benefit from both an individual work-space and the inspiration of the group effort.

The best calling times are evenings, from 5:30 p.m. to 9:30 p.m., Monday through Friday. If a patron is interrupted at dinner, the staff should politely apologize, and arrange to call back at a more convenient time.

Cancellations/Renewals

In selling subscriptions with a credit-card charge, you will have to accept occasional cancellations. If you indicate that this is an irrevocable, final sale, you will decrease total sales by a much greater percentage than the actual cancellations you'll receive. Cancellations come from many sources—they come from brochure sales as well as telephone sales. Patrons move out of town, don't like their seats, or sometimes, are flat broke. Once in a while, you'll receive a cancellation from a patron who feels he or she was pressured to buy, but these are generally too few to worry about.

The number of renewals you get from telephone sales will relate to the strength of a prospect list. Those who have been to the theater will probably enjoy the season more than those who haven't. It is therefore imperative that you have access to last season's single-ticket buyers. On making a sale, it's a good idea to follow up with an information package thanking the patron for his or her order, and describing the excitement that surrounds the upcoming season. This way, the new patron will be building interest in the plays prior to receiving the credit-card invoice.

Newsletters are also a good idea during the season. The more background you can provide about the play, the better it's enjoyed, and the greater your chances for renewals. Curtain speeches, backstage tours, and other activities that make the subscriber feel part of the family are always worthwhile.

Closing

Our subscribers are too important to rest on the uncertainty of direct mail. Brochures, although convenient for fulfilling a choice to subscribe are not forceful or reliable enough to sell our product. To meet rising costs, our audiences must grow. We have to *create* subscribers, not simply find them. Our theaters are alive with fresh, exciting work that's effectively packaged with tempting incentives. We've designed the product to sell, but too often stop short of selling it. With the telephone as a tool, we can reach a ready market, and persuasively convince those who are uncertain to subscribe.

PART IV:
Specific Application of the Marketing Principles by Discipline

Linda Kinsey

THEATER: A CASE HISTORY

McCarter Theater is located in Princeton, a university town of 25,550 people in central New Jersey. In recent years, McCarter has emerged as New Jersey's foremost performing-arts center, annually presenting professional drama, dance, music, and film series as well as numerous special events, including an annual production of *A Christmas Carol.*

In the spring of 1979, Nagle Jackson, formerly artistic director of Milwaukee Repertory Theater, assumed leadership of McCarter. He dedicated himself to building a resident professional acting company — a company whose members would make their homes in the community and become part of that community.

His artistic vision spelled a significant change for the established subscription audience of 9,000 patrons who were accustomed to seasons highlighted with "star" attractions and a company of actors whose faces changed with each production. The new artistic direction meant building a new audience—an audience which would respond and eventually become committed to a resident company of gifted but largely unknown actors, performing varied roles in classic and contemporary plays.

For two seasons (1979–80 and 1980–81), the subscription campaigns showed disappointing results. By 1980, the subscription base had slipped to 8,200, which was a cause for some alarm and certainly a source of frustration for the management and artistic director. By the beginning of the 1981–82 season, subscription for the drama series had begun to show improvement—they increased to 8,835. Encouraged that we had finally seen the last of the "dog days," and that our product was finally catching on, we contented ourselves with the theory that the audience development for McCarter's drama program was a long-term challenge.

In the fall of 1981, McCarter's board of trustees requested a five-year plan that called for, among other improvements, a significant increase in the area of earned income, specifically for the drama program. Of the $2.3 million annual budget, we earned 64%. The board wanted a plan that would improve that ratio significantly. An "earned-income committee," comprised of representatives from the board of trustees and key staff members, was established to review the situation and then make recommendations.

It was clear that drama subscriptions was one area that could stand improvement. Of the 17,232 available seats, only 8,835 had been sold on subscription the previous season. We needed to generate a quantum leap in both the numbers of subscribers and the income from subscriptions. Several other ideas, such as increasing ticket prices, increasing group sales, and increasing single-ticket sales, were discussed.

Each idea was explored, and a proposal was created for the trustees suggesting the following general plan: that we invest our energies and money in improving the subscription base; that we combine that effort with a substantial increase in ticket prices. (McCarter's single-ticket prices were lagging behind the local and national average for theaters of similar size and quality); that we more aggressively pursue group sales through the hiring of a commissioned salesperson.

A plan to improve single-ticket sales was rejected out of hand. It was reasoned

Linda Kinsey has been Director of Communications for McCarter Theatre in Princeton, N.J. since 1980. Prior to McCarter she served as Marketing Director for the Denver Center Theatre Company in the Denver Center for the Performing Arts; Public Relations Director for Image Dynamics, Inc., a national advertising agency; and Audience Development Director for Baltimore's Center Stage. She frequently consults for FEDAPT in the area of audience development.

"The optimum time to begin the renewal effort was during the second-to-last show of the season."

that single-ticket sales are too intimately connected with the popularity of a given show to be able to quantify the results of a broader, more expensive single-ticket advertising campaign.

Instead, we addressed ourselves to researching and quantifying various marketing techniques that could help us realize a substantial increase in subscriptions. We were spending approximately $12.29 to attract each of our 8,835 subscribers. Certainly a bigger, more expensive direct-mail and advertising campaign would yield more impressive results, but once again, these results would be difficult to quantify. The idea of telephone marketing was proposed. Research revealed that many theaters were using telephone marketing as a component of their subscription drives and doing so quite successfully. We asked a well-known telemarketing company to present a proposal to McCarter. Based upon the demographic and historical information we supplied, they projected that they could attract 4,200 new subscribers and earn $217,000! This appeared to be the shot in the arm we needed to attain our goal.

In December of 1981, we presented a proposal to the board. We were confident that this proposal would result in a 45% net increase in income and a 35% increase in the subscription base in one season. The proposal included a telemarketing component. Some concern was expressed over this method of selling, but the numbers finally spoke for themselves, and the trustees committed their support to the plan.

Although this chapter focuses on the planning and implementation of the 1982–83 drama subscription drive, it is important to understand that we also conduct subscription campaigns for our music, dance, and film series. These campaigns take place simultaneously in the spring, summer, and fall, and must be carefully orchestrated with the drama subscription campaign to maximize their effectiveness.

Our staff, luxuriously large by most standards, included at the time of the campaign a full-time director of communications, a seasonal (September to May) publicity manager, a full-time graphic artist, a full-time subscription manager who worked with an additional staff of two, and part-time labor as necessary to process all the subscriptions.

The drama season is comprised of five plays each running seventeen performances in a 1,077 seat house over a three-week period from September to April. (*A Christmas Carol* is offered annually on a single-ticket basis and is not part of the series.)

The proposed 1982–83 season was scheduled to open with Edward Albee's *A Delicate Balance,* followed by Shakespeare's *Hamlet,* James McLure's *The Day They Shot John Lennon,* Chekhov's *The Three Sisters* and close with Noel Coward's *Blithe Spirit.* We were delighted with the play selecton; the variety was sure to be appealing to our current subscribers and attractive to prospective subscribers. However, looking ahead, we reasoned that in view of the fact that we were anticipating a rather large influx of new subscribers for the 1982–83 season, it might be better to open the season with a comedy, thereby "hooking" our new subscriber for the rest of the season, since everyone loves a good comedy!

We involved Managing Director Alison Harris in our discussions, and she suggested that an informal recommendation be made to Nagle Jackson to move *Blithe Spirit* up to the opening slot of the season. This was because of our concern over opening with a serious drama and the impact that might have on so many new subscribers.

We approached Mr. Jackson with the idea, and he agreed to think about it in terms of the artistic ramifications such a decision might have on casting and guest directors. His willingness to consider such a change should be noted. In the end, he deferred to the communications department recommendation. This meant that he trusted our instinct, judgement, and knowledge about the development of an audience for his drama program.

Copies of the plays were distributed to everyone who would be working on the campaign, and Mr. Jackson discussed his feelings about each choice—invaluable information for developing copy and graphics to represent the season to the community.

Ticket Prices

The established single-ticket price structure called for the previews to be least expensive; Friday and Saturday evenings most expensive; and Thursday evening, Sunday evening, Sunday matinees, and the Saturday (4:30) twilight to be midway between the two.

Each week during the season, our box-office publishes weekly ticket-sales reports listing subscribers, single-ticket, and group sales on a series-by-series basis. These reports are helpful in establishing the single-ticket buying pattern. In reviewing these reports, we discovered that Sunday matinees were at least as popular, if not slightly more popular, than Friday and Saturday evenings.

With that great a demand for seats, we reasoned that Sunday matinee single-ticket prices should be made equal to those for Friday and Saturday evenings, thus increasing our potential gross in the matinee series. Once we shifted Sunday matinees into the higher price range, we then increased single-ticket prices across the board by $2. The shift in pricing and the $2 increase did result in rather substantial price increases for our subscribers, particularly those who attend Sunday matinees.

We knew the subscription prices would be of the utmost importance to the success of the campaign. It had proven useful in the past to structure discounts to favor the renewing subscriber if he renewed by the announced deadline. To offset the sharp increase in subscription prices, we decided to offer a 30% discount to renewing subscribers (35% to renewing senior citizens, students, and Sunday matinee subscribers), and a 20–25% discount for new subscribers until June 30. We would reduce discounts on a series-by-series basis for the fall as they became close to capacity on subscription.

With a goal of 12,000 subscirbers in mind, we evolved a preliminary plan that called for an intensive renewal effort, a spring "target" effort, a telemarketing effort and a fall direct mail effort.

The Budget

To accomodate the extraordinary expense involved in the telemarketing campaign (we expected our expenses to average 50% of our income), we endeavored to keep our other costs as low as possible. We spent $108,000 in F.Y. '82 to attract 8,835 subscribers through direct mail and advertising. Our F.Y. '83 goal for the same activities was only 7,780. We had produced an expensive four-color brochure for the 1981–82 season, which we used in a massive direct-mail effort in the spring. To cut costs, we planned a much more modest brochure for the 1982–83 season to be used in specific target mailings in the spring. The size and scope of the fall campaign was to be contingent upon the success of the renewal, spring, and telemarketing campaigns.

We arrived at a total expense figure of $64,100 for the mail/advertising components of the campaign, and $111,115 for the telemarketing component of the campaign. We allocated the $64,100 as follows:

Renewal	$11,800
Spring Mail	$22,050
Fall Mail	$30,250

Each aspect of the campaign was assigned a specific goal:

Renewal:	6200 (70%)	$285,000 income
Spring "target":	680	33,700 income
Telephone subs:	4220	217,500 income
Fall direct mail:	900	45,000 income
Totals:	12,000	$581,200 income

McCarter Theatre. Christine Baranski and Paul Shenar in *Blithe Spirit*. Photo: Cliff Moore.

The specific planning of the campaigns took place throughout December and most of January. We knew that in order to achieve our goals, we needed a campaign that would insure a 70% renewal rate, attract 1,580 new subscribers through mail and advertising, and secure an environment where 4,200 new subscribers could be gained through telemarketing.

The Renewal

The renewal effort was projected to attract a 70% return. We started from the ground up and began to examine the effectiveness of all aspects of our past campaigns. Although not computerized, our box-office had, through coding, successfully tracked the results of our previous campaigns. An analysis of these carefully kept records revealed valuable information about our past successes and failures and also helped us to identify our key zip-code areas immediately.

From box-office forms to brochures, we reorganized our price charts, slicked-up our billing forms, and cleared up our order forms—all for the purpose of making renewals as easy as possible for our customers. From past campaigns, we had already learned that the optimum time to begin the renewal effort was during the second-to-last show of the season. (This was also necessary from a "cash flow" perspective.)

We had learned that we should plan to bill our customers at least twice, and that we should plan a renewal phone-athon using volunteers to capture all the procrastinators who were as yet unrenewed by the deadline.

McCarter Theatre. Penelope Reed, Mercedes Ruehl and Stacy Ray in *The Three Sisters*. Photo: John Cox.

Specific elements of the renewal—first billing

BROCHURE (Included plans for new season—titles and dates, subscriber benefits, order form for friends of renewing subscribers*, price charts, deadline.)
     * We had successfully used this idea for many seasons. We offer friends of renewing subscribers the opportunity to subscribe at the renewal discount, if they do so before the renewal deadline. This seems to encourage groups of neighbors and friends to attend the theater together.

BILLING FORM (A six-part NCR form, no carbon required, was developed to speed processing, record-keeping, and filing. The top copy was sent to each renewing subscriber with seat locations and the special renewal discount price typed in. The deadline for renewing at that special discount was clearly displayed. All the customer had to do was enclose a check or charge-card number for the total amount, and mail it back to our subscription office in the enclosed post-paid envelope. The second billing notice was also part of the six-part form.)

PRICE CHART (This was a pick-up from the brochure, which we hoped had been given to "friends of renewing subscribers"! Another price chart was enclosed for the renewing subscriber who chose to change series or upgrade seats, thus requiring a change in the subscription price.)

CHRISTMAS CAROL ORDER FORM (A subscriber benefit is the opportunity to purchase popular *Christmas Carol* tickets in advance of the public, at a discount.)

RETURN ENVELOPE (A stamped return envelope was enclosed with the first billing only. This is a small investment and a great convenience for the customer.)

DRAMATIC LONDON SWEEPSTAKES ENTRY (To make subscribing irresistible, and to build a good reference list for future telephoning, we solicited a local travel agency for a free trip for two to London. To enter the contest, you did not have to purchase a subscription, but you did have to supply us with five names, addresses, and telephone numbers of individuals you thought would be interested in McCarter. (I stole this idea from the Guthrie Theater in Minneapolis!)

MAILING ENVELOPE (We chose a 6x9 window envelope to accommodate our NCR forms, and printed a provocative message on the outside. Each of these envelopes was stamped, rather than metered, to give them a more important look.

LETTER (An invitation to renew, clearly outlining the advantages of renewing by the deadline—a veiled threat that several thousand customers were waiting to grab their seats! Each of these letters was individually signed to make it appear more personal.)

Renewal—second billing

BROCHURE (same as first billing)
LETTER (urged immediate response)
RETURN ENVELOPE (not post-paid)
BILLING FORM (second copy—a different color than the first, with a deadline reminder clearly displayed.)
MAILING ENVELOPE (metered, not stamped, and printed with an urgent message.)

The Renewal Phone-athon

From our past experience, we knew we needed three evenings, staffed with approximately twelve volunteers per evening, to call all as yet unrenewed subscribers to encourage last minute renewals. Fortunately, because we were expecting to begin a telephone marketing effort immediately following the renewal, we had the use of the telephones that were installed in our rehearsal hall for that purpose. McCarter staff and members of the McCarter Associates (our volunteer group) were signed up to call the customers. We provided dinner to our volunteers (we called from 6 to 9 P.M.), and a packet of information including a script for the caller. Box-office staff members were on hand to answer questions and deal with problems. We set up a large blackboard where we could record our results, and we purchased a bell that we rang each time a caller "scored" a subscription. In other words, we created an exciting atmostphere for the callers to work in. The results were gratifying.

A time/task schedule was then developed so it would be clear to all involved what was expected and when.

Time/Task

January 25—Copy due for all elements of renewal
        Brochure: Linda (communications director), Christine (communications intern), Nagle (artistic director)
        Price Charts: Jim (subscription office manager) and subscription office staff (two people)
        Carol Order Form: Linda and Jim
        London Sweepstakes: Linda
        Envelope copy: Linda, Christine
        NCR Forms: Jim and subscription office staff
January 29—Copy to typesetter—Rob (graphic artist)
February 3—Brochure and inserts to printer—Rob
February 17—Deliver printed materials in-house
February 18—Begin processing subscriptions—NCR forms—Jim and staff
        Sign letters: Linda, Christine, Veronica (publications manager), Pam (publications advertising manager)
        Affix stamps, mailing and return envelopes: same
March 8—Stuff renewal—(first wave)—all
March 15—Mail renewal—all
April 5—Mail second notice: Jim and subscription office staff
        Begin calling volunteers for phone-athon: Linda
April 29—Mail follow-up card to subscribers we can't reach over the phone: Linda, Christine, Pam
April 30—End renewal

The Spring Drive

The 1981–82 season had been well received critically and had attracted several thousand single-ticket buyers. We had developed a ticket envelope for box-office use which enabled us to retrieve all single-ticket buyers' names, addresses, and telephone numbers so that they could be coded and added to our mailing list. In addition, we had kept several seasons' lapsed subscribers on our list so that we could have the opportunity to target a message specifically designed for them.

> "Offering friends of renewing subscribers the same discount seems to encourage groups of neighbors and friends to attend the theater together."

> "Each renewal letter was individually signed to make it appear more personal."

The spring campaign therefore would be divided into two phases: the ''priority'' phase—mailed to target groups who were familiar with McCarter in ''advance of the public''—and the direct-mail (key zip codes and in-house list) phase.

The "priority" campaign elements

BROCHURE (Included announcement of new season, list of plays, directors and dates, subscriber benefits, price chart with discounts clearly displayed, photos of previous season's most popular shows. Clearly displayed deadline with price increase threat; order form).

RETURN ENVELOPE (Printed with subscription office address).

MAILING ENVELOPE (Clearly displayed ''priority'' message).

LETTER: Each target group had a letter specifically designed to speak to them:

> Single-ticket buyers
> Lapsed subscriber
> Princeton faculty/staff
> Target neighborhoods within fifteen mile radius
> London Sweepstakes entries
> McCarter Associates (non-subscribing)

These combined lists added up to 20,000 names. Each letter was individually signed to make the message more personal. A mailing house was engaged to handle this mailing, because speed and efficiency was of the utmost importance. However, all the signing and stuffing were handled in-house by staff and volunteers. The mailing house affixed the labels, sorted the pieces into zip code, and where possible, carrier-route sequence, and delivered them to the post office.

The ''mass-mail'' component of the campaign was far simpler: Two weeks after the ''priority'' campaign was mailed, 100,000 self-mailer brochures (same as were included in target packets) were dropped into key zip codes and mailed to the McCarter in-house list. We hoped that this combined effort would yield 680 new subscribers by June 30.

A timetable was again developed, showing the date each task was to be completed and by whom.

Time/Task Schedule—Spring

February 17—Copy for spring brochure and target envelope to Rob.
                Linda and Christine begin design.
March 1—Copy to typesetter—Rob
March 3—Letters in house, begin signing—Linda, Staff
March 8—Brochures and mailing envelope to printer
March 15—Begin stuffing—Linda, Staff
March 23—Deliver target packets to mailing house
March 26—Press conference to announce season—Veronica
April 1—Mail to priority lists—Crell (Direct-mail house)
April 9—Print out McCarter list and deliver to Crell
April 15—Mail 100,000 to key zips and in-house lists

Because we were trying to attract new subscribers, it was important that we develop a strong publicity plan to support the mailing efforts. What we wanted was increased visibility for the theater, the artistic director, and the new season during the campaign. We developed a publicity schedule that began with a press conference to announce the season and continued with individual interviews on radio, television, and in print. In addition, a series of press releases was planned to carry us over the ''slow news'' times. Basically, we endeavored to keep McCarter constantly in the news throughout the duration of the campaign—from April 15 through June 30.

Advertising

To support the mailing efforts, we decided to run a modest print advertising campaign in newspapers popular in our target areas. A schedule of ads was developed to run during the last three weeks of the campaign. The focus of the ads would be the coming price increase on June 30. Remember, we guaranteed that the spring prices would be valid only through the end of June. Although we did not anticipate raising prices in all series, we kept our options open and used that fact to encourage subscribing before June 30. In the end, we raised prices in only two series and kept the pre-June 30 prices in all others. There were no complaints from the public.

Speaking engagements

In addition to our publicity efforts, we endeavored to create excitement about the new season by scheduling several speaking engagements in the community. Both Artistic Director Nagle Jackson and Managing Director Alison Harris were called upon frequently to address area groups. Although no specific subscription goal was set for this aspect of the campaign, much valuable visibility and favorable PR was gained.

The Telephone Campaign

The telemarketing campaign was handled by an independent company. They supplied an on-site manager who in turn hired and trained a staff of callers. We were responsible for supplying the leads, fifteen telephones, paying a fixed-rate commission on every subscription sold, and absorbing all overhead expenses such as phone bills, supplies, and casual labor. We were also responsible for processing the subscriptions through the box-office. An average of twelve callers and one campaign manager worked Sunday through Friday evenings from 5 p.m. to 9 p.m. They placed an average of 3,000 calls per week.

As telephone marketing was an entirely new arena for us, our first shot at projecting expenses was somewhat naive. It was not difficult to figure out what we'd have to pay in commissions if the staff reached their projected goals, but projecting our overhead expenses proved to be much more difficult. Princeton is located on the dividing line between two area codes. It was necessary to make many more toll calls than we expected, and the telephone bills soared. In addition, we found it essential to hire part-time labor for six weeks to add telephone numbers to borrowed mailing lists—telephone books are absolutely taboo as sources for callers, and keeping the campaign supplied with good leads was time-consuming and costly.

Through manipulation of lists, we were able to operate both the telephone campaign and the direct-mail campaigns simultaneously. We began our telephone component approximately one month after we began the ''priority'' campaign, calling the names on our general mailing list first and then, lapsed subscribers and single-ticket buyers. The telephone manager did not call any list that was currently in use for the direct-mail effort. Several weeks were allowed to pass before those lists were used.

The Fall Campaign

As previously stated, we considered the size and the scope of the fall campaign to be contingent upon the results of the renewal, spring, and telephone campaign efforts. In June, with all aspects of the renewal, spring, and telephone campaign efforts reaching or exceeding their goals, we felt we'd be safe to plan a modest fall campaign. The strategy included a direct-mail component, an advertising component, and a publicity component.

Direct Mail

Rather than produce an individual brochure for the drama series, we decided to feature the drama series in the fall edition of our *Calendar News,* a twelve-page newspaper we mail out four times a year to promote our various events. Normally, we mail the *Calendar News* to the 55,000 households on the McCarter in-house mailing list.

For this mailing however, we increased the circulation to 250,000 households. The mailing therefore consisted of 55,000 in-house names, 180,000 key zip-code households, and 15,000 names borrowed from a local summer theater. They were, of course, coded to track their results.

Advertising

Again, we viewed advertising as support for the direct-mail effort, and we selected media (print and radio) from the areas into which we were mailing. We chose to run a series of ads beginning shortly after Labor Day and ending three weeks later with the opening of the first show of the season. We pushed discounts, convenience, and the fact that subscribing was the only way to guarantee seats, since subscriptions were flooding in. We did not include an order form in our ads, preferring to devote the limited space to graphics and sales copy to encourage the convenience of telephone ordering.

Publicity

Because there was such a short period of time in the fall in which to sell subscriptions (the season opened in the last week of September), we needed to develop as much visibility as quickly as possible for the subscription campaign. Several interviews—radio, print and television—were planned for the artistic director or the guest director of the first show and members of the acting company beginning right after Labor Day and continuing through the opening. We planned a major open-house on September 12 where backstage tours, entertainment, and information about the coming season's activities would be presented. In addition, a series of press releases were planned focusing on the new season, the plays, the casts, the directors, the designers. These too would be issued over a three-week period of time. We developed a timetable and assigned tasks as we had with the renewal and the spring efforts.

Fall Campaign Timetable

July 23—Copy due for *Calendar News* to Rob—Linda, Pam
July 30—*Calendar News* to typesetter—Rob
       Order printout of mailing lists—Linda
       Select and arrange zip-code mailings—Linda
       Arrange ''open-house'' meeting
August 2—Brainstorm story ideas and begin preparations for publicity campaign
        —Linda, Nagle, Alison, Pam
August 13—Open-house Meeting
       Print *Calendar News*—Rob
August 16—Ship *Calendar News* to mailing house with labels
August 20—Publicity manager returns. Finalize PR campaign plans—Veronica
       Design ads—Rob
       Produce radio spot
September 8—Begin print advertising and radio promotion—Linda
       Begin feature press—Veronica
September 9—Deliver press release focusing on subscription and new season
        details
September 10—Final Open-house meeting—make final preparations
September 12—Open-house
September 15—Send out release on *Blithe Spirit* cast
September 22—Send out release on *Blithe Spirit* director and designers
September 29—Open season

    The details of the drama campaign thus determined, we produced a master ''time/task'' calendar, overlaying the dance, music, and film campaign schedules. It adhered faithfully to our master plan and happily, all ran smoothly.

The Results of the Campaigns

McCarter Theatre. Harry Hamlin in Hamlet. Photo: Cliff Moore.

	Projected Results			Actual Results		
Renewal	6200	Subs @ $46 Avg =	285,000	6154	Subs @ $46.24 =	284,560
Spring Mail	680	Subs @ $50 Avg =	33,700	924	Subs @ $50.82 =	46,957
Telephone	4220	Subs @ $52 Avg =	217,500	3819	Subs @ $53.68 =	205,400
Fall Mail	900	Subs @ $50 Avg =	45,000	536	Subs @ $53.70 =	28,788
	12,000		$581,200	11,433		$565,705

As you can see from the above chart, the renewal projections were accurate; we renewed exactly 70% of our audience and earned just $440 less than projected. The spring mail effort fared better than expected. The personalization of the promotion—the fact that the letters were individually signed rather than xeroxed, and mailed in an envelope with the brochure, was as important as the quality of the mailing lists we used. Our hard work had paid off.

The telephone campaign fell somewhat short of its goal. In early September, we experienced our first real difficulties—many of the calling staff returned to college or their winter employment, leaving the campaign short-handed. It proved nearly impossible to attract a new staff because of the short time left to the campaign. Had we been able to continue with a full complement of callers, I have no doubt that the campaign would have reached its goal.

I must additionally note that in our experience, with the money available to our single-ticket campaigns, we can expect to sell between 1,800 and 2,200 single tickets per show. With some trepidation, we projected that we could sustain an average of 2,000 tickets per show, even though we knew many of our new subscribers would be culled from that single-ticket pool. In fact, the first two shows of our season broke all single-ticket records. To explain this increase, we feel we must turn to our telemarketing campaign. Certainly the first two shows of our season were popular (*Blithe Spirit* and *Hamlet*), and were well-received critically. But popular and critically well-received shows are the rule, not the exception, in our programming. We only increased our single-ticket advertising budget to keep pace with inflation. We did, however, speak directly to over 70,000 people on the telephone. This direct and aggressive approach seems to be responsible for not only 3,900 new subscribers, but the increase in single-ticket sales we are now experiencing.

What remains to be tested is the "quality" of the subscribers attracted through our telemarketing effort. Will they renew in predictable numbers via our usual mail efforts? Will they renew at all given the fact that many of them had no past experience with this type of entertainment? Will they only respond to aggressive approaches such as those employed by the telemarketing team? Our renewal will prove interesting.

The fall campaign showed disappointing results. Apparently, we were our own competition. The decision to include the drama series in the circular we used to promote all our events proved too distracting for our customers. Single-ticket sales for our events fared *very* well, but at the expense of our drama subscriptions.

Switching *Blithe Spirit* and *A Delicate Balance* proved worthwhile. Indeed, our "no-show" rate has decreased sharply over last season. Our new subscribers seem to be hooked!

In summary, had the board of trustees not insisted that we find a way to significantly increase income, we probably would have continued to pursue drama subscriptions in a slow and methodical way, taking no extraordinary risks, and being satisfied with a 5% or 10% increase in the subscription base each year. In fact, we *were* challenged to improve the income and subscription bases. We met that challenge not with a knee-jerk reaction, but with careful planning, hard work, and follow-ups.

Developing an audience for any program requires continuous planning, and a re-evaluation of the product and goals, and the methods used to reach those goals. Although it may appear that a disproportionate amount of time was spent planning the 1982–83 drama campaign, we've learned from past experience that a properly planned campaign can eliminate most risks and ensure a greater degree of success.

Ivan Sygoda

DANCE: THE MARKETPLACE FOR EMERGING COMPANIES

A dance presentor once said to me, "I can't afford an inexpensive company." It took me a long time to understand what that remark meant and what its implications were. I had assumed, as you might, that if rising costs put the larger, better-known companies out of the reach of many sponsors, they would surely turn for their programming to the smaller, less expensive but equally interesting companies like the ones I work with at Pentacle,[1] or probably, like yours.

The assumption was rash. Presentors with tight budgets depend on the drawing power of familiar names. Their technical and promotional costs can be just as burdensome for an "unknown" as they are for a highly visible company, but they know that ticket sales are likely to be lower. The mathematics of the situation are cruel, and so one has to sympathize to a certain degree. Furthermore, I think those of us who live and work in New York are somewhat blinded by the dazzling array of choreographic and performing talent routinely available here. Most presentors across the country have neither the means nor, unfortunately, the desire to research what you and I perceive to be an almost infinite number of choices. It often seems that the same names keep cropping up on their season flyers—Taylor, Tharp, Ailey, Nikolais, Joffrey, Pilobolus and the Trocks, not to mention an impressive assortment of international ethnic companies.

It's easy to conclude that everything conspires to keep young and emerging artists out of the marketplace. The litany of complaints can be spelled out like a rosary:

"It's hard to get bookings. I don't know how to do it. Besides, I hate making those phone calls. I'd rather be making dances. I can't find anyone to do it for me. I can't afford anyone to do it for me. Few people seem to be interested in emerging talent anyway. Even if they *are* interested, they don't have any money. Presentors have dreadful taste. They pander to the lowest common denominator. Audiences are dense. Critics are denser. I can't get reviewed. I can't get listed. I can't get a grant. I can't keep my dancers."

It sounds familiar, doesn't it? Nevertheless, there is a lot of dancing going on all across the country—more dancing in more places than ever before. And it isn't all Paul Taylor and Twyla Tharp either, even though they certainly get their share of bookings. It may be someone you never heard of from Fargo. It may be the choreographer across from you in the Jacuzzi. It could be you—which is the point of this chapter.

You're here and the work is there. All you have to do is get from point A to point B. It's embarrassingly simple and extraordinarily complicated. This very book is a source of frustration. Each chapter is a success story—someone else's success. Each chapter chronicles a different artist doing a different kind of art in a different place under different circumstances. And so you say to yourself, "That doesn't apply to me."

Well, it does and it doesn't. As an artist, you know that assembly-line techniques

Ivan Sygoda is the Director of Pentacle, a New York-based not-for-profit service organization which provides fiscal and administrative services to performing artists and companies. He majored in French at Brown University and at the Sorbonne, and eventually earned an M.A. in Romance Languages at Princeton University. While teaching at Wheaton College, he became responsible for booking, coordinating and publicizing campus dance residencies and organized a multi-college consortium for participation in the NEA Dance Touring Program. He joined Pentacle in 1976 as Tour Manager, and became Director (with Mara Greenberg) three years later. He conceived and produced "Men Dancing" at the Theatre of the Riverside Church in 1981 and 1982, and was a contributing editor to the *Poor Dancer's Almanac,* second edition. He has been a selection panelist for the Pennsylvania State Council on the Arts, the Colorado Dance Festival and several Dance Theater Workshop Choreographer's Showcase series, and is currently a National Endowment for the Arts Dance Program Panelist. He also writes an ongoing column on data base management for the Radio Shack *Microcomputer News.*

Photo: Cora DuBack

---

[1]Pentacle is a New York City based service organization which provides administrative and management services to performing artists and companies.

"It doesn't make sense to 'package' your uniqueness in someone else's carton."

don't apply to creativity. You can't churn it out like bottle caps. The same principle applies to the various "management" problems and techniques discussed in this book. In every case, creative minds analyzed a situation, determined its unique aspects, and applied a tailor-made solution. You know how to do this, because you do it every day in the rehearsal studio and onstage. In other words, you already possess the analytical and synthetical tools you will need to solve your own marketing problems.

Even if there were someone else to help or to do it for you—an in-house company manager, a booking agent, a marketing consultant, a paid professional publicist, a whole battery of experts — the process still has to begin and end with the artist and the art. It still has to begin and end with you.

This can't be emphasized enough. Look around you. Success of the sort you want is based on uniqueness. You won't get very far by being a clone of anyone else. Art is about originals. That's why you work so hard to find, develop, and refine your own voice, your own style, your own particular kind of energy. It doesn't make sense to "package" your uniqueness in someone else's carton. That would obliterate your hard-won gains. Also, it probably wouldn't work. Thus, there is a very real, practical use for the sort of self-examination that must underlie your efforts to enter the dance marketplace.

Who are you? What is your art about? Who is your audience? What are your strengths? Where do you want to go with your art? Where do you *not* want to go with it? Do you like to teach? Do you like children? There are a hundred questions and as many answers to each as there are different choreographers. Success for you will be something quite different, perhaps, from success for another artist. How do you define success for yourself?

It's too easy to say, "I want to be like Paul Taylor." He's famous, well-regarded, has a great company, and works a lot. And you *could* be something like Paul Taylor—if your work is theatrical and will project in a large proscenium house, accessible so that audiences of all sorts will find in it whatever undefinable thing it is they look for in events they pay money to see, astounding in the sense that theater goers can't possibly believe that any but superbly trained performers could accomplish the technical wizardry they are witnessing. Someone's got to be the next Paul Taylor. Why not you?

Fine. You've got your work cut out for you. Hard work, but the steps are reasonably straightforward. First, you've got to arm yourself with the tools you are expected to have in the national dance marketplace—superb photographs (8» × 10» glossies and color slides), an attractively designed promotional brochure, ad slicks, a beautiful and colorful poster for the presentor to distribute, a sheaf of rave reviews from major papers, and a track record of unfailingly delivering, technically smooth, and emotionally satisfying performances to sold-out houses.

Then you take these tools into the marketplace—the annual round of booking conventions, the perennial round of letter-writing and phone solicitations to major sponsors, the ceaseless follow-up work, the road trips, the occasional wining and dining. Then, with time and genius and a lot of bruises, you can be Paul Taylor. It only took him thirty years.

But not everyone can or *should* try to emulate Mr. Taylor (or Ms. Tharp or whomever). There are other kinds of excellences, and other kinds of satisfactions, and other ways of being successful in the field. Not everyone can or should be "popular." Perhaps that's what we're really talking about here. Think back to your high-school days and all that adolescent agony about acceptance. Maybe you were popular in that context, maybe you weren't. But you made assessments about the values involved, about what was important and real—and what wasn't. This isn't so terribly different, nor is the process any less agonizing.

Perhaps you're a choreographer's choreographer in the way that James Joyce was a writer's writer. You'll never be on the hit parade, but that doesn't mean you won't be admired and respected by your peers. Perhaps your work is by its nature cerebral or difficult, destined for those whom Stendhal called "the happy few." Maybe you're one of those exciting artists exploring the movement possibilities of "non-dancers." Maybe you're on the cutting edge, forging a path that the next generation will tread. You might be any of dozens of wonderful, important, worthwhile things, none of which are presently compatible with immense national popularity or even notoriety, which can be just as hard to achieve.

So where do you begin? You begin with what you do well, which is most likely performing, teaching, and/or choreographing. Performing involves the most compromises. Given the facilities likely to be available, it's almost impossible for your art to look exactly the way you want. The space is too small, or the lighting is nonexistent, or the floor is a nightmare, or your lead dancer pulled a muscle, or the sound system stinks. Or, more probably, all of the above at once. You just want to do your art, and there you are contending with amateurs, incompetents, and fools. But every single heartless, show-business cliché applies—The Show Must Go On, and when it's over, You're Only As Good As Your Last Show, and The Audience Is Always Right. No excuses. You only get one chance to make it work, and so you have to learn where possibility ends and impossibility begins. The line is different for each artist. You're hungry for work, and so you'll tend to say yes. But there are times when you should have said no. It can't help your career if you look bad onstage.

Right? Of course. But think again about what makes you look good or bad in performance. Is it really the technical accoutrements, the lighting, the sound? It goes without saying that a proper floor is important to the performers' physical health. But haven't you been bored to tears in major, well-equipped houses and excited beyond description by things you've seen in the most god-awful holes? I have, and the longer I stay in this business, the more I believe that good art can happen anywhere artists are generous. It's not unfair that artists have to perform in inadequate surroundings; it's merely a great nuisance. What's unfair is that artists are expected to be infinitely more generous than everyone else except saints and other visionaries. What's more, they have to be generous on cue and on call, usually at 8:00 p.m., with a matinee the next day at 2:00.

If this challenge excites you, then perform as much as you can, anywhere you can make your work fit. Exposure is crucial, even if it doesn't pay its way at first. You're making an investment in your career, just like a doctor-to-be in medical school.

Consistency is also important. It's devilishly hard to build a performing company out of a collection of dancers. From this point of view, it's perhaps better to work together twice a week, but every week for a year, than to group activity more economically, but in a way that makes it impossible to keep your momentum going. Momentum is an intangible but very real thing. One event feeds the next in ways that are impossible to predict or plan. Be ready for the opportunities which may arise from unexpected sources — somebody's sister-in-law who works in a senior-citizen center that brings in performing artists, and who saw you perform at an outdoor festival you were invited to because your ex-boyfriend's brother got a job at a bank.

This is how a lot of meaningful work gets to happen. By serendipity, by being in the right place at the right time and having your brochure with you. Here's a fact that will give you cause for hope: By simply being a dancer/choreographer, by taking classes, going to concerts, reading posters, and talking to your friends, you are exposed to more viable leads for paying work than almost any manager sitting at a desk. Managers and agents may well have lists of presentors, halls, and festivals. But you know so-and-so who danced there, taught there, who knows the director personally, whose sister studies there, whose Aunt Millie is the mayor's secretary there—whatever. Don't laugh. You've heard of the "old-boy network," which is supposed to operate in the world of high finance? Well, there's an artists' network that's just as extensive. When the artist/teacher at College X needs a replacement teacher or has funds for a small performance, he's not really likely to start calling agents and managers. He'll ask around among fellow artists. Do you call an agent when you need a dancer?

So don't hesitate to ask your peers where they've been getting work. The variety of possibilities might surprise you—hospitals, senior centers, youth centers, private schools, factories, corporate headquarters, parks, shopping malls, prisons, halfway houses, piers, beaches, public pools, public libraries, resorts, cruise ships, military bases, day-care centers, plazas, piazzas, and porticos. Someone you know

"You've heard of the 'old-boy network' of high finance? There's an artist's network that's just as extensive."

and respect has performed in every one of these places.

If your peers run out of suggestions, use your eyes. The walls are plastered with notices of alternative spaces and places where performances and classes are happening. The imaginativeness and resourcefulness of some of the brightest young minds are there for all to see and be inspired by. I remember being struck a year or three ago by a lamppost sign advertising lunch-hour dance classes for business executives. What an excellent way to build audience awareness and exposure among people who are likely to be consumers of culture, while earning money.

The free and special-interest papers are also a good field to mine for ideas, as are all those catalogues of neighborhood classes. Adding some little twist or slightly changing the focus of something you already do may make it a perfect class or workshop to offer a group with special needs.

A dancer I know teaches a variety of posture classes at the New School in New York City. She thought of it first and then made it work. Here's another idea, only slightly far-fetched: There are bowling leagues all over the city peopled with weekend athletes suffering from aching muscles. Offer a movement warm-up class at the bowling alley at the start of the tournament. You'll probably meet some resistance at first, but if you can cajole the management into trying it just once, for free, maybe the bowlers will come back for more, and pay for it.

This sort of research, then, can lead in two directions:

1. Self-production of concerts, workshops, classes, and lecture-demonstrations in places off the beaten track and for audiences who don't get frequent exposure to non-traditional or experimental dance and
2. Paid employment made available to you by other professionals, be they dance professionals, such as teachers or fellow artistic directors, or other types of professionals, such as health and welfare officials, educators, city administrators, and so forth. In either case, the market will not be handed to you on a silver platter. You have to invent it, create it, or discover it.

Any place you can possibly perform in front of people is a place where your art can happen. Furthermore, you don't necessarily need an engraved invitation, at least not on public property. I remember being quite impressed with a dance company that set up shop on a plot of grass right next to the line of people waiting to get into a free Shakespeare performance in New York's Central Park. The head of this company was Marta Renzi. It could have been you.

You probably won't be paid to perform the first time. But maybe the second time, you will. Through it all, you've got to ask questions: Who's in charge here? Who has authority? How do I get to them? Your greatest resource is not the expensive directories, but the local phone book, which is free.

If you're like many artists I know, the idea of phoning someone about getting work is intimidating. You're probably afraid you'll say the wrong thing and spoil your chances forever, especially when it comes to talking about money. Here's a thought that might make the task a little bit easier at the beginning: The person on the other end of the line is likely to be only a bit more experienced than you are at arranging performances. The college dance teacher you may be dealing with is a thoroughly professional teacher, but only an amateur presentor of dance companies, if he invites only one outside company per year to give a performance at the college. The local parks commissioner is a thoroughly professional administrator of trees and equestrian statues, but an amateur booker of outdoor concerts. This will certainly be true in those situations where you are creating a marketplace for performance art.

The consequences of this are enormous. You have as good a chance, if not better, at entering into productive contact with that person as the slickest agent going. You can talk artist-to-artist or professional-to-professional with a knowledgeability and immediacy that a booking agent will never have. You can transmit your excitement and concern directly. You can seize upon opportunities occasioned by chance remarks and questions. You can make an impression far beyond the capabilities of the fanciest brochure imaginable.

There is another side to this coin, however. Large companies dealing with major presentors can make many assumptions. They know that these presentors have experience and knowledgeability concerning the needs and expectations of dance troupes. You can't make these assumptions if you are bringing your art into new venues. The person you are dealing with may well share your enthusiasm and belief in the value of the project, but he is unlikely to understand fully why you can't dance on concrete or warm up under a tree. For your part, you have to realize that meeting each of your legitimate demands will cost the presentor money—to rent or build a stage, to rent lights or a sound system, to hire a crew, to pay for a space. As a rule of thumb, if your fee is x dollars, the presentor will have to spend that much again to meet his own costs of presentation.

Explaining your needs and negotiating their fulfillment are also part of your marketing efforts. Try to remember that you are dealing with another human being who has as much good will as you do, but who is speaking from a different context. It's easy to sound self-righteous and to take a lot for granted, but it will be counter productive to do so. In some ways, presentors need educating as much as audiences do. It will take patience to explain things you think are self-evident, and foresight to anticipate technical and scheduling problems. You will not always be able to get what you need, either in terms of money or facilities.

Money. Whole books have been written on the subject. How does one decide what something is worth? I have no idea, so let's go on to the next question. What should you charge for your services? This question, in turn, raises a host of other questions, chief among which is: What does it actually cost you to deliver classes, workshops, lecture-demonstrations, and performances? If you've been working independently, you probably don't know the answer, because your professional life and your personal life have been intertwined to a great degree. You should get in the habit of carefully logging your professional expenses and saving your receipts. This will come in handy at tax time and also give you an accurate idea of how much it costs you each year to be a dancer/choreographer/teacher.

Ideally, you want the fees you earn in the course of the year to cover your expenses to keep you alive for 365 days, and enable you to put something away for your old age. If you could know in advance all the work you'd be getting for the year, it would be a simple matter to add and divide and then apportion the amounts among the people paying you. Unfortunately, the answer is usually unpredictable.

Here is one way of setting fees. It is based on a number of assumptions and precedents, some of which are possibly outdated, but at least it will give you a starting point. It stems from the days of the Dance Touring Program, when companies set weekly, all-inclusive fees for standard length residencies (whole-week and half-week). Furthermore, it is based on the assumption that you are being paid for your time as opposed to your effort. In other words, if a presentor is buying your time for a week, he can expect to receive a week's worth of assorted dance activities, be it one performance and ten classes, or two performances and seven classes, and so forth. It's up to you to establish the formulas and equivalences, so that you can determine what it is reasonable to do in one day. Next, the salary rates for dancers are based more or less on AGMA guidelines. (AGMA is the American Guild of Musical Artists, the craft union for dancers and opera singers.) This is because the National Endowment for the Arts legislation specifies that workers involved in federally funded projects be paid at prevailing union rates, whether or not they are union members and whether or not the companies employing them are under union contracts. We'll beg the question of whether these rates are realistic, at the same time affirming that all dancers everywhere should be paid much, much more. In any case, these are the rates that the large companies use in setting their own fees. And finally, this pay schedule provides for a week of rehearsal for each week of paid work, because dancers should not have to rehearse for free, although they often do.

Weekly Fee, Royal American Dance Company
Salaries (1 week res., 1 week reh.):

Artistic Director @$500/wk. × 2 wks.	$1,000
4 Dancers @410/wk. × 2 wks.	3,280
Technical Director @$450/wk. × 1 wk.	450
Total salaries	4,730
Fringe benefits (15%)	710
Food per diem @$32 × 6 persons × 7 days	1,344

Housing: 3 doubles @$40 × 7 nights	840
Misc. expenses (cabs, phone, gels, laundry, etc.)	300
TOTAL (NET)	$7,924

Let's look at what we've got so far. In one sense, this is bare-bones budget because none of your recurring or ongoing expenses are reflected in it—your dance classes, studio rental, costume design, sound-tape production, lighting-design fees. But in another sense, it leaves some room to maneuver. If you're just starting out as an artistic director, you probably don't have your dancers on salary yet. So there's $710 to play with. (If you don't know what is at issue here, ask someone soon.) But if your company goes through dozens of pairs of jazz or pointe shoes, add a significant amount in the miscellaneous line. If your art requires special sets or technical equipment, add appropriate amounts for freight and rental. Close your eyes and imagine your way through the whole projected itinerary, door to door. You'll catch a half-dozen items that must be anticipated—the cab to the airport, the extra night's lodging because the flight connections are not feasible, the iron you have to buy on tour because the old one broke, a six-pack for the crew, etc.

Per diems are non-taxable to the degree that dancers can document on-the-road expenses in that amount. Since dancers are seldom in tax brackets where this is a major problem, it sometimes makes more sense to take the per diem money and add it to the pool available for dancers' salaries. Furthermore, these salaries do not have to be $410 per week. We've budgeted a residency week at $410, a rehearsal week at $410 and seven days of food per diems worth $224 per dancer. This totals $1044 per dancer. It might make sense, depending on that dancer's individual employment situation, to pay four weeks at $261 per week. Or to phrase all this more cynically, when you get back home and count the money, the salary pool will be what's left. Divide it up in whatever way seems fair, reasonable, and to everyone's maximum advantage.

A dance company that uses a booking agent to get it dates has to build in a commission, usually 15–20% of the gross fee. Here's a mathematical trick. If you take the net fee you calculated ($7,924) and multiply it by 1.25, you get $9,905. If you then subtract a 20% commission from that number ($9,905 × .20 = $1,981), you are left with the original net amount ($9,905 - $1,981 = $7,924).

In other words, that booking agent has to command a fee of approximately $10,000/week for the company to net the $8,000 it needs to meet its expenses. Assuming such a fee is feasible in the first place, you will remain financially "competitive" in the marketplace if you add a similar percentage to your own costs to meet ongoing expenses.

So here we are with a weekly fee of $10,000 for the Royal American Dance Company, five dancers, one techie. Plus transportation, of course. Companies used to try to build anticipated transportation costs into an all-inclusive fee. This has become almost impossible because of the airlines' fluctuating fare structures and unpredictable discount regulations. You can never be sure that a discount rate will be available to the city you have to visit, or that it will apply to your final routing. If I am absolutely forced to build airfare into a fee quote, I use the regular economy rate and add something for inflation. But I usually express my willingness to pass along the savings if and when I can confirm a discounted fare.

Ten-thousand dollars per week, plus allocated transportation costs, is indeed a fair fee for a touring company of five dancers, and any artistic director quoting this fee should not feel embarassed because it *seems* large. I hope I have shown that it is really not large.

The next question is: Can you command such a fee? The answer is best illustrated by a bad joke. The presentor asks the dancer, "What is your fee?" and the dancer responds, "$10,000 per week." The presentor then says, "But we only have $400," and the dancer says, "We'll take it." And sometimes you will. For the exposure, the prestige, for the chance to appear in an interesting city, for the opportunity to break in a new work on the road, because Aunt Martha lives there, because your ex-husband doesn't, because if you don't get to dance you'll go crazy.

But remember what we said above about saying no. If they want an outdoor performance in the swimming pool and you only dance on pointe, say no. If they want

"Being on the road is lonely, often boring. The accommodations are mediocre, the food is worse, and the TV is full of evangelists."

Limon technique and you're pure Cunningham, say no. If they want classes for children and you hate the brats, say no. But don't hang up yet! Recommend a friend who does what they want. Your good deed will come home to roost some day.

But if they say yes and you say yes, remember the following: Marketing isn't only press kits and flyers and photos. You are marketing your company from the moment you leave the studio until the moment you crawl back home. Your only two choices are to market it well or badly. Here are some examples, all culled from real life:

You are marketing your company when you first arrive in the small theater which is the presentor's pride and joy. You announce, in the hearing of the tech crew, that it is a dump. You are marketing your company when you so thoroughly litter the van the sponsor makes available to you as a courtesy that he will never have the free use of it again. You are marketing your company when the students overhear you chortling about what club-footed clods they are. You are marketing your company when you make it perfectly plain to the local newsstand operator that his town is a pestilential backwater hardly worth being a dot on the map. If you commit enough of these crimes against hospitality, your audience will not have eyes or inclination to see how good you really are onstage.

Audiences may prove unsophisticated, perhaps even ignorant and occasionally rude or thoughtless, but they are never dumb. They smell a lack of genuineness onstage from a mile away, and have an unerring instinct that lets them know when an artist doesn't respect them. And if you can't respect your audience in a very basic way, you have no business being in this business.

As the artistic director of a company, large or small, the onus is on you. You set the tone onstage and off. And that tone is as crucial a component of your promotional efforts as all the rest put together. It's hard being out on the road. It's lonely, often boring. The accommodations are mediocre, the food is worse, the bed is never right, the schedules are impossible and the TV is full of evangelists. Maybe, just maybe, the shower is better than the one you have at home.

An artistic director who fails to be a true leader, especially when things go badly and the pressure is on, can do more to destroy a company and its professional possibilities than all the obtuse reviews and splintered floors put together. I do not mean that you are expected to be a Pollyanna on the road, spreading joy and sunshine from town to town. You are there to work hard, and you have legitimate demands and expectations (which you should have clarified before leaving home). What I am saying is that you are a guest wherever you go, and that your host is more likely than not to be an enlightened amateur, ill-equipped to deal with unexpected circumstances and difficult situations. Make the best of whatever comes your way, and do it graciously. If there are things your host ought to learn about presenting dance, then educate him. This is very different and far more useful than telling him off.

This is important for everyone in the dance community. In spite of the vaunted dance boom, modern and post-modern dance in America is a fragile thing. It is not proving as acceptable as we think it should be by now. We have, by and large, failed to make people understand what it is we are trying to accomplish onstage. Audiences are still nonplussed by abstract works, made anxious when we dance to silence, scandalized when we speak or vocalize in any way, become restless at repetition, censorious when dancers don't point their feet, scornful when they wobble, and positively venomous if they weigh more than Margot Fonteyn.

But you've got to keep doing your work—for yourself, and for all of us. Any time good and real dance happens anywhere, it increases the likelihood that dance will happen there again. The people will catch up to you.

You want to be an artist, and you find you have to be a pioneer as well. You have to start all over from ground zero whenever the curtain goes up—if they have a curtain. The risk is complete and total every time. One chance to make an image or an emotion penetrate that dreadful wall of noise, inattention, boredom, fear, ignorance, vanity, and distraction. One shot at beating death. That's what you're really selling. You will eventually succeed, because in the long run, everyone desperately needs you to.

"The market will not be handed to you on a silver platter. You have to invent it, create it, or discover it."

John Simone

BALLET AND THE ART OF MARKETING

The intent of this part of the chapter is to provide a perspective on the experiences of a ballet company in a particular region of the United States (The Hartford Ballet) relating to the creation, implementation, and results of a marketing plan. While every ballet company has its own unique artistic goals and exists in its own singular geographic and demographic region, there are some universal conclusions that can be extrapolated from an analysis of the ingredients that contributed to one company's marketing successes and failures.

Considering the great number of ways the term "marketing" is used, the following is the definition of a marketing plan for the purpoes of the analysis:

1. Define your product (Art)
2. Define your market (Audience)
3. Define your goals (they must be measurable)
4. Develop your strategy (list your techniques)
5. Develop a plan of evaluation.

NOTE: The order in which the above steps progress is extremely important. Additionally, it is essential to have a clear, objective understanding of your resources at any given moment.

My focus will be mostly on the development of a home audience of ticket buyers with only occasional references to touring. After a brief summary of the conception and results of the Hartford Ballet's first ten years of marketing plans, each step will be analyzed in greater depth.

The School of the Hartford Ballet has existed since 1960. During its first twelve years, it grew into a multi-faceted institution that offered numerous programs and classes to an enrollment of over 600 students. Concurrently, a performing ensemble of semi-professional (that is to say, semi-paid) dancers was created. In addition to offering an annual *Nutcracker,* this group performed extensively in the school systems throughout Connecticut. In the summer of 1972, Michael Uthoff was hired as artistic director and the Hartford Ballet became a professsional ballet company employing ten dancers for a forty-week contract. At this time, a ten-year plan was developed to gradually increase the size and scope of the company by creating a larger home audience, a contributions base, and a national touring market.

The intent was to develop a national reputation through touring that could be utilized at home to build the local audience. Once the company's resource of shorter repertory ballets was secure, the talents and number of its dancers had increased, and its organizational and financial base was solid, it would be ready to produce larger full-length works. These would appeal to and attract a larger market, further extend the artistry of the dancers, and place the company in a more prominent position in the field of American dance.

In many ways, this plan worked. The company toured extensively throughout the United States, and was purportedly the most actively toured ballet company in 1975 and 1976. The number of dancers increased from ten to twenty-five. The company produced a full-length *Carmina Burana* in 1978, a unique re-staged version of *Nut-*

John Simone was a founding member of the Hartford Ballet and performed as a principal dancer with the company from 1972-1979. During much of this time he assumed the position of company representative and established employment guidelines and management procedures between the artists and the company's administration. From 1977-1979 Mr. Simone was employed as company manager for the Hartford Ballet. In 1980 he left the company to accept the position of Development Director for the Boston Repertory Ballet. Upon his return to Hartford in 1980 he was appointed Administrative Director of the Hartford Ballet and in 1981 he was appointed Managing Director. Mr. Simone holds a Bachelor of Arts degree from Trinity College in Hartford, Connecticut.

Photo: Gary W. Sweetman

"The Hartford Ballet believed that a national reputation developed on tour would help build a home audience."

Hartford Ballet. Fabric.

cracker in 1979, and a full-length *Romeo and Juliet* in 1980. The attendance in Hartford grew from 8,000 in 1972–73 to 64,500 in 1979–80. Despite this apparently successful realization of a long-range plan, the attendance for the two subsequent seasons fell off to 53,500, and the subscription base of approximately 1,700 essentially remained flat from 1978 to 1982. The reasons for this audience attrition and non-growth of subscribers can be found in an analysis of how the Hartford Ballet created, implemented, and evaluated its marketing plan.

As was mentioned earlier, the Hartford Ballet believed that a national reputation developed on tour would help build a home audience. The underlying assumption here was that the home market understood and wanted dance, and that once the company had demonstrated its quality through a demand for tour bookings and the resulting positive reviews, ticket sales in Hartford would increase. Ticket sales *did* increase, but further analysis showed that it was not only because of the market's acceptance of the company's reputation and growing artistry, but more significantly because of the product.

Ticket sales in Hartford increased only slightly from 8,000 in 1972 to 13,000 in 1977. Up to this point, the company had offered basically the same season (product) of repertory performances and the *Nutcracker* each year. Virtually all of this modest increase was due to an increase in sales for the *Nutcracker* which, in 1975, had been "packaged" differently — it had new sets and costumes. This first dramatic increase in sales occured in 1978 when the company offered a new product—appearances by guest companies.

At this time, the Bushnell Memorial, the major performing-arts theater in Hartford where the Hartford Ballet performs, had its own dance subscription series that featured guest companies. In the 1977–78 season, the Hartford Ballet incorporated this series into its own. That year, attendance went from 13,000 to 20,500. The intent was, and still is, to help educate and build the Hartford dance audience by bringing in the best of modern and clasical dance that was available and economically feasible. Additionally, it was hoped that popular companies like Alvin Ailey, American Dance Theater, Twyla Tharp Dance, and Pilobolus would help build a subscription base. Once a person subscribed to the series, even if it was because of the guest performers, they would be able to see that the Hartford Ballet compared favorably to these world-renowned companies. Although the second year of programming guest companies in the series with performances by the Hartford Ballet produced a 50% increase in subscriptions, a significant statistic was emerging. The attendance to the Hartford Ballet repertory performances, a very important component of the company's artistic program, had not increased since the first year of the company's existence.

In the 1978–79 season, when the Hartford Ballet introduced its new full-length *Carmina Burana*, it was the first time the company incorporated live music into a subscription event and the production included 100 singers onstage, the assumption was that these performances would appeal to a larger market. This proved to be true. Subscriptions increased by 50%, and the three performances of *Carmina Eurana* sold out. The apparent success of this season further encouraged the company to move forward with its long-term plans.

The strategy used was founded in the belief that if a full-length production and live music increased sales, then doubling the number of full-length productions and having live music at all performances of the Hartford Ballet would double sales. In the evaluation process that produced this line of reasoning, certain points were either ignored and/or misinterpreted. Although the 1978-79 season was an artistic and critical success, the subscription base of 1,750 represented only 33% of total capacity, and again, attendance at repertory performances was less than 60% for two performances. The decision was made to produce new sets and costumes for a restaged *Nutcracker,* create a new full-length *Romeo and Juliet,* repeat *Carmina Burana,* and offer four different repertory evenings with live orchestra accompaniment for all performances. The total number of performances increased from nineteen to thirty-five.

As defined earlier, a marketing plan must incorporate a clear understanding of resources. The 1979-80 season had a basic economic problem—the allocation of scarce resources. Such an amibitious season not only required staff with sufficient time and experience to make it work, it also needed a strong subscription base so that the projected goals could be achieved without overtaxing the administrative staff and the promotional budget.

The expectation was that the 30,500 single-ticket buyers from the previous season could be converted into subscribers. However, two-thirds of these people attended only *Carmina Burana* and *Nutcracker*. The company perceived that these single-ticket buyers, having thoroughly enjoyed the performances, would be prime targets for the 1979-80 dance series. Another assumption made about the market was that it would want to see *Carmina Burana* again the following season. It certainly was true that *Carmina Burana* was so rich in textures and utilized such a diversity of dance, music, and singing that one would benefit from a second viewing. But the perception held by the people intimately involved with the production did not necessarily transfer to the general public.

As for *Nutcracker,* it is truly a different animal. It is much more a holiday tradition and a spectacle than it is a dance event in the eyes of the audience. As it turned out, subscriptions did not increase for the 1979-80 season and the company was faced with 80% of the available seats left to sell before the start of the season.

Despite what would have appeared to be an impossible task, the season was apparently successful from a gross sales point of view. Ticket sales increased from 39,500 to 64,500. But two of the eight events, *Nutcracker* and *Romeo and Juliet,* accounted for 41,000 of the tickets sold, while the other six events sold at an average of 50% capacity. These six events included *Carmina Burana* and five works of a repertory nature. The belief that the people who were attracted to the larger, more spectacular ballets could be converted into subscribers or attendees at repertory performances was not realized. In fact, it can be argued that *Nutcracker* and *Romeo and Juliet* contributed to the disappointing attendance at the other events.

Because of the excitement created by these two works, they enjoyed an abundance of publicity. In a sense, this cast the rest of the season into a promotional shadow and made the selling job more difficult, since all the events were targeted toward the same market. If the repertory events were geared, say, to a student audience at a much lower price, and perhaps in a different theater, perhaps the sales effort would not be in competition with the larger productions. Unfortunately there is no smaller theater appropriate for dance repertory in Hartford that is also economically feasible. With the single-ticket buyer having such a wide range of choices, and *Nutcracker* and *Romeo and Juliet* dominating the public awareness, these two productions sold very successfully *at the expense of* the other events.

In evaluating the 1979–80 season and planning for 1980–81, it was not completely understood that the Hartford Ballet had at least four different products on its hands that attracted different segments of the market. Guest companies that attracted people who were aware of them from national media attention; repertory performances that appealed to, and were understood by, a narrow window in the market; full-length productions, which would have a broader following the first year than the second year; and the traditional *Nutcracker,* riding the coattails of the Christmas spirit, this fourth product also benefits from the commensurate increase in spending during the holidays. Buoyed by the strong sales for the *Nutcracker* and *Romeo and Juliet,* subscriptions were budgeted to increase 25%.

The conviction continued to be held that single-ticket buyers to spectacular events could be converted into subscribers. Although an evaluation of attendance to repertory events demonstrated that the goals needed to be lowered, the optimism generated by these specific previous successes prevailed. Also, as goals were being developed, the state of the economy was not taken into consideration. No contingency was factored into the budget to take into account the financial woes that were besieging the nation. Clearly, though, the state of the economy would have an effect on ticket buyers' disposable income.

Artistically, the 1979–80 season had been a success beyond anyone's expectations. The quality of all aspects of the performances, the choreography, dancing, music, sets, and costumes, was praised by both the critics and the audience. The monumental effort put forth in the creation and selling of so much in one year, however, had drained the company's human and financial resources. Although no major new works were planned, the 1980-81 season was as ambitious from a selling

"The conviction continued to be held that single-ticket buyers to spectacular events could be converted into subscribers. Spectacles may increase sales, but not necessarily develop an audience."

> "If the ballet can be done with smaller and lighter sets, there will be a greater number of potential performing spaces."

Hartford Ballet. *Allegro Brillante.*

point of view as the previous one. The lack of financial resources and staff to properly sell the year, the inability to convert the people who attended *Nutcracker* and *Romeo and Juliet* into subscribers, and the weak economy, all contributed to sales dropping from 64,500 to 53,500 in 1980–81.

The primary lesson that can be learned from this is that spectacles created by a ballet company may increase sales, but not necessarily develop a dance audience. This is not to say that a full-length ballet with imaginative sets and costumes is not an integral part of the art form of dance, or that it lacks artistic integrity, but because of its popular and showy nature, the market (audience) can perceive it simply as an entertaining event and not be motivated by the positive experience to see other types of dance offerings.

Therefore, should a company only concentrate on popular full-length productions? Not necessarily. Both artistic growth and economics weigh heavily in such a consideration. Generally, repertory performances provide more challenge and opportunity for the dancers' creativity. In a given evening, one dancer may have to create many different roles in distinctly varied styles of dance. The fact that any given repertory piece is only one of four ballets on a program and can be produced relatively inexpensively, gives the choreographer the freedom to experiment and explore new vistas without the specter of failure hanging over him. A full-length production that costs $250,000 or more can cause a company to be more conservative in developing an artistic concept.

Expensive, full-length productions may not be able to break even at the box-office. With funding sources becoming harder to find, the financial planning of lavishly produced ballets is very crucial. One possible way to have a full-length production pay for itself is to take it on tour. Today's dance sponsors are looking for productions that are recognizable and "easy" to sell and affordable at the same time. The planning of a new, large work can be modular in concept. If the ballet can be done with less or smaller and lighter sets, then the cost of touring can be kept down, and there will be a greater number of potential performing spaces. The major cost of any new work is in the creative period. Once it is in performance, the longer the run and/or tour, the more opportunity there is to realize a return on the initial investment.

A common complaint heard throughout the dance world (and many other worlds for that matter), is that there is never enough time, money, or people to do things right. Unfortunately, this reality is not likely to change throughout the 1980s. All anyone can do is marshall his resources, work within identifiable limits, and apply those resources where they will achieve the best results.

The performing arts sector has discovered that a strong subscription base is the backbone of its organizations (in addition, many ballet companies have found a second backbone in a well-attended *Nutcracker*). The Hartford Ballet, even with all the emphasis on touring, remains connected to subscription as an important income base. We learned that each subscription sale tends to cost less in terms of direct advertising and promotional costs than a single-ticket sale, and the cost of keeping a subscriber for more than one year is even less costly.

A good marketing plan, like a good professional training program in the ballet school, is an investment in the future. Spending the time and money to get to know the subscribers, how old they are, what their level of education is, where they live, where they work, and what motivates them to attend, is essential.

Concurrently, it is just as important to keep the subscribers informed about the company. In 1983, the Hartford Ballet began a program of pre-performance lecture/dinners for subscribers. The only cost to the ballet is time. The subscribers are offered the incentive of a price-fixed meal in the subscription brochure at an extra cost of $10 for each opening night. This money is then paid out proportionately to the restaurant after each dinner. Before each dinner, the subscribers listen to the choreographers and/or dancers who provide wonderful insights into what they are about to see. The people who have attended these dinners have said that their understanding of the ballets was greatly enhanced by this exposure. Word-of-mouth has been so tremendous regarding this program that the last lecture/dinner was sold out with a long waiting list.

Dance is the newest and one of the least understood of the performing arts in the

United States. Although the language of dance is universal, many people do not attend because they fear they will not be able to understand. This is obviously more true of abstract repertory performances where there is no familiar story or elaborate sets upon which the dance-company management can build a campaign. The different events performed by the Hartford Ballet are different packages offered to a customer for use in his leisure time. Consumers are literally bombarded with thousands of such offers daily—most are more tangible products than dance. The key is to understand what type of people would be inclined to attend various dance performances being offered, and to create messages that are directed to each identified target so that the potential customer will want to buy your package.

If a company wants to build an audience for different types of dance productions, it must first identify the market's sensitivities and determine which aspects of the dance appeal to which types of people. Everyone likes to go on vacation, but one person's paradise could be another's hell. Some people look for fast-paced night-life and want to spend money; others prefer quiet, nature, economy, and exercise. For these reasons Las Vegas and the United States National Parks use very different approaches in their respective efforts to create messages that will match "customers" with their respective packages. This is analogous to a company like the Hartford Ballet.

Like Las Vegas, the spectacular productions of the Hartford Ballet have a lot of action and extravaganza with elaborate sets and costumes. A majority of the people in the audience will attend because these are special events. Therefore, they should be promoted as such. This is not to say these productions are tacky or gawdy. One only has to emphasize the spectacular nature of the production to get them in their seats. The reality that beyond the magnificent sets and costumes are dancers who are creating and communicating subtle and powerful statements will become apparent during the performance. The artists will make sure that the audience leaves with more than it came with — an experience that can be digested and become nourishment to the soul.

Hartford Ballet. *Hansel and Gretel*.

Perhaps the same things that lure people to the National Parks can be used to attract an audience for repertory. The exhiliration of hiking through the verdant countryside, breathing fresh air, and feeling all the senses tingle from the experience can all be felt at a performance. The beauty of a dancer using a well-disciplined body to express emotions in an architecturally lit space in consort with the changing rhythms and melodies of music can be as profound an experience for some as confronting the Grand Canyon.

The point is to understand the various levels of appeal these dance products offer to the general public. Once this has been carefully defined in the context of the specific marketplace, the process of creating the particular messages to different segments of the population through the appropriate medium can begin. Do not assume that the people who attend the *Nutcracker* and *Romeo and Juliet*-type of full-length specials will want to come to repertory performances, or vice versa. Of course, there is the possibility that a large-scale ballet, choreographed around a popular story, could share an evening with other selected repertory. With time, continued communication through newsletters (the names of single-ticket buyers are to be cherished and nurtured) and different programming, these two different types of ticket buyers may begin to understand and enjoy more forms of dance. Eventually they may become subscribers.

Creating goals within the identifiable limits of your resources is essential to a properly formulated marketing plan. For a plan to unfold in its necessary chronology, resources will be utilized every step of the way. Every goal that is not attained will inevitably create an unplanned drain on resources and impair the proper implementation of the remaining elements of the plan.

An unattained goal may deplete the resources necessary for market research, and this will severely hamper the ability to define the market properly. A marketplace must be successfully analyzed in order to determine the product-definition for sales components. This is not to say that the product, which in this case is dance, should be molded to appeal to the market, but rather that the sales image of the product conveyed to the public should appeal to the potential ticket buyers.

Underachieved goals that restrict resources can have a disastrous effect on

"Underachieved goals can have a disastrous effect on strategic planning."

Hartford Ballet. *Carmencita Variations.*

strategic planning. The best laid plans of arts administrators will be foiled if the means do not exist to carry them out. If the strategy is to educate the audience (especially the single-ticket buyers), with regular mailings of newsletters and other informative sales literature, and the time and money does not exist to produce these mailings, then a wonderful opportunity will slip away. No matter how successful the event was that created these single-ticket buyers in the first place, the long, hard-fought process of building a subscription base will have to begin from scratch once again.

The potential for such an unfortunate possibility to occur makes the evaluation process all the more imperative. The artistic director, top management, the marketing director, and members of the board must all collaborate in this evaluation process. Each person will bring different concerns, plans, and knowledge to bear that will directly influence the ultimate goal of selling tickets. A forum that allows for the exchange of information and the identification of problems will help everyone achieve a better understanding of the different components of the organization, and will expedite the development of a strategy to satisfy everyone's needs while reaching set goals. Statistical information is a prerequisite for defining these goals.

Marketing decisions must be grounded in a resource of empirical data. The first way to define your market is to find out where they live. Every ticket order should have the person's name, address, and phone number (work and home). Compiling the number of ticket buyers by zip code will not only provide a demographic profile of the audience, but will also help in the development of an advertising schedule. If ticket buyers are concentrated in certain areas, then focus a direct-mail campaign on these zip codes. Local newspapers in these areas would be effective vehicles for print advertising.

To build an audience economically, you must determine which sales tools are producing the best response. Order forms should be coded so that when they are returned, the box-office can record whether the form was from a brochure, a newspaper advertisement, a handout, or a flyer. If radio or television is used, the times the spots are run should be obtained, if possible, and the box-office personnel should note any significant increase in telephone sales following the run of the commercials. All phone callers should be asked how they heard about the performance, and the responses should be recorded and compiled.

Sales data will show the fluctuation in attendance, not only from night to night of the same production, but also from one production to another. Different times of the year may be more popular than others. This information will help in planning future schedules. In the case of the Hartford Ballet, sales data demonstrates that repertory events are not as popular as fully staged productions.

The collective analysis of this data by the key members of the organization can lead to the creation of effective strategies. A board member, in charge of marketing for a local busines that is trying to attract the same market as a ballet company, may have used some successful techniques that would work for dance. Another board member who is a professional financial planner can help predict the impact of the economy on sales. If it seems evident that the market prefers a ballet with a plot-line, the marketing director may suggest the idea of a ballet that is a trilogy in an effort to find solutions to increasing reportory attendance. Assuming Part One is successful the first year, people will come back the next for Part Two, and so on. Perhaps word-of-mouth will help increase sales. The artistic director may find that this idea stimulates his search for subject matter in previously unexplored choreographic vistas. It worked for *Rocky,* why wouldn't it work for ballet? The top manager, with the most thorough overview of the organization, will most effectively facilitate the synthesis of these ideas in relationship to costs and available resources.

This type of collective evaluation process has proved helpful to the Hartford Ballet, particularly regarding the concept of helping to build a home audience through a national touring reputation. An analysis of the yearly attendance statistics revealed that increased touring did *not* increase ticket sales at home. The marketing director pointed out that the local media was reticent to cover touring stories. Therefore, it was difficult to inform the public of the company's touring activities. Furthermore, no conclusive evidence appeared to link the public's knowledge of a tour reputation with their desire to attend a performance. In fact, because touring kept the company out of Hartford for many weeks of the year, it was more difficult to maintain a continued and visible presence at home.

This information lead some members of the board to question the reason for touring. Both the artistic director and managing director pointed out that the home season alone could not provide enough work for the dancers. Touring allowed the company to be able to offer a contract long enough to keep and attract talented artists. Although this analytical exercise only served to disprove a theory, it did help the board achieve a better understanding of the necessity for touring.

Evaluation means listening carefully to the voice of experience. It provides the chance to learn from mistakes and explain unexpected triumphs. It requires the resource of timely and accurate data. Art is created inspirationally and intuitively, yes, but it is also created by hard work, discipline, and years of training. The same is true of a marketing plan for a ballet company. It must have a foundation of knowledge and discipline before it can create beautiful results.

David Levenson

MUSIC: PRODUCT, MARKET, MEDIA, MESSAGE

From the spring of 1972 until the summer of 1980, I was Director of Press and Public Relations of The Cleveland Orchestra, a job that entailed responsibility for ticket sales, press relations, promotions, and special events. In 1972, Lorin Maazel, who had spent the majority of the previous fifteen years conducting in Europe, was appointed the orchestra's music director, succeeding George Szell. During Mr. Szell's twenty-four-year tenure, the orchestra had been acclaimed as one of the world's few *great* orchestras.

At that time, the orchestra's general manager (to whom I reported directly) was Michael Maxwell, an elegant and articulate New Zealander whose strong vision of the orchestra—what it was and what it should continue to be—acted as the bridge between Mr. Szell's death (1970) and Mr. Maazel's advent (1972). Mr. Maxwell's primary concern was with the larger canvas, the broad sweep, the bigger chunks of the picture.

In 1975, he was succeeded by Kenneth Haas. Mr. Haas, still (in 1983) the orchestra's general manager, is firm, direct, and literate. He possesses a clear understanding of the orchestra's needs and goals, his staff's objectives and direction, and how to mesh the two. Haas, unlike Maxwell, is interested not only in the larger structure of programmatic ideas, but also in the details of their implementation.

The Cleveland Orchestra is operated by the Musical Arts Association, a not-for-profit corporation whose president is Alfred M. Rankin, a prominent Cleveland lawyer who possesses a keen mind and the ability to see all possibilities and viewpoints. He has an unbounded devotion to the orchestra. The chairman of the board's public-relations committee was Dorothy Humel. Miss Humel ran a business, yet found time for her many philanthropic activities. And it was with her, on behalf of the board, that I worked most closely.

When I arrived in Cleveland and heard my first concert by the orchestra (an indescribably translucent performance of works by Gustav Mahler, conducted by Pierre Boulez), I was immediately struck by the horrible sight of only half the hall filled. This on the first night of the week's series of three concerts! Since Mr. Szell's death, both subscription and single-ticket sales had fallen off dramatically; public awareness of the orchestra, its concerts and subsdiary events, had diminished. Yet, this was clearly a great orchestra. ("But if a tree falls in the forest and no one is there," asked my logic professor, "does it make a sound?")

Cleveland is a much maligned city. A metropolis of vast cultural resources (world-class museum and orchestra; opera and ballet companies; art galleries; renowned regional theater; etc.), accomplished educational institutions, medical facilities of enviable quality, professional sports teams, libraries of uncommon depth, beautiful parks, and comfortable residential areas. Among its prominent and long-standing traditions is a profound commitment to its cultural institutions, both in attendance, contributions, and hard work.

These, then, were the players and the setting I was given that night in April of 1972 as I listened to Mahler's Symphony No. 10 and viewed a half-empty hall.

David S. Levenson has been Managing Director of the Asolo State Theater (Sarasota, Florida) since 1980. He is concurrently a Professor of Theatre Management of The Florida State University and works closely with the Asolo/FSU Conservatory of Professional Actor Training, teaching courses in theater management and dramatic literature. Prior to joining Asolo in 1980, he was Director of Press and Public Relations for The Cleveland Orchestra (1972-1980), and previously worked with the orchestras of Boston and Baltimore. He has been a lecturer at Ohio State University's Studies in Arts Administration program, a member of the Music Advisory Panel of the Ohio Arts Council, and a technical consultant for the American Symphony Orchestra League and the Ohio Arts Council. He currently serves on the Theater Panel of the Florida Fine Arts Council. A Theater Arts graduate of Boston University, Mr. Levenson has worked as a stage manager and assistant director for Sarah Caldwell's Opera Company of Boston and the American National Opera Company.

Immediately upon my arrival, General Manager Michael Maxwell detailed the vision that he, the board, and Mr. Maazel had for the orchestra. It was to continue to be a ''world-class'' orchestra. This meant that it would accelerate its touring (both internationally and domestically), renew its recording activities, initiate television programming, and continue its strong radio syndication. But first we needed to fill its winter home, Severance Hall.

I had had the good fortune of working with two other orchestras (Boston and Baltimore), and had evolved a quartet of words that always assisted me in beginning my work: *product, market, media, message.*

Surely the product could hardly be improved upon. Its new conductor was among the most acclaimed in the world. But yet, in my investigation of the *product*, I perceived several ''obstacles'' that prevented audiences from attending concerts. These ''obstacles'' were ascertained through surveys, both formal and informal (asking dozens of neighbors in my large apartment complex).

And so began the litany. ''Yes, I know The Cleveland Orchestra is great, but I don't go to concerts because...''

1. I don't know enough about classical (or symphonic) music,
2. I'm afraid to come out at night and park my car on city streets,
3. I like to relax when I go out for entertainment, and listening to symphony music requires too much work,
4. It's too expensive,
5. When we go out, we don't like to run from dinner to concerts,
6. It's so difficult (or confusing) to buy tickets,
7. I understand that you have to buy a subscription to all twenty-four concerts, and we don't want to go that many times,
8. I don't go out much at night, and you only have evening concerts,
9. (My personal favorite) Well, everyone knows you can't get tickets to The Cleveland Orchestra because their concerts are always sold out.

A clear profile was evolving. Most notable was the fact that each person responded with great admiration for the orchestra, but for a variety of reasons, it was *inaccessible* to them. So, in my investigation into the *product,* it was obvious that the quality of the orchestra was not a problem, but other matters were.

Working with several board members, we received a large grant from the Cleveland Foundation, a foundation committed to sustaining Cleveland's cultural life. Because of this grant for audience development, we were able to work on a variety of projects which otherwise would not have been possible, and we now could fund the kind of research and support needed for success. Market research, copywriters, designers, photographers, mass mailing (printing of brochures, handling, lists, postage, etc.), and newspaper-radio-television advertising were extended to the proper proportions. With our financial burden now assumed by this grant, we could do what was necessary for an all-out campaign.

The Product.

Since the product we had (albeit great) was not ''selling,'' we developed a ''secondary product.'' In answer to the question, ''what is our product?'' we united all activities then in existence at Severance Hall and supplemented them with others. We arrived at a slogan that expressed our *entire* product, ''IT'S ALL AT SEVERANCE HALL!'' We devised a ''package'' before a single brochure was mailed or radio/television spot placed. A package included an entire evening of ''entertainment,'' and related to those qualms and queries of my survey:

1. You can park in a well-lit, attended lot adjacent to the hall,
2. You can have dinner at a restaurant inside the hall,
3. You can attend an ''Informal and Informative'' (the slogan used) pre-concert talk (not lecture) given by Klaus George Roy, the orchestra's distinguished program annotator, who discusses that evening's program,
4. The Concert. It's not work, it's enjoyable, amusing, moving, entertaining, tuneful, etc.

In addition, we offered series of twelve concerts, six concerts, and a new three-concert sampler series; the orchestra's remarkable and dedicated women's committee initiated a five-concert matinee (11 a.m.) series; and we pushed student and senior-citizen tickets.

Another aspect of our new product was Lorin Maazel, the new music director. Here was the potential of another kind of product, one which could be utilized best vis-à-vis his predecessor. A great conductor, George Szell (or so it was perceived by the media and public) rarely made public appearances off the podium or gave interviews. At 42, Lorin Maazel was young, handsome, stylishly dressed; he was charming, articulate, humorous, urbane, and on fire with the professional opportunity now given him. His understanding of the power and use of the media was deep and accurate. His wife, pianist Israela Margalit, was informal, intelligent, attractive, very outgoing. They had a young son. They were ''jet-setters'' (that wonderful 1970s phrase).

The ''secondary'' product was the conductor beyond his role as musical leader. Here's a man, a father, a warm, charming individual—just like you Mr./Mrs./Ms. Ticket Buyer. He is a human being with all the concerns, needs, and responsibilities you have. This second product, beyond our entertainment package, was another link with the public who may not have been reached through the first. Mr. Maazel's persona made him, and hence the orchestra, *accessible* to the public.

Step one had been taken. Without varying our *actual* product, we had constructed a new one, or *so it seemed to the public.*

Market

Next we identified our audience, or the *market.* Past audiences had traditionally come from the east side of Cleveland, from three or four of its suburbs. Age range was older (50 and up); economic status was upper income. Using the traditional computer tools, we collated the zip codes where our current subscribers lived and measured them against the potential in each area. We discovered that within certain communities, we had perhaps 100 subscribers from a potential base of 3,500; in others, we found that we had attained almost 75% of the potential audience. In still others, we had very few. Up until that time, we had ignored the more affluent/ educated/culturally oriented neighborhoods of Cleveland's west-side suburbs and surrounding cities; had all but ignored its campuses; had done little with its younger and middle aged (that is, 25–35 and 35–45) populace.

We targeted certain potential zip-code areas, using the 1970 government census, which at the time was relatively current. We identified certain age groups. We had ''reshuffled'' our *product* and thought we knew where we felt a potential audience was hiding.

Media

I've always felt that in addition to looking at the *product* in too confining a manner, we looked too traditionally at the definition of *media.* We utilized the usual ones, sending out hundreds of thousands of direct-mail brochures heralding our ''entertainment package,'' we ran full newspaper ads and PSA spots (and even paid for some) on radio and television. But we extended our use of the traditional media. While the music and entertainment pages are very important, and were the heart of our effort, we looked at the newspaper in toto: women's pages, financial section, sports page, gossip column, front page, etc., etc. We investigated every program on television. We established an even firmer relationship with our fine-arts radio station. (One of Cleveland's great cultural assets is its fine-arts radio station, WCLV. Robert Conrad, the voice of orchestra radio broadcasts, devised a new format for our spots, encompassing the entertainment values of our concerts.)

Beyond this exceptionally supportive station, we came to establish a relationship with a rock station WMMS. In 1972, this was an unheard-of tactic. This contact would prove to be a gold mine. In the search for new audiences, we felt we were completely missing those between 16 and 30 years of age. This audience neatly focused on this progressive rock station; they had their ''ear.'' We had worked with WMMS on several occasions and discussed audience cross over—whether their audience was interested in our music, whether our audience listened to their station. We found that their listeners owned the best and most up-to-date audio equipment,

"Break all the stereotypes... avoid those hideous words 'classical' and 'cultural'."

"The sale of recordings is often stimulated by tours, as is an orchestra's ability to attract television programming."

that many did go to our concerts, and that many more would go if they felt that certain "classical concert" barriers (i.e. dress, conduct) were eliminated. So, they co-produced a new series, an informal *special* concert series with a narrator. WMMS devised (in their language) spots for their audience. They plugged our regular concerts, played our music, and on one memorable afternoon, they interviewed Lorin Maazel. Two worlds, seemingly galaxies apart, met, and discovered that their worlds were one—music was the universal language.

Other forms of *media* were actively pursued. Maazel appeared at high schools (of course the newspapers, etc. were there), he spoke and spoke and spoke to groups (older, younger, retired, civic, cultural), he played tennis with a pro (nice picture on the sports page), his wife decorated their house (it was photographed in both papers), their European trips and tours appeared frequently in the gossip columns, and on one golden day, a photograph of Mr. Maazel and his small son appeared on the front page of both Cleveland dailies. And on and on...

The Message

The *message* grows organically out of the other three elements and is, in a way, the easiest to devise. It is the mirror image of the *product,* attached to a specific *market,* using the appropriate and entire *media.* The overall guiding force was simple: Break all the stereotypes the symphony orchestras had labored under for decades, those that had diminished its audiences and constipated its growth. The *message:*

1. we've got a great orchestra;
2. it plays beautiful, moving music (avoid those hideous words "classical" and "cultural")
3. it's relaxing and part of an entertainment package;
4. you don't have to spend hundreds of dollars;
5. (in the person of Lorin Maazel) it is the work of people just like you. In sum, it is both an enjoyable and accessible experience.

Augmenting the effort to sell our Severance Hall concerts (and we did) were other activities, most notably foreign tours. Many orchestras tour internationally, for good reason. The sale of recordings is often stimulated by these tours, as is an orchestra's ability to attract television programming.

But most important, at least to me, is its impact *at home.* While on our seven foreign tours (twice each in Europe, the Orient, and Central and South America, and once to Australia/New Zealand) my tasks were three-fold:

1. assist local presenters in promoting our concerts;
2. send the word back throughout the United States;
3. get reports back to Cleveland.

Number three was always the most important. It is of inestimable value to ticket sales when the London or Sydney or Mexico City or Tokyo critics and audiences laud your orchestra. Our tours, for the most part, preceded season openings, and their successes stimulated sales at home. It is the press agent's nirvana for bdwVppers and radio/television stations to send representatives on tour. Barring this, I devised a system to transmit reports back to Cleveland. The wire services are a perfect way of touching all the papers. I would call into programs on WCLV at specified hours to give capsule versions of concerts and reviews. These were aired frequently. European-based, American television crews sent footage to Cleveland's TV stations. All of this is equally effective for tours throughout the U.S.

At this point, let us not forget the much overworked director of development. His unenviable task is to raise millions of dollars annually. All of the activities described above relate directly to fund raising efforts, (and so does every thing else that the marketing department does), for they create the *environment* in which these activities will flourish or fail.

None of my activities would have been possible without leadership from the top. The general manager and music director must articulate a coherent and unified vision of the orchestra, its goals, and its aspirations. Both must have a *realistic* understanding of what the media can do (and here I was very lucky); both must be available to discuss plans and problems and participate in their implementation.

Similarly, a board of trustees and its public-relations committee must make the financial and emotional commitment to the effort. The three major figures (board of trustees, music director, general manager) must agree on the activities that should be undertaken, the image that must be perceived, the mission in the community, and the cost. And they must all commit to it.

The survival of any arts organization is a reflection of its community's desire for it to survive. But an arts organization must identify and respond to the community's needs. At The Cleveland Orchestra, the community's interests are expressed through a citizen's advisory committee (a new one each year) that sits in consultation with the management and board and reflects the interest and displeasures of the community.

In my estimation, a board of trustees has three major tasks:
1. to appoint both the artistic and managerial leaders;
2. to assure the economic survival of the organization;
3. to address long-term needs (i.e. summer facility, long-range plan, endowment, etc.)

Its public relations marketing committee should be made up of a group of people (some of whom are perhaps not even board members) who act as resource for ideas and guidance. When a program is devised, they suppport it (meaning very often they support the cost) at the full board level. A good chairman of such a committee will be informed of all activities, will be supportive, and will never interfere with the daily operations of the department.

The general manager has three major responsibilities: 1. He must oversee the organization's budgetary planning and its implementation; 2. He must give direction to the staff (with the artistic leader) for the planning and implementation of the artistic goals; 3. He must, along with the staff, foster the environment in which the artists and artisans can create the product.

A marketing/press director must have access to both the artistic and managerial leaders. Both leaders must spend time defining their joint goals, conveying them to their marketing director and be available to participate in their execution. Above all, they must have a *realistic* idea of the limitations of the media and the fallibility of marketing directors, as well as having access to and power over the media. (To date I know of no marketing director who owns a radio or television station or a newspaper.)

Realistic goals (i.e., subscription growth), timetables, and budgeting vary with each organization. In general, I find a three-year plan to be realistic. Once "signed up," a subscriber must be kept in contact with the orchestra apart from concerts if you hope to re-subscribe him. Newsletters help in this way. Re-subscription plans should be developed. A subscription notice followed by a reminder letter—why not coming from the music director?—plus a telephone campaign, will get as many as possible to re-subscribe. Analysis of and renewed contact with old subscribers who haven't yet re-subscribed is also valuable.

For me, examination was most important. Set within the confines of my office, surrounded by timetables, budgets, census data, code analysis, etc., proper investigation of the *product, market, message, media* was the most valuable thing I did. In retrospect, I asked myself a number of important questions and didn't confine myself to any on prejudice, taking nothing for granted.

- PRODUCT. What is it? If it's not selling now, what else around it can be sold? What is the public now buying? What don't they like about my product? Is it accessible? What makes it inaccessible?
- MARKET. Where and with whom are we now successful and why? Have we reached the maximum potential in each area? Have we ignored one or more age groups, economic groups, geographical areas? Have we arbitrarily decided that they won't like our product (remember the rock audience)?
- MEDIA. Use them all and use all of them. No, it's not redundant. Use the arts pages and use the rest of the newspaper as well. As you target your potential audience, see where they get their information from. Find new audiences. God bless the fine-arts stations, but don't forget the rock stations, the all-talk

stations, etc. Use media in its broadest context—as an avenue to contact people. Find the right medium for the specific group.

• MESSAGE. Avoid the clichès ("the arts enrich the spirit", or "it's good for you" doesn't sell tickets). Look at what movies and television do to attract audiences.

The largest corporations have the advantage of seemingly unlimited money, hence the availability of specialized advertising agencies and research firms. One agency analyzes the product, another the market, another a campaign, another the most efficient use of the media, another zip codes, etc. Generally speaking, arts organizations do not have that luxury. A good marketing director enjoys all of the tools of his trade. He has the knowledge, experience, imagination and expertise to deal with an entire campaign, from conception to implementtion. He should have the ability to compile budgets, write copy, work with designers (a good one is worth his weight in gold), proof, write and produce spots, etc. He must work well with those who set the patterns and create the product, since they are often the best source of ideas. Some of the best ideas I received came from the orchestra members themselves. And again, let us not forget about the key relationship with the director of development. Every effort should be made to enhance and reinforce his projects and programs.

Perhaps there hasn't been an original idea in marketing since the snake pushed the apple on Eve. We all use the same principles, whether we're selling music, theater, dance, opera, beer, cosmetics, cars, politicians, etc. What can be new is the skillful and creative use of the principles of marketing and the way the pieces of the puzzle are arranged and manipualted—for they are never asembled the same way twice.

Edward Corn

OPERA: THE PEOPLE'S THEATER

"the opera's not over til the fat lady sings..."

That celebrated, rallying cry from the world of basketball, whatever it may mean, reflects many popular beliefs about opera: It is an unreal world filled with dragons that sing, fat ladies in breastplates pretending to be beautiful heroines, stories screeched out in languages no one understands. Opera, according to this view, is an arcane entertainment for the wealthy, the snobbish, the highly educated, the fanatic, and/or the demented. Audiences, similarly, are entirely composed of bored husbands, bejewelled dowagers ("glitterbosoms," as they were called by the late director of the Baltimore Opera, Robert Collinge), and cheering/booing, lovers/haters of some particular singer.

There are, it must be admitted, some performances that fit the image. This writer remembers a notorious opening-night *Norma* at the Metropolitan Opera not long ago when the air was so filled with the odor of blood lust that one might as well have been attending a bullfight as an opera. The intended victim — an internationally famous soprano — was impaled on the points of the picador even before a strangled note could escape her throat. But I also remember the atmosphere of electricity in the Met lobby the night John Dexter's new *Aida* opened, when the most violent debate concerned the artistic qualities of the production for a change—not the coiffures, or gowns, or the best restaurant for supper.

Faced with the ubiquitous jokes about opera that pervade television and the comic pages and help to shape the derisive perceptions of the average citizen, should the marketing director of your neighborhood opera company simply throw up his hands and apply for a job at McDonald's? Or can the mental picture of opera in this country be changed?

Our hapless marketing director must apply the classic marketing approaches to the job: He must identify the potential market and then develop strategies to reach and motivate that market. But, before I delve into a discussion of the idiosyncratic application of standard marketing approaches to the mad world of opera, it may be helpful to explore a few personal thoughts about the origins and growth of opera in the United States. Perhaps we can find a few clues as to why an art form that is the "people's" theater in Europe has traditionally been the butt of the "people's" jokes in this country.

As we near the end of the twentieth century, it is easy to forget that not so long ago we were a country of new arrivals, of recent immigrants from Europe's old cultures. It was only natural that the immigrants would want to enjoy the music theater that had meant so much to them in the Old Country. Given the years of training needed by opera performers, it was more sensible to import French troupes to New Orleans and Italian companies to New York than to try to assemble local productions (although there were, from early colonial days, American groups that performed English operas and then, original ballad operas). The performances by visiting opera companies were, of course, sung in the language of the composer, librettist, and performers—not in English.

It is the opinion of this writer that opera in the United States drifted away from the

Prior to becoming General Director of the Minnesota Opera Company, Edward Corn's professional music career began in 1955 as an assistant to the manager of the St. Louis Symphony Orchestra and assistant to the public relations director of the St. Louis Municipal Opera. A series of positions with increasing responsibilities brought him, in 1969, to the position of Manager of the Western Opera Theater (touring and educational subsidiary of San Francisco Opera). In 1972 Mr. Corn became Manager of the San Francisco Opera, and in 1975 he was appointed Director of Planning and Public Affairs for the Metropolitan Opera of New York. In 1977 Mr. Corn assumed the responsibility of the Manager of the Opera Company of Philadelphia, which brought him, three years later, to the National Endowment for the Arts as the Director of the Opera-Musical Theater Program. Before joining the Minnesota Opera Company, Mr. Corn served as Executive Director of Wolf Trap Farm Park for the Performing Arts. Mr. Corn holds an AB degree from Yale University.

"The audience for opera became a strange mixture of believers and snobs, those who genuinely loved the art and those for whom attendance was a symbol of class distinction."

average person and became the isolated hunting preserve of the upper classes as immigrants were assimilated into the mainstream of American life. It was further removed from them as they stopped speaking their native languages and adopted the ways of their new homeland. At that point, opera's very foreignness became a badge that the wealthy could flaunt to distinguish themselves from the masses. By appreciating opera, the wealthy demonstrated that they had the leisure to travel to other lands, to learn the exotic ritual of opera, and to acquire foreign tongues; and that they could spend the necessary money to build themselves opera houses and then buy the gowns and carriages they said were requisites for attendance of performances.

And so, the audience for opera became a strange mixture of believers and snobs, of those who genuinely loved the art and those for whom attendance at opera was a symbol of class distinction. For a myriad number of reasons, everyone in the mixture put up walls to isolate opera from the general public. Only in very recent years have Americans once again recognized that opera is the most fulfilling of all the performing arts. It is the one theatrical experience in which the audience's emotional response can be heightened to a state of ecstasy through its affect on all the senses.

Opera is, it must be admitted, a peculiar and unnatural art form. It demands from the spectator a total suspension of disbelief—how, otherwise, can one accept the convention of singing instead of speaking? But music so intensifies the drama, so heightens the emotions and passions, that they become vicariously as thrilling and unbearable to the spectator as the desire and love and hatred he has directly experienced outside the world of opera.

Opera, like all religions, is a bit frightening to the uninitiated, and, unfortunately, its false priests have too often inspired fear by insisting that one must have special training and equipment even to attend performances. Nonsense! Opera is music and drama and the visual arts, and it is the magic of theater. All these forms should be accessible to anyone with the eyes and ears and open mind to admit them. As with any other human activity, however, from cooking to lovemaking, one will enjoy opera more if one has some knowledge of it and experience with it.

Let us return to some thoughts about the development of opera in the United States. An interesting parallel situation was occurring as opera was isolated behind the closing doors of money, education, dress, and status. In city after city, a voice teacher or a conductor or a stage director was founding an opera workshop at the local college or university. Singers were attracted to the workshop, which eventually grew and scheduled full productions, and soon there was community support for a civic opera company. Twenty-five years ago, opera in the United States meant almost exclusively the Metropolitan Opera — its New York and Philadelphia seasons, its national tour, and its radio broadcasts. Large companies existed in San Francisco and Chicago, but the grass-roots movement was still in the seedling stage at the colleges and universities.

Today, any American city of any size at all has its own resident opera-producing company (Jackson, Mississippi, for example, has two). This writer remembers a performance about ten years ago in a Southern city for which the same individual was producer, conductor, stage director, and set and costume designer. But today, the generation who founded the workshops and then directed almost all aspects of the burgeoning companies' work is being succeeded by professional artistic directors and managers. And at the same time, the old-fashioned press agent is giving way to the professional marketing director.

Until a few years ago, the public relations director (often the manager or director of the company) wrote a few press releases and mailed them out, placed advertisements he had designed in the newspapers, arranged an interview or two with the visiting stars, and lit up the press agent's cigar. The Metropolitan Opera, often unfairly villified as a museum for the preservation of old operas and outmoded management and production styles, deserves much of the credit for leadership in advancing opera toward twentieth-century marketing concepts. About the same time that the Met was changing its approach to producing opera under the triumvirate of Anthony Bliss, James Levine, and John Dexter, it was also putting into place a modern marketing plan under the direction of Patrick Veitch (now head of the Australian Opera). The Met's leadership made full and sophisticated use of such tools as market surveys; carefully directed planning, copywriting, and graphics; designed direct-mail campaigns of many varieties; offered multi-layered subscription plans, and sophisticated ticket services. Since then, most opera companies throughout the country have developed marketing techniques that can take advantage of data-processing equipment. No longer is the all-purpose opera director threatened by the marketing director who can harness such techniques and make them work.

Let us examine two other exclusively operatic problems for their instructional value. First, the problem of marketing new works. On Broadway, virtually all presentations are advertised as "a *new* drama," "a *new* comedy," or "a *new* musical." But how often will the phrase "a *new* opera" attract customers? Operatic audiences have been conditioned to want to see the same two dozen works over and over again. How many excesses of stage direction have been indirectly stimulated by this narrow interest? But as more American opera companies dedicate their efforts to keeping the art form vital through the infusion of new works into the repertory, marketing directors will have to find ways to persuade the public to try contemporary lyric theater.

Are there examples of successful strategies for the marketing of new works by opera companies? Probably many, but two examples come to this writer's mind:

1. The Minnesota Opera Company, of which I was recently made General Director, was founded twenty years ago almost exclusively to produce new operas. With that as its publicly promulgated purpose, the Minnesota Opera Company tried to build an audience from the segment of the ticket-buying public interested in the fresh, the challenging, even the avant-garde. This was a difficult task in a relatively small community like Minneapolis/St. Paul; in recent years, there has been extreme pressure on the company to mix both traditional opera and musical theater into its repertory. Now, therefore, it is far from clear what Minnesota Opera stands for. To clarify our mission, we will offer three discrete festival seasons when we move into the new Ordway Music Theater in 1984–1985 (which is being built for the Minnesota Opera, the St. Paul Chamber Orchestra, and the Schubert Club)—traditional grand opera in fall, new and contemporary works in the spring, and operetta and a classic musical in summer. Marketing considerations were the principal concern in establishing this configuration. Now, new works can be marketed on their own terms.

2. Western Opera Theater, the touring and educational subsidiary of the San Francisco Opera, had by the early 1970s established the ultimately desirable relationship with many of its sponsoring communities: They accepted whatever repertory the company offered with confidence that each opera would be produced with style and quality. Thus, Western Opera Theater was able to introduce new works painlessly. I specifically remember Ernst Krenek's *What Price Confidence,* a piece composed in tone rows rather than traditional musical key-signatures. It was so successful — because of the elegance of the staging (by a young director, David Ostwald) as well as the quality of its music and libretto—that sponsor requests kept it in the repertory for several seasons beyond the original plan.

The second problem unique to opera marketing relates to the "if only I had known..." syndrome. This writer vividly recalls being in innumerable small towns in the West years ago with Western Opera Theater. At least twice a week, after a performance, members of the company would be approached with the comment, "I would have come to see opera long before now, if only I had known I would enjoy it so much." This is a marketing problem: How do you encourage people to try something that is preceded by such a gray cloud of dismal expectations? How can we remove from opera the inaccurate preconceptions resulting from so many decades of bad press? Two thoughts occur, although there surely are many more:

1. Hit the problem head-on. Say — in your repertory, your advertising, your graphics—that you are *not* a company that appeals only to the wealthy, the highly educated, the European travellers. Say that you exist for the people. Take your performances into non-traditional locations, even into the streets,

> "Opera, like all religions, is a bit frightening to the uninitiated."

Minnesota Opera Company. *The Jealous Cellist and Other Acts of Misconduct.* Photo: Peter B. Myers.

as Western Opera did with *The Threepenny Opera*. As you reach non-traditional audiences, word-of-mouth will then do your marketing job for you.

2. Direct your marketing to those people who attend theater, sports, films. Create an audience that is interested in living and the arts, even if it has so far been afraid of opera. Use discount tickets, two-fers, group packages; reach people through employee-recreation programs, clubs, service organizations. And show your attractive young artists to them, to counter the false image of opera as a stuffy, silly art form.

These are some of the problems our opera marketing director (now as often a woman as a man, at last) must overcome. He or she must still make decisions about the potential audience: Should marketing efforts be directed mostly to the traditional opera-goers, those in the upper-income brackets, the season subscribers, the music lovers? Or should some money be spent to reach new and untested audiences, those who attend sports events or buy books, for example? What about the young and the senior citizens? What proportion of funds budgeted for marketing should be spent to promote the sale of season subscriptions, and what percentage should be reserved to encourage single-ticket sales? Should it be assumed that new works will not sell well, and should the company then try to cut its losses by spending only a minimal amount on marketing? What kind of mix should be established between advertising in print media and electronic? How much of the company's budget should be allocated to advertising?

Quality is still the best sales tool of all, and fine productions will consistently draw ticket purchasers. A community-wide feeling of excitement about a company's work will do more to increase sales than any advertisement or any review of a single production. And word-of-mouth is still the most effective way to let the public know about anything.

One of my personal concerns is that marketing not become an end in itself. The marketing director and the company's board and general director must work together to decide on the company's mission, and also to decide how much they will attempt to lead and how much to follow their audience's tastes. There is nothing worse than a cynical marketing director. He must know why the job is being done and must know when to stop. And, finally, the good marketing director must find ways to evaluate the campaign — to know what is working and what should be modified or eliminated.

Today's marketing director is part of a team of managers who are changing the image of opera in America, who are developing a new American tradition of music theater. For all our sakes, let us wish them well.

"There is nothing worse than a cynical marketing director."

Frank Jacobson

PERFORMING ARTS CENTERS

The Arvada Center for the Arts and Humanities sits inside a seventeen-acre park overlooking the metropolitan Denver area. This multi-disciplinary facility, owned and operated by the city of Arvada, Colorado, opened in 1976. It produces and presents 600 events a year in its 500-seat theater; 10,000 square feet of gallery space, classrooms, and studios; and in the 1,000-seat outdoor amphitheater. Patrons can park easily in the expansive open lot, and can, if they wish, walk to the adjacent restaurant—a quaint, converted farmhouse reminiscent of Arvada's earlier agricultural days.

A physical gem of an arts center both in design and setting, it has, however, had certain identity problems from the day the initiative for the center began, almost ten years ago, in 1973. The identity problems of any arts center must be taken into account prior to initiating any marketing strategy.

Arvada is a community of 87,000, approximately twenty minutes from downtown Denver and as much as forty-five minutes from other suburban areas. Because Arvada is part of a 1.5-million, metro-area population, the Arvada Center can rely on a significant arts-interested public from the entire Denver metropolitan area. In fact, our audience research indicates that between 50% and 60% of our attendees come from outside the Arvada city limits.

Perception about the city of Arvada itself, both by its residents and the metro-area populace, evoke the common expression, "but in Arvada?" whenever the center is mentioned. How do you build an identity for a center located in a community that was once known only for its nationally famous celery? Historically, Arvada was a small agricultural community; today, it is primarily a residential community with vestiges of its previous farming economy still visible on the outskirts of town. It does not have a well-developed commercial or industrial economic base. In fact, only 19% of its work force actually works in Arvada, the majority commuting to Denver or other adjacent communities. Consequently, except for the Arvada Center, the city is not distinguishable from any other residential community. Sometimes, it has been difficult for people to conceive of Arvada as a home for an arts center.

Perception about the nature of the center presents a different problem—that is, the "community center" versus the "community arts center". The "community center," in the most general sense, usually connotes recreational activity: swimming pools, basketball courts, and theater and art activity designed more for the leisure time of the participants than for the cultural enhancement of the observers. The Arvada Center, on the other hand, is a community arts center. It integrates and balances its arts programming by combining professional, semi-professional, and community based activities.

In summary, the underlying considerations in our marketing strategy were this need to draw on the Denver populace, the perception about Arvada, and the confusion over the nature of the facility.

Frank Jacobson has been Executive Director of the Arvada Center for the Arts and Humanities since 1979. He came to that post after four years with the Western States Arts Foundation where he was General Manager of Budget and Planning. Initially appointed as a Program Director for the Foundation's regionally based touring program, Mr. Jacobson was promoted in 1977 to Director of Programs. Mr. Jacobson has a Master of Fine Arts degree in Directing from Boston University School of Fine Arts and a BA in Speech and Theatre from the University of Wisconsin. He has served as assistant professor of drama at the University of Montana and was Managing Director of the Montana Repertory Theatre from 1973-75. Currently, Mr. Jacobson is President of the Metropolitan Denver Arts Alliance, and has served as a panelist for both the National Endowment for the Arts and the Colorado Council on the Arts and Humanities. In 1980, he received an award as an Outstanding Young American.

"Programming diversity presents marketing problems similar to those of a department store."

In setting out to develop our audience, it was critical that we take two initial steps:
1. to articulate our institutional purpose and goals;
2. to establish a program plan that directly related to them.

From there, we would then be able to communicate an institutional identity to the public. Our marketing strategies emanate from this identity.

The key to marketing our activity lies in our programming diversity—we are a kind of department store for the arts. This diversity presents the Arvada Center with marketing problems similar to those of a department store—i.e., we have many different products to sell: theater, music, dance, children's theater, a visual-arts gallery, a historical museum, a range of classes and workshops, and a variety of events within each of these categories. And, like the department store, if we get the people in to buy one product (for example, a jazz concert or play), they will at least look around in other departments. This may mean walking through the gallery, or picking up brochures on classes, or the classical concert series. In marketing this diversity, we put greater emphasis on advertising performing-arts programs which we believe will draw greater audiences than the education and gallery/museum programs. The goal, however, is that our consumers will be attracted to other events as well—if not now, then eventually.

Surveys of our audiences support this thesis. If they come and enjoy one event at the center, they will come back to other events. Obviously, diversity is not enough. The quality and professionalism of our events, whether it be our local chorale or the internationally known Tokyo String Quartet, must be at a consistently high level to establish a credible reputation with the public. If people consistently experience high-quality events at our center, they will more willingly attend events without "name" recognition for the sheer pleasure of attending a quality arts event.

Marketing Management Planning Process

We begin our planning process each year in September, ten months prior to the annual summer program, and twelve to thirteen months prior to the fall/winter/spring season. Looking over the available touring companies' promotional materials, attending the regional booking conference, and negotiating dates and fees, is traditionally a process that can take us until January, February, or even into March. During this same period, our resident artistic directors from our theater and music groups are reviewing plays and music repertoire.

Because the Arvada Center is interested in multi-disciplinary activities, and because scheduling for the 600 events a year can be very complex, the center's management staff and I meet regularly throughout the planning period to discuss the future calendar of events. The staff consists of the three program directors (performing arts, gallery/museum and education), the marketing director, development director, and executive director (myself).

I charge the program directors with the responsibility of presenting the marketing staff and me with program possibilities that fit within the framework of the existing year's budget. We analyze the program presentation for its balance, quality, excitement, and thematic values. We then review its audience sales-potential and cost-effectiveness. Some programs require little more than a press release to fill the house, while other events may require several thousand dollars of advertising expenses to do the same thing. There must be a balance between the artistic sensibilities and the financial realities. It is up to the staff to sort this out before presenting the program and its costs to the Arvada Arts Council Board, the advisory body for the Arts Center. The Arts Council Board provides additional feedback to the staff on the selection and pricing.

Between February and April, the marketing staff creates the marketing strategy for the upcoming season. A season-ticket brochure is designed and readied for the early spring and late summer mailing. It is most efficient to have season-ticket ads designed at this time, so that they can be correlated with the design in the brochure. Advertising schedules are reviewed. Season ads usually run from mid-August through the first week in October.

The marketing staff also determines the packaging of a series, its pricing, and the method of brochure distribution.

While these areas are the domain of the marketing staff, a consensus is sought with the other program directors regarding design copy, marketing themes, positioning, packaging, pricing, and sales objectives.

Pricing Process

Pricing is integral to our budgeting process. A team approach is used to make determinations, involving the performing-arts director, the marketing director, and myself. It is particularly important that the marketing staff agree with the sales objectives that evolve from this process, because they are charged with responsibility of creating the strategies to earn the revenue.

The pricing formula is based on a policy of attracting as large an audience as possible at the most "reasonable" ticket price. We review several other factors in determining our ticket prices: what our competition is charging, the fee of the artist in relation to our hall, what we have charged in the past, and our own audience surveys.

Individually, the three of us involved in pricing chart out our own projections of audience size and our average ticket price. With only 500 seats, we have found it best to have only one price for our house and a discount for full-time students, senior citizens (62 and older), and children (12 and under). After we have made our separate tabulations, we review the figures together and come to an agreement. If we are considerably apart in our projections, we review historical records to see if we can make a determination from similar events.

The perennial problem is evaluating whether we have priced the event correctly. If we sell out an event at $8.00, would we still sell out the same event at $9.00 or more? It is not unusual for us to ask our staff and board members how much they would pay to see a particular event. We prefer to have our house filled at $8.00 per person than to have 80% of it filled at $10.00 per person. Even though the gross is the same, we prefer to have the increased exposure to more people. Another factor is that a sold-out house makes everyone feel good—the performers, the staff, the board, and the audience. Audience members at a sold-out event feel that they made the right choice in attending the event, and lucky that they have a seat.

We never budget at 100% capacity—even when we know we have a potential sellout. We do this for two reasons:

1. The risk is too great, and the odds are against selling out. Since it is difficult to hit the revenue mark on every concert or play (with some being above and some being below), a sellout can sometimes help make up the difference on those events that did not do as well as expected.
2. You can be a hero with your board for doing better than your projections. It surely beats getting fired because you did not hit the mark of your revenue projections.

Be conservative with your revenues. Revenues are more difficult to control than expenses.

We budget revenues for each event individually and then run a tally of the overall discipline, i.e., music, theater, and dance. Multiplying the estimated attendance by the average ticket price, we get the projected revenue: A (attendance) × P (average ticket price) = R(revenue).

Total up the attendance and revenue projections and compare them to last year. If your marketing strategy is similar to the prior year, attendance and revenue should not vary by too wide a margin. It was reassuring to discover, when we made our next year's projections, that after reviewing fifteen events independently, we came within four percentage points of the previous year's percent capacity. Because we were not planning to alter our marketing strategy very much for the next year, this helped confirm our attendance and revenue projections.

Pricing must go hand in hand with attendance projections. Use past years to explore the history of your patrons. Graph out statistics. See if the visual graphics begin to reveal patterns. Does your audience taper off or go up with ticket increases? When does it taper off? At what price level does it taper off? Survey your audience. Ask what they consider to be reasonable a ticket price, and at what price they feel the ticket is getting to be too expensive.

"Audience members at a sold-out event feel that they made the right choice in attending the event, and lucky that they have a seat."

"The more seats you have to sell, the more ticket-discount programs you may need to create."

Discounts

We discount tickets for one main reason—accessibility to our events. We feel we have an obligation to keep our ticket prices affordable to a wide cross section of people with varying ages and income levels. Further, we recognize that not every event will sell out, so if we target audiences with discounts, we can attract more people to our programs.

Discounting ticket prices, particularly to the less popular events and performances in the middle of the week, is a very common practice among performing-arts organizations. The more seats you have to sell, the more ticket-discount programs you may need to create. We discount tickets for subscribers, groups, senior citizens, full-time students, children under 12, and other special audiences who may not normally attend the Arvada Center.

We offer the potential subscriber savings of up to 30% off the regular ticket price. Discounts are an incentive to buying a series—in our case, four or more events.

Group-sales discounts operate under the same principle as subscriptions, offering an incentive to purchase a large number of seats at one time. Groups buy blocks of tickets for four primary reasons: social, educational, fund raising, or to save money. We seek out groups who generally fit into one or more of these categories.

Letters are sent and phone calls are made to service and civic clubs, churches and synagogues, and to schools — our primary targets for group sales. We have established our group discounts on a competitive basis with the other performing-arts organizations in the area. Typical discounts to groups in the Denver metropolitan area run from 10% to 25% off the price of tickets. Groups buying large numbers of tickets hate to get stuck with seats they can't sell, but our policy is that we will help sell any of their remaining tickets if we are sold out for the performance. Generally, if we are sold out two weeks prior to the event, and the organization who has purchased a block of tickets cannot sell all the tickets they originally agreed to take, our box-office will make these tickets available to the public at the regular ticket price. After the event, we will refund the discounted group rate to the organization for all tickets we sold at the regular price. This way, the group feels you are helping them out of a bind when they have contracted for more tickets than they can handle.

We also utilize "two-for-one" coupons in various promotional entertainment and dinner-club coupon books. In such a coupon book (which is purchased by the consumer at a fixed rate and at no charge to the participating organization, company, restaurant, or store), are an assortment of discount coupons redeemable for goods, services, and events. We choose to be included in those books that are oriented toward entertainment and leisure-time activity.

Entertainment/dinner-club activity coupon books are a free form of advertising and help sell seats that might otherwise stay empty. We only make available those events we are relatively sure will not sell out or which historically have not been as popular. We would rather sell a seat at half price than not at all. Tickets are always subject to availability. We usually will not honor discounts if less than 10% of the house is unsold forty-eight hours or more prior to the event.

The Newcomers Club and Welcome Wagon also help distribute discount coupons to new residents of the area. This is a good public relations program to introduce new audiences to the center.

Promotion Process

Our promotion process includes a mix of direct mail, print and radio advertising, press releases, feature coverage, public service announcements, and calendar listings.

Direct Mail

Several years ago, we found ourselves doing an inordinate number of mailings every month. Because of our high activity rate, every program director wanted to send out invitations, postcard reminders, education catalogues, newsletters, or calendar listings. We were competing with ourselves. We thought a more efficient method would be an Arvada Center magazine, a publication which was more than a newsletter and which could also help create an overall image.

We needed our own mouthpiece to promote our own events, create the multi-disciplinary image we sought, and provide some educational and entertaining background on this activity for our audiences. We wanted to create a publication that would be used often and kept around the house for an adequate period of time. Thus, we evolved *Center Magazine* which now combines all previous mailings, including our education-class catalogue. Circulation goes to our mailing list of approximately 20,000, and another 5,000 are used as the event program. The magazine is also available at our information desk. We will publish six issues in 1983. When enough advertising is developed, our long-range objective is to publish an issue every month. We debated long and hard as to whether the magazine was to be sent only to members and subscribers, and to be used as our concert/theater program. The promotional opportunities at this point suggest that we should send the magazine to our entire mailing list. Our board strongly supports the publication. It turns up in doctors' and dentists' offices, in libraries, and at other pick-up points strategic to promoting the awareness of the center and its events.

Center Magazine has thus become our primary direct-mail piece outside of our annual subscription brochure. We have found, however, that we are somewhat limited when promoting our exhibition openings and receptions. Therefore, on some occasions during the year, we will mail special reception invitations to promote these kinds of activities.

With the help of a computerized mailing-list system, we are able to separate out the various interests of our patrons. We can code names by the interest category checked off by the patron: Dance, Music, Theater, Visual Arts, Museum, Education/Classes, Memberships, etc. We record patron names, addresses, when tickets are purchased, and code the names according to event. Subscribers and donors are kept in the same file. Each series and level of contribution have their unique codes. On occasion, we will mail out special flyers to advertise certain activities, particularly those events like workshops, which have a smaller targeted audience requirement. In these cases, we find it more cost-effective to use a smaller list and publish a special flyer. Often our rate of return for registration is much higher.

Advertising

Advertising weekly in the two major, daily Denver newspapers has become essential in terms of competing with the ever-increasing arts opportunities in this area. Advertising three times a week would probably be ideal because of higher visibility and to keep up with out competition, but currently, our budget will only allow one time a week. Ideally, we should be advertising in Wednesday morning and Sunday's papers, as well as the Friday weekend arts and entertainment section, in which we now regularly appear. We find that most events run successfully with two to three weeks of advance advertising, although this depends on the number of seats we have to sell and how much other activity is going on at the center.

Our ads primarily promote the name of the event, the time, the cost, and the date. Since the direction of the center advertising is to promote our multi-disciplinary image and create visibility for our many different activities, we generally promote at least three events in a single ad, rather than running separate ads for each event.

Free Promotion

The most effective promotional tool for the Arvada Center is the newspaper feature article. If a newswriter makes an event sound appealing, and the center is given a lot of space with photographs, interest is always greater, and calls and attendance always increase for that event. Creating the right relationships with the news media and gaining their respect for your work, is to me the most important element of good marketing and promotion. A good publicity person knows how to create good working relationships with the media. We don't get features for every event, of course, but generally, the news media is cooperative with the Arvada Center and provides us with excellent coverage. Our staff person consistently visits the major newspapers every week and has generated those excellent working relationships without being overbearing.

"Our magazine turns up in doctors' and dentists' offices, in libraries and other strategic points."

We mail an average of five press releases and public-service announcements per week to over seventy media contacts, and another forty publications receive notice of our events on a monthly or quarterly basis. Volunteers help our staff weekly with this major effort.

As many events as the Arvada Center produces and presents, it is essential that our press materials be planned and well organized. It is difficult not to compete with ourselves. Each media contact will not print every release, but our hope is that each will select several releases for print. With so many potential contacts, the news release is one of our greatest promotional strengths.

Packaging

Packaging is a means of increasing the frequency of attendance by patrons. In its most simple form, it involves the offering of season tickets to a series of events. Over the last three years, we have offered the following types of series: classical music (small ensembles and soloists), chamber orchestra, chorale, a combination of chamber orchestra and chorale performances, series of five center-produced plays, series of five one-person plays called *Meet the Great Americans* (James Thurber, Louisa May Alcott, Groucho Marx, Albert Einstein and Harry Truman), a seven-event summer Pops series in our outdoor amphitheater, and a fall/winter/spring series of five Pops events, and a dance series.

This type of series-packaging is fairly typical of many art centers, but we attempt some unique aspects at the Arvada Center. The total performing-arts program is a combination of center-produced activity and the presentations of touring companies. We mix national, regional, and local artists together on the same series. This is a great advantage to local companies, who are all too often overlooked and given less status than national/regional touring groups. Inclusion of the local companies and artists in our series raises their stature and image in the eyes of the community.

Another example of product packaging is our attempt to put together groups of artists who are not generally seen together. For example, we are contracting a local jazz group to perform with our resident chorale. Both groups have their own following but might not attract each other's audiences to their respective preformances. By programming them together, we have introduced new audiences to new arts programs which they might not otherwise attend. The resident chamber orchestra's joint performance with the chorale gave them a tremendous boost. The groups perform independently on the program, but the highlight of the performance is the works they do together. Poet Maya Angelou was contracted for a residency at the Arvada Center doing two evening performances of her own writing and music and two more evenings in collaboration with a local dance company who premiered a new work utilizing Miss Angelou's poetry and music.

Promoting thematic program activity is also packaging. We promoted a program entitled, ''America in the 1930s''. This gave us an opportunity to explore the 1930s through music, dance, theater, film, radio shows, exhibitions, workshops, classes, lectures, panel discussions, and seminars. We designed a commemorative poster which carried the schedules of the events, and we used the graphic from the poster on the cover of our magazine, which included articles describing our activities. The objective was to persuade people to attend one or more of the events and come back for further enjoyment and exploration of the 1930s. We were even able to tie in a fund-raising event with the 30s theme by setting our casino night in that decade. Patrons were encouraged to dress in their appropriate 30s garb—from knickers to black tie.

We have packaged activities in other ways: mini-subscriptions to seasonal activity, e.g., the ''Spring Getaway'' package of five mid-season events for the price of four and the ''Choose Your Own Subscription'' series whereby a customer can select four to seven events at a substantial savings.

A writer for a local magazine ''packaged'' the center for his readers when he wrote the following:

Thus it is possible for an average hopped-up citizen to straddle a potter's wheel in the morning, attend a board conference for lunch...paint a brace of nudes during siesta, leap around the ballet studio during the afternoon thunderstorm, check out the galleries at tea time, and attend the theater after dinner...all under one roof.

(*Denver Magazine*, Sept. 1977)

This sums up the unique quality of the Arvada Center for the Arts and Humanities. We try to capitalize on the multi-disciplinary nature of the center—"Come take a class, visit the gallery, and see a live performance". Packaging events is second nature to us now; our audiences have come to expect it. And when we are in between exhibitions, and the main gallery is closed during an evening's performance, we hear comments from our patrons who insist that we have short-changed them. Competition for audiences gets increasingly difficult with the growing marketing sophistication and effectiveness of other area arts organizations. It is the staff's responsibility, therefore, to stay ahead of the market, anticipate the trends, and effectively and creatively find ways to keep building our audiences.

PART V:
Marketing Problems and Alternatives

Ruby Lerner

UNIQUE CONSTITUENCIES: REGIONAL COMPANIES

As Yet Unimagined

In terms of marketing, there is nothing more important for an organization than defining its mission and goals. This clarity is essential, for everything that the organization does will proceed from an extensive institutional analysis and the statement of purpose which emerges from that analysis. There are now in existence a number of arts organizations whose stated aims extend beyond appealing to a traditional arts audience, whose work seeks to address the needs and concerns of special constituencies. Many of these organizations choose to remain small, many are committed to touring to reach their audiences, and almost all seek to build a kind of performing art that will be integral to people's daily lives.

Roadside Theater of Whitesburg, Kentucky, is one such arts organization. Whitesburg, "Home of 1199 Friendly People and 1 Grouch," as a local billboard wryly proclaims, is located in the heart of coal-mining country. Roadside is part of The Appalshop, which also houses Appalshop Films, June Appal Recordings, Headwaters Television and the Mountain Photography Workshop. The Appalshop is the largest employer in a non-coal-related industry in the county. The work of all the components that comprise The Appalshop could be classified as local and regional, with regionalism defined as Kentucky poet, essayist, and farmer Wendell Berry put it: "...as *local life aware of itself.* It would tend to substitute for the myths and stereotypes of a region a particular knowledge of the life of the *place* one lives in and intends to *continue* to live in. The motive of such regionalism is the awareness that local life is intricately dependent for its quality but also for its continuance, upon local knowledge. Without a complex knowledge of one's place, and without the faithfulness to one's place on which such knowledge depends, it is inevitable that the place will be used carelessly and eventually destroyed. Without such knowledge and faithfulness, moreover, the culture of a country will be superficial and decorative, functional insofar as it may be a symbol of prestige, the affectation of an elite or 'in' group. And so I look upon the sort of regionalism that I am talking about not just as a recurrent literary phenomenon, but as a necessity of civilization and survival." ("The Regional Motive" in *A Continuous Harmony.*)

A widely acclaimed group, Roadside Theater has been primarily a touring theater, with extensive performing throughout the Southeast, including a popular summer revival tent tour closer to home, in the hollows of eastern Kentucky and western Virginia. Just recently, The Appalshop finished building a new home in Whitesburg. Complete with meeting rooms, a gallery, a dark room, a film-screening room and a 150-seat theater, it is a cultural center for central Appalachia. Although only in operation for a few months, Roadside is already performing to standing-room-only crowds.

The tools of the trade—brochures, press releases, the telephone, the media—are all there to assist you. They serve to *re-enforce* your personal efforts, not *substitute* for them. And that is the major difference between a more traditional arts organization and one that serves special constituencies. The tools are the same, but there

Ruby Lerner is currently the Executive Director of Alternate ROOTS, a coalition of small performing arts organizations located throughout the South devoted to making their art where they are, out of who they are and what their communities are. Prior to ROOTS, she was the Audience Development Director at the Manhattan Theatre Club in New York for four years. Ms. Lerner spent two years in North Carolina's Visiting Artist Program. She serves on the National Endowment's Expansion Arts Performing Arts Panel, the Board of Advisors of the Institute on Cultural Affairs of the Martin Luther King, Jr. Center for Nonviolent Social Change in Atlanta and the Board of Directors of the Alliance for Cultural Democracy (formerly NAPNOC).

"The direct-mail responder profile has been ascertained—generally over 35, well educated, in an upper-income bracket, and white."

must be a difference in the degree to which the tools are utilized.

The plans and methods Roadside utilized to fill its house are by no means astounding, but they do serve to illustrate the point. For three years prior to having their own space, monthly press releases were sent to the local newspaper, even though Roadside rarely performed at home. They sent these to build an awareness of who they were and where they were touring, to begin to build an identity as a local theater of which the area could be proud, and to also prepare for the time they would have their own performance space. This was a crucial investment activity with no immediate pay-off, but with the long-range goal of creating local pride in the theater's achievements, and a keen sense of building and planning for the future. For their recent performance, two pieces appeared in the local newspaper, one each week for the two weeks preceding the performance. The theater management ran a paid advertisement during those same two weeks. They also ran radio spots on local stations, and a member of the company appeared on a local television show. They printed and distributed about twenty posters to schools, libraries, and local businesses. They called the leaders of civic organizations, including the local home-extension group, a local women's club, and a women's service sorority, among others. A representative of the theater went to every *local* high-school English class to speak about Roadside. No magic there—just a lot of smart planning and personal effort on the part of a number of individuals.

It is important to note here that direct mail was not one of the tools that Roadside utilized to fill its theater. It is crucial to state that direct mail would not be viewed by Roadside as a substitute for any of the work they did, merely as a re-enforcement. Because Roadside has been a touring theater, they have not yet built a local mailing list. This is the one missing tool that will be invaluable to them in the future. There is no way to overestimate the value of building a strong mailing list to a small organization. There is no room for carelessness with regard to collecting the names and addresses of *every single individual* who attends your events. This is true for all arts organizations, whether large or small, mainstream or alternative, but it is especially true for organizations dealing with special constituencies, because they will probably be unable to relocate those individuals any other way. Outside of that 2% sphere, their names may not show up on the mailing lists of other arts organizations or professional journals. It is up to you to be diligent in your efforts.

Roadside Theater is able to perform to standing-room-only crowds in Whitesburg, Kentucky, because it is part of the life of its community, not separate from it. Michael Kustow, formerly of the National Theater of Great Britain, recently observed that the "American theater doesn't have an audience, it has customers." If one concurs, even partially, with that statement, it is fair to repeat, *the medium is the message.*

As to the kind of relationship Roadside seeks to build with its audience, Dudley Cocke of Roadside states, "All of Roadside's material comes from central Appalachia, most all from a six-county area where Virginia and Kentucky back up on one another. In that sense we are more a local than regional theater. We've drawn our style from church services and from the area's musical and storytelling traditions. One of our shows end with a hymn that Ron Short originally wrote for his grandmother's funeral. Several weeks ago a woman, whose only connection and experience with us was through our theater, called to ask Ron to come sing that hymn at her father's burial. So, in that most personal of moments, when her father was being laid in the ground, Ron sang. Although Ron and the family had never met, neither felt unnatural or out of place. The distance between Roadside's performance and those people's lives was imperceptible."

There is a fundamental precept in arts marketing that any arts group is addressing only about 2% of the general population. For many organizations like Roadside, this fundamental precept is untenable, as their defined *mission* addresses their work to a specific constituency of the 98% majority. Direct mail, for example, is a science, and the responder profile has been ascertained—generally over thirty-five, well-educated, in an upper-income bracket, and white. If you choose to utilize this marketing tool, that will more than likely be the profile of the individual who responds. But even many traditional organizations seek to diversify their audience beyond that profile. Their hope is to create drama in their audiences, to reach out beyond the 2%, to encourage in the audience-mix a conflict of values which is resolved by the shared act of participation in the event. Do the principles of traditional marketing strategy apply when addressing special constituencies? And is it necessary to utilize tools different from those used to reach the 2% in order to reach special constituencies?

Before these questions can be answered, it is necessary to establish a larger context in which they may be addressed. In 1964, Alvin Toffler, author of the later *Future Shock,* wrote *Culture Consumers.* This was early in the movement to dot the country with performing-arts centers, regional theaters, and local arts councils. He presaged, ''The time will come, sooner or later, when the process of bureaucratization will advance to excess and begin to standardize our cultural production. We must be prepared for this eventuality. At that point, we may, figuratively speaking, have to tear down the centers and councils we are now building and reorganize the culture industry in ways as yet unimagined. This should not dismay us, for the process of growth, decay and regeneration in society is unending.''

It is my hypothesis that we are currently entering an exciting time—that period of reorganization of the culture industry of which Toffler writes. And that means that we must look at how the industry has operated to date and what its assumptions have been.

Arts management techniques and tools have gotten increasingly sophisticated since the writing of Toffler's book. This has produced several problems—the prizing and rewarding of organizational ability over creative impulse. When does the tail start wagging the dog? Fundamental questions have often become obscured. Are the style and methods of support for the vision consonant with the vision itself? By style, I refer to the internal management structure of the organization. Aren't the organizational model that has been selected and the operating style of the group merely extensions of the organization's stated mission? For example, the corporate model is the currently extolled management model for an arts institution. What are other possibilities? Where can you look for other models? How do you determine which model is best for you?

Why does it seem so difficult to identify other useful organizational models? Is this because we must redefine success and failure with regard to alternative models? Is survival—the sheer act of continuing—success? The business model is successful at self-perpetuation. But are other models perhaps more responsive to organization as organism, to a process of birth, growth, aging, and even death? And significantly, even if you start out with an alternative operating style, isn't there an assumption that as you ''grow up'' institutionally, you will want to adopt a more hierarchical organizational structure?

I certainly don't have the answers to all these questions, but I think that one of the most hopeful aspects of this current time of reorganization of the culture industry will be the appearance of a multiplicity of operating styles, new models, and an abundance of choices for fledgling groups.

In one sense, all art is constituency art. The 2% certainly represents a special constituency, as does any segment of the larger community—black, Spanish-speaking, Appalachian, disabled, etc. The organization's operating style and its structure as an organization, which proceeds from its stated mission, is a signal to prospective participants. Several additional questions arise at this point: Is there an optimum-size audience for the kind of work you want to do? Is bigger better? If growth is desirable, what is the best way to prepare the organization and its current supporters for this growth so that the current supporters are not alienated in the growth process?

Once these questions have been dealt with, it is then necessary to look at both the principles and tools of traditional marketing to determine whether they apply to an organization addressing special constituencies. The principles of traditional marketing are unassailable. They relate to a comprehensive knowledge of one's community, a detailed plan of action with objectives, and thorough, ongoing analysis.

As for the tools of traditional marketing, I would like to talk about ''altering the balance.'' Recently, in arts marketing, we've become enamored of direct mail, telemarketing, and when affordable, extensive use of the media. There is certainly nothing wrong with these tools, and they are all extremely valuable, but it is a fact that many of the tools of traditional marketing have long been used to manipulate us.

> "The corporate model is the currently extolled management model for an arts institution. What are other possibilities?"

"I am talking about returning to a time when person-to-person contact was one of our greatest strengths in the arts."

They have told us which soap to buy, which car to buy, which candidate to vote for, which art to buy. We have witnessed a gradual depersonalization in the way we attract people to our arts organizations.

When I speak of altering the balance, I am talking about returning to a time when person-to-person contact was one of our greatest strengths in the arts. This is such a simple tenet, but it seems to have been mostly forgotten in this current era of marketing sophistication. It is a tenet, however, that organizations relating to special constituencies cannot afford to forget.

There is and always will be a *big* difference between a personalized letter from a magazine firm exclaiming, ''You, Ruby Lerner and the Lerner family may have already won....'' and an actual conversation. The medium is the message, and person-to-person contact carries the message that we see people as individuals, not as customers. When we communicate person-to-person, we are saying, ''Your ideas are valuable to me—you are valuable to me.'' There is a good reason why politicians, despite all the money they spend on the media and direct mail, *still* get out there and shake hands and kiss babies. They know that there is no substitute for their physical presence.

Communication should build more than just knowledge and action. It should build a spirit and solidarity, a sense of belonging to the organization. For many groups addressing special constituencies, there is the sobering possibility that they literally will be *building their audience one by one.* This requires time, tireless effort and the long-term commitment to the non-quantifiable goal of engendering good will in the community they seek to serve. It means becoming an arts organizer, which is what we all must become if we are to build a broad-based constituency for the arts in this country.

Becoming an effective arts organizer has very little to do with whether precanceled stamps yield a better return than bulk-rate indicia, and is not so easily taught in weekend seminars. But this one-by-one method is an honest, organic way to build an organization. How do you do this? There are no secrets, no surprises, no tricks. You do it by being visible in your community; by schlepping twenty miles out into the country to church suppers; by attending meetings of non-arts-related community and civic groups; by talking to every Lion, Tiger, Optimist, and Pessimist club that will have you; by locating strategic people in the segment of the community you wish to reach and asking them for help; by going to people *before* you expect them to come to you. In other words, you will achieve support only by becoming a citizen of the community of which you are a part.

Rena Shagan

TOURING

On The Road: A Marketing Perspective

This chapter is about how a performing-arts organization markets itself for touring, the process usually called "booking." The material here is aimed primarily at the person who will be doing the marketing; however, many questions are raised that will require input from an organization's artistic and managerial staffs and its board of trustees. We'll begin by defining some terms basic to the booking process, then indicate questions that must be answered before an organization can proceed further. We'll also look at producing printed materials for marketing tours, will discuss the mechanics of booking and putting together a tour, and finally touch on the needs and expectations of the sponsor. The material included does not by any means tell the whole story, but it is an indication of how the process works.

Touring plays a more or less important role in the life of performing-arts organizations, whether they are dance companies, chamber-music ensembles, opera companies, orchestras or theater companies. The kind of touring a company does will very much depend upon the importance touring income and activity play in the survival of the company. Dance companies and chamber-music groups who rely on touring as a major source of income tend to tour more widely, more frequently, and for longer periods of time than theater companies whose income base is not as dependent on this type of income. For example, regionally-based theater companies traditionally have longer resident seasons than dance companies and are therefore prone to feel they have more choice about where and how to tour. They are more likely to opt for shorter tours and for keeping their touring closer to home.

The word "touring," however, is really a catch-all term for a wide range of activities that occur when a company leaves its home base to provide a performance, set of performances, or arrange other activities. In fact, "touring" can mean something quite different to a well-established organization than it does to a small, new one.

Before we talk further about how one markets companies for touring, we should define the different types of activities that occur under the general label of "touring."

Rena Shagan is presently General Manager for the State Ballet of New York (formerly the Eglevsky Ballet Company). Previously she acted as Administrator for 5 by 2 Plus—A Modern Dance Repertory Company, Bert Houle-Sophie Wibaux Mime Theatre and worked for the Bill Evans Dance Company and American Ballet Theatre II. Shagan developed subscription campaigns for Dance Atlanta and acted as a consultant to the Joffrey Ballet and the Los Angeles Music Center. She wrote the only existing book on marketing companies for touring in the arts, *A Blueprint for Booking and Tour Management;* and trained multidisciplinary personnel in conferences sponsored by the Southern Arts Federation, Mid-America Arts Alliance, FEDAPT and other organizations. She is presently on the Boards of Dance/USA, the American Arts Alliance and has served on the National Endowment for the Arts Dance Panel.

- *Tour*—A tour is a series of performances and/or other activities performed by a company in different places on the road. The company does not return to its home city during the tour. A tour can be made up of one-night stands and residencies, and can range in length from a few days to several weeks or even months.
- *One-Night Stand*—A one-night stand is a single performance for one sponsor which is part of a tour.
- *Run-Out*—A run-out is a term generally used to mean a performance in a nearby town or city that does not entail an overnight stay. A run-out always involves a performance, but the short trip might also include other non-performance activities (for instance, teaching a master class).

"Don't expect your phone to ring just because you send out a good brochure."

The first thing a company needs to do in the marketing process is to take a long, hard look at itself. The initial question to be addressed is, why does the company want to tour in the first place? Is it for financial reasons; for getting better known nationally or in a particular region; is it to provide work and performance experience for its artists? Maybe it's the desire to tour a particular production or body of work that the artistic staff deems important or because government or private-sector funding is available for a tour. Whatever the reason or combination of reasons, the rationale should be articulated, because it will dictate the circumstances of the tour. For example, if a theater company is touring strictly for financial reasons, it might decide to tour a well-known crowd pleaser that requires only a few actors and a minimal set. This would enable the company to do one-night stands easily and efficiently, pay fewer salaries, and have a limited number of pre-production costs, while controlling transportation and per diem expenses.

After it considers the reason for touring, the company needs to ask itself a second series of questions that will have a great impact on the actual marketing process:

1. What production(s) or body of work will be toured?
2. What will be the minimum length of an individual engagement on the tour? (i.e., one-night stand/one week, etc.)
3. How many weeks will the tour run—maximum and minimum?
4. How will the company and its equipment travel?
5. Where will the tour go?
6. When will the tour take place?
7. How much will the tour cost the company?
8. What can the company reasonably charge its sponsors?
9. Are there other revenues available to partially fund the tour (i.e., NEA or other grants, corporate support, etc.)?

Once an organization has answered those questions, it has gone a long way towards determining the strategy it will employ to market the tour.

Targeting Sponsors

The company should now have a good idea of what, where, and how it is touring, and what it must charge. The next step in the process is targeting prospective sponsors. Once you know where, it is necessary to figure out to which sponsors you should direct the mail and telephone campaigns that must follow. How large or small your list of perspective sponsors should be is dependent upon your answers to the questions posed above. For example, a large ballet company with a relatively high fee, which has decided that its minimum length engagement with one sponsor is half a week, will probably find fewer sponsors in a geographical area able to accommodate its fee, length of engagement, and technical requirements, than a small, five-person, modern dance company willing to do one-night stands. The smaller company will be in a position to target a far larger universe of possible sponsors, because it can offer its performances less expensively and probably has less stringent technical requirements than the ballet company.

You can get your information on which sponsors to approach from a number of sources. One of the best and most eye-opening lists is the one compiled by the Association of College, University, and Community Arts Administrators (ACUCAA). The ACUCAA is a national organization of sponsors. Members range from organizations with presenting budgets of half a millon dollars and 3,500-seat facilities, to those with budgets of $10,000 and 250-seat theaters. The ACUCAA list is valuable not only for the many sponsors' names, addresses, and phone numbers, but also for its inclusion of house sizes and producing budgets. So to go back to our earlier example, a large, costly ballet company can see at a glance from the ACUCAA list which member in a particular state has the resources to book their company. The small, relatively unknown modern dance company will be able to ascertain which large sponsors with 3,000-seat facilities will probably *not* book them, because they are looking for better-known attractions to fill their large theater.

Other lists are also available. The regional arts agencies (for example, Western States Arts Foundation) all have lists of sponsoring organizations in their areas, and some are keyed to type and size of sponsor. Dance Theater Workshop, a New York

City service organization serving individual artists and companies, has a national mailing list of dance sponsors. *Dance Magazine Annual* and *Musical America,* both published once a year, include lists of sponsors. Many of the mailing lists mentioned above are available on computerized labels. The appendix to this chapter indicates where these resources are available.

Job Description

Some people believe that having a booking person who knows the decision-makers at sponsoring organizations is key to bookings. I'm not at all convinced that this is really the case. On the one hand, it is true that a person who has been booking for a number of years has built up a network of contacts. He probably has special relationships with some sponsors and can call upon them on a personal basis. If sponsors have been happy with the company(s) they have booked from the experienced booking person before, he can sometimes get them to book a new, unknown company on a trust basis. On the other hand, there is a great deal of turnver in the personnel of presenting organizations. The faculty member who was chairperson of the performing-arts presentation committee at a particular college may very well not be in the same position next year. The same goes for the executive director of the performing-arts center. In addition, it has been my experience that decisions on what to present are being made more and more often by committees. Frequently, they decide what types of attractions they would like to present—i.e., one dance company, one orchestra, one chamber-music group, one chorus, etc., and then choose among a number of companies in each category. Therefore, the neophyte booker has the opportunity to establish his own contacts in this industry. Remember: how well-known a company is and how good its artistic product is perceived to be, its price, its size, its ability to be there when the sponsor has access to the theater (and availability), and even the personality and ability of the booking person are all really crucial for securing a booking.

The primary duties of a booking person are:

1. Meet with the artistic director, general manager, and board of trustees to ascertain touring priorities and budget.
2. Oversee production of marketing materials.
3. Procure mailing lists and oversee mailings.
4. Make telephone calls to sponsors.
5. Send follow-up letters and materials.
6. Negotiate fees and services, and construct the tour routing.
7. Attend booking conferences.
8. Keep a file system of sponsor contacts and correspondence.

If I were looking for someone to market (i.e., to book) a company for touring, I would look for someone who:

- Had a real enthusiasm and understanding of the work of the company.
- Had enough personal confidence to deal with the reality that the company will not be booked by most of the sponsors solicited.
- Was persistent and not easily discouraged, able to call and to converse easily with strangers on the phone and in person.

Materials

In order to market a company successfully for touring, an organization needs to have materials describing what it is offering to prospective sponsors. Materials can range from a four-color brochure to a self-produced packet. How elaborate these materials are depends on who the company is, and how much touring is desired. A well-known company can probably send out something quite simple—almost an announcement—as can a company that is just touring a mainstage production for a couple of weeks and has a good idea of who its sponsors will be. Those companies that need to tour quite a lot will have to reach many sponsors in order to get the number of bookings they need. This type of organization will have to put more money and effort into its mailings. In either case, it is unfortunately true that the quality of a company's work and its professionalism is often judged by the way it

"If you are spending money on marketing materials, they must be produced by professionals."

sells itself, and not on its work. For this reason, whichever way a company proceeds, the image it presents can make or break it.

• *Alternative I*

Let us assume for the moment that you are associated with an organization that needs to tour a great deal. What should be included in your sales materials? The marketing tool that enables you to reach the greatest number of sponsors in a cost-effective manner is the booking brochure. A booking brochure must be based upon a concept. If your organization is a dance company, you will probably be marketing the company's name, the choreography of a particular person, and/or the kind of dance the group performs. In the case of a chamber-music ensemble, the name of the group, personalities involved, and the kind of music they play would be important. Theater and opera usually market a production or series of productions.

A booking brochure should be built around an idea. What is unique about the company/production, why is it special, what does the company/production do that nobody else does? Put yourself in the sponsor's place. What does he want to know about the company that will separate your organization from the 100 other entities competing for this sponsor's bookings?

Try to get all the information on one mailing piece. Include excerpts from reviews as part of the brochure's text. Five pieces of paper in an envelope will probably get lost in the shuffle on somebody's desk or at a meeting of the campus committee. Be sure to include your fees with the booking brochure, because they are important. A sponsor wants to know not only how good you are, but how much you cost. Make your brochure short and concise. Remember, you are not trying to tell the whole story, but merely trying to get the sponsor interested and ready for your telephone follow-up. Don't expect your phone to ring just because you send out a good brochure.

The booking brochure should be produced as part of your company's overall marketing plan—discussed elsewhere in this book. In this way, the company can take advantage of lower printing costs and the reuse of type, logos, and pictures. As has also been mentioned earlier, if you are spending money on marketing materials, they must be produced by professionals. A booking brochure is not a job for the company's artistic director.

The brochure must be produced so that it can be mailed at the not-for-profit bulk rate. It can either be a self-mailer—a self-contained promotional piece, with the company's name, address, and not-for-profit stamp on the front—or it may be designed to be sent in an envelope. Before putting your materials into production, check with the post office for acceptable size, folds, weight of paper, etc., for not-for-profit bulk mail.

Many organizations have found it helpful to have business reply envelopes or postcards inserted into large-scale mailings. This gives a sponsoring organization the ability to request further information and a follow-up telephone call from the company. A company will know, therefore, right from the start of the booking process, the name of a number of organizations that may possibly be interested in sponsorship.

The business reply envelope or postcard usually provides space for the sponsor's name, organization, address, telephone number, best time to call, and a brief message. Reply envelopes or postcards can either have postage pre-paid by the company, or a space can be left for the sponsor to affix a stamp. The latter alternative is obviously less expensive for the company. I don't really think a sponsor will fail to ask for additional material for lack of a stamp. Again, be sure to check with the post office for rules and regulations governing this type of mail.

• *Alternative II*

Alternative II is usually useful for companies that tour for brief periods each year and generally know who their sponsors are in a particular area. If you are associated with this kind of organization, you can choose this strategy. In this case, you might put together a packet of materials that could be enclosed in a folder. A picture and/or the company's name or logo could be printed on the front. Into this folder would go a letter to the sponsor (personalized if possible, if you have access to a word processor) describing the company and the production/work being presented. This is the place to point out the unique quality of the company or production and what it offers that might be of special interest to the sponsor. The packet also should include a fact sheet further describing the production, technical requirements, crew, lighting, price, several good reviews, and a picture or two of the company in performance. While this kind of approach is much less expensive than going with a full-fledged booking brochure, it is crucial that each piece of material in the packet be well-written, clear, and precise. The reviews should be offset carefully, and the pictures should be of good quality.

Mailing

Allow two to three weeks for a bulk-rate not-for-profit packet to get to sponsors. Materials sent first class obviously get there much more quickly. Some people stagger the mailing of their materials so that telephone follow-ups can occur at appropriate times.

The Booking Process

Telephone Calls

Your mailing must be followed up by a telephone call, which is the heart of booking. It is the direct contact between the company and prospective sponsor. Remember, sponsors are busy people. Not only are they receiving lots of calls from many booking people covering all of the art forms, but they are also producing their own series. Make up a telephone presentation before you call; you might even practice it with a tape recorder to see what you sound like. But in any case, plan in advance what you want to say, and then tailor it to the person you are calling.

In the first telephone call, identify yourself as a representative of a particular company and remind the sponsor that he should already have recently received information from them. Try to talk about the unique qualities of the company. Give the sponsor some good reasons to book: what does your group do that is special, how much do they cost, when will they be in the area (if you have that information), and especially in what ways do they meet the sponsor's needs. Do try to discuss specific dates or a time frame; for example, ''We could be in your area during the last week in October.''

In this first call, you shouldn't make any attempt to negotiate the fee. I prefer to simply state the fee and then say that of course it is somewhat negotiable, depending on a variety of factors such as travel distance, number of performances, etc. It is also important to mention whether you have any federal, state, regional, or private support to tour and how much this will decrease the sponsor's fee. If the sponsor says the price sounds high, you might talk about getting a number of organizations in the community together for a joint sponsorship. For example, a presenting organization and a school district might jointly sponsor a theater company. The company could offer children's performances and master classes in addition to public performance(s) in order to make the engagement financially viable.

Try to use this first call to ascertain how the sponsor makes decisions and how long the process takes. Keep things moving—don't give the sponsor an opportunity to say ''no.'' The sponsor may suggest that you send additional information or reviews. This gives you another opportunity to contact the sponsor and allow him to see the company name and information a second time.

It is also a good idea to remind sponsors that they are in a position to request funds from their state arts agency for presentations. Just about every state arts agency has monies put aside for this purpose. It is also worthwhile to suggest the possibility of soliciting local corporations and foundations that might want to help support performance activity in their community.

If you are a conscientious booking person, you will repeat this procedure hundreds of times during each booking season. At the same time that you are giving the sponsor information about the company, you are getting information on their facility, what kind of programs the organization usually presents, what has been successful for this sponsor, special needs, and the like.

> "In the first call, you shouldn't make any attempt to negotiate the fee."

"The most cost-effective routing moves a company from its home base in a loop, a figure-eight, or in a circle around its home area."

Consortium booking or block booking is a fairly new phenomenon. A group of sponsors within an area (for example, the states in the New England sector), get together and invite many different companies to submit proposals for a tour in their area. The rationale here is that if a group of sponsors within a certain geographic radius book a company for a period of several weeks, they will have a more cost-effective tour and thus be in a position to offer a lower fee to all of the sponsors in the consortium or block.

Follow-Up Letter

Each phone call should be followed by a letter to the person with whom you spoke. The letter should reiterate the information you gave on the phone about the unique qualities of the company/production, the special things it does, the price and the time it will be in the area. These letters, composed of previously designed paragraphs, can be put onto a word processor and then a few personal lines can be dropped in at the end. Along with the letter, you will want to send reviews or other materials that seemed to be of interest to the sponsor during the course of your conversation.

Keeping Records

As you make your calls, note the response of the sponsor on an index card or other established filing mechanism. Jotting down a brief summary of the prospect's response will give you an idea when to call next and what to say. Note whether the sponsor seems interested, wants additional information, or anything else pertinent. If a sponsor is not interested, indicate why not. Then put those cards away—you can try them again next year. All of the other interested sponsors are worth another follow-up call later on in the process.

Follow-Up Phone Calls

The big secret in this process is patience and persistence. You may make a number of follow-up calls to a sponsor over a several-month period before you finally find out that they have decided to book anything, and they may very well not book your company. That's why so many calls and follow-ups are necesary so that you contact them before they have chosen a specific company. Try to get an idea from the sponsor of the timing involved in their decision-making process. Be diligent in sending requested follow-up materials.

Many times sponsors are not in or can't be reached. Sometimes you can spend an entire morning on the phone and not reach anyone. Don't get discouraged. Most people booking a tour are on the phone a good part of every day for several months. Peristence and hard work are the way to get bookings. To repeat for emphasis: Each time you call back, you must emphasize the special qualities of your company, and why the company would like to come to the sponsor's location.

Booking Conferences

Booking conferences are meetings held by organizations of sponsors. At these meetings, company reprsentatives are given the opportunity to meet with prospective sponsors face to face. If your organization does not intend to tour very much, always uses the same sponsors, or is very well known, then booking conferences are probably not for you. However, if you need to tour a great deal, are not very well-known or want to build your national/regional image with sponsors, then attending a booking conference might make sense.

At a booking conference, each performing-arts organization is given a table on which to display its materials, signs, etc. Sponsors walk around, pick up materials from the tables, and talk to company representatives. At a booking meeting, it is important to present the company in a well-organized, attractive table display. Simple, well-designed signs or displays (they need not be elaborate or expensive) indicate something positive about the company you represent. Well-produced video tapes, played on VCR's equipped with earphones, are an excellent tool to use at a booking meeting, especially in the fields of dance, opera, and theater. The tapes give you an opportunity to demonstrate visually to the prospective sponsor how good the company really is. Slides and musical tapes can also be helpful.

If a prospective sponsor does stop at your table to chat, note down his name on the list of convention attendees, and what was discussed. A friendly note and a thank you for stopping by the display should be sent immediately after the conference, along with another copy of the company's materials. A list of organizations sponsoring booking conventions appears in the appendix.

How To Put Together a Tour

Tours string together a series of several individual engagements into a connected routing. The best routing (i.e., the most cost-effective) moves a company from its home base in a loop, in a figure-eight formation, or in a circle around its home area. Obviously, it wouldn't make economic sense for a company to spend a week performing in Minneapolis, return home to Chicago, and then spend another week in the twin city of St. Paul. If you have decided to tour in a five-state area then take out your map and pinpoint a routing that makes sense geographically and in terms of the sponsors who fit into your marketing strategy. The tour probably won't work out exactly as you plan, but at least you should have an idea and structure to work from during your planning process.

Even one definite booking gives you an edge. It enables you to say to a prospective sponsor in an adjacent area, "The company will be appearing at Slippery Rock Teachers College on February 15th. Would you be interested in an engagement just before or after those dates?" You would be surprised at the impact it has on a sponsor to know that a compatriot in an adjacent area is presenting your company.

Begin looking for additional sponsors in both "en route" and adjacent areas. For example, a company based in Atlanta is planning to tour in Tennessee, Georgia, Kentucky, and South Carolina, and sends out a mailing accordingly. It gets a booking in Knoxville, Tennessee. The marketing person should then send company materials again, first class, to all those sponsors on your list in Tennessee, with a covering letter saying that the company will be in Knoxville on certain dates. He should follow up this second mailing with the necessary phone calls. At the same time, he would do a mailing and phone follow-up for those states adjacent to Tennessee, as well as those en route from the home state, Georgia. A booking for a tour can't be done without a good atlas of the entire United States and of each state individually.

Don't make absolute commitments on specific dates until the tour begins to shape up. You don't want to be in a position of having locked in dates, only to find out that you would have to go several hundred miles out of your way that particular week, although it would work perfectly two weeks later in the tour. However, when the routing does begin to shape up, you will want to go to contract as quickly as possible. This is the time to negotiate fees and activities. You should have enough flexibility in your fee so that it can be reduced slightly, or so that you can make up for a small loss one week with a larger fee the next. Additional services such as a children's performance, master classes, etc., can also be used to help "close" on a sale.

From a Sponsor's Viewpoint

Once the company has signed a contract with a sponsor, the sponsor has the responsibility of presenting it with the proper technical equipment, staff, lighting, etc., as prescribed in the contract. On the other hand, the company has responsibilities that extend far beyond showing up and performing.

Sponsors, whether they are on campus or in the community, invest a large chunk of their organization's money in your company's performance/residency. Not only must the sponsor usually pay the company a set fee regardless of how many people come to the scheduled event, but they must also pay for advertising in local newspapers, radio, and TV. They supply a theater or other appropriate setting in which the company can perform, hire a crew, ushers, ticket-takers, print programs, etc. Anyone who has produced a home season already knows the challenge involved in this type of operation.

Sponsors always need press materials. Since sponsors must pay for the perform-

"A sensational-looking poster helps the sponsor sell tickets to your performance."

ance/residency by selling tickets, the box-office is their biggest worry. A company must provide a sponsor with press materials well in advance of the engagement. It is not too soon to send the materials as early as the spring preceding a fall tour. Many sponsors present organizations as part of a series and print a season brochure to sell subscriptions long in advance of the scheduled dates, so they need information early.

The materials for publicizing the company should be produced as part of the company's overall marketing plan. They may be a version of what the company uses at home. In any case, the materials you send should look as professional as possible. Get a good professional photographer to take your press pictures, and a professional copywriter to compose your press stories and bios. The posters and flyers that the sponsor will use to advertise the company's appearance should also be produced by professionals. A sensational-looking poster that successfully communicates what the company does, and which is exciting enough to persuade people to attend, helps the sponsor sell tickets to your performance. Be sure to leave several inches at the bottom of your standard poster/flyer for information to be included by the specific presenting organization.

The general consensus is that a company must supply a sponsor with at least the following basic information for publicizing a performance:

- Five different 8x10 glossy photographs
- Biographies of artistic director, leading performers
- Sample press releases on company/production, feature stories
- Description of company and history
- Posters
- Ad slicks
- Two written public service announcements, 10-second and 30-second (PSAs)
- 35MM color slides for television PSAs with company name or logo
- If possible, a well produced 30-second audio tape casette for radio PSAs.

This chapter has tried to provide an outline of the booking process and some guidelines for success. The basic techniques and tools described in this material have been, of necessity, quite general. Every situation is different—an established company versus one with unknown work, a large company versus a small company, a theater versus a chamber-music ensemble, but the process is sufficiently similar for all companies so that it is possible to supply at least the general outline for successful booking. Now it is up to you, the reader, to tailor the information to the goals and needs of your organization.

Joseph Golden

SPONSORS AND PRESENTORS: COMMUNITY GROUPS

Seats vs. Souls; or, Who's Trying to Sensitize My Psyche?

Marketing the arts is one thing. It is surely a demanding, sometimes maddening, and often unpredictable adventure in the stimulation of appetite and action—the end result being (please, heaven!)—the filling of seats, and of galleries, and of institutional coffers. The goals are clear; the effect, for better or worse, is measurable.

But marketing a community to itself is another thing. The premise is that, like an iceberg, a large mass of talent, interest, and creative energy floats just below the surface, mostly unseen. This large mass may not feel comfortable in the rarified atmosphere above the surface and remains, therefore, unresponsive to the inducements and seductions of traditional arts-marketing techniques.

How do we get at that large mass and thereby broaden the market?

A solution would be either to lower the water or raise the iceberg. Lowering the water may be a task only the Lord can perform. But maybe there's a method of raising the iceberg. And doing so depends on how many marketing pathways we are willing to follow, how specifically or loosely we define marketing, and how many hats we are prepared to wear.

The Cultural Resources Council of Syracuse and Onondaga County, Inc., which this writer is privileged to serve as Executive Director, is like some mythological character, a creature with three heads. A tax-exempt, not-for-profit private agency, it is, simultaneously, several different things. First, it is an arts-service organization that provides the familiar cluster of programs (arts calendar, festivals, awards, technical assistance) for the citizens of Onondaga County. Second, it is the agency that manages a three-theater performing-arts complex—the Civic Center—which houses about 1500 events and attracts in excess of 325,000 persons annually. It is also a presenting organization, offering attractions large and small for adults and young people in entertainment media that range from the American Ballet Theatre, to B.B. King, to puppet festivals, to travelogue films. The neuroses that might be expected to attend this mix of functions has not yet surfaced, nor is it likely to. What keeps the three heads in more or less synchronous behavior is CRC's elegantly, if a bit amorphously, stated goal—to identify, develop, and promote all manifestations of the arts as experiences central to the life of the community.

To accomplish this goal, operating with three heads does not seem at all bizarre. Two of them work with a nice sense of compatibility, since there is very little awkwardness in shifting one's faculties from the role of facility manager to the role of presentor and back again.

But it's that third head, so radically different from the other two, that significantly alters our institutional mission and that obliges us to stretch the concept of marketing beyond its familiar parameters. We are also, as noted above, an arts council—one of the more than 3,000 community-based service agencies in the United States committed to sensitizing and expanding the psyches of the many organizations and sub-communities that somehow feel alienated from the mainstream of professional cultural delights.

Dr. Joseph Golden is Executive Director of the Cultural Resources Council of Syracuse and Onondaga County, and Managing Director of the Civic Center of Onondaga County, a three theater performing arts complex. During the past 17 years, he has served as theater and community resources consultant for the New York State Council on the Arts and for the National Endowment for the Arts, and as an independent advisor to community arts agencies, city planners and municipalities around the country. Dr. Golden was for seven years co-producer and host of two television shows on the arts. He is the author of several books and numerous essays on theatre practice and television, and 25 plays for both adult and children's theatre. He has an A.B. degree from Tufts University, an M.A. from Indiana University, and a PhD. from the University of Illinois. He is a graduate of the Harvard Business School Institute in Arts Administration, the IAAM seminar of facility management and the Syracuse University workshop on financial administration. He is the recipient of the 1980 Arts Management "Career Service" Award.

So, while two of our heads vigorously apply most of the traditional and novel marketing strategies to get bodies into seats for concert and theater events, our third head is fussing less with filling seats and more with winning souls and making converts. It helps to bridge the gulf that often exists between local community amusements and diversions, and the more sophisticated experience of the "establishment" arts institutions—as it were, between the beer hall and the concert hall.

Right up front, we acknowledge the inanity of expecting everyone in town, despite the most canny marketing strategies, to become overnight devotees of Gustav Mahler or *Swan Lake*. Further, we acknowledge the solid and intrinsic value of the avocational, ethnic, and educational enterprises generated by local amateurs, most of whom extract considerable social and cultural values from their exercises. And finally, we are compelled to acknowledge that the process of sensitizing and developing new audiences, of significantly raising the arts consciousness of a total community, may extend well beyond the lifetime of this writer, or even this writer's children.

Nonetheless, one of the most profound challenges to professional arts managers is surely to penetrate and proselytize among the "others"—the 95–97% of a community's citizens who may appear to be indifferent to, or unprepared for, the blandishments of the many marketing techniques and philosophies so cogently discussed in this book.

Civic Center of Onondaga County, Syracuse, New York.

We discovered long ago, as no doubt many others have, that a player in a local amateur theater group is not necessarily a subscriber to the professional LORT (League of Resident Theatres) operation in town, or that an enthusiastic practitioner of a Hungarian *Csardas* dance is going to be turned on by the offerings of the local ballet company, or that a blue-collar lathe operator—who is incidentally an occasional Sunday painter or potter—is a regular visitor to the local art museum, or that a zealous benefit chairman of the Jewish Community Center will have even a remote grasp of the complex arrangements entailed in booking a "big star" as a fund raiser.

It is almost as if the informal or avocational arts (and non-arts) community was a cluster of isolated planets, whirling in independent orbits, experiencing little or no gravitational pull toward the major professional arts institutions that do, in fact, represent the models of excellence.

A major thrust of this agency is the adoption of a marketing strategy with a wholly different wrinkle, a completely different goal—*selling a community to itself.* This takes the form of creating programs and showcases designed gradually to reinforce the ego and celebrate the creative energy of those individuals who view their effort as isolated from the traditional concert-loving or museum-going crowd, and who are, therefore, not readily susceptible to arts-marketing campaigns, no matter how provocative or clever.

So while hats No. 1 and No. 2 worry over lease agreement details with promoters, or concoct ideas that will produce enough box-office revenue to at least break even on a Vienna Symphony Orchestra performance, hat No. 3 is busy implementing programs to enhance, teach, or salute those communities of interest that are typically viewed as remote from mainstream culture.

Four examples, described briefly below, may illuminate our oblique approach to marketing the arts, particularly in the areas of community theater; ethnic traditions; "closet" visual artists; and a wide assortment of civic, social, fraternal, educational, and religious organizations that occasionally rub shoulders with the arts. We do not, incidentally, claim any pride of originality. Many of our programs are done elsewhere, although perhaps not with the same philosophic objective.

A Marketing Goal: Attainable Professional Excellence.

Community Theater

Local amateur theater/musical groups offer a maddeningly complex dilemma. On the one hand, they are contentious, jealous, uncooperative; on the other, dedicated, energetic, and often unusually deft. They tend to operate on and protect their special piece of turf, and are often reluctant to share information, mailing lists, or equipment, or to invite supervision by an outside professional.

Although we knew we could never suppress — or eliminate — certain traits characteristic of amateur theater groups, we suspected that a strong dose of professional guidance and obligatory cooperation might begin to help them develop a new empathy with the community's Equity theater by imbuing the amateurs with a more mature sense of professional competence than they had previously known.

To this end, we created Summerfest—a summer season of seven local theater groups packaged under our aegis, as producer. A professional technical staff, publicist, house-management personnel, and box-office were now deeply involved in the implementation of the summer package. Training was given in move-ins and take-outs, pre-planning sessions were held to establish lighting and sound designs that would make more efficient use of time (and thus money). Tickets were ordered for the entire season, obliging each company director to think hard about scaling and income; budgets had to be prepared and submitted to the producer; and a promotion campaign was mapped out in detail, indicating the sequence of display ads, news releases, special features, and photo sessions. In other words, the local groups were induced (or seduced) into behaving like pros. We were, in short, "marketing" the idea that a higher degree of excellence was attainable by the application of some basic discipline. (By the second season, in fact, company directors were meeting privately to figure out how to share sets, props, costumes, and even a "universal" light plot, the cost of which could be divided up among the groups.)

After four years of Summerfest, the gap between them and the LORT operation was beginning to close. The operating mentality of the amateurs is slowly beginning to parallel the mentality of the pros.

A Second Marketing Goal: Pride.

Festival of Nations

Ethnicity—a pride in cultural origins—has enjoyed an unusual revival over the past several years throughout the country. The revival has been no less visible in Syracuse where nearly three dozen national heritage organizations proudly retain their links with the "old country." These organizations are formidable. They are not only cohesive and strong, but they also represent collectively slightly more than 75% of central New York State's population—a demographic factor with more than a few political implications.

Prior to 1969, a few of the ethnic organizations—Polish, German, Ukrainian, Scottish, and Italian—sponsored "field days" at different times during the year. Robust and friendly affairs, they nonetheless isolated themselves from one another and from the community at large, evoking an unfortunate and inaccurate schism between "blue-collar ethnic stuff" and "real art." This distortion of value, we felt, had to be altered; a different perception of the existence and worth of traditional folk art had to be "marketed."

The strategy to accomplish this was relatively easy. We invited the groups to accept being organized into a festival under the guidance of professional directors, stage managers, sound and light technicians, publicists and others. This would be a major international celebration under one roof over a two-day period, that would create an ethnic and entertainment mix with broad appeal.

The invitation was accepted. In 1982 (the fourteenth festival year), thirty-five national heritage groups participated by displaying national dress, offering tasty edibles, performing traditional dances and songs, and demonstrating unique crafts.

That the program is successful—about 12,000 normally attend—is irrelevant. The effect on the participants and the general community is what counts. Sensitive to the new level of public expectations, the ethnic groups upgraded or remade their costumes; rehearsals for their live performances became more intense, obliging many choral or dance directors to re-explore their own roots to ensure accuracy; ethnic groups that felt they were too small or too scattered—persons of Estonian, Latvian, or Macedonian descent, for example—banded together in order to share the spotlight. By encouraging organizational continuity, the festival generated the

"We acknowledge the inanity of expecting everyone in town to become overnight devotees of Gustave Mahler."

> "Individuals who view their own artistic efforts as isolated from the traditional concert-loving or museum-going crowd are not susceptible to arts marketing campaigns, no matter how provocative or clever."

formation of national heritage clubs—the Japanese-American Cultural Exchange Society, the India Association, and others. Some groups became brave enough, having tasted the heady experience of public approbation, to rent the large concert hall in town to present evenings of traditional music and dance.

And from the response of the public—through individual comment, letters, editorial statements, press coverage, and ticket sales—the notion being marketed was getting through: That authentic traditional folk music, dance, and crafts are an intrinsic part of a community's cultural texture; that bona fide ethnic arts offer a purity and historic dimension as valid as anything in a symphony's repertoire; that ethnic traditions cannot be relegated to a low spot on a cultural totem pole, but are, rather, part of the spectrum of cultural diversity. They are bright and luminescent chips in a community's artistic kaleidoscope. With each year of the festival, that Hungarian *Csardas* dancer is perceived as less an ethnic and more an artist, more the alter ego of the ballet dancer than the opposite.

Just as we are marketing the notion that amateur theater groups can aspire to high professional competence, so we are selling pride of identity to the ethnic groups. Professionalism and pride are only two of the ingredients to use in selling a community on the strength of its own artistic muscle, thus gradually heightening a community's susceptibility and favorable response to traditional arts-marketing strategies.

A Third Marketing Goal: Discovery.

"On My Own Time"

The man who refills the bottle cap machine at a local brewery has been dabbling in pastel drawings for years, unknown to his fellow workers and bosses. The pediatrician's secretary occasionally escapes from the wails in the waiting room by thinking about the glaze she will choose for the finished ceramic piece that is about to enter her kiln. The insurance-company executive, strolling to the coffee machine, frowns over his failure last night to accomplish a secure weld on one component of the freeform metal structure he's creating in his garage.

The bottle-cap filler, secretary, and insurance man have three things in common. First, they are "closet artists"—men and women who live double lives as wage-earning 9 to 5 company employees and as creative artists who practice their skills on their own time. Second, they tend to be deferential about their artistic efforts, accepting the role of "one who loves"—an amateur. And third, like the community-theater actor or Hungarian dancer, they sense and much too often accept, the gulf that exists between themselves and the sanctioned "establishment" artists, who are exhibited in the community's major museum.

The three types of employees identified here can be multiplied many times over. There is not a factory, bank, department store, or hospital that does not harbor among its work force, men and women who retreat from the dull world of gear boxes and interest rates into the real and fulfilling world of the visual arts and crafts.

We felt it was both appropriate and essential that we flush them out and make them visible; that we create a program that produces, for both the worker and the boss, the great discovery that authentic artistic abilities lurk in unlikely places. They may be found on assembly lines, in reception rooms, within the typing pool, or at the cashier's window.

The program, called "On My Own Time," accomplishes just that. In its ninth year, and now involving twenty-four major commercial, medical, and educational institutions, the program provides tools to set up the mechanism a company needs to invite employees to submit works of art. It assists in the arrangement of in-house exhibitions of the works (in corridors, employee lounges, cafeterias, each work is carefully labeled with the name of the artist and his department); provides a training session, conducted by a professional art store or gallery manager, to teach basic techniques of matting, framing, and displaying. The program organizes and dispatches to each company a panel of professional artists/judges to identify the best works; arranges to have the selected works put on exhibition in the community's major art museum; and schedules a gala opening for the artists, their families, and their bosses—many of whom, incidentally, confess that they have never before set foot in the community's major art museum.

The impact of the "On My Own Time" program is not yet accurately measurable. A few developments are intriguing, however. As a result of being selected and receiving favorable comment, several employees left their full-time jobs to pursue the ephemoral career of full-time artists; companies have begun to elevate the importance of the in-house exhibition by sponsoring receptions, giving awards, and purchasing works; company officers have begun attending the gala opening to bask in the reflected glory of an employee's achievement; and company officials admit that their *pro rata* share of the program's cost is one of their most fruitful fringe-benefit investments.

- *Discovery:* Louis, standing at the next lathe, is not just a lathe operator anymore. He's different now—he's an artist.
- *Discovery:* The myth of the blue-collar worker or typist as a 9 to 5 drone begins to dissolve. They now possess the power to create beautiful things.
- *Discovery:* The local art museum is not a walled and forbidding fortress. It's a place in which a lathe operator or typist are welcome.
- *Discovery:* Top management perceives the multi-dimensional nature of many of their employees and sees that the loading dock foreman can magically transform a piece of wood into a soaring eagle.

Professionalism, pride, discovery. These phenomena are as critical to a healthy mileau for the arts and as central to the goals of a marketing strategy as the more typical objectives of increasing subscription sales for an opera company or a ten-year campaign to build an endowment.

Final Example of an indirect marketing approach: Sharing with laymen the mysteries of theatrical skills.

Production Planning Seminar ("Where Do I Go From Here?")

The first three examples of marketing are related to the arts—performing, visual, or ethnic. The Production Planning Seminar reaches for a totally different constituency, to share with them the basic, usually theater-based skills required to mount a public event successfully.

The cosmos of a community as we know, embraces a constellation of clubs and societies — social, civic, professional, commercial, fraternal, educational, and religious—that will, at least annually, "go public."

Read the calendar of community events published weekly in the local press. There are lectures, fashion shows, benefits, bazaars, pancake breakfasts, talent nights, book reviews, poetry readings, product-display meetings ("industrials"), political debates, awards or installation ceremonies, alumni reunions, and a host of other occasions that attract the public's attention. This calendar always invites them to an event that launches, culminates, explains, or dramatizes the institutional mission unique to the agency that sponsors the event.

Comprised mostly of volunteers, these sponsoring agencies constitute a wide band of energy, influence, and diversity—qualities that are rarely channeled in support of arts agencies. These agencies are, after all, just several more "clubs" in a community's human infrastructure. And wouldn't it be delightful, we mused, if some of these agencies could be sensitized to the role and contribution of the arts?

Fortunately, these social, civic, and service organizations have become increasingly aware of the need to develop basic skills, to become adept in planning, staffing, budgeting, fund raising, promotion, ticket sales, and transmitting their special message (in a space or on a stage) in an orderly, attractive, and compelling form. In other words, they must learn to apply the principles and techniques that are the basic language of arts-producing agencies.

The object, then, was to bring together the two elements—the enthusiastic but untutored community service and business groups, and the veterans who were professionals in preparing for and putting on a show.

The Production Planning Seminar was introduced seven years ago. It has become an annual event drawing representatives from organizations as disparate as the

"Authentic artistic abilities lurk in unlikely places— on assembly lines, in reception rooms."

"A player in a local amateur theater group is not necessarily a subscriber to the town's professional operation."

YMCA, American Dairy Association, Onondaga Community College, Holiday Inns, United Methodist Church, General Electric, Jewish Community Center, Miller Brewing Company, Cortland Historical Society, P&C Food Markets, Planned Parenthood, and a Convention & Visitors Bureau.

The basic message transmitted to these agencies is that the only difference between producing *Aida* and an Ebony Fashion Show is one of degree. Both need intensive planning, a realistic budget, a committed staff, a methodical and attractive promotional campaign, good internal cash controls, and an organizational structure that makes clear who's in charge of what.

Seminar alumni have reported to us on their successes and failures. They have sent us copies of "right" budgets and upgraded brochures as evidence of their new skills; advised us of changes in the composition of their boards that has produced more fund-raising clout; and, on several occasions, proudly informed us of their successful battle with state and federal bureaucracies to become 501(c)(3) agencies. At least one took the bold step of booking our 2100-seat concert theater to present a benefit event and, at least in this case, made money.

The object of this side-door marketing is simple: A new rapport develops between a food market chain and an arts agency, between a motel operator and a legitimate theater. Sharing with them certain basic production skills—the kind that can apply directly to their own enterprises—produces a germinating bond between the arts and the rest of the world, a kinship that had not hitherto existed. The revelation that arts principles and practices can make a local G.E. products show more exciting, can begin to reduce certain barriers that often exist between engineers and artists.

The four programs cited here as parallel or oblique marketing strategies do not come, alas, without price tags. But the price is not dollars—each of the four is financially self-sustaining by both direct and indirect revenues. The real cost is in staff time, energy, and patience. To achieve the four marketing goals—professionalism, pride, discovery and skill—among community theaters, factories, ethnics, or clubs, the Cultural Resources Council staff must become counselors, teachers, handholders, disciplinarians and cheerleaders, in addition to their regular administrative and technical duties. They must produce a series of publications that explain how, why, and when; they must maintain a library of current documents on management, budgets, and promotional techniques; they must provide one-to-one technical assistance to help novices prepare funding requests or evaluate a proposed poster design; they must somehow squeeze out a few extra minutes or hours onstage to give neophyte groups a sense of security and confidence. Finally, they will agree to attend and to critique a final run-through of a PTA Follies.

These are the price tags. And we are willing—indeed, as an arts council, we are obliged—to pay the price. But we believe it to be a profoundly good investment, and recognize that any measurable return on the investment may be a decade or a generation down the road.

We are "marketing" a tenuous product—a reinforced community ego. By such reinforcement, we hope gradually to create a climate in which a community's perception of the arts is sharper, deeper, and more hospitable to the products of arts institutions.

We contend that the best way to market the ego and to create the climate is to demonstrate to as many people as possible, especially those who seem to believe they are alienated from the traditional purposes of the arts, that they possess (or can cultivate) the intuition, taste, skill, and critical judgment basic to a flourishing arts scene.

If understood, trained, and rewarded, it is possible to win the souls of the amateur theater actor, the balalaika player, the lathe operator, and the motel manager, and to count them as allies in the battle for the survival and growth of the arts.

And this is the ultimate issue. Survival and growth, not selling and gain, are the overriding imperatives of the 1980s. Arts administrators—opera company directors, facility managers, arts council executives — who fail or are reluctant to acknowledge the profound need to employ populist strategies to achieve elitist goals, to identify and channel the creative energies that pulse in the shadows of the major institutions, or to bring into sharp focus the valiant but untutored efforts of community amateurs that hover on the periphery of our cultural vision, these people are gambling with the survival and growth of their own organizations.

It makes sense politically, fiscally, socially, and artistically to cultivate, teach, endorse, assist, display, and sponsor the ambitions of those who constitute the unseen part of the community's cultural iceberg. If nothing else, there is a purely pragmatic reason for this. The community arts amateurs, the ethnics, the labor force, and the special interest clubs, associations and societies constitute a formidable chunk of the population. They add up to an impressive number of voters and taxpayers, and are a potent source of allies in the increasingly hazardous battle of survival.

Never before have those of us who presume to keep the flame of humanism and sanity alive needed so much more fuel for our fire. It can be suicidal not to seek it out aggressively.

In sum, the more a professional administrator can help make a total community aware of the depth and diversity of the hidden artistic resources of its citizens, the sooner the citizens of that community will become more willing targets for traditional arts-marketing strategies.

PART VI:
Appendices

Appendix A

REPRESENTATIVE MARKETING CAMPAIGNS

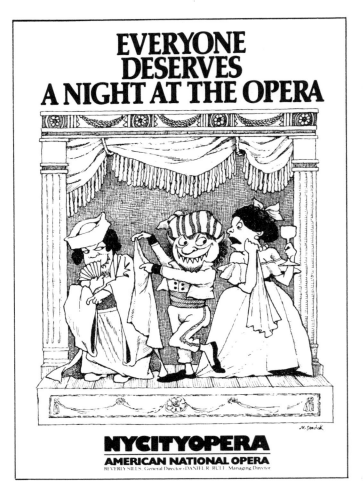

Season Brochure

Program Cover

A consistent graphic identity is essential to effective marketing. For a recent New York City Opera season, Maurice Sendak's whimsical, highly identifiable drawings provided an excellent focal point for brochures, posters, program covers and advertising formats.

Mefistofele

Alceste

The Merry Widow

Hamlet

The Magic Flute

Candide

Advertising Format

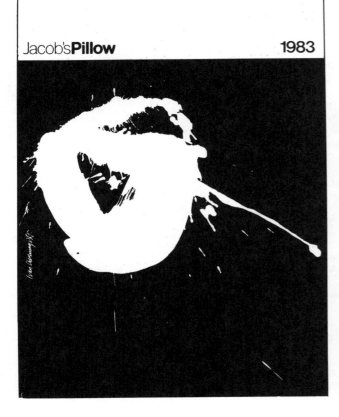

Jacob's**Pillow**   1983

Program Cover

Using only abstract brushstrokes, the design firm of Chermayeff & Geismar effectively evokes *dance* by evoking *motion*. This striking graphic identity system was used by the Jacob's Pillow dance festival for its 1983 season, and illustrates the principle that good marketing graphics needn't depend on photography. Reproduced here in black and white, each element actually sported a different, immediately identifiable color.

School Catalog Summer 1983

Ballet Project June 19-July 23
Jazz Project June 19-July 23
Modern Workshop July 31-August 19

Fifty-first Season
Liz Thompson, Executive Director
Ted Shawn (1891-1972), Founder

From the Artistic Director:
Jacob's Pillow is a very special place. Inside and out, it is a place of magic. Here students become a part of the continuum of dance history. They see the most exciting dance of the 80's performed in the first theatre built for dance in this country, live on a campus where many of the buildings were constructed by the pioneers of American dance and dance in studios where Cynthia Gregory, Alvin Ailey, Amanda McKerrow, Carolyn Adams, Douglas Dunn and Edward Villella have worked.

Many of our students have gone on to join major companies such as The Paul Taylor Dance Company, Joffrey Ballet, Rosalind Newman and Dancers, American Ballet Theatre, Martha Graham Dance Company, Dance Theater of Harlem and Twyla Tharp

and Dancers while others have performed in such Broadway shows as "Dancin'" and "West Side Story."

In order to remain a valuable resource for the dancer of the 80's, we have reshaped our curriculum this summer. Each of our three programs in modern, ballet and jazz have a specific focus while all offer a variety of classes to enhance the quality of a dancer's education.

This summer Jacob's Pillow begins its second half century. Dance history has been and will continue to be made here. We hope you will join us.

Jacob's**Pillow**

School Catalog

Pillow
Box 287S
Lee, MA 01238
Address Correction Requested

1983 Festival Season

**Subscribe to
the best season
of your life**

The**New**Jacob's**Pillow**

Fifty-one and feisty

An American Folktale

The story of Jacob's Pillow is a renowned American folktale; the story of a man with a dream, but a man with enough pluck and practicality to make it happen.

Fifty-one years ago Ted Shawn decided to show America that male dancers were as tough and hardy as America's pioneers. He bought an 18th century farmhouse, 150 acres of woods, and selected eight potential dancers from the physical education class he was teaching at Springfield College. Together they cleared the land and constructed the cabins; many of which stand today. The dances that they learned under Shawn's direction were based on American themes and demanded enormous strength and muscularity to execute.

Area people expressed interest in the goings-on, and so Shawn opened rehearsals to the public, charging 75¢ for a lecture, a look at dancing and a cup of tea. This was the beginning of a festival that has subsequently become a major force in international dance.

Having made his point about male dancers, in 1942 Shawn built the 618-seat Ted Shawn Theatre, America's first dance theatre, and launched a new crusade—to bring the best dance from all over the world —modern, ballet and ethnic—to the Berkshires. The Pillow has offered hundreds of premieres, as well as American or world debuts for dancers and dance companies; it is a crusade that continues.

Season Brochure

Design: Chermayeff & Geismar Associates

Advertising Rate Card

IT'S YOUR TURN

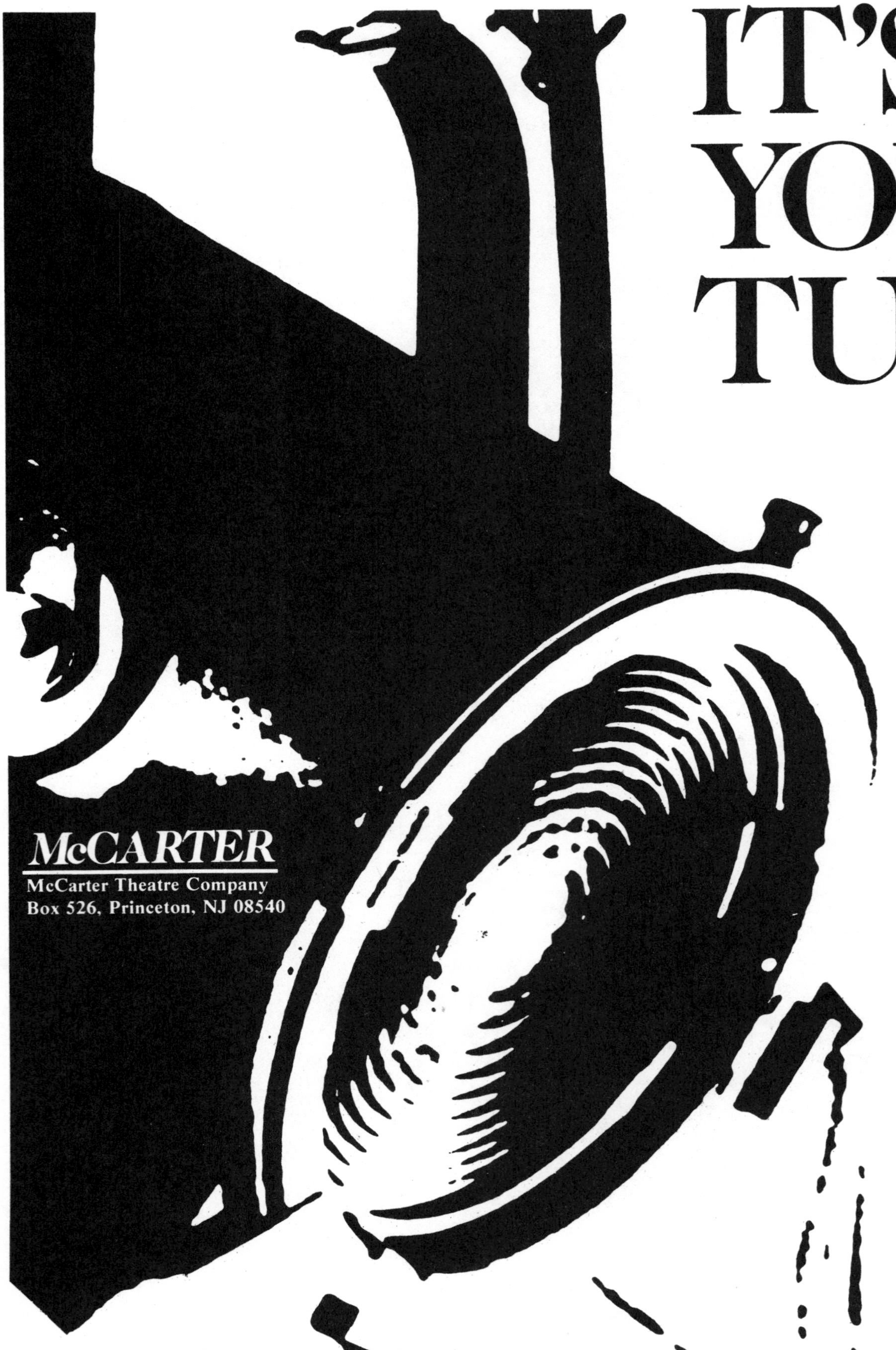

McCARTER
McCarter Theatre Company
Box 526, Princeton, NJ 08540

Non-Profit
U.S. Posta
PAID
Permit No.
Plainfield,

ACT NOW!

One simple visual message—theatre lights—were used throughout the McCarter Theatre's 1978-79 season for real cost savings and graphic continuity. Design: DANA.

Subscriber Services & Benefits

McCARTER

Shirley Knight

Innovative Productions of the Classics

Michael Allinson, Meg Wynn Owen, Patrick Horgan in Design for Living

The great dramas of the past are the cornerstone of a McCarter season. Classics can vividly remind us of our cultural heritage, and, through innovative productions, give us insights into contemporary life. Recent McCarter productions of classics have included: Shakespeare's *Romeo and Juliet*, set in Italy's *risorgimento* period, *The Winter's Tale*, and the "Empire style" production of *Much Ado*

*Ellen Holly,
Al Freeman, Jr. in
'Tis Pity
She's a Whore*

About Nothing, which all went on to open the American Shakespeare Theatre's student seasons in Stratford, Conn.; John Ford's *'Tis Pity She's a Whore*, which travelled to Chicago's Goodman Theatre; Brecht's *Mother Courage*, which featured Academy Award-winner, Eileen Heckart; Noel Coward's timeless masterpiece, *Design for Living*; Lillian Hellman's New York Drama Critics' Award-winner, *Toys in the Attic*, which marked the renowned American actor, Pat Hingle's debut as a director; Jean-Claude van Itallie's sensitive new translation (commissioned by McCarter) of Chekhov's *The Sea Gull* and Tennessee Williams' *A Streetcar Named Desire*, with Shirley Knight returning to the stage as Blanche, after winning the Tony Award in New York.

McCarter Rediscoveries

Each season, McCarter selects one or two plays by important

playwrights of the past which are rarely seen, but worthy of reinvestigation. Some of the "McCarter Rediscoveries" include: *Beyond the Horizon* by Pulitzer Prize-winner Eugene O'Neill, which was televised nationally on WNET's "Theatre In America" series; George S. Kaufman and Edna Ferber's *The Royal Family* with George Grizzard, Rosemary Harris, Eva LeGallienne, and Sam Levene, which continued on to great acclaim on Broadway and won a Tony award for its director, Ellis Rabb; Clifford

Richard Gere, Morris Carnovsky

Odets' *Awake and Sing* which brought the distinguished American actor, Morris Carnovsky, to the McCarter stage; *The Heiress*, Ruth and Augustus Goetz's adaptation of Henry James' story, which won 6 New Jersey Drama Critics' awards including one for Maria Tucci in the title role and for its director Michael Kahn; and *The Torch-Bearers*, featuring a cast of favorites including Peggy Cass, Tovah Feldshuh, Farley Granger and Dina Merrill.

Eva LeGallienne

Photos by Cliff Moore

A "family" look and strong use of black
helped these Pennsylvania Ballet
newspaper ads stand out on a busy
page. Design: DANA.

From Isadora to a Galaxy Beyond

Pennsylvania Ballet.

2 Weeks Only!
October 29 - November 8

4 Premieres
"In Celebration of Women Choreographers"

Dances of Isadora Duncan—
  with guest artist
  Annabelle Gamson
Shakers—
  Humphrey/traditional
Resettings—Driver/Purcell
Galaxies—Houlton/Schönberg

Shubert Theatre,
  250 S. Broad St., Philadelphia
Times: Tuesday through
  Saturday, 8 p.m. with
  matinees on Saturday and
  Sunday at 2 p.m.
Tickets: $19.50 $15.00 $10.50 $6.00
Visit the Shubert Theatre Box
Office, or charge your tickets
by phone to your Visa, MC, AX.

Chargit, tollfree 1-800-223-0120

World
Class
Dance

Returns
to the
Shubert
Theatre

Pennsylvania Ballet.

Get ready for down-home fun,
explosive drama and haunting high-
land romance as Pennsylvania
Ballet opens its 18th season. Hailed
by critics as "perhaps the best
resident company in this country,"
Philadelphia's own world class
company comes home Oct. 15
through 25 with: the Philadelphia
premiere of **Square Dance,** Balan-
chine/Vivaldi, Corelli; Mendelssohn.
The Moor's Pavane, Limon/Purcell;
and **Scotch Symphony,** Balanchine/
Mendelssohn. Also, coming soon:
**In Celebration of Women Choreog-
raphers** (an all-premiere program),
Oct. 29-Nov. 8

Convenient order in 3 ways:

• **Visit** the Shubert Theatre
  Box Office
• **Mail** your check, choice of
  date/time and section, and a
  self-addressed, stamped
  envelope to:
  Shubert Theatre,
  250 S. Broad St.,
  Philadelphia, PA 19102
• **Charge** by phone to your
  Visa, MC or AX.
☎ **Call tollfree 1-800-223-0120
  or in Phila. call 665-8051.**

Times: Tues.-Sat. eves. at 8 pm Sat. & Sun. mats. at 2 pm
Tickets: $19.50 (Orch. ctr.; Balc A- K), $10.50 (Balc L-P),
  $15.00 (Orch sides), $6.00 (Family Circle)

Appendix B:

RESOURCES

Appendix B

Douglas Eichten
A PLAN FOR PLANNING

I. Organization Goals

A. Analysis

1. Why do we exist?
2. What are we now?
3. What do we want to be?
4. What position do we want in our market?
5. How long should it take to reach these goals?

B. These goals dictate the market plan.

II. Situation Analysis

A. Marketplace

1. Problems and opportunities:
   —the economy
2. Competition from other theaters, other performing arts, other entertainment, including cable TV.
   —their budgets and income
   —performance schedules
3. Understand demographics of community—1980 census.
4. Total makeup of the community: climate, corporations, communities, military, religions.
5. Sources: public library, advertising agencies, chambers of commerce, local government, arts board, census bureau

B. Your audience

1. Audience demographics
   a. Methods
      —in-house handout
      —telephone survey
      —some informal research
      —in-house surveys
   b. Major factors
      —information needed
      —budget available
      —time available
      —sample size
   c. Survey information must not just be "interesting to know," but must be actionable.

          —set clear objectives
   d. Demographics
      —Age (match categories with radio study categories)
      —Sex
      —Education (use basic census breakdown)
      —Occupation (use census categories)
      —Income (use broad breakdown by household)
      —Residence (use zip code)
      —Other arts attendance
   e. Thoroughly discuss cross-tabulations before study begins.
2. Attitude toward organization
   a. focus groups
   b. in-house studies
3. Audience preferences
   —Be careful of asking audience to indicate artistic selections.

C. Product

1. Describe artists and events—what are we promoting.
2. Describe last season and this new season, and compare them.
   —advantages
   —disadvantages
   —general conclusions
3. Pricing plans and packaging used in the past.

D. Sales Programs

1. Which used in the past:
   —season tickets   —part-season packages
   —group sales   —corporate sales, etc.
   —student sales
2. Which communication tools used to promote them.
3. Results—Cost-analysis, *all* costs compared to income—staff included.
4. Staff needs to vary by sales programs and should be considered a tool, not a gimmick. Include staff costs in all budgets.

E. Description of last season's market plan.

1. Objectives
2. Results
3. Carryover

III. Set Marketing Objectives

A. Audience maintenance — renewals — ongoing programs — relationship building—plans to increase frequency

B. Audience expansion—TARGET AUDIENCE

1. Recognition that the number of new people attending our events each year is directly related to the efforts and funds we expend on attracting them.
2. Our resources are limited, causing us to focus our attention on those most likely to attend.
3. Those most likely to attend are those people who are most like those who now attend.
4. Develop objectives relating to who we will be seeking, how many will attend, how we will attract them.

C. Audience development—group plays—tours—easily accessible events—student programs—adult groups and corporate programs.

D. Audience enrichment — newsletters, workshops, symposiums, parking, programs.

E. Overall attendance and revenue goals for season and for each separate event.

IV. Sales Programs: Plans

A. Select appropriate mix of programs to meet organization financial and other objectives.

—past history
—current needs—goals
—expected outcome

B. Assign goals for each program

C. Renewal rate objectives

D. Amount of new buyers needed—realistic

V. Strategy

A. Define target audience for each sales program—separate campaign for each.

B. Message guidelines: Develop what you want to say to target audience.

1. Be sensitive to the language used—must be appropriate to event promoted.
2. Image—be sensitive to audience general attitudes toward your organization.
3. Graphics—consider how message can benefit from graphics—they can also confuse.
4. Colors—use of color can add beauty, truth, excitement—also is expensive.
5. What *has* to be said *has* to be included.
6. The sell—don't forget to ask for the money.
7. Expectation: Promotion of event should be honest. If the people, even at a fine event, expect much more than they receive, they will be extremely disappointed. If they experience much more than they expected, the attendance is likely to be low, because the message is weak.
8. Logo concept: A simple, bold, graphic seen over and over causes instant recognition and support for promotion by an event.
9. Communication
   —for the purposes of a marketing plan, we should consider four levels of communication. Each level could be reached by one communication device, however, they are often used to evaluate role of a wide variety of communication tools in a campaign.
   a. *Awareness*—General awareness of the existence of your product.
   b. *Comprehension*—Knowledge of the who, what, where, when, concerning your product.
   c. *Conviction*—Knowledge causing potential buyer to consider a purchase.
   d. *Purchase*—Knowledge of pressure causing buyer to buy.

C. Select communication tools for each sales program—based on goals, budget, message, target audience.

1. Message Match Up:
   Examples • awareness—billboard
   • comprehension—newspaper
   • conviction—direct mail
   • purchase—phone call

2. Target Audience Match Up:
   - direct mail and telemarketing—lists selected by zip code or interest
   - radio/TV—selection by age and sex
   - magazines—selection by interest

3. Tools:
   - Publicity
   - Word-of-mouth
     —comp tickets
     —season ticket performance scheduling
     —testimonial ads
   - Public service announcements
   - Billboards
   - Transit advertising
   - Newspaper ads
   - Magazine ads
   - Displays/tents/bookmarks
   - Pont-of-purchase advertising
   - TV (PSA and ads)
   - Radio
   - Theater programs
   - Posters/handbills
   - Newsletters
   - Personal sales—group sales
   - Telephone campaigns
   - Direct mail—customer lists—prospect lists—rental lists
   - Complimentary tickets for press and opinion leaders.

D. *Coordinated activity schedule of tools selected:*

1. Countdown to curtain for complete campaign
2. The ideal message chain

E. *Analyze cost of each tool at level needed*

F. *Goals for each tool*

G. *Consider staffing needs—costs*

H. *Cost-benefit analysis of each sales program—cost per dollar of income—return on investment*

VI. Budget

A. *Determine priority ranking of sales programs*

B. *The "15% guideline"—make sure you have enough—smaller needs more—percentage of income goal.*

C. *Submission of budget to management for cutoff decision*
   —balance with other areas
   —what can I get if I spend another $100

VII. Develop Monitoring System — to prepare for next marketing plan and identify need for mid-course adjustments.

A. *Sales reports*

B. *Coded messages*

C. *Staff reports*

D. *Box-office involvement*

Ivan Sygoda

DANCING FOR DOLLARS

The major presenters' organizations include ACUCAA, ISPAA, and NACA. Each one sponsors one annual convention, and several organize a series of regional conventions. Each one publishes a list of its members and associate members. (Members are the colleges, universities, community-arts organizations, and arts centers that present touring performing-arts attractions. Associate members are the agencies, managers, and companies with attractions to promote.)

Membership overlaps to a small degree, but by and large, each of these organizations has a unique "tone" that colors the sort of energy to be found at its conventions. The brief descriptions that follow are entirely subjective, and are written from the point of view of the author, whose job it is to represent small and emerging dance companies.

ISPAA (International Society of Performing Arts Administrators, P.O. Box 7518, The University of Texas at Austin, Austin, TX 78712, 512/471-2787), meets annually in New York City in December, immediately before the ACUCAA National. ISPAA has begun coordinating exhibit hall with ACUCAA. Of all the organizations, ISPAA has the smallest proportion of colleges/universities as opposed to reconverted vaudeville houses and festivals. Probably the least likely to book small companies.

ACUCAA (Association of College, University and Community Arts Administrators, 6225 University Avenue, Madison, WI 53705, 608/233-7400), sponsors a huge annual convention each December in New York City as well as Midwest and Northeast regional conventions each autumn. As its name implies, a good mix of colleges and community-based houses. The typical attendee is the staff person responsible for organizing a multi-genre town-and-gown subscription series for a 1000-seat auditorium. This means that most small companies will not be of interest. However, a certain number of these people are personally committed to young artists, new work, and innovations in choreography. Caveat: the dance and theater departments at these colleges may well have budgets and interests compatible with small companies, but as a rule, the faculty members involved do not attend these conventions.

WAAA (Western Alliance of Arts Administrators, P.O. Box RRR, Citrus College, Azusa, CA 94704, 213/335-0521), meets annually in September in rotating cities in the west. Mostly colleges and universities from Colorado west, including some from western Canada. Proportionally the most amenable to emerging artists, and the most "social" gathering, with easiest access to people. Air fare makes this an expensive one for eastern companies.

SAE (Southern Arts Exchange, Southern Arts Federation, Suite 122, 1401 Peachtree Street, N.E., Atlanta, GA 30309, 404/874-7244), sponsored every October in Atlanta by the Southern Arts Federation. A large proportion of attendees are from county and city arts councils with modest budgets and older, conservative audiences. Many regionally based companies are represented and booked. Problematical for out-of-region emerging artists.

NACA (National Association for Campus Activities, Box 11489, Columbia, SC 29211, 803/799-0768; formerly NECAA, National Entertainment and Campus Activities Association), sponsors a mammoth annual convention each February in rotating cities, to which will henceforth be appended their annual Arts & Lectures Conference, and many regional conventions. In contrast to the above, NACA meetings are attended by students shepherded by their campus activities advisors. On paper, the budgets and facilities involved are a perfect match for the prices and offerings of small and emerging companies. In reality, the students change every year, making it difficult to build relationships, and they are often ignorant about their own technical facilities. Finally, they can be distressingly unadventurous in their programming. The Arts & Lectures Conference is supposed to isolate those attendees truly interested in "culture" (as opposed to James Bond movies, hypnotists, cabaret acts, and rock bands), but attendance has been disappointing up to now.

The membership lists of these organizations are a valuable resource made available to paid-up members. The following publications also contain names, addresses and numbers of potential sponsors:

Dance Magazine Annual (Dancemagazine, 33 West 60th St., New York, NY 10023, 212/921-9300) $20.00. Lists many presenters, festivals, local, and regional arts organizations. Also useful as a resource list of managers, agents, and service organizations.

Dance College Guide (Same publisher as above) $10.95. Lists the dance departments with contact names for North American colleges and universities. Latest edition, 1982–83. A must for small companies and emerging artists.

Community Arts Agencies: A Handbook and Guide (American Council for the Arts, 570 Seventh Avenue, New York, NY 10018, 212/345-6655) $7.50 plus $2.00 shipping. Contains a large listing of local arts councils and a description of their activities. The latest edition is 1978, and so many contact names will be outdated.

International Directory of Theater, Dance, and Folklore Festivals, by Jennifer Merin and Elizabeth B. Burdick (Greenwood Press, 51 Riverside Avenue, Westport, CT 06880) A large and varied listing of festival presenters by country, cross-referenced by annual dates. Latest edition, 1979, with additions to 1981.

Great Lakes Arts Alliance, Resource Directory: Presentors of Performing Arts, (GLAA, 11424 Bellflower Road, Cleveland, OH 44106, 216/229-1098) $5.00. Listings for Illinois, Indiana, Michigan, and Ohio, and a model presentation of such information.

Most of the above references themselves contain listings of additional references which will prove useful.

Following is a list of SAAs and RAAs (state arts organizations and regional arts organizations), mostly public and semi-public agencies, by state. Their personnel are usually well-informed about arts activities in their region and can often suggest leads, contacts, and other resources. Many of these agencies publish rather comprehensive lists of presenters both large and small, available for the asking. Ask.

The Dance Program at the National Endowment for the Arts is staffed with committed, knowledgable, and overworked people. If personnel and address changes make any of the above information outdated, they will supply current facts. Address: Dance Program, National Endowment for the Arts, 1100 Pennsylvania Ave. N.W., Washington, DC 20506. Call (202) 682-5435.

Finally, your most important resource is the local Phone Book. Browse through city, county, and state listings for departments of Cultural Affairs, Arts, Recreation, Parks, and so forth. Every municipality will have different names for similar agencies. The mayor's information office should be able to point you in the right direction. You might also try the headquarters of local elected officials.

Almost any one of all these resources contains more leads than you can deal with in a month or two. You can accumulate names and addresses of potential presentors until the millenium, so get on the phone!

**List of DTP
Coordinating
Organizations
For the 1980-1981
Touring Season**

**Affiliated State Arts Agencies
Of The Upper Midwest**
For: Iowa, North Dakota, South
Dakota, Wisconsin, Minnesota
Mike Braun
Affiliated State Arts Agencies of the
Upper Midwest
430 Oak Grove Street, Suite 402
Minneapolis, MN 55403
(612) 871-6392

Alabama
See: Southern Arts Federation

Alaska
Nancy Starling
Arts Alaska, Inc.
430 W. 7th Ave., Suite 2
Anchorage, AK 99501
(907) 272-3428

American Samoa
American Samoa Arts Council
Office of the Governor
Pago Pago, American Samoa 96920

Arizona
See: Western States Arts Foundation

Arkansas
See: Mid-America Arts Alliance

California
Carolyn Evans
Program Mgr.,
Touring & Sponsor Development
California Arts Council
2022 J St., Sacramento, CA 95814
(916) 445-1530

Colorado
See: Western States Arts Foundation

Connecticut*
John Ostrout
Connecticut Commission on the Arts
340 Capitol Avenue
Hartford, CT 06106
(203) 566-4770

Delaware
Joseph Brumskill
Delaware State Arts Council
9th and French Streets
Wilmington, DE 19801
(302) 571-3548

District of Columbia
Bill Hasson
D.C. Commission on the Arts and
Humanities
1012 14th Street, N.W.
Washington, D.C. 20005
(202) 724-5613

Florida
Sherron Long
Fine Arts Council of Florida
Division of Cultural Affairs
Department of State, The Capitol
Tallahassee, FL 32304
(904) 487-2980

Georgia
See: Southern Arts Federation

Guam
Office of the Governor
P.O. Box 2950
Agana, Guam 96910

Hawaii
Barbara Furstenberg
University of Hawaii
College of Continuing Education and
Community Services
2530 Dole Street, 4th Floor
Honolulu, HI 96822
(808) 948-8242

Idaho
See: Western States Arts Foundation

Illinois
Cordelia Burpee, DTP Coordinator
Illinois Arts Council
111 North Wabash Avenue
Chicago, IL 60602
(312) 435-6765

Indiana
Andrea Olin-Gomes
Indiana Arts Commission
155 East Market
Indianapolis, IN 46204
(317) 633-5649

Iowa
See: Affiliated State Arts Agencies of
the Upper Midwest

Kansas
See: Mid-America Arts Alliance

Kentucky
See: Southern Arts Federation

Louisiana
Jodie Glorioso
Louisiana State Arts Council
P.O. Box 44247
Baton Rouge, LA 70804
(504) 342-6467

Maine*
Gigi Ledkovsky
Touring Coordinator
Maine State Commission on the Arts
and Humanities
State House
Augusta, ME 04330
(207) 289-2724

Maryland
Oletha DeVane
Maryland Arts Council
15 West Mulberry
Baltimore, MD 21210
(301) 685-6740

Massachusetts*
Tom Wolf
Executive Director
New England Foundation for the Arts
25 Mount Auburn Street
Cambridge, MA 02138
(617) 492-2914

Michigan
Jack Olds
Michigan Council for the Arts
1200 6th Avenue
Detroit, MI 48226
(313) 256-3717

Mid-America Arts Alliance
For: Arkansas, Kansas, Missouri,
Nebraska, Oklahoma
Jonathan Becker
Mid-America Arts Alliance
Suite 550
20 West 9th Street
Kansas City, MO 64105
(816) 421-1388

Minnesota
See: Affiliated State Arts Agencies of
the Upper Midwest

Mississippi
See: Southern Arts Federation

Missouri
See: Mid-America Arts Alliance

Montana
See: Western States Arts Foundation

Nebraska
See: Mid-America Arts Alliance

Nevada
See: Western States Arts Foundation

**New England Foundation for the
Arts**
Erika Zaccardo
New England Foundation for the Arts
25 Mount Auburn Street
Cambridge, Ma 02138
(617) 492-2914

New Hampshire*
Clinton Baer
New Hampshire Commission on the
Arts
40 North Main Street
Concord, NH 03301
(603) 271-2789

New Jersey
Estelle Hassenberg
Middlesex County Cultural Heritage
Commission
841 George Road
North Brunswick, NJ 08902
(201) 745-4489

New Mexico
See: Western States Arts Foundation

New York
Mary Ann Doyle
New York State Council on the Arts
80 Centre Street
New York, NY 10013
(212) 488-2892

North Carolina
Miller Sigmon
North Carolina Arts Council
North Carolina Department of
Cultural Resources
Raleigh, NC 27611
(919) 733-7897

North Dakota
See: Affiliated State Arts Agencies of
the Upper Midwest

Ohio
Ira Weiss
Performing Arts Coordinator
Ohio Arts Council
50 West Broad Street
Columbus, OH 43215
(614) 466-2613

Oklahoma
See: Mid-America Arts Alliance

Oregon
See: Western States Arts Foundation

Pennsylvania
Suzanne Wood
Pennsylvania Council on the Arts
Room 216, Finance Bldg.
Harrisburg, PA 17120
(717) 787-6883

Puerto Rico
Institute of Puerto Rican Culture
Apartado Postal 4184
San Juan, Puerto Rico 00905
(809) 723-2115

Rhode Island*
James D. Johnson
Rhode Island State Council on the Arts
344 Westminster Mall
Providence, RI 02903
(401) 277-3880

South Carolina
See: Southern Arts Federation

South Dakota
See: Affiliated State Arts Agencies of
the Upper Midwest

Southern Arts Federation
For: Alabama, Georgia, Kentucky,
Mississippi, South Carolina,
Tennessee
Jeff Woodruff
Southern Arts Federation
225 Peachtree Street, N.E.
Suite 712
Atlanta, GA 30303
(404) 577-7244

Tennessee
See: Southern Arts Federation

Texas
Jane Koock
Texas Commission on the Arts and
Humanities
P.O. Box 13406, Capitol Station
Austin, TX 78711
(512) 475-6593

Utah
See: Western States Arts Foundation

Vermont*
Ellen McCulloch-Lovell, Exec. Dir.,
Vermont Council on the Arts
136 State Street
Montpelier, VT 05602
(802) 828-3291

Virgin Islands
Wyn Heftel
Virgin Islands Council on the Arts
and Humanities
Caravelle Arcade
Christiansted, St. Croix
U.S. VI 00820
(809) 773-3075

Virginia
Lindsay Nolting
Virginia Commission of the Arts
400 East Grace Street
Richmond, VA 23219
(804) 786-4492

Washington
See: Western States Arts Foundation

West Virginia
John R. Hennen
Community Arts Coordinator
West Virginia Arts and Humanities
Council
Science and Culture Center
Capitol Complex
Charleston, WV 25305
(304) 348-3711

Western States Arts Foundation
For: Arizona, Colorado, Idaho,
Montana, Nevada, New Mexico,
Oregon, Utah, Washington,
Wyoming
Michael Holden
Western States Arts Foundation
141 E. Palace Ave.
Santa Fe, NM 87501
(505) 488-1166

Wisconsin
See: Affiliated State Arts Agencies of
the Upper Midwest

Wyoming
See: See Western States Arts
Foundation

*Member of the New England Foundation for the Arts

BIBLIOGRAPHY

American Institute of Graphic Arts (AIGA). *Graphic Design for Nonprofit Organizations*

Association of Community, University, and College Arts Admistrators. *ACUCAA Handbook* (the marketing and fund raising chapters). 1982.

Alexander, J.H., ed. *Early American Theatrical Posters.* Hollywood, Calif: Cherokee Books, n.d.

Andreasan, Alan R. "Non-Profits: Check Your Attention to Customers," *Harvard Business Review,* May–June, 1982.

Arnold, Mark. *Dialing for Dollars: A Direct Approach to Subscription Sales.* Performing Ideabooks, vol. 1, no. 1; Theatre Communications Group, 1981.

Ashford, Gerald. *Everyday Publicity: A Practical Guide.* New York: Law-Arts Publications, 1972.

Barrell, M.K. *Technical Production Handbook: A Guide for Sponsors of Performing Arts Companies on Tour.* Western States Arts Foundation.

Barry, John F. & Sargent, Epes W. *Building Theatre Patronage.* New York: Chalmers Co., 1927.

Baus, Herbert. *Publicity in Action.* New York: Harper and Brothers, 1954.

Biegel, Len and Lubin, Aileen. *Mediability: A Guide for Nonprofits.* Washington, D.C.: Taft Products, 1975.

Burke, Clifford. *Printing It.* Wingbow Press, 1972.

Capbern, A. Martial *The Drama Publicist.* New York: Pageant Press, 1968.

Center for Arts Information. *Graphically Speaking* (a bibliography and source list), 1981.

Clay, Roberta. *Promotion in Print: A Guide for Publicity Chairmen.* South Brunswick & New York: A.S. Barnes and Co., 1970

Craig, James. *Production for the Graphic Designer.* Watson-Guptill.

Dawson, Prieve, and Mokwa, eds. *Marketing the Arts* Praeger Publishers, 1980.

Foundation for the Extension and Development of the American Professional Theatre (FEDAPT). *Subscription Guidelines* Rev. ed. New York, 1977.

Goldovsky, Boris and Wolfe, Thomas. *Touring Opera: A Manual for Small Companies.* National Opera Association Monograph Series.

Keller, Mitchell. *The KRC Guide to Direct Mail.* Public Services Materials Center, 1980.

Kotler, Phillip. *Marketing for Non-Profit Organizations.* Prentice Hall, 1975.

Langley, Stephen. *Theatre Management in America.* New York: Drama Book Specialists (Publishers), 1980.

Levine, Mindy and Frank, Susan. *Get Me to the Printer: On Time, On or Under Budget and Looking Good.* A.R.T./New York, 1981.

MacIntyre, Kate. *Sold Out: A Publicity and Marketing Guide.* Theatre Development Fund, 1980.

McArthur, Nancy. *How To Do Theatre Publicity.* Berea, Ohio: Good Ideas Co., 1978.

Metropolitan Cultural Alliance. *Getting in Ink and on the Air: A Publicity Handbook.* Rev. ed. Boston: Metropolitan Cultural Alliance, 1978.

Mitchell, Arnold. *Marketing the Arts.* Melo Park, Calif.: Stanford Research Institute, 1962

Moore, Lou and Kassak, Nancy, eds. *Computers and the Performing Arts.* Theatre Communications Group, 1980.

National Association of Broadcasters. *If You Want Air Time: A Publicity Handbook.* Washington, D.C.: National Association of Broadcasters, 1977.

Newman, Danny. *Subscribe Now! Building Arts Audiences Through Dynamic Subscription Promotion.* New York: Theatre Communications Group, 1977.

O'Brien, Richard. *Publicity—How To Get It.* New York: Harper & Row, 1977.

Ogilvy, David. *Confessions of an Advertising Man.* Atheneum, 1980.

Roman, Kenneth and Maas, Jane. *How to Advertise.* St. Martin's, 1976.

Shagan, Rena. *A Blueprint for Booking and Tour Management.* (Contact FEDAPT for publishing information.)

Shapiro, Benson P. ''Marketing For Non-Profit Organizations'', *Harvard Business Review,* September–October 1973.

Skal, David J., ed. *Graphic Communications for the Performing Arts.* Theatre Communications Group, 1981.

U.S. Postal Service. *How To Prepare Second and Third Class Bulk Mailings.*

Voegli, Thomas J. *Handbook for Tour Management.* University of Wisconsin–Madison: Center for Arts Administration.

White, Jan V. *Editing By Design.* 2nd ed. R.R. Bowker, 1982.

Wolfe, Thomas. *Presenting Performances: A Handbook for Sponsors.* American Council on the Arts.

ABOUT FEDAPT

The Foundation for the Extension and Development of the American Professional Theatre (FEDAPT) is a not-for-profit service organization offering a process of Management Technical Assistance to professionally oriented theatres and dance companies. FEDAPT's staff, together with a core of working professionals from the theatre, dance and related performing arts disciplines, provides an intensive system of management consultation. FEDAPT helps develop the management structure that is essential to the continued artistic growth of theatre and dance throughout the United States.

FEDAPT supplements its one-to-one consultancies with a variety of programs and workshops designed to assist performing arts managements and boards of trustees. These programs include an annual National Conference on Theatre and Dance Management, and a series of week-long seminars that constitute the Theatre and Dance Middle Management Program. FEDAPT also sponsors the Commercial Theatre Institute which is designed to present information on the mechanics of producing commercially on or off-Broadway.

Other FEDAPT publications are: *In Art We Trust; The Board of Trustees in the Performing Arts,* compiled and written by Robert W. Crawford; *Investigation Guidelines for Developing and Operating a Not-for-Profit Tax Exempt Resident Theatre; Box Office Guidelines;* and *Subscription Guidelines.* For more information contact: FEDAPT Publications, 165 West 46th Street, Suite 310, New York, New York 10036. (212) 869-9690.

Market the Arts! has been made possible by grants to FEDAPT's Publications Revolving Fund from the W. Alton Jones Foundation, The Xerox Foundation, and the Inter-Arts Program of the National Endowment for the Arts.

NOTES